CAMPAIGNS OF WORLD WAR II
DAY BY DAY

CAMPAIGNS OF WORLD WAR II DAY BY DAY

CHRIS BISHOP & CHRIS McNAB

amber
BOOKS

This edition published in 2006 by
Amber Books Ltd
Bradley's Close
74–77 White Lion Street
London N1 9PF
www.amberbooks.co.uk

Reprinted in 2007

A catalogue record for this book is available from the British Library.

ISBN 1-905704-08-9
ISBN 978-1-905704-08-8

Project Editor: Mariano Kalfors / Charlotte Berman
Design: Graham Curd

Printed in Singapore

Picture credits:

TRH: 12t, 12b, 13, 16, 20t, 21, 24t, 25, 29, 32t, 32b, 36, 37, 40t, 40b, 41, 44t, 44b, 45, 49t, 52t, 53, 56b, 60, 61b, 64t, 64b, 65, 68t, 69t, 72, 76, 81, 84, 88, 92t, 97, 105, 108, 109, 112t, 113, 116t, 116b, 117, 120b, 124, 125t, 125b, 128, 140b, 144, 145, 148, 152t, 152b, 153, 156t, 157, 160t, 160b, 164, 165t, 168t, 168b, 170, 176t, 176b, 177, 186t, 186b, 191t, 194, 195, 196, 197, 206t, 206b, 207, 210t, 214, 215, 226, 227t, 227b, 234t, 234b, 235, 239t, 239b, 242t, 242b.

TRH/IWM: 24b, 49b, 73t, 77, 80t, 80b, 93, 104, 129t, 132, 133, 136, 137, 156b, 238, 243.

TRH/DOD/IWM: 8-9, 20b, 28b, 33, 48, 52b, 56t, 57, 61t, 68b, 69b, 73b, 89, 92b, 101, 112b, 121, 136t, 141, 149t, 78-179, 187, 191b, 198, 203, 210b, 219t, 230b, 243.

TRH/US DOD: 120t.

TRH/ US Air Force: 129b.

TRH/US Army: 85, 100, 161, 165b, 183.

TRH/USNA: 28t, 28b, 140t, 149b, 218, 222, 223, 230t, 231.

TRH/US Navy: 17, 182b, 190, 202, 219b.

TRH/USMC: 211.

Contents

Introduction

From western Europe to the steppes of Russia and the jungles of Southeast Asia, on land, at sea and in the air, World War II was six years of unprecedented conflict.

In *Campaigns of World War II Day by Day*, Chris Bishop and Chris McNab document the bravery and sacrifice, cruelty and terror that millions of servicemen and women, as well as ordinary people, experienced and endured on a daily basis.

This comprehensive reference volume is divided into two parts, the war in Europe and North Africa and the war in the Pacific. Within each section every campaign is described in detail, and is expertly analysed. Black-and-white and colour action images, detailed maps and illustrations provide an evocative, and often harrowing, insight to the war.

Exhaustive chronologies show how the war progressed from one day to another; beginning as a purely European affair and ending with the cataclysmic use of atomic weapons in Japan.

World War II remains the largest military conflict in history. This book tells the day-by-day story of the campaigns of that tumultuous era.

THE WAR IN EUROPE AND NORTH AFRICA

The Blitzkrieg begins
Poland is overrun

September 1939: Hitler takes a gamble that he can launch an attack on Poland without triggering another European conflict.

On 31 August 1939 Hitler ordered the invasion of Poland. The following day the UK and France demanded the instant withdrawal of all German forces and, in the face of the contemptuous silence with which this was greeted in Berlin, consulted on how best to implement their promises to Poland. That they must be implemented was unanimously agreed, but how, when and where this would happen were matters for lengthy discussion, and indeed remain the subject of controversy. As a result of the agreement an ultimatum was sent – and ignored. At 1100 on 3 September 1939, British Prime Minister Neville Chamberlain broadcast the news that Britain was now at war with Germany.

Luftwaffe in action

At 0445 on 1 September, bombers and fighters of the Luftwaffe crossed the Polish frontier and began their systematic destruction of the Polish military infrastructure. The first Blitzkrieg had begun.

Poland was an ideal theatre for warfare. In addition to being fairly flat, her frontiers were much too long for them to be well defended. She was, moreover, flanked by her enemy on both sides – East Prussia to the north and the newly occupied Czechoslovakia to the south – and the most valuable areas of the country lay between those flanks. Poland, in fact, protruded like a tongue into hostile territory – and in September 1939 her armies were deployed in that tongue, instead of behind the river lines of the Vistula and San where their defences would have been stronger. But the fatal weakness in Poland's defences lay in her lack of armour, for the bulk of the army consisted of 30 divisions of infantry supported by 11 brigades of horsed cavalry and two motorised brigades. Against them were to be launched six German armoured divisions and eight motorised divisions, together with 27 infantry divisions whose main role would be to engage the attentions of the Polish infantry while the German mobile forces raced around the flanks to strike at the centres of control and supply.

One hour after the Luftwaffe had struck, Army

The Germans organised an SS unit in the free city of Danzig during August 1939 and at the outbreak of hostilities it joined the Danzig police in an assault on the Polish-held post office and the Westerplatte fortress.

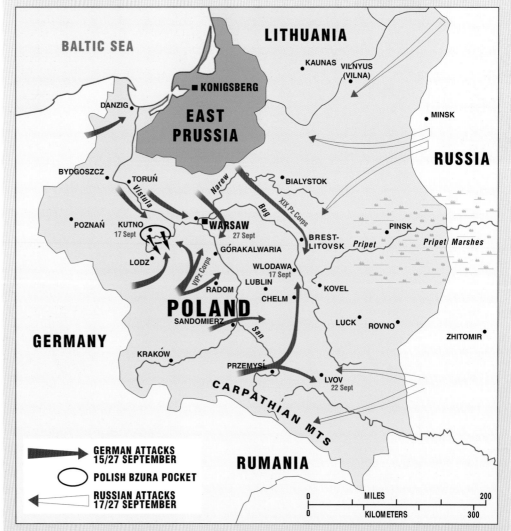

ENCIRCLEMENT: THE FIFTH PARTITION OF POLAND

GERMAN ATTACKS 15/27 SEPTEMBER
POLISH BZURA POCKET
RUSSIAN ATTACKS 17/27 SEPTEMBER

The German plan was to defeat the Polish army in a classic battle of encirclement. The Poles fought stubbornly, but the professionalism and numerical superiority of the German army made the result a foregone conclusion.

Poland fielded about 100 PZL P23 Karas light bombers in 1939 but they had little impact. 327 Polish aircraft were destroyed, many on the ground, and 98 flew to neutral Romania as the defeat of Poland became inevitable.

The Polish army was poorly equipped and its troops poorly led. Despite weak strategic direction and a reckless enthusiasm for offensive tactics, the Polish soldiers resisted for 36 days. Sixty-six thousand Polish troops were killed in action and 130,000 wounded.

Group South under General Gerd von Rundstedt smashed its way forward: the 8th Army on the left wing driving for Lodz, the 14th Army on the right aimed for Krakow and the line of the River Vistula, and the bulk of the armour of the 10th Army under General Walther von Reichenau in the centre piercing the gap between the Polish Lodz and Krakow Armies, linking with 8th Army mobile units and racing on for Warsaw.

By 4 September, 10th Army spearheads were 80km (50 miles) into Poland, curving up towards the capital and isolating the Lodz Army from its supplies, while to the south 14th Army tanks had reached the River San on each side of Przemysl.

Meanwhile, Army Group North under General Fedor von Bock was driving down from Pomerania and East Prussia: the 4th Army along the line of the Vistula towards Warsaw, and the 3rd Army along the line of the Bug towards Brest-Litovsk, Lwow and eventual junction with the 14th Army coming up from the Carpathians.

Frantic efforts

Thus two massive encirclements would take place, the outer intended to block any escapees from the inner, and at the end of the first week only the immediate confusion of battle masked the extraordinary success of the German attack. The inner pincers had certainly met successfully, but the chaos inside the trap was such that no-one could be sure what was happening. Polish columns marched and counter-marched in frantic efforts to make contact either with the enemy or with their own support, and in doing so raised such clouds of dust that aerial observation could report nothing but general movement by unidentified forces of unknown strength, engaged in unrecognisable activity in pursuit of incomprehensible aims.

Fighting at Bzura

As a result there was some doubt at German headquarters whether or not the bulk of the Polish forces had been trapped, therefore 10th Army armour was wheeled north to form another block along the Bzura, west of Warsaw. Here was fought the most bitter battle of the campaign, but it could only end in defeat for the Poles. Despite their desperate gallantry, they were fighting in reverse against a strong, well-entrenched enemy who had only to hold on to win, and after the first day they were harried from behind by troops of the 8th Army from the southern group and of the 4th Army from the north. It is hardly surprising that only a very small number managed to break through the German armoured screen to join the garrison at Warsaw, where they soon found themselves again cut off from escape to the east by the outer encirclement.

From this double encirclement only a small fraction of the Polish army could hope to escape, and on 17 September even this hope was dashed. The contents of the secret clauses of the Russo-German Pact signed the previous month were cruelly revealed when the Red Army moved in from the east to collect its share of the spoils; Poland as a nation ceased to exist and a new international frontier ran from East Prussia past Bialystok, Brest-Litovsk and Lwow as far as the Carpathians.

Panzer I armoured command vehicle, Radzymin, 27 September. A young German tank crew commander leads a column of German armour along the road to Warsaw. The white cross was used as a recognition sign on German vehicles during the Polish campaign.

The Blitzkrieg begins
Chronology

The invasion of Poland was the trigger for World War II. It also illustrated Germany's new talent in mechanised warfare. In under four weeks the entire Polish defence collapsed under the tactics of Blitzkrieg.

1939

August 31st
Adolf Hitler gives the final orders for the invasion of Poland.

September 1st
In the early hours of the morning, German air units begin preparatory bombardment of Polish defences. At around 6.00am over 50 divisions of German armour and infantry cut across the border in two main army groups: Army Group North attacking across northern Poland from northern Germany and East Prussia, and Army Group South driving towards Warsaw and through the Carpathians from Silesia.

September 3rd
The British prime minister, Neville Chamberlain, announces that Britain is at war with Germany.

September 8th
German units begin to enter the outskirts of Warsaw, having advanced nearly 321km (200 miles) in a week.

Below: Polish civilians dig trenches in September 1939. The Poles concentrated much of their defence on the frontiers, so were easily bypassed and encircled by German armour.

Right: An anti-Nazi leaflet from the early days of the war. On 9 September 1939 alone British bombers dropped over 12 million propaganda leaflets on Hamburg, Bremen and the Ruhr.

German soldiers remove Polish street signs. The German occupation aimed at eradicating Polish culture, especially in the anonymously named 'General Government' territory, formerly central Poland and heavily administered by the SS.

September 9th
The retreating Polish Poznan army launches a counter-attack against German forces around Kutno on the Bzura.

September 17th
From the east, Soviet forces invade Poland, striking towards Vilnius and Bialystok. The isolated pocket of Polish resistance around the river Bzura finally falls to German forces north of Lodz. Over 170,000 Polish soldiers are taken prisoner.

September 18th
Vilnius falls to the Soviets. The Polish government flees across the border into Romania and is interned.

September 19th
Soviet and German forces meet at Brest-Litovsk.

September 22nd
Bialystok and Lwow fall to Soviet forces.

September 27th
The defence of Warsaw finally collapses. The carve up of Poland between the Soviets and the Germans begins.

September 28th
Polish troops holding out at the Modline fortress some 36km (20 miles) from Warsaw finally surrender after an 18-day siege.

September 29th
Molotov and von Ribbentrop sign the 'German-Soviet Boundary and Friendship Treaty', dividing Poland into eastern and western zones under the control of the Soviets and Germans respectively.

October 2nd
The final element of the Polish defence, a unit of 4500 men under Admiral Unruh in the Pûbwysep Hela peninsula north of Danzig, surrenders to German forces.

International Events 1939

September 3rd
In the UK, 1.5 million citizens – mainly children, pregnant women or women with young children – are evacuated from the major cities in expectation of German air raids. Britain's armed forces are mobilised.

September 4th
The British RAF loses seven aircraft during ill-conceived raids on German naval bases at Wilhelmshaven and Brunsbuttel.

September 10th
Canada declares war on Germany.

September 11th
Over 150,000 British troops are shipped over to France to bolster the European defences against Germany.

September 15th
Russia and Japan sign a peace treaty which ends their conflict over the border of Mongolia and Manchuria.

September 17th
A German U-boat, *U-29*, sinks the British aircraft carrier *Courageous* off the Hebrides.

September 22nd
The Romanian prime minister Armand Calinescu is shot dead by Nazi terrorists.

Incredible victory
Battle of the River Plate

Hitler's 'pocket battleships' were expressly designed to be fast enough to outrun any vessel their guns could not sink.

Although history affords no example of war against commerce in itself defeating a major maritime power, the Kaiser's fleet had come close enough to success against the UK to encourage Hitler to try again. Among ships built expressly for the purpose were the three 'Deutschland' class 'pocket battleships' (more correctly 'armoured ships'). They were designed with long range and economical diesel machinery to give a speed greater than that of any more powerful ship, while armament and protection were on a scale that was to be more powerful than any faster ship.

Toward the end of August 1939, before the actual outbreak of hostilities, two of these ships, KMS *Deutschland* and KMS *Admiral Graf Spee*, together with their dedicated supply ships, left for their war stations in the North and South Atlantic respectively. Beginning with the 5050 grt Booth liner *Clement* near Pernambuco on 30 September, the *Graf Spee* destroyed several independently routed merchantmen during wide-ranging depredations over the next few months. No fewer than eight separate Anglo-French hunting groups were formed to catch her.

Raider warning

On 2/3 December 1939 two British ships, *Doric Star* and *Tairoa*, were sunk in mid-ocean. Each transmitted a raider warning and position that, when plotted, indicated that the German ship's course was toward the rich traffic in the Rio de Janeiro – River Plate area. This region

Deutschland's *guns in action during her successful commerce-raiding cruise in the North Atlantic. The elusive German raider sank the British armed merchantman* Jervis Bay *before returning to Germany.*

was in the ambit of Commodore Henry Harwood, whose South American Cruiser Division was known as Force 'G'. Having picked up the merchantmen's distress signals, Harwood was convinced that Captain Hans Langsdorff, in the *Graf Spee*, was making for the Plate estuary and at a speed that indicated arrival on or about 13 December. He accordingly concentrated his three available cruisers, the 203mm (8in) HMS *Exeter* (flag) and the 152mm (6in) sisters HMS *Ajax* and HMS *Achilles* (the latter New Zealand-crewed) some 240km

(150 miles) off the Uruguayan coast on 12 December and thoroughly briefed his captains regarding his intentions.

Sure enough, at 0608 on 13 December *Ajax* sighted the enemy, unexpectedly to the north-westward. Langsdorff was, in fact, loitering in expectation of intercepting a small convoy whose presence he suspected through papers taken from a further British ship, the *Streonshalh*, sunk on 7 December without any transmission. Backlit by the early dawn, Harwood's ships had been sighted by *Graf Spee* at 0530 and, taken to be the convoy, were already being approached.

Harwood was presented with a formidable adversary. Against him Langsdorff could deploy six 280mm (11in) guns in two triple turrets and eight 150mm (5.9in) weapons.

Within 150-200mm (8-6in) gun range, the German ship's 80mm (3.15in) vertical armour would prevent vital damage. Only in speed did the British have the advantage and this was used to good effect, the three cruisers working in two divisions. *Exeter* approached from the south while the two faster light cruisers worked around to the east; each division could thus spot the fall of

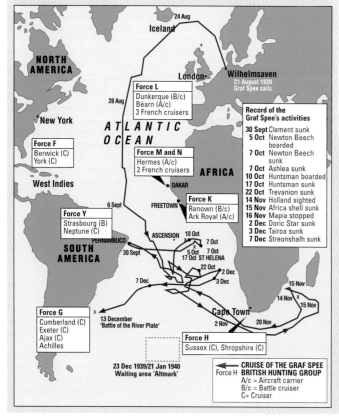

LANGSDORFF: TO CATCH AN OCEAN RAIDER

Force L
Dunkerque (B/c)
Béarn (A/c)
3 French cruisers

Force F
Berwick (C)
York (C)

Force M and N
Hermes (A/c)
2 French cruisers

Force Y
Strasbourg (B)
Neptune (C)

Force K
Renown (B/c)
Ark Royal (A/c)

Force G
Cumberland (C)
Exeter (C)
Ajax (C)
Achilles

Force H
Sussex (C), Shropshire (C)

21 August 1939
Graf Spee sails

Record of the Graf Spee's activities

30 Sept	Clement sunk
5 Oct	Newton Beech boarded
7 Oct	Newton Beech sunk
7 Oct	Ashlea sunk
10 Oct	Huntsman boarded
17 Oct	Huntsman sunk
22 Oct	Trevanion sunk
14 Nov	Holland sighted
15 Nov	Africa shell sunk
16 Nov	Mapia stopped
2 Dec	Doric Star sunk
3 Dec	Tairoa sunk
7 Dec	Streonshalh sunk

13 December
'Battle of the River Plate'

23 Dec 1939/21 Jan 1940
Waiting area 'Altmark'

CRUISE OF THE GRAF SPEE
BRITISH HUNTING GROUP
A/c = Aircraft carrier
B/c = Battle cruiser
C= Cruiser

Captain Hans Langsdorff handled his ship with considerable skill, ranging across the South Atlantic and into the Indian Ocean and leaving the Allied navies completely confused. He sank only nine merchant vessels, but he did so without the loss of a single life and, in the process, tied down four enemy battleships, four battlecruisers, six aircraft carriers and more than twenty cruisers. He was handicapped by his ship having only one seaplane, the famously unreliable Arado Ar 96. This broke down for the final time on 11 December, so he could no longer see over the horizon just as a British cruiser squadron approached.

Graf Spee's 76mm (3in) armour belt and heavily protected turrets were proof against the 150mm (6in) guns of Ajax and Achilles except at close range. By contrast neither of the British light cruisers could have withstood a few hits from Graf Spee's main armament.

shot for the other and, it was hoped, force *Graf Spee* to split the fire from her main battery.

Langsdorff opened fire at 0617 at about 17,350m

out of action. Badly on fire and listing to starboard, she struggled gamely on, steering from local control and firing only from her after turret. At 0640 her condition was so

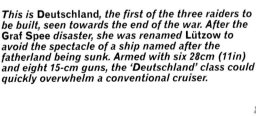

Exeter was badly damaged by Graf Spee and returned to England to refit after temporary repairs were carried out in the Falkland Islands. She was subsequently deployed to the Far East and sunk by Japanese cruisers in the Java Sea on 1 March 1942.

(56,922ft) and, after some initial uncertainty, concentrated on the main threat, *Exeter*. He enjoyed a further advantage over the British in having one of only two ships in the German fleet fitted with a radar that could be used for gunnery purposes. Within minutes *Graf Spee* had found the range, three 280mm (11in) shells smashing *Exeter's* bridge and putting her forward turrets

dire that she fired a salvo of torpedoes to cover a manoeuvre designed to open the range.

Despite his obvious success Langsdorff, an ex-destroyer man, seemed very concerned at the torpedo threat posed by the two light cruisers. Their feints resulted in his changing course by steps from the original south-east, through east and north eventually to west, i.e. back

towards the Uruguayan coast. While *Exeter* had hit the German only twice, the light cruisers had scored a possible 13 times and, while their 152mm (6in) shells caused little significant damage, the psychological effect on Langsdorff was considerable.

Dubious shelter

At 0716 *Graf Spee* had made a sudden turn as if to finish off the still present *Exeter*, but had been immediately closed by the others which deterred her at the cost to *Ajax* of three hits, which deprived her of the use of two turrets. With *Exeter* obliged to steer southward to the dubious shelter of the Falklands, the two light cruisers were dodging main and secondary battery fire at ranges down to 7300m (23,950ft) and, as the German patently could not be stopped, lost bearing and took up a shadowing role with the idea of a further attack after dark. *Ajax* was now down to three guns and only 20 per cent ammunition. Surprisingly, Langsdorff was obviously determined to make for Montevideo instead of the more obvious sanctuary of the open ocean, and fired only when the British

approached too closely. Early on the morning of 14 December he duly entered neutral waters with a still fully battleworthy ship and 36 dead (the British had suffered 72).

International law obliged the ship to leave within 24 hours but the Germans asked for more, to effect necessary repairs. This accorded with British aims to delay her even more to allow the concentration of reinforcements. The diplomatic battle was matched by careful use of misinformation that appeared finally to convince Langsdorff that the aircraft-carrier HMS *Ark Royal* and a battle-cruiser awaited him.

On the morning of 17 December *Graf Spee* moved out into international waters in the estuary, her crew left and she was blown up, the resulting column of smoke clearly visible to the British ships outside. These comprised just the *Ajax*, *Achilles* and the newly-arrived *Cumberland* (able to steam on only two shafts).

On 20 December the disillusioned Langsdorff shot himself. Napoleon had once observed that morale was to *matériel* as three was to one. Never was it more true.

This is Deutschland, the first of the three raiders to be built, seen towards the end of the war. After the Graf Spee disaster, she was renamed Lützow to avoid the spectacle of a ship named after the fatherland being sunk. Armed with six 28cm (11in) and eight 15-cm guns, the 'Deutschland' class could quickly overwhelm a conventional cruiser.

Incredible victory
Chronology

The destruction of the German battleship *Graf Spee* was one of the earliest Allied victories of the war, and an embarrassing blow to the German naval fleet. Pursued across the South Atlantic by Royal Navy warships, she was finally scuttled in the Uruguayan port of Montevideo.

1939

August 21st
The *Graf Spee,* under the command of Captain Hans Langsdorff, sails from Wilhelmshaven with its supply ship *Altmark*. Its destination is a waiting area in the North Atlantic.

September 27th
Graf Spee and and the battleship *Deutschland*, both now stationed in the North Atlantic, are given free rein to attack Allied shipping passing between the Americas and the UK or British territories.

September 30th
The *Graf Spee* moves into the South Atlantic and sinks her first merchant ship, the *Clement*, off the coast of Brazil.

October
The *Graf Spee* sinks four more Allied ships during the month.

November
Graf Spee sails around the coast of Africa, sinking the oil tanker *Africa Shell* off the coast of Madagascar on November 15th. By November 20 she is heading back to a waiting area in the mid-South Atlantic. A large Royal Navy cruiser squadron including the cruisers *Cumberland, Exeter, Ajax* and *Achilles* are in pursuit.

December 13th
Having destroyed three more ships in the South Atlantic – the *Doric Star, Tairoa* and *Streonshalh* – the *Graf Spee* heads for the River Plate area of Uruguay for a last combat patrol of the South American

*The **Graf Spee** lies scuttled off Uruguay, having been destroyed by her own crew rather than the enemy. Captain Langsdorff's later suicide was a sad end to a naval career which began in 1912 and included combat experience at the Battle of Jutland in World War I.*

shipping lanes. She is spotted on the morning of the 13th by the British cruiser squadron under command of Commodore H.H. Harwood.

6.14am
Graf Spee opens fire upon the heavy cruisers *Ajax* and *Exeter* which are attacking from the north while the cruiser *Exeter* manoeuvres to the south.

6.40am
The *Achilles* is damaged by shell splinters from the *Graf Spee*'s 11in (28cm) and 6in (15cm) guns.

6.50am
The British cruiser *Exeter* is badly damaged by German shellfire. Only one of its turrets its operable and it is on fire.

7.25am
Ajax loses two turrets to accurate gunfire from the *Graf Spee*.

7.40am
Ajax and *Achilles* pull away from engagement to avoid further damage. They shadow the *Graf Spee* out of range of her main armament.

7.50am
Exeter peels away from the action and diverts to the Falkland Islands.

8.00am
Despite comparatively light damage to his ship, Langsdorff turns the *Graf Spee* towards the port of Montevideo in Uruguay. The remaining British cruisers follow her closely.

12.00pm
Graf Spee enters Montevideo harbour. Langsdorff intends using the stop to make repairs to his ship. The British authorities put diplomatic pressure upon the Uruguayan government, and consequently Langsdorff is given only 72 hours in which to make his repairs and leave Uruguay.

December 17th
Langsdorff is led to believe that a large Royal Navy forces awaits him outside Montevideo. Feeling his position hopeless, he orders the *Graf Spee* to be scuttled.

December 20th
Langsdorff commits suicide.

International Events 1939

September 17th
The Soviet Union invades eastern Poland in support of German operations in the west of the country.

September 21st
A directive from Reinhard Heydrich, head of the Reich Security Main Office (RSHA), orders Polish Jews to be concentrated into ghetto areas. It is a measure to facilitate the 'Final Solution' – the deportation and extermination of European Jewry.

September 27th
Warsaw falls to the Germans and Poland effectively surrenders. The former Polish leader, General Wladyslaw Sikorski, sets up a Polish government in exile in Paris.

September 29th
Lithuania, Latvia and Estonia sign 'mutal assistance' agreements with the Soviet Union.

October 14th
The British battleship *Royal Oak* is sunk by *U-47* at Scapa Flow.

November 30th
The Soviet Union invades Finland. Finnish troops under the command of Field Marshal Karl von Mannerheim inflict appalling casualties upon the Russian aggressors as the campaign develops.

December 3rd
Finland appeals to the League of Nations for help in resisting the Russian invasion.

December 4th
The USSR does not recognise the League of Nations intervention, saying that the USSR is merely supporting the new Finnish People's Government as proclaimed by its leader Otto Kuusinen.

December 14th
The Soviet Union is expelled from the League of Nations.

*The **Admiral Graf Spee** in August 1939. German 'pocket' battleships were engineered to be within the weight restrictions imposed on German military shipping by the Versailles treaty of 1919.*

Battle for Finland

The winter war

In 1939 the USSR expands its border at the expense of several neighbouring countries. But Finland refuses to be coerced.

Poland was not the only country that figured in the secret clauses of the 1939 Russo-German Pact. They also mentioned the Baltic republics of Estonia, Latvia and Lithuania, together with Finland, placing them all within the sphere of interest of the USSR. Joseph Stalin, having watched Hitler's army conquer one small nation so spectacularly, seems to have felt that it was time for the Red Army to bring him similar gains.

Political pressure and geographic realities were enough to persuade the three Baltic republics to sign treaties of mutual assistance, which allowed the USSR to establish garrisons and bases within their borders. However, Finland felt herself protected in her most vulnerable area by the Gulf of Finland and Lake Ladoga, and by the wilderness of forest, swamp, lakes and sheer arctic distances that made up her eastern frontier, stretching from Lake Ladoga up to the Arctic Ocean. The Finns also believed that the spirit and training of her armed forces would be enough to hold the first onslaught, and that the sight of their own David fighting off the Soviet Goliath would evoke active aid from the rest of the world.

Overwhelming odds

When, on 28 November, after two months of verbal bullying by Molotov and defiance by the Finnish leaders Paasikivi and Tanner, the USSR broke off negotiations and attacked the Finnish defences two days later, it looked at first as though the Finns had been right. Certainly, all Western Europe and the USA applauded the Finnish stand – and Finnish military successes at first exceeded all expectations. Despite the size of the Finnish army (at its peak, never more than 16 divisions), despite its acute shortage of artillery and heavy ammunition, despite its shortage of transport, signals equipment and total lack of armour, it held the Soviet attack which came up through the Karelian Isthmus, along the whole of the Mannerheim Line (the main Finnish defences) from the Gulf of Finland to the River Vuoksi. The Finnish II and III Corps, in fact, beat back the Soviet 7th and 13th Armies, inflicting astonishing losses on the Red Army infantry by the accuracy of their rifle and machine-gun fire, and on the Soviet tanks with petrol bombs. By 22 December, after six days of pointless battering against a seemingly impregnable line, the Soviets broke off the

The long columns of Soviet troops pressing into central Finland were cut to pieces in December. Chopped into pockets ('mottis') some 30,000 Soviets were killed or captured around Suomussalmi, many frozen to death after their supplies ran out. The Soviet 44th and 163rd Divisions were annihilated.

FINLAND: RUSSIAN ASSAULT

The Winter War was fought in a sparsely inhabited land of forest and swamp with a savage winter climate. From south of Oulu the countryside was heavily wooded and bad going for mechanised units. Following the German invasion of Russia in 1941 Finland swiftly recaptured the territories it lost in 1940, only to lose them and other areas after World War II.

action and withdrew to re-group and to re-think.

Matters had not gone so well for the Finns north of Lake Ladoga. The six divisions of the Soviet 8th Army crossed the frontier and advanced implacably to the line of Finnish defences between Kitelä and Ilomantsi. But in doing so they had given some hostages to fortune: incredibly, the Soviets had no ski troops, whereas every Finnish soldier was well

Finnish troops were desperately short of equipment but their difficulties were exacerbated by the sheer variety of different weapons provided by friendly countries. The Suomi M1931 was Finnish-made and one of the best SMGs available. It was tough, accurate, reliable, and always in short supply.

trained on skis and many were expert at using them in a military context. Soviet divisions thus found themselves cut off from communication and supplies; small formations were decimated, some units annihilated.

Finland defiant

Much farther north at Suomussalmi, the Soviet 163rd Division was surrounded until 29 December, when it broke completely; the survivors fleeing across the frozen wilderness leaving 11 tanks, 25 guns and 150 lorries to the elated victors.

But of course, it could not go on. Firstly, although the UK, France, the USA and Sweden all professed a desire to help, they produced very little of it – the first two because they needed all their resources for their own use, the others because of their

This Soviet soldier wears the standard army greatcoat and high boots. The curious cap is the budionovka, which proved impractical in Finland, fur caps being much warmer. The red colour patches indicate arm of service.

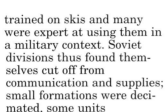

The Soviet attacks in December 1939 were so poorly managed that Finnish machine-gunners were presented with thick waves of Soviet infantry with no effective support from tanks or artillery. The ensuing bloodbath stopped the Red Army in its tracks.

carefully cultivated neutrality; and secondly, when plans were laid to send British and French reinforcements in, Sweden refused to allow them passage.

By early January, Stalin had decided to bring it all to an end. Command was given to General Semyon Timoshenko, siege artillery, was brought up, and on 15 January 1940 the systematic destruction of the Mannerheim Line began.

Finnish troops spent their

days in the trenches connecting the strongpoints and their nights desperately trying to reconstruct smashed concrete boxes and obliterated gunposts. Very soon they also had to spend every night trying to beat off Soviet tanks. Sheer exhaustion spelt the end of the Mannerheim Line, and in due course of every other Finnish line of defence.

The road to Helsinki

By the beginning of March the Soviets had driven them back to Viipuri, and from there the Finnish line curved back almost to Tali and on to Vuosalmi, then to the waterline at Taipale on Lake Ladoga. On 3 March Timoshenko sent a battalion and a brigade across the ice to Vilajoki. So the Finnish positions were turned, and the road to Helsinki open.

On 13 March, bowing to the inevitable, Prime Minister Ryti signed the Treaty of Moscow, which returned the Russo-Finnish border more or less to where Peter the Great had drawn it in 1721.

The Soviet 14th Army launched a vigorous offensive aimed at Petsamo to forestall a possible Anglo/French landing. But the Finns could not stop the Soviet advance and they fell back towards the Norwegian border.

Battle for Finland: Chronology

The Russian conquest of Finland demonstrated the terrible inadequacy of Soviet tactics in 1939. It cost the Soviets over 200,000 dead to suppress the country, the heroic Finns less than 25,000 to resist.

1939

November 30th

Russian forces invade Finland. Using five armies they cross into Finland along the entire length of its southern and eastern borders, and Helsinki is heavily bombed. Finnish troops under the command of Field Marshal Baron von Mannerheim resist doggedly.

December 1st

Russia establishes a Finnish Soviet government at Terijoki under the leadership of Otto Kuusinen.

December 5th

The Russians reach the 'Mannerheim Line' across the Karelian isthmus, a line of emplaced fortifications reaching from the Gulf of Finland to the southeastern tip of the country. There the Russians are held.

December 9th

Amphibious assaults and air raids on Helsinki cease as the Finnish winter weather deteriorates. The weather provides the acclimatised Finnish soldiers with their greatest tactical advantage, and they have greater capabilities of manoeuvre in the sub-zero conditions. The Russians of the 163rd and 44th Divisions, however, enter and take the town of Soumussalmi in the northeast of Finland, the region where Finnish forces are most thinly spread.

December 15th

The Russian offensive in the south and southeast effectively grinds to a halt, stopped by the arctic weather and Finnish talent in defence. Amphibious assaults across the Gulf of Finland are repelled, protecting Helsinki, and the Mannerheim Line holds strong. Soumussalmi is

Above: The Finnish population rapidly mobilised to dig extensive infantry trench systems. Note the zig-zag configuration to prevent small-arms fire being directed along the entire length of the trench.

Below: The defeated Finnish defenders of Kuhmo return home after the signing of the Finnish–Soviet peace accord on 13 March 1940. They had inflicted massive losses on the Russian 54th Division.

Finnish women work flat out manufacturing snowsuits for ski-patrol soldiers. Cloth shortages forced many citizens to relinquish their cotton bedsheets for the purpose.

retaken. In the extreme north the 14th Army takes the town of Petsamo but is unable to do the same with Nautsi.

December 17th-31st
Following the recapture of Soumussalmi, Finnish troops actually cross the border into Soviet Karelia. They – and the cruel Finnish weather – inflict a massive defeat on Soviet units, killing around 27,000 soldiers and decimating the Russian 163rd and 44th Divisions.

1940
January 2nd
A further Russian offensive in the Karelian isthmus ends in failure.

January 7th
Soviet units adopt defensive tactics as repeated offensives are crushed by the Finns, though constant air bombardment continues (weather permitting). Stalin makes a change in command. From now on Russian forces will be led by General Semyon Timoshenko. He begins to make preparations for a decisive offensive.

January 28th
While the Finns on the Mannerheim Line prepare to receive a new offensive from

Timoshenko's units, other Finnish units gain ground against the Soviet 54th Division at Kuhmo.

February 1st
The Soviet Seventh and Thirteenth Armies begin their offensive against the Mannerheim Line, first pounding the Finnish lines with an artillery barrage of 300,000 shells.

February 11th-17th
The Soviet Seventh Army finally break through the Mannerheim Line at Summa after improving their tactics and training. The Finnish Army is put into a general retreat northwards and has only 15 divisions left.

February 23rd
The Soviets deliver the terms of surrender to Finland, making severe territorial claims to the whole of the Karelian isthmus/Lake Lagoda region and also requiring the Finns the protect the Russians from any external threats to its northern border.

March 5th
Finland enters into negotiations with the Soviet Union over the peace terms. On March 12th the Soviet agreement is accepted in the

Finnish Diet by 145 votes to three.

International Events
1939
December 5th
In the US, President Roosevelt requests defence expenditure to total $1.3 billion.

December 8th
As the UK attempts to impose a naval blockade of Germany, the US government protests at what it sees as a restriction on international free trade.

December 14th
The Soviet Union is expelled from the League of Nations following its invasion of Finland.

December 24th
Pope Pius XII issues a guarded call for peace, striving to remain apolitical.

1940
January 8th
Food rationing is introduced in the UK.

February 14th
The British government announces that it will be arming all merchant vessels.

February 15th
Hitler issues a directive to

U-boat commanders giving them licence to attack any merchant ship destined for British-controlled waters, even if it is flying a neutral flag.

February 28th
Three rotors from the German Enigma encoding machine are recovered by Allied divers from a scuttled U-boat off Scotland. The catch is a vital step forward in breaking the Enigma code.

Breakthrough at Sedan

10 May 1940: The long awaited German offensive in the West begins. The French border defences are outflanked.

Shortly after 0230 on the morning of 10 May 1940, 64 men of the German army crossed the Dutch frontier; this was the pinpoint of invasion. Three hours later glider-borne troops dropped over the Belgian border to capture and demolish the huge fortifications at Eben-Emael. After another five minutes the 30 divisions of Army Group 'B' under General Fedor von Bock flooded forward across the frontiers from Maastricht up to the coast at the Ems estuary, while to the south General Gerd von Rundstedt's Army Group 'A' of 44 divisions, including the main striking force of seven Panzer divisions under General Ewald von Kleist, struck forward into the Ardennes – the wooded country that French military commanders had been proclaiming impassable

for tanks since 1919. With an almost suicidal alacrity that brought tears of joy to Hitler's eyes, the Allied armies in the north – five divisions of the British Expeditionary Force, eight divisions of the French 1st Army on their right and seven divisions of the French 7th Army up on the coast around Dunkirk – left the defensive positions they had spent the bitterly cold winter so arduously preparing, and moved forward to join the Belgian army in accordance with the Dyle Plan, which envisaged a defensive line

A few sorties by these monstrous tanks caused the Germans momentary alarm since they were impervious to the standard 37mm (1.46in) anti-tank gun. Unfortunately French logistic arrangements beggared description and many were captured as they ran out of fuel.

The armoured formations that achieved such startling success in 1940 represented a small proportion of the German army. The bulk of the infantry divisions were equipped much like their fathers in 1918 but they faced a very different opposition. The British and French armies were not the competent, victorious forces of 20 years before but had deteriorated to a very low professional standard.

GERMAN GAMBLE: THROUGH THE ARDENNES

The German plan was an audacious gamble that had captured Hitler's imagination but alarmed several of his senior commanders. Success depended on the German armour debouching from the Ardennes forest before the French could deploy a blocking force. In the event, the German spearheads reached the Meuse in two days. Like the Second Empire before it, the Third Republic perished to the sound of gunfire at Sedan.

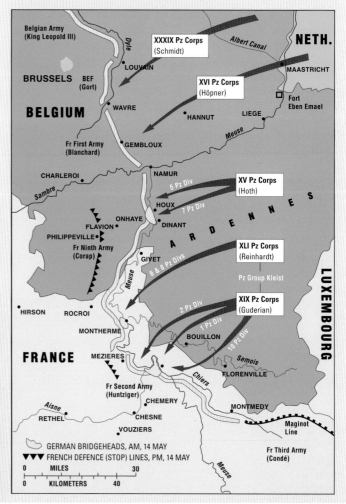

Armed with a 37mm (1.46in) gun that could penetrate the armour of only the lighter German tanks the H-39 was hopelessly outclassed in 1940. The German army captured hundreds of them and pressed them into service later in the war on anti-partisan operations in the USSR and Balkans.

running along the Dyle and Meuse rivers. There were obviously some difficulties to be overcome on the way, for the Luftwaffe was busy overhead all the time and this was the occasion for the baptism of Allied troops by dive-bombing – it took time for them to become accustomed to the nerve-shaking howl that accompanied it. Moreover, roads were soon choked by refugees fleeing ahead of von Bock's advancing infantry.

Nevertheless, by the evening of 14 May, the Allied line was formed. From the mouth of the Scheldt to just north of Antwerp stood three divisions of the French 7th Army; the 80km (50 miles) south-east to Louvain were held by 13 divisions of the Belgian army; between Louvain and Wavre the front was held by the BEF and from Wavre to Namur by six divisions of the French 1st Army. Some of the battalion and brigade commanders

were dismayed by the fragmentary nature of the defences they now occupied – especially compared with those they had just left – while the divisional and higher commanders were alarmed by news of events further to the south. But as yet none of them was aware of the fact that von Bock's slowly advancing army group was in fact 'the matador's cloak', tempting the mass of the Allied armies forward into the trap which would release von Kleist's Panzer group for the killing thrust.

Race to the Meuse

This was not merely the plan; it soon became the reality. Crashing through the 'impassable' Ardennes as though on a peacetime exercise and brushing aside the French light cavalry unit that had been sent out to 'delay' them, the three divisions of General Heinz Guderian's XIX Panzer Corps were across the French fron-

tier and had reached the Meuse on each side of Sedan by the afternoon of 12 May. By evening German armour controlled the right bank of the river up as far as Dinant. They were across the river within 24 hours (French High Command estimates, once they had got over the shock of the German arrival on the Meuse, were that the crossing would take at least four days to organise and two to carry out). By the morning of 14 May, Guderian had two bridgeheads consolidating, while up at Dinant the 7th Panzer Division of General Hermann Hoth's XV Panzer Corps (commanded by Generalmajor Erwin Rommel) had formed yet another bridgehead in the face of desperate but sporadic French resistance.

Screaming Stukas

Early on 15 May the flood burst into France. From each of the bridgeheads the Panzers roared out, preceded

on every advance by a cloud of screaming Stukas, covered against attack from British or French fighters by marauding Messerschmitts. Refugees choked the roads, harried by Luftwaffe fighters, bullied by frightened and demoralized soldiers or gendarmes of their own side, or forced into the ditches by strange, ominous, foreign vehicles manned by blond young giants who waved triumphantly at them, rarely deliberately harming them but leaving an impression of invincibility. That evening, German Panzers were reported only 19km (12 miles) from Laon, and when Edouard Daladier, then France's Minister of National Defence, ordered a counterattack, the French commander-in-chief, General Maurice Gamelin, replied that he had no reserves because the bulk of French strength was locked up in the outflanked Maginot Line. At the same time Gamelin announced that he could no longer take responsibility for the defence of Paris, and he issued orders for a general retreat of all French forces in Belgium. A copy of these orders came, solely by good fortune, to the notice of the British commander-in-chief, Field Marshal Lord Gort, enabling him to ensure that the BEF divisions on the Dyle were not left there on their own.

The breathtaking pace of the German advance quickly demoralised the French army. While the French high command manoeuvred pins on their maps, the bewildered soldiers began to surrender. There were several gallant stands but there was no strategic co-operation.

Breakthrough
at Sedan: Chronology

On May 10th, 1940 German forces invaded the Low Countries. In only four days they were breaking through the Franco–Belgian lines at Sedan and penetrating the French interior.

1940
May 10th

German forces invade Belgium and Holland. The invasion utilises airborne forces to capture key bridges and other strategic positions in advance of German armoured columns punching across the borders. The powerful Belgian fortress at Eben Emael with a garrison of 2000 men falls to only 89 German paratroopers. Rotterdam and The Hague are also assaulted by advanced paratroop units.

May 11th

Allied forces, including the British Expeditionary Force and three French armies, make defensive arrangements in Belgium in a desperate

German troops parade victoriously through Paris after the fall of France. France became the most popular foreign destination for garrisoned German troops, with its abundant supplies of excellent wine and food and good weather in the south.

attempt to stop the German advance. They make a defensive line moving down from positions just south of Rotterdam, though Antwerp, cutting just east of Brussels, then following the River Meuse to terminate around Sedan on the western edge of the Ardennes forest. The greatest concentration of troops is around Louvain near Brussels, but the Germans send the Twelfth Army through the supposedly impassable Ardennes to assault the southern defences around Sedan.

May 14th

The XV, XLI and XIX Panzer Corps establish three bridge-heads on the River Meuse at Dinant, Montherme and Sedan without any substantial opposition. The Allies are being outflanked in their southern defences. Later in the day the XV Panzer Corps at Dinant and the XIX Panzer Corps at Sedan break through the light Allied defences and push into France.

Anxiety is etched onto the faces of these French refugees. Gridlocks of civilian vehicular traffic caused huge problems for the Allied armies trying to outmanoeuvre the German advance.

May 15th

XLI Panzer Corps at Montherme joins its neighbouring Panzer Corps to drive deeper into France. The breakthrough at Sedan also allows the Germans to bypass the French Maginot Line to the south. The French had been relying on the Belgian forces to protect their northern border.

French prisoners of war prepare for a potato dinner. Large numbers of French prisoners, and free citizens, were sent to Germany itself where they worked in industry and construction. Many of these positions were filled voluntarily by Frenchmen looking to escape the austerity of living in an occupied land.

May 15th
Dutch forces surrender to the Germans following intensive bombing raids on Rotterdam.

May 17th-18th
Brussels and Antwerp fall to German forces. The Allies are in full retreat towards the French and Belgian coastline.

May 21st
British and French forces attempt to cut off the German advance through a pincer attack around Arras. The attack comes too late in the battle and is itself outflanked by German Panzer divisions cutting down from the north.

May 28th
King Leopold of Belgian instructs his armed forces to surrender. The rest of his government has moved to Paris. German forces now advance to the Belgian coast.

International Events 1940

May 8th
The British Prime Minister Neville Chamberlain resigns his office after a violent Commons debate and a vote of no-confidence passed by the House.

May 10th
Winston Churchill becomes the new British prime minister. He incorporates opposition leaders into his war cabinet and forms a coalition government to raise the handling of the conflict above party politics.

May 14th
Rotterdam is bombed by the Luftwaffe, a raid which kills nearly 1000 people and leaves 78,000 homeless.

May 16th
Ninety British bomber aircraft attack German military targets on the Ruhr and in Belgium, the largest single Bomber Command operation to date.

May 18th
The Italian dictator Benito Mussolini predicts Italy's inexorable involvement in the war.

Escape from Dunkirk

Nightfall, 26 May 1940: The Germans have stormed Calais and the French 1st Army, the Belgian forces and the BEF are hemmed in with their backs to the sea.

When the Germans broke through the Allied line in France during May 1940, there were still considerable French forces to the south of the breakthrough, and even larger forces – including the British Expeditionary Force – to the north. Between them, could they not first manoeuvre to channel and then contain the German breakthrough, then counter-attack from both north and south and so cut the enemy spearheads off from their main sources of supply and support?

Muddle through

In the depths of their despondency, the French leaders were reluctant to admit the practicability of such a scheme, pleading lack of air strength unless Churchill were to abandon all thought of retaining RAF fighter squadrons for the defence of Britain and send them all to France instead. Even then it seemed most likely that the German forces would be either on the Channel coast or in Paris – or both – in a matter of days, in which case the British and French armies to the north most probably faced early dispersion and disintegration and, unless a general armistice saved them, possibly physical destruction. Churchill was home by the morning of 17 May, but before he left he managed to instil something of his own dogged courage into the

French leadership, so that they at least agreed to order some form of counter-attack on the German spearheads as he had suggested. But at the pace of Allied military planning it was four days before it could be attempted, and even then it was bungled. By the evening of 20 May General Heinz Guderian's tank spearheads had reached Abbeville at the mouth of the Somme, and at

An abandoned Renault R-35 light tank lies among burned out vehicles. As the German 18th Army fought its way into Dunkirk the Luftwaffe provided round-the-clock air strikes against which there was little defence.

The BEF of 1939–40 was a far cry from the magnificent army of 1914. Utterly unprepared to wage war in Europe it was ignominiously defeated by the very opponent it had beaten in 1918. Fortunately Lord Gort, the Commander-in-Chief, ignored the ill considered orders emanating from London, and fell back to Dunkirk. He saved the BEF to form the nucleus of a new British army.

DUNKIRK: FLEEING FROM EUROPE

GREAT BRITAIN

DOVER

North Sea

27 May
Calais pocket
surrenders

OSTEND

BRUGES

DE PANNE
BRAY DUNES

NIEUWPORT

28 May
Belgian army
capitulates

GRAVELINES

FURNES

DIXMUDE

GHENT

CALAIS

DUNKIRK

BERGUES

ROULERS

BOURBOURG

WORMHOUDT

BELGIUM

1 Pz Div

WATTEN

POPERINGE

YPRES

BOULOGNE

CASSEL

COMINES

MENIN

COURTRAI

ST OMER

HAZEBROUCK

ARMENTIERES

ROUBAIX

Army
Group B

AIRE

BEF

2 Pz Div

PREMESQUES

LILLE

ETAPLES

6 Pz Div

10 Pz Div

MONTREUIL

8 Pz Div

3 Pz Div

ETHUNE

LA PASSEE

CARVIN

4 Pz Div

FR First Army

Scarpe

ST POL

7 Pz Div

5 Pz Div

DOUAI

DENAIN

VALENCIENNES

NOYELLES

ARRAS

ABBEVILLE

FRANCE

CAMBRAI

DOULLENS

German
bridgeheads
established

BAPAUME

Army
Group A

FRONTLINE, 25 MAY

German infantry divisions consolidate

FRONTLINE, 28 MAY

Somme

FRONTLINE, 31 MAY

PERONNE

AMIENS

0   MILES   30

0   KILOMETERS   50

The crowded beach at Dunkirk where 224,717 British troops were brought off by the Royal Navy and hundreds of volunteer civilian craft. Over 100,000 French soldiers were also evacuated but chose to return home after the surrender.

this point their line was as attenuated as it ever would be. On 21 May four British infantry brigades and the 1st Army Tank Brigade were launched southwards from Arras, in theory supported by two French infantry divisions on one flank and one light mechanised division on the other, while equally strong French forces were assumed to be attacking up from the south to meet them.

Evacuation planned

In the event, only the British forces and the French light mechanised division moved at all, and they quickly found themselves blocked by Generalmajor Erwin Rommel's 7th Panzer Division, which after a brisk battle drove them back to their original positions and threatened them with encirclement. By the evening of 23 May Field Marshal Lord Gort was withdrawing the British brigades farther north, and two days later it became evident to him that

The Vickers Mk VI light tank was armed with twin machine-guns and was designed for reconnaissance. It remained in service until 1942.

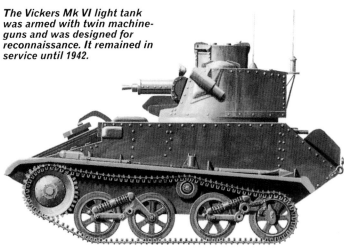

only a rapid retreat to the coast and evacuation to England would save even a quarter of his command.

Battle on the beach

On his own responsibility he issued the necessary orders; the British III Corps withdrew to the beaches on each side of Dunkirk, the I Corps fell back to hold the western flank with one French division on their right and the British II Corps on their left, while the Belgian army held the eastern end of the perimeter. However, on 28 May King Leopold of the Belgians signed an armistice with the Germans, the Belgian army ceased to exist and a large gap yawned on the left of the British positions – filled during that night by a manoeuvre of extraordinary difficulty carried out with admirable efficiency by the 3rd Infantry Division under command of Major-General B. L. Montgomery. It is not too much to say that this opera-

tion saved the British Expeditionary Force. Now Operation Dynamo began – the attempt to evacuate the British army and as many French soldiers as

possible from the trap into which they had been lured. Over a thousand boats took part in this evacuation, varying in size from a Royal Navy anti-aircraft cruiser down to yachts which were sailed across the Channel by their owners from a hundred tiny slips along the south coast or along the reaches of the Thames. At least 50 of these craft were sunk; many of the yacht owners were killed or wounded; but an astonishingly large number of soldiers were saved to fight again, and to form the basis of new armies.

The highest hopes before the evacuation began were that perhaps 50,000 men might escape capture or worse; in the event 338,226 reached the shores of Britain during those miraculous nine

days, of which, on Churchill's insistence, over 100,000 were French. He had returned to Paris on 31 May, and there agreed that British troops would share in holding the rearguard with French formations, and that French troops in the bridgehead would be evacuated in the same proportion as the British. As it happened, French formations were fighting furiously to the south of the bridgehead (thus holding back powerful German forces which would otherwise have been free to attack Dunkirk), and these never reached the sea. Many of those that did arrive towards the end of the operation refused the chance to escape, and the last ships to

Photographed by their commander Erwin Rommel, from his Fieseler Storch command aircraft, 7th Panzer Division heads for Rouen. After Dunkirk there were still 140,000 British troops left in France. Rommel's men took the surrender of the 51st Highland Division at St Valéry.

sail were thus almost empty. As quite a large number of French troops who did get away quickly decided that they did not care for life in Britain and chose to return to France (where most of them soon found themselves in German prison camps), Churchill's well-meant gesture was to a great extent wasted.

But, to the British people, the escape of the bulk of the BEF at Dunkirk was nothing short of a miracle.

Escape from
Dunkirk: Chronology

The evacuation of British forces from the beaches of Dunkirk was an exceptional military escape act which saved Britain from subsequent defeat and occupation by the German forces. Over 338,000 Allied servicemen were rescued, including 113,000 French soldiers.

1940

May 20th
Churchill advises the Admiralty to assemble a fleet of vessels suitable for the evacuation of the British Expeditionary Force (BEF) from the French coastline. In Paris, General Maxime Weygand takes over from General Maurice-Gustave Gamelin as the supreme Allied forces commander in France.

May 24th
Hitler orders his advancing Panzer forces not to pass the Lens-Béthune-St Omer-Gravelines line. The reasons for the halt are unclear, but it nonetheless gives British and French troops retreating to Dunkirk an invaluable time-gap in which to reach the coast.

May 24th
The Luftwaffe commences a heavy bombardment of the Allied positions around Dunkirk. It maintains this bombardment until the end of the Dunkirk evacuation on June 4th, but loses over 200 aircraft to RAF sorties from southern England.

May 25th
German forces take Boulogne and the Allies concentrate in the Dunkirk pocket.

May 26th
Hitler reverses his stop order, but the delay has meant that German forces cannot reach Dunkirk before the retreating Allies. At 6.57pm Operation Dynamo, the evacuation of British forces from Dunkirk,

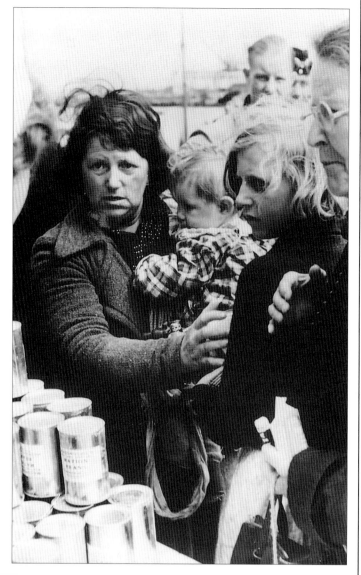

Above: French refugees receive food at Le Havre. A sad fact of the French refugee situation was that 350,000 refugees were Jews who had fled Germany in the late 1930s.

officially begins. Over 850 minor British civilian vessels participate, ferrying troops from the shoreline to the waiting offshore naval ships, or carrying the troops back to the UK itself.

May 28th
The Belgian Army protecting the Allies' right flank surrenders before the onslaught of the German 18th and 6th armies. Belgium has been defeated in only 18 days, yet its holding action gives the Allies the opportunity to make an escape. By the end of the 28th 25,473 British troops have been evacuated.

A German anti-aircraft unit in western Europe. Allied air opposition over France was restrained after Air Chief Marshal Dowding's decision to retain many fighter units in the UK for the forthcoming defence of the British mainland.

A neat line of destroyed Allied vehicles on the beaches at Dunkirk. The British Army was forced to leave behind 84,500 vehicles in France, as well as 2500 field guns, 77,000 tons of ammunition and 165,000 tons of vehicle fuel.

May 29th
Over 47,000 British troops evacuate from Dunkirk on the 29th alone.

May 30th
120,000 Allied soldiers evacuate from the Dunkirk beaches. The figure includes 6000 French soldiers.

May 31st
150,000 Allied soldiers – including 15,000 French – transported back to the UK.

June 1st
The defence of the Dunkirk perimeter passes to the French XVI Corps.

June 4th
Operation Dynamo officially ends. In total 338,226 Allied troops had been rescued from imprisonment or death at the hands of the German forces. The total included 113,000 Frenchmen. Some 40,000 French soldiers, however, become POWs as German troops take Dunkirk.

June 5th
The German Operation Red begins – the final onslaught intended to break French resistance along the Somme, Seine, Aisne and Moselle rivers and push through to Paris. By June 12th the German Army Group B under General Gerd von Rundstedt breaks through French defences.

June 10th–25th
The Allies conduct further evacuation operations along the French coastline. Prior to June 15th, the evacuations are concentrated in northern ports such as Le Havre and St Valery, but with the launch of Operation Ariel on the 15th, southern ports in Biscay are also used. Nearly 250,000 Allied troops are rescued during these operations.

June 14th
German forces enter Paris after the capital is declared an unfortified city. French defences throughout the country collapse under the final German onslaughts.

June 22nd
French general Charles Huntziger signs an armistice agreement with the Germans. Humiliation is heaped upon the French by having them sign the armistice agreement in the railway carriage used to sign the German capitulation at the end of World War I.

International Events 1940

May 22nd
British code-breakers working at Bletchley Park in England break the Luftwaffe's 'Red' key cipher from the Enigma enciphering machine. They accomplish this using a mechanical computing device known as a 'Bombe'.

May 26th
The British government begins the requisitioning of scrap and surplus metal for use in war production industries.

June 10th
Italy declares war on Britain and France. Mussolini declares that 'We take the field against the plutocratic and reactionary democracies who always have blocked the march and frequently plotted against the existence of the Italian people.'

June 11th
The island of Malta experiences its first German air raid, beginning one of the heaviest bombing campaigns of the war.

June 12th
The Royal Air Force bombs Milan and Genoa in response to Italy's declaration of war against Britain and France.

June 14th
In Poland, the infamous Auschwitz concentration camp receives its first inmates, some 728 prisoners from Tarnow.

June 20th
In the Far East, Japan warns French colonial governments in Indochina against helping anti-Japanese actions by the Chinese Nationalist government in Chungking.

Skies of glory
The Battle of Britain

22 July 1940: the German army prepares to invade Britain. First the Luftwaffe must win aerial supremacy then the army can land and the war will be over.

Following the invasion of Norway and the fall of France and the Low Countries in May and June 1940, and as the RAF set about dressing its wounds, the Luftwaffe moved up to bases along the coasts facing the United Kingdom. For the all-out air attack, intended to eliminate RAF Fighter Command in preparation for Operation Sea Lion, an invasion of the islands, the Luftwaffe disposed its forces in three air fleets. Luftflotte III was based in north-west France, Luftflotte II in north-east France and the Low Countries, and Luftflotte V in Norway and Denmark.

By early July the German air forces facing the UK fielded about 2800 aircraft, comprising 1300 Heinkel He 111, Junkers Ju 88 and Dornier Do 17 bombers, 280 Junkers Ju 87 dive-bombers, 790 Messerschmitt Bf 109 single-seat fighters, 260 Messerschmitt Bf 110 and Junkers Ju 88C heavy fighters and 170 reconnaissance aircraft of various types. Of these totals roughly half were combat-ready.

At the head of Fighter Command, Air Chief Marshal Sir Hugh Dowding divided his air defences into three Groups: No. 11 in the south under Air Vice-Marshal Keith Park, No. 12 in the Midlands under Air Vice-Marshal Trafford Leigh-Mallory and No. 13 in the north under Air Vice-Marshal Richard Saul. A fourth Group, No. 10 under Air Vice-Marshal Quintin Brand, was added soon after to cover the south-west.

Dowding disposed a total of 640 fighters at the beginning of July 1940, including 347 Hawker Hurricanes, 199 Supermarine Spitfires, 69 Bristol Blenheim night-fighters and 25 Boulton Paul Defiants. Slightly over half his strength was deployed in the south, the key airfields of Biggin Hill, Kenley, Croydon, Hornchurch, Manston and Tangmere forming a defensive ring around London and the Thames estuary. To provide early warning, the south and east coasts were covered by a network of radar stations, which could detect approaching raids at a distance of about 160km (100 miles).

The German attacks of July, aimed principally at shipping and coastal targets in the south, proved something of a strain on the British pilots who were obliged to fly standing patrols over the convoys until the German tactics were recognised for what they were, and orders given not to engage enemy fighters unnecessarily. British losses in the July combats amounted to 77 fighters, of whose pilots about half survived.

The RAF had a considerable advantage fighting over its own territory. British pilots who bailed out could quickly return to action while German aircrew were captured and German aircraft that crash-landed could be studied for their intelligence value. However, the remorseless onslaught against the RAF's frontline airfields was beginning to succeed by late August. Meanwhile, elements of the German army practised embarkation drills with varying degrees of enthusiasm.

THE BATTLE BEGINS: ATTACKS ON SOUTHERN ENGLAND

The Battle of Britain began at the start of August 1940 with a series of German air strikes on coastal shipping and Channel ports. On 11 August the Luftwaffe started to raid inland, concentrating on frontline airfields and the vital radar stations. The tempo increased until by mid-August the Luftwaffe was mounting up to 1800 sorties a day. The UK's security depended on a dwindling number of irreplaceable young pilots.

The onset of the main assault on 8 August was competently countered by Park's squadrons, whose pilots quickly spotted the weaknesses of the Junkers Ju 87 and Messerschmitt Bf 110, and designed effective tactics to deal with them. The appearance of large formations of Messerschmitt Bf 109s, which were superior in most respects to the Hurricane, caused the British controllers, where possible, to order their Spitfires against the enemy fighters, while the Hurricanes fought the

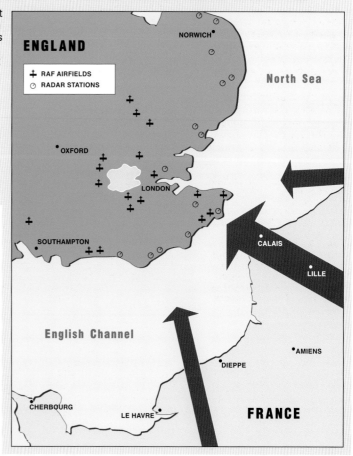

This Hawker Hurricane Mk I (left) flew in 85 Squadron, which was commanded by Squadron Leader Peter Townsend who shot down six enemy aircraft during the Battle. Highly manoeuvrable, if slower than its opponents, Hurricanes shot down more enemy aircraft than all the other defences put together.

This Supermarine Spitfire (right) Mk IIA was flown by Squadron Leader D. O. Finlay when 41 Squadron was based at Hornchurch in December 1940. Air Chief Marshal Dowding had resisted demands to send his Spitfires into the battle for France, thus husbanding his most modern fighters for the battle to come.

slower, lower-flying bombers. By now raids were penetrating farther inland, and on 15 August Luftflotte V attempted to attack targets in northern England, but suffered so badly that such raids were not repeated during the Battle.

A reappraisal of the tactics being employed by the Luftwaffe led to a marked shift during the next phase of the attack, which began at the end of August. Following complaints by the Bf 109 pilots that they were badly handicapped when employed in the bomber-escort role, the Jagdgeschwader were allowed to resume 'free chase' tactics over southern England, frequently catching the RAF fighters during take-off or landing, or as they returned short of fuel and ammunition after combat.

This was unquestionably the most successful phase from the Luftwaffe's viewpoint and would have quickly

brought the defences to their knees had the Germans persisted. However, exasperated at continuing losses, Goering ordered the attack to switch from the RAF to the British civilian population with a massive attack on east London in the late afternoon of 7 September.

Turning point

This marked the turning point of the whole battle, and the easing of pressure on the fighters allowed them a much-needed respite. In the course of further heavy daylight attacks on London, particularly on 15 September and on south east England at the end of the month, the Germans took a heavy beating; the British fighter pilots no longer had to fight over their airfields and could concentrate on the great armadas making their way ponderously towards some unfortunate town or city.

It was at this time that the

differing tactics favoured by Park and Leigh-Mallory came into sharp focus, the former advocating use of single squadrons (because of the short time available in the south to assemble larger forces) and the latter favouring the committing of whole fighter wings to battle. Both men were probably justified in their own combat environments and it must be said that, given adequate warning, Park himself tried to employ two or three squadrons simultaneously. There were, however, occasions when Leigh-Mallory's wing tactic failed to operate efficiently as a result of the time taken to assemble.

The daylight Battle of Britain cost the Luftwaffe a total of 2020 aircraft destroyed, and more than 5200 aircrew killed or missing. Nevertheless, whereas the British could regard the final outcome of the Battle of Britain as a resounding

victory, it was by no means the end of the air assault, which now continued (with very different results) under cover of darkness.

The cost of victory in the daylight Battle of Britain was heavy. Considerable damage was suffered at many of the key airfields, of which some were temporarily abandoned for operational purposes. The cost in aircrew lives was heavy, more than 500 men being posted killed or missing, yet on the last day of the Battle (31 October) Fighter Command possessed eight more squadrons in the frontline than on the first day, and replacement pilots were arriving from the training schools twice as fast as in July to continue a tradition that would forever be remembered by a grateful nation: survival had been achieved through the prowess of just 3030 airmen.

The Luftwaffe raids on Britain were conducted by three main types of bomber: Heinkel He 111H-3, Dornier Do 17 and Junkers Ju 88. The Heinkel 111 (right) was a very successful medium bomber, destined to serve throughout the war. Fortunately for the British, the Luftwaffe lagged behind in the development of four-engined heavy bombers.

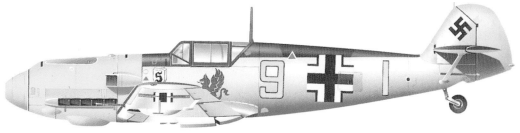

Armed with two or three 20mm (0.8in) cannon and a pair of 7.92-mm (0.31in) machine-guns, the Messerschmitt Bf 109 (left) was fast, agile and would serve until the end of the war. The Bf 109s achieved their greatest successes in early September 1940, swooping under the British radar to catch RAF fighters as they landed.

Skies of glory
Chronology

In 1940 Reichsmarschall Hermann Göring boasted to Hitler that he could pound the UK into submission by air power alone. He had not reckoned on the extraordinary resilience and talent of the Royal Air Force.

1940
June–August 12th
The Luftwaffe concentrates most of its efforts upon Allied shipping in the English Channel and North Sea, destroying some 30,000 tons of merchant vessels.

August 12th
German fighters and bombers

Below: A scene of total destruction in London after a German bombing raid. The heaviest standard German bomb was the SC2000 weighing in at 1953kg (4306lb).

make their first dedicated attacks against British fighter squadron airfields and Chain Home radar stations. Hitler's aim is to destroy the Royal Air Force and so strip the UK of air supremacy for a forthcoming German invasion, Operation Sealion. Sealion is announced in Führer Directive 17 (July 16th) with the intended invasion date between September 19th and 26th.

August 13th
'Eagle Day' – the launch date of a four-day Luftwaffe

Above: A group of British evacuees board a train to take them out of the city. Around six million British children were evacuated during the course of the war, more than any other European country.

The rise of German night-bombing in late 1940 led the UK to develop dedicated night-fighting aircraft, such as these Bristol Beaufighters.

operation intended to destroy the RAF and its radar installations – is set back to the afternoon because of poor weather in the morning. When finally launched, the raids are inconclusive. The attacks include some heavy bombing of Portland, Andover and Southampton, but the Germans lose 40 aircraft in combat.

August 15th
The Luftwaffe loses 74 aircraft during what became known as 'Black Thursday'. Unescorted Luftflotte V bomber units flying from Norway and Denmark are so heavily decimated that the survivors are effectively withdrawn from any further significant contribution to the battle.

August 17th
Volunteers from Bomber Command are sought out to replace heavy losses among RAF fighter pilots.

August 19th-24th
Air activity is reduced by a period of very poor and overcast weather. During the lull Göring decides to switch tactics, concentrating on engaging and destroying RAF fighter aircraft in the air, luring them up through attacks on priority airfield targets. Göring is unaware that RAF fighter strength is almost double what he believes – 600 fighters instead of 300.

August 24th-31st
British airfields suffer one of their worst sustained periods of bombing. Nearly 200 RAF fighters are destroyed, though the Luftwaffe loses nearly 330 aircraft in the same period.

September 3rd
Operation Sealion – the planned German invasion of the UK – is postponed because of disappointing returns in the Battle of Britain. Its date is set back to September 21st.

September 7th
The Luftwaffe bombers switch their attention away from British airfields to concentrate on the bombing of London. It is the Luftwaffe's worst strategic decision, allowing the RAF to recover its losses and operate more effectively against the enemy squadrons.

The 7th sees the heaviest German bombing raid to date, involving 348 bombers and 617 fighters.

September 15th
Now officially known as 'Battle of Britain Day', September 15th sees the RAF meet one of the largest concentrations of German aircraft seen so far in the war. Two separate German bombing raids are attacked by over 300 RAF fighters. Eighty German aircraft are lost and the myth that the RAF is almost defeated is shattered. From this date onwards Germany's efforts are redirected mainly towards the night-bombing of cities, though occasional attacks on air bases continue.

September 17th
Operation Sealion is indefinitely postponed.

International Events 1940

August 18th
The US and Canada establish a Joint Defense Board.

September 2nd
The UK acquires 50 old escort destroyers from the US in return for US use of British naval ports in the West Indies.

September 9th
Aircraft of RAF Bomber Command attack several city targets throughout Germany and Europe, including Hamburg, Bremen and Boulogne.

September 10th
Italian forces begin building up a force of 200,000 troops in Albania prior to the invasion of Greece on October 28th 1940.

September 12th
The US Secretary of State is warned by Ambassador Joseph Grew that the limited US oil embargo of Japan could lead to Japan taking severe retaliatory measures.

September 13th
Italian forces in Ethiopia invade the neighbouring British colony of Kenya.

October 5th
Premier Konoye of Japan predicts a state of war between Japan and the US 'if the United States refuses to understand the real intention of Japan, Germany, and Italy in concluding an alliance for positive cooperation in creating a new world order and persists in challenging those powers'.

Operation Judgement
The raid on Taranto

While the Japanese navy was planning its attack on Pearl Harbor, the Royal Navy prepared to launch a very similar operation.

On the night of 11/12 November 1940, 21 Fairey Swordfish torpedo-bomber biplanes of the Fleet Air Arm struck at the Italian fleet in Taranto harbour and, in the first major and successful strike by naval aircraft, effectively redressed the balance of sea power in the Mediterranean in British favour.

Italy's entry into the war in June 1940 and the subsequent elimination of the French fleet had given the Axis superiority at sea in the Mediterranean, a situation that seriously threatened British convoys sailing to the

fleet to battle on 21 October (Trafalgar Day) with a British fleet of four battleships and battle-cruisers, two carriers (HMS *Eagle* and *Illustrious*), 10 cruisers and four destroyer flotillas. Despite the sailing of two convoys through the Mediterranean, the Italian fleet (comprising five battleships, 14 cruisers and 27 destroyers) declined to leave its base at Taranto; moreover, following a number of near misses from Italian bombers, the carrier *Eagle* was suffering mechanical troubles, necessitating the transfer of her Swordfish aircraft to the *Illustrious*.

Three of the 'Zara' class cruisers were lying in the centre of the Mar Grande when the Swordfish made their attack. In addition to their main armament each carried 16 dual-purpose 100mm (3.92in) guns, a powerful anti-aircraft battery in itself.

Wave-top recce

The action was accordingly postponed, and as a preliminary step a reconnaissance of Taranto was ordered on 10 November. A Martin Maryland of No. 431 Flight,

RAF, flown by Pilot Officer Adrian Warburton, was despatched from Malta that day and, following an epic wave-top tour of the enemy port carried out in the face of intense flak, full details of the Italian fleet's dispositions were reported back to Rear Admiral Lumley Lyster, the flag officer aboard *Illustrious*. The same evening the crew of a RAF flying-boat reported that a sixth Italian battleship had also entered Taranto.

Encouraged by the survival of the Maryland, Lyster decided to launch a strike against the Italian ships where they lay, and on the evening of 11 November two waves of Swordfish flew off *Illustrious* at a position 275km (170 miles) southeast of Taranto. The first formation, led by Lieutenant

Vittorio Veneto was not hit during the Taranto raid but her sister ship Littorio suffered three torpedo hits leaving her under repair until April 1941. Capable of 30 knots and armed with high velocity 381mm (15in) guns, these magnificent battleships seriously threatened the British position in the Mediterranean.

UK with vital supplies from the dominions east of Suez. Moreover, following Italy's attack on Greece in October that year, undisputed use of the Aegean and Adriatic by the Axis powers posed considerable difficulties in the support of any British foothold in the Balkans that might be considered.

Key to any operations in the central Mediterranean by the Royal Navy lay in the continued use of Malta, both as a naval and air base, and it was with a fine sense of history that it had been intended to bring the Italian

TARANTO: NIGHT OF THE SWORDFISH

2300, 11 Nov 1940
Main direction of Swordfish torpedo attacks

Mar Piccolo

Cruiser   Cruiser

Second wave

Mar Grande

Torpedo nets

TARANTO

Fiume
Zara
Duilio
Gorizia
Littorio
Cesare
Vittorio Veneto
Doria
Cavour

First waves

Ballon barrage

San Paulo

Diga di Tarantola

Diga di San Vito

━━ SHIPS CRIPPLED

0   1 MILE

The Italian air force failed to detect the approach of the British fleet to within range of Taranto. A few lumbering flying boats came near, but were shot down by British Fulmar fighters operating under radar control. So the raid achieved complete surprise and sank half the Italian navy's battleships, altering the balance of power in the Mediterranean at a stroke. The British were lucky: after storms earlier in the week only 27 of the 90 barrage balloons protecting the ships were still in the air on the night of the attack, and the Italian torpedo nets did not extend deep enough to protect the ships properly.

The Fairey Swordfish was armed with a single 45.7cm (18in) torpedo or 8 x 27.2kg (60lb) rockets. It was capable of only 222kmh (138mph) at sea level and was extremely vulnerable to enemy fighters and flak.

Commander Kenneth Williamson, comprised 12 aircraft (six with torpedoes, four with bombs and two with bombs and flares); the second wave of nine aircraft (five with torpedoes, two with bombs and two with bombs and flares) led by Lieutenant Commander John Hale followed 40 minutes later.

Despite the obvious significance of the Maryland's appearance over the naval base on the previous day, the Italians were evidently caught completely unaware when Williamson's aircraft swept into Taranto harbour; added to this was the fact that the balloon barrage, which had been expected to cause some embarrassment during the attack, had been almost wholly destroyed by

storms the day before. Moreover the Italians had decided against the use of anti-torpedo nets on the pretext that they restricted the movement of their ships.

Two flares quickly disclosed the position of the new battleship *Littorio* (35,000 tons), and with three torpedoes she was promptly sunk at her moorings. Two older battleships, *Conte di Cavour* and *Caio Duilio* (both of 23,600 tons) were also hit, the former never to sail again, and the latter beached to prevent her sinking. In the inner harbour a heavy cruiser and a destroyer were also hit. In due course the gun defences came into action and two Swordfish were shot down, including that flown by Williamson himself, although he and his crewman survived to be taken prisoner. Another Swordfish failed to release its torpedo.

At a single blow, half Italy's battlefleet had been put out of action, a blow from

which the Italians never fully recovered. On numerous occasions during the following three years their fleet declined battle with the Royal Navy, having been deprived of capital ship superiority. In the naval Battle of Cape Matapan on 28 March 1941, when a powerful force of Italian battleships might otherwise have severely crippled Admiral Sir Andrew Cunningham's Mediterranean Fleet, the two

enemy capital ships (albeit one of them damaged) sought safety by flight, leaving three cruisers and two destroyers to be sunk by the Royal Navy. In the subsequent evacuation of Greece and Crete by British forces, losses among ships of the Royal Navy were grievous, being in the main inflicted from the air. Had the bulk of the Italian battlefleet been intact at that time losses would have been immeasurably worse.

The Italian navy included large numbers of well-armed destroyers. Like most classes of Italian warship they were built for speed, but the lightness of these destroyers' design betrayed them after the Battle of Sirte when two foundered in heavy seas.

HMS Eagle, seen here after Taranto, was unable to take part in the raid as planned. She had sustained considerable damage from numerous near misses during enemy air attacks off Calabria. Some of her Swordfish and their crews were transferred to Illustrious for the attack.

Operation Judgement
Chronology

Despite using obsolete Swordfish biplanes, the British airmen who attacked the Italian naval base at Taranto managed to alter the balance of power in the Mediterranean theatre. Three major Italian battleships are put out of action in only a few minutes, and four other vessels damaged.

1940

October 21st
First date set for Operation Judgement, the British air assault upon the Italian naval base at Taranto. The attack is postponed, however, after a fire aboard the aircraft-carrier *Illustrious* and technical problems on the aircraft-carrier *Eagle*.

November 9th
Illustrious moves into position in preparation for the Taranto raid. A Swordfish aircraft is forced to crash land after engine trouble.

November 10th
The British force comes under bombardment from Italian aircraft as it approaches Malta. There is little damage and an Italian bomber is downed. Another Swordfish is lost to engine malfunction.

November 11
A further Swordfish is lost to mechanical failure, the third is as many days. Contaminated gasoline is discovered as the source of the problem. Nevertheless, the operation is given the go-ahead and around 10.00pm the *Illustrious* launches the first wave of Swordfish from a position off the Greek island of Cephalonia, 290km (180 miles) off southern Italy.

10.58pm
The first aircraft begin their assault at Taranto. Two flare-launching aircraft mark out the targets for the approaching torpedo planes.

11.14pm
The Italian battleship *Cavour* is struck by a torpedo from the Swordfish L4A. The aircraft is brought down by anti-aircraft fire, but both crew members survive.

11.15pm
The *Doria* is hit by two torpedoes near the bows. Shortly afterwards the battleship *Littorio* is struck on her starboard bow following a bold attack by Lt. N.M. Kemp around dense barrage-balloon protection. The starboard stern is hit by another torpedo from aircraft L4M. The final two torpedo runs of the first wave are unsuccessful, one torpedo launched against the *Vittorio Veneto* sinking and

*The Italian battleship **D**uilio lies crippled in Taranto harbour the morning after **O**peration Judgement. **D**uilio was deliberately run aground at the bows to prevent her sinking. She was refloated within a month by expert salvage and repair teams and fully repaired within six months.*

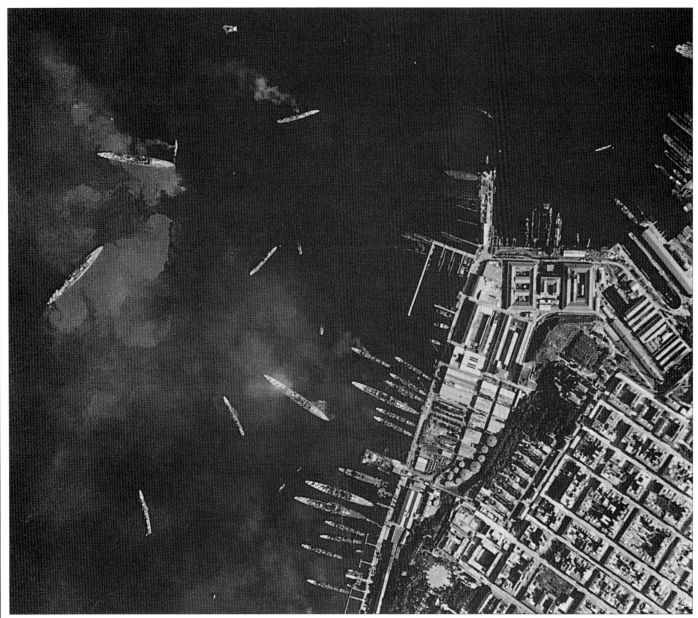

A British high-altitude reconnaissance photograph of Taranto harbour after the British attack. Pools of oil are clearly visible spreading out around the damaged shipping, the result of torpedo strikes.

exploding on the floor of the harbour, the other hitting the *Libeccio* but failing to explode.

11.35pm
The second wave of aircraft move into position for their attack.

11.50pm
Flares are dropped over the target area. The two flare-dropping aircraft go on to attack the harbour's oil depot without success.

12.00 Midnight
The battleship *Caio Duilio* moored in Mar Grande is struck by a single torpedo near the bow.

**November 12th
0.01am**
The *Littorio* – already sinking from earlier attacks – is struck once again. Swordfish E4H is downed by anti-aircraft fire, the co-pilot being killed. The *Vittorio Veneto* escapes damage in a further assault, this time by Swordfish E5H (Wellham-Humphreys). The *Trento* is hit by a bomb dropped from L5F, but the bomb does not explode.

1.22am
The Taranto defences sound the all-clear. The attack is over.

3.00am
All apart from two Swordfish return to the *Illustrious*.

International Events
1940
October 21st
British Prime Minister Winston Churchill makes a radio broadcast to the French people, imploring them to resist German occupation and be assured that 'We seek to beat the life and soul out of Hitler and Hitlerism - that alone, that all the time, that to the end.' In the UK, the city of Liverpool experiences its 200th air raid of the war.

November 6th
Franklin D. Roosevelt is re-elected as President of the United States.

November 9th
In Alsace-Lorraine the Germans begin the forcible expulsion of nearly 200,000 French citizens.

November 11th
The Dachau concentration camp conducts its first mass execution, killing 55 Polish academics. Well over 40,000 inmates would die in Dachau by the end of the war.

November 11th
In Paris students demonstrate around the Arc de Triomphe against the German occupation. The demonstration is brutally dispersed by German military units.

November 12th
Hitler issues political orders for bringing Spain into the Axis alliance. Hitler was eager to use Spain as a launch pad for an attack on Gibraltar and for control of the Mediterranean sea lanes. Spain's leader, General Franco, maintained Spain's 'non-belligerency' despite pressure from Hitler.

O'Connor's victory
Operation Compass

December 1940: the Western Desert Force is preparing to counter-attack the Italian armies that are menacing Egypt.

The Italian invasion of Egypt in September 1940 ground to a halt at Sidi Barrani, 96km (60 miles) short of Mersa Matruh, having apparently run out of petrol, water and perhaps energy. The leading Italian formations then spent the next two months building a number of fortified camps running in a quadrant out into the desert from Maktila on the coast to Sofafi at the top of the Escarpment.

On 9 December General Richard O'Connor launched Operation Compass, a 'five-day raid' by both divisions of the Western Desert Force. It was intended to attack two or more of the fortified camps, menace the others on the Escarpment, shell Italian barracks and garrisons in Sidi Barrani and Maktila, and, if all went well, advance as far as the frontier wire and destroy any other enemy installations there. They were then to collect as many prisoners as possible before withdrawing either along the coast to Mersa Matruh or down into the desert.

It caught the Italians totally by surprise, with the majority of the garrisons in the course of preparing breakfast. Ponderous and irresistible, the line of Matildas appeared over the crest half a mile from the main entrances to the camps, brushed aside any vestige of defence put up against them, burst through the gateways and fanned out across the camp areas like avenging furies. They were impervious to any fire, even from the Italian artillery.

Nibeiwa was in British hands by noon, the Tummar camp to the north by evening and the camp nearest to the coast surrendered the following morning without firing a shot. Meanwhile Sidi Barrani had been occupied, the forward patrols of the 7th Armoured Division were probing westwards to the wire, and by the evening of 10 December one of the greatest problems facing Western Desert Force was dealing with some 20,000 prisoners.

Bardia was surrounded by the Australians by 17 December and assaulted by them on 3 January; by the

The Italians christened the desert highway between Sollum and Sidi Barrani 'The road to victory'. That it certainly became, but not in the way they had hoped. Here a Fiat CR 42 fighter lies wrecked on a captured airstrip. The Italian markings have been stripped off by souvenir hunters

evening of 6 January the last Italian defences had collapsed, thousands more prisoners were trudging eastwards, and one British armoured brigade – the 7th – had reached El Adem on their drive to seal off Tobruk. Their vehicles desperately needed overhauling, the drivers' eyes were red-rimmed and everyone was hungrier and thirstier than they had believed possible – but they were winning and this made up for everything.

The Australian 19th Brigade and the riflemen of the 7th Support Group arrived on the Tobruk perimeter on 12 January, the other two Australian brigades following on the 17th. On 21 January, covered by the guns of the Support Group and the small-calibre fire of the tanks, the Australian infantry mounted

HERCULEAN EFFORTS: THE RACE INTO LIBYA

O'Connor's staggering victory was made possible by the Herculean efforts of his troops. In the long race across Cyrenaica the wear and tear on men and machines was severe and by the end of the operation only 20 per cent of British vehicles were still operational.

Capable of no more than 13kmh (8mph), the ponderous Matilda tank was all but invulnerable to the Italian anti-tank guns. The Matilda regiment sent out from England headed the attack on the Italian camps around Sidi Barrani. The tank's only disadvantage was the inability of it's 40mm (1.57in) gun to fire high-explosive shells as well as anti-tank rounds.

Italian regular troops wore a grey/green uniform but the army in North Africa generally wore the colonial khaki uniform. This officer wears the lighter cordellino twill uniform and carries a Beretta pistol. For field service dress the cap badge was supposed to be embroidered in black.

the first attack on Tobruk. It was all over in 36 hours: few of the Italian posts were held with any degree of determination, and the naval garrison around the port gave up without a shot fired.

The following morning new orders reached the men of Western Desert Force: they were now to mount a raid on Benghazi, so their advance must continue westwards – the Australians moving on Derna, 7th Armoured Division concentrating at Mechili, on the Trig el Abd, south of the Jebel Akhdar bulge. They were there by 2 February.

Excitement kept them all going. They were driving vehicles in dire need of service and maintenance, over appalling country about which almost nothing was known except that it led in the right direction. They had aboard the vehicles two days' supply of food and water, just enough petrol to get them to the target area and as much ammunition as they could find room for.

But the leading armoured cars were chasing an astonished garrison out of the fort at Msus by the afternoon of 4 February, the first cruiser tanks arrived there the following morning, and by that afternoon guns and infantry of the Support Group had raced down to Antelat and then across the coast road at Beda Fomm. By 1600 a battalion of the Rifle Brigade was established across the road with gun positions in support to their rear and armoured cars patrolling the stretch of beach on their left.

Altogether, the force consisted of about 600 men.

Italian counter-attack

When the morning came one small attack was launched against the British lines by 13 M13 tanks, which had been brought up to the head of the column during the night; but it was met by a storm of fire. When the smoke of battle cleared, the astonished watchers saw 13 smouldering and stationary Italian tanks, some with their tracks blown off, some with their crews shot by fire, one stopped only metres from the tent from which the action had all been directed. In ten weeks, General O'Connor's force had advanced 800km (500 miles) and destroyed the Italian 10th Army, taking 130,000 prisoners including seven generals – at a cost to themselves of 550 killed or missing, and 1373 wounded.

The Milizia Volontaria Per La Sicurezza Nazionale, popularly called 'Black Shirts', were Mussolini's Fascist militia. They fought under the command of the Italian army but retained their distinctive shirts, collar patches and black fezzes with tassels.

It was a remarkable feat by any standards and now, despite the condition of their equipment, all the men of the force were sure they could drag themselves farther, on and into Tripoli, thus driving the Italians completely out of North Africa.

With this in mind, O'Connor's chief staff officer dashed back to Cairo. He arrived early on the morning of 12 February and at 1000 was ushered into General Wavell's office. All the maps of the desert that had previously covered the long wall were gone; in their place was a huge map of Greece. "You see, Eric," said Wavell, gesturing towards it. "I am planning my spring campaign!" Developments in the Balkans had conspired to rob O'Connor and his men of their greatest victory.

O'Connor's victory
Operation Compass: Chronology

Operation Compass provided a much-needed morale boost to the British people. A quarter of a million Italian soldiers are defeated by a British force numbering 36,000 in Egypt and Libya, setting the tone for Italy's poor North African campaign.

1940
September
Italian forces in Libya under the command of Marshal Graziani cross into Egypt. They occupy the coastal town of Sidi Barrani and arrange a series of fortified military camps south of the town into a defensive line. The camps are called East, North and West Sofafi, Nibeiwa, Tummar East, and Tummar West.

Below: An Italian column moves along a North African coast road. The quality of training in most Italian divisions in 1940–41 was woefully inadequate. This factor, rather than a want of bravery, accounts for many of the problems experienced by Italy in North Africa.

December 6th–8th
Major-General Richard O'Connor, commander of the Western Desert Force in Egypt, launches the preparatory stages of Operation Compass, originally planned as a 'five-day raid' against Italian positions. The 7th Armoured Division, 4th Indian Division and New Zealand Division, together numbering 36,000 men, move from their bases around Abar el Kanaysis and Mersa Matruth and advance some 112km (70 miles) to the offensive's start line at 'Piccadilly' to the southeast of the Nibeiwa fort.

December 8th–9th
The Royal Navy begins an offshore bombardment of Italian positions at Sidi Barrani and Maktila on the northern coast.

Above: A battery of 25-pdr field guns opens up on enemy positions. The 25-pdr was an excellent weapon on par with the German 88mm (3.45in) Flak, having a range of 12,250m (40,189ft) and muzzle velocity of 518mps (1699fps).

Italian troops inspect a position. In mid 1940 the Italian Army in total had 43 divisions of infantry, with two motorised divisions and 11 'self-transportable' divisions capable of motorised movement.

December 9th
Operation Compass is launched. The 7th Armoured Division strikes between the camps of Sofafi and Rabia and the northern camps and drives north to cut the Libyan coastal road at Buqbuq. Simultaneously the 7th Royal Tank Regiment and 4th Indian Division attack and take the camps at Nibeiwa and Tummar West.

December 10th
Tummar East falls, the last of the northern camps. The Italians at Sidi Barrani are effectively surrounded, with another British unit – Selby Force – advancing westwards along the coast road. Selby Force has ejected the Italian 1st Libyan Division from Maktila, and proceeds to take Sidi Barrani. Over 38,000 Italian soldiers are taken prisoner. The Italian XXI Corps, which escaped the net, are put into retreat.

December 11th
The Royal Navy switch their bombardment to Sollum, west of Buqbuq, to restrict the speed of the Italian retreat along the northern coast. The Catanzaro Division is later caught between Buqbuq and Sollum, taking heavy losses and giving the Allies another 30,000+ prisoners to deal with.

1941
January 22nd
The Allied advance reaches and takes the key strategic port at Tobruk, providing the Allies with greater logistical security for their further advance across the Africa. They have advanced over 200 miles since the beginning of Operation Compass against Italian forces numbering around 250,000 soldiers, and have taken 130,000 Italians prisoner.

International Events
1940
December 10th
Two German spies are hanged in Pentonville jail, London. Jose Waldberg and Carl Meier are the first spies to be executed in the UK. Efficient British intelligence ensures that almost all German spies in the UK are compromised during the war.

December 11th
The UK makes further requests for US aid. The British ambassador Lord Lothian tells US officials that 'with your help in airplanes, munitions, in ships and on the sea, and in the field of finance now being discussed between your Treasury and ours, we are sure of victory'.

December 17th
President Roosevelt publicly announces that the US will lend arms and other military equipment to the UK as part of what became known as the Lend-Lease scheme.

December 19th
The British Purchasing Commission places $750 million-worth of orders for war supplies with the US government, including an order for over 12,000 aircraft.

December 27th–29th
London suffers a horrific series of bombing attacks from German aircraft dropping mainly incendiary devices. On the 29th, Roosevelt announces that the US must become the 'arsenal of democracy', giving full impetus behind the Lend-Lease scheme.

This Sturmgeschutz III of XL Panzer Corps, from List's XII Army, passes at the foot of the Acropolis in Athens in 1941. From the joint commencement of both operations, it had taken under a month to occupy the Balkans. The German victory was highly symbolic. It was a victory that caused the almost fatal weakening of the British Empire forces in North Africa.

Panzer Division advanced from Petrich, first to Stip and then to Skopje. On 8 April, Colonel-General Paul von Kleist's I Panzer Group drove northwest along the valley of the Nisava to capture Nis, pressing on the next day along the River Morava towards Belgrade. On the same day, LI Corps of Field Marshal Max von Weichs' II Army struck south from Styria to take Maribor and then drove on to Zagreb, with a division veering west to Ljubljana. On 11 April, the 8th Panzer Division crossed the Drava River from Bares, driving down towards Belgrade from the northwest.

Croat sympathies

The German advance was rapid, owing to the panic and confusion amid the Yugoslav ranks, which were under-equipped and badly demoralised. Weichs' units were advancing into Croatia. The Croats had long rebelled against the Serbian majority, which had for years ruled Yugoslavia with an arrogance towards minorities. The Croat Ustase formations threw down their arms, and on more than one occasion, welcomed the advancing German units.

By 10 April, Zagreb was firmly in German hands, and two days later the mayor of Belgrade officially

Hitler strikes south

The invasion of the Balkans

Yugoslavia's stand against Hitler was rewarded with instant invasion but the German foray into the Balkans became more extensive as the Greeks doggedly resisted the Italian advance from Albania.

On 25 March Yugoslav Foreign Minister Aleksander Cincar-Markovic signed a pact with Hitler guaranteeing Yugoslavia's frontiers in return for neutrality and the demilitarisation of the Adriatic coast. But neither Hitler nor Prince-Regent Paul, Yugoslavia's ruler, had correctly gauged the temper of the Yugoslav population.

On 27 March, Yugoslav tanks moved into Belgrade, and the radio announced the immediate exile of Paul; the assumption of the throne by the 17-year-old King Peter II, and the renunciation of the pact with Germany. The coup was greeted with much rejoicing in Belgrade.

Hitler was gripped by anger. He issued orders to the Wehrmacht commanders to prepare 'for the destruction of Yugoslavia'.

Operation Marita

Field Marshal Siegmund List's Twelfth Army had moved from Romania into Bulgaria to carry out Operation Marita, the invasion of northern Greece. In view of the presence in Greece of British and Anzac units, there was now no point in limiting Marita to Thrace and Macedonia.

Operations Strafgericht (Punishment), the invasion of Yugoslavia, and Marita both began on 6 April with strikes against Belgrade by the Luftwaffe. By the following evening 17,000 people had been killed. On the same day, Piraeus harbour in southern Greece was congested with the convoy AFN 24, which had brought more units to support the Anzac Corps advancing towards the Kozani area. The Luftwaffe bombed the port and parachuted mines, blocking any escape route out of the harbour for the convoy.

Meanwhile, the 9th

German motorcyclists from XLI Motorised Corps enter the Yugoslav capital on 12 April, six days after Operations Strafgericht and Marita had begun.

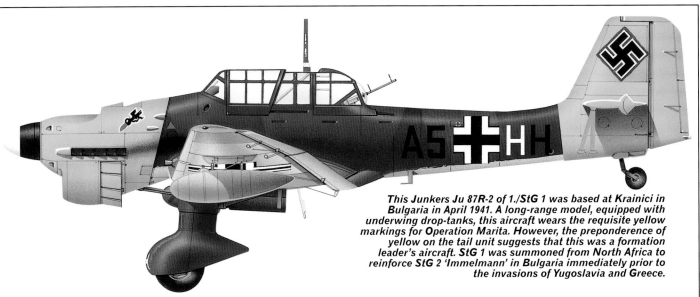

This Junkers Ju 87R-2 of 1./StG 1 was based at Krainici in Bulgaria in April 1941. A long-range model, equipped with underwing drop-tanks, this aircraft wears the requisite yellow markings for Operation Marita. However, the preponderance of yellow on the tail unit suggests that this was a formation leader's aircraft. StG 1 was summoned from North Africa to reinforce StG 2 'Immelmann' in Bulgaria immediately prior to the invasions of Yugoslavia and Greece.

surrendered his city to an SS captain who had driven his company ahead of the main column of the German XIV Corps. Early on 14 April the Yugoslav army capitulated. Its chief of staff formally requested an armistice, and King Peter and his government flew to Athens. The Monastir Gap was now open for the German invasion of Greece.

The invasion of Greece

From Bulgaria, the German XX Corps of List's Twelfth Army drove south from the Arda region into Thrace, isolated the two fortresses at Nymphaea and Ekhinos, annihilating the Greek Evros Brigade. Then XXX Corps turned east towards the Metaxas Line over the River Nestos – all in one day. To their east the 2nd Panzer Division had first driven west into Yugoslavia at Strumica, then hooked south across the border. By the morning of 9 April, it had reached Salonika behind the

two spurs of the Metaxas Line, destroying the remnants of the outnumbered rearguard and precipitating the collapse of the entire Greek Eastern Macedonian Army. The first German patrols had come through the gap as early as 8 April. General Maitland Wilson had brought up New Zealand machine-gunners to support the the British 1st Armoured Brigade and to extend the defences of the Vevi Gap inside Yugoslavia through which the Germans intended to penetrate.

General Wilson was in an unusual situation, commanding Commonwealth troops in a foreign, albeit friendly, country. In addition to the knowledge of his own weaknesses, he knew from day to day not only the enemy's order of battle, but also their local intentions, thanks to Ultra, the deciphering of the German Enigma code.

As early as 7 April, Wilson had known of German planning regarding List's army in

Thrace and Macedonia. The following day he knew what formations would drive through the Monastir Gap to attack the British and Anzac forces under his command. Wilson knew that his units were not strong enough to withstand them. Therefore, he would not repel the invader, but withdraw so that as many of his forces as possible might survive.

By 12 April he knew that the victors of Salonika were about to outflank him on the east. He ordered the evacuation of the Vevi Gap and by 14 April those who had got away were joining New Zealanders along the line of the Aliakmon River and the passes around Mount Olympus. They held the German assault for four days until 18 April, when Wilson learned through Ultra that German armour was driving for Ioannina and the Thessaly region, thus outflanking him again, this time on the west.

On 19 April Anzac and

British troops were streaming back past Thermopylai. Royal Navy ships were evacuating base personnel from Piraeus. However, 50,000 men could not be lifted from one port alone, so the 4th Hussars went south to keep the bridge over the Corinth Canal open and to guard the beaches on the Peloponnesian coast for a mass evacuation.

Greek captitulation

General Alexander Papagos advised his King on 21 April that the Greek army could fight no more. The rearguards at Thermopylai held on until 24 April, then slipped away. General Wilson left Athens on 26 April and crossed the Corinth Bridge. For the next two days, only the Luftwaffe could harass the evacuation, sinking one transport and two destroyers on the same day. But the Royal Navy carried on and 26,000 men were evacuated over the next two days. On 28 April, the 5th Panzer Division and the SS 'Leibstandarte Adolf Hitler' crossed the Corinth Canal, and the panzers headed for Kalamata. No ships could rescue the 7000 Imperial troops still there. The Imperial Expeditionary Force had lost nearly 12,000 men, including 900 dead and 1200 wounded. The RAF lost 209 aircraft, including 137 destroyed on the ground. The Royal Navy lost two destroyers and 25 other ships. Rightly or wrongly, the British had kept their promise to defend Greece.

A machine-gun armed German paratrooper near Corinth in May 1941. An airborne assault launched on 26 April and supported by gliders attempted to capture the Corinth Bridge.

Hitler strikes south: Chronology

On October 28th 1940 Italy invaded Greece. Though their forces were numerically superior to those of the Greeks, they suffered a crushing defeat. It was left to Germany to take over the Balkans.

1940
October 28th
Italy invades Greece with over 200,000 soldiers. A combination of talented Greek resistance and British Royal Air Force air cover puts them into retreat in only two weeks.

1941
March 25th
Yugoslavia's ruler Prince Paul signs allegiance to the Axis, but is overthrown two days later in a coup led by nationalist Yugoslav generals Bora Mirkovic and Dusan Simovic. Simovic becomes head of government, and renounces Yugoslavia's membership of the Tripartite Pact.

March 26th
Hitler tells senior officers in Berlin, 'I have decided to destroy Yugoslavia'.

April 6th
German units begin the simultaneous invasion of Greece and Yugoslavia, code-named Operation Marita. The invasion forces include 24 divisions of troops and 1200 tanks.

April 8th
The Yugoslavian capital Belgrade is flattened by a massive German bombing raid resulting in an estimated 30,000 dead

April 9th
Greece. The 'Metaxas Line' – a chain of defences on the north-eastern corner of Greece defended by four Greek divisions – is encircled and defeated by units of the German 12th Army. The

Below: A German Hauptsturmführer gives an interview to a radio war correspondent following the capture of Belgrade, Yugoslavia. The German forces who remained in Yugoslavia as occupying forces would fight a bitter anti-partisan war which resulted in nearly one million Yugoslavian dead by the end of the war.

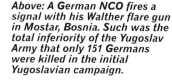

Above: A German NCO fires a signal with his Walther flare gun in Mostar, Bosnia. Such was the total inferiority of the Yugoslav Army that only 151 Germans were killed in the initial Yugoslavian campaign.

Germans also capture the vital port of Salonika, preventing the Allies reinforcing their units in northern Greece from the sea.

April 10th–16th
Greece. The 160km (100-mile) long defences in the Vermion Mountains known as the 'Aliakmon Line' are defeated. The line had been held by three divisions of British, Australian and New Zealand troops.

April 12th
The Allied troops from the Vermion line are redeployed to more southerly defensive positions around Mount Olympus

April 12th
The Yugoslavian capital Belgrade is captured by the

The greatest obstacle to the German advance in the Balkans was often the terrain, particularly in Greece where local fighters were able to spring ambushes from mountain positions before disappearing back into the familiar landscape.

Germans. Yugoslavian forces had been entirely overwhelmed throughout the country by a German assault from Austria, Hungary, Romania and Bulgaria, and an Italian push up from northern Albania.

April 14th
Yugoslavia. Greek units in Albania are cut off from their homeland after German forces decimate Yugoslav units in the Monastir gap and push through into northern Greece.

April 16th
Allied units are in full retreat throughout Greece. The retreat is, in part, due to requests from the Greek commander-in-chief General Alexander Papagos to the British Prime Minister Winston Churchill that Allied troops pull out to save Greece from being destroyed by the Germans.

April 17th
The Yugoslavian army surrenders and the Yugoslav

leadership signs an unconditional surrender.

April 20th
The Greek Army surrenders to the German and Italian forces.

April 26th
Greece. German airborne units make a parachute assault against the bridge spanning the Corinth Canal. Their aim is to capture the bridge and to cut off the retreating Allies, but most of the Allies had already escaped further south. The bridge was also accidentally destroyed during the action.

April 27th–30th
Retreating Allies begin to reach the south coast of Greece and are evacuated by waiting Royal Navy vessels in Operation Demon. Some 51,000 Allied soldiers manage to escape. Athens is occupied on the 27th and Greece capitulates.

International Events 1941

March 24th–April 25th
German and Italian forces advance over 500 miles across north Africa from El Agheila in Libya to the Halfaya Pass in Egypt. En route they capture the coastal towns of Benghazi, Derna, and Barnia, depriving the Allied forces of crucial ports. Tobruk, however, remains isolated but tenaciously defended.

March 28th–29th
Italian and British navies clash in a large action off the coast of southern Greece, subsequently known as the Battle of Cape Matapan. The battle is a resounding British success, with five Italian ships sunk for the loss of just one British aircraft from the carrier *Formidable*.

April 1st–18th
Iraq. The government of Regent Faisal is deposed in a pro-Nazi coup d'état led by the nationalist politician Rashid Ali.

April 6th
Allied forces capture Addis Ababa, the capital of Ethiopia, from the Italian East African Army.

April 13th
The Soviet Union and Japan sign a five-year non-aggression pact.

April 7th
The UK cuts all diplomatic ties with Hungary, arguing that Hungary has effectively become a base of operation for Axis forces.

April 24th
After three nights of continual bombing, the British coastal city of Plymouth is left with 30,000 homeless people.

Death from above
The airborne invasion of Crete

April 1941: as the German army advances remorselessly through Greece, its attention turns to the largest of the Greek Islands, Crete.

By the end of April 1941 the last of the Allied survivors of the disastrous Greek campaign had arrived in Crete, and as it was obvious to many that the island would certainly be the next target of Hitler's aggression, the wounded, unfit and non-combatant were evacuated to Egypt. Major-General Bernard Freyberg, VC, then assessed the forces at his command and set about deploying them for the defence of the island.

He posted two brigades of his own New Zealanders (the 4th and 5th) around the vital Maleme airfields and supported them with three Greek battalions. In the Suda Bay area Freyberg left some 2000 men of the Mobile Naval Defence Organisation and added one British, one Australian and one Greek battalion; to the Retimo section he sent three Australian infantry battalions and their machine-gun support, plus two more Greek battalions; and to Heraklion he sent the two remaining battalions of the British 14th Brigade, one Australian battalion, a medium artillery regiment with rifles but no guns, and two more Greek battalions.

A new intensity

By May 7 they were all in position, numbering some 15,000 British, 7750 New Zealanders, 6500 Australians and 10,200 armed Greeks. By the end of the month another British infantry battalion, 22 elderly tanks and 49 pieces of artillery had joined the garrison from Egypt.

They all trained, dug defences – and waited. At dawn on 20 May they heard a new note in the intensity of the early morning Luftwaffe 'heat' – a hum like that of an approaching swarm of bees. As it rose in a crescendo, the New Zealanders at Maleme saw a huge fleet of transport aircraft coming towards them across the sea, and as these arrived overhead the sky blossomed with a thousand parachutes – and the Battle for Crete began.

Assault on Maleme

Operation 'Merkur' called for airborne landings, in two waves, at four places along the north coast of Crete. Gliderborne soldiers and paratroops would assault and capture Maleme airfield and hold it until 5th Mountain Division units could be flown in; the 3rd Paratroop Regiment would drop around Galatas and Khania and then, reinforced by the men from Maleme, drive east and take control of the Suda Bay area. The second wave would consist of two more paratroop regiments with their artillery who would drop at Retimo and Heraklion during the afternoon. In the meantime, seaborne support would arrive off Maleme during the evening, more the following morning off Heraklion, and once Suda Bay was in German hands as many Panzers as possible would be landed. Altogether 22,750 elite German troops were to be put ashore, carried and protected by over 1200 aircraft.

Yet by the end of the first day it seemed to their commander, General-leutnant Kurt Student, that this powerful force was about to suffer the first German defeat since 1918. They were being beaten by the remarkable shooting of the New Zealanders and Australians, many of them farmers who had shot for the pot since childhood. Several of the paratroop units were wiped out before they hit the ground, only those fortunate enough to be dropped away from Freyberg's concentrations escaping.

Victorious German paratroopers on Crete: The 7th Air Division sustained nearly 50 per cent casualties during the attack on Crete, mostly during the first day. Although the German parachute arm was to be expanded later in the war, it was never to attempt another opposed landing of this kind.

CRETE FALLS: 20-31 MAY 1941

The three airfields at Maleme, Retimo and Heraklion were the key to Crete. The Germans gambled that by using all available paratroops together against all three airfields they would capture one of them. Then ground troops could be flown in by transport aircraft.

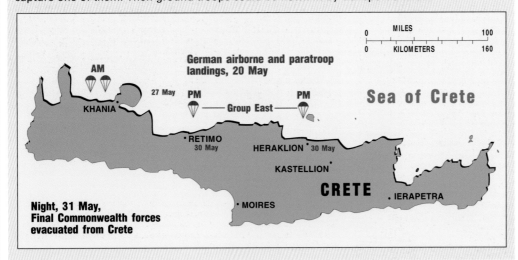

One such unit was from the Assault Regiment, dropped by mistake so far west of Maleme that it could take no part in the immediate battle. But the men coalesced and marched west towards Tavronitis Bridge, arriving in time to help beat off a New Zealand counter-attack – and worry the New Zealand commander. Lieutenant Colonel Andrew, VC, DSO, commanding 22nd New Zealand Battalion around Point 107, realised that the nearby German force was powerful and, now, concentrated. As his radio sets had broken down he was out of touch with two of his companies, had grave doubts about the other and could get only weak and sporadic communications from his HQ. Feeling that dawn might bring such an attack as might overwhelm his decimated battalion, Andrew withdrew to his reserve position in order to have his flanks covered by his neighbours. In doing so he uncovered Point 107 and with it a corner of Maleme airfield.

Costly move

It is not too much to say that this move lost the Allies the Battle of Crete. By noon, Student had realised that Maleme airfield was now his for the taking. He sent in all his remaining paratroops, plus more mountain division units, in Junkers Ju 52s, which flew unhesitatingly through devastating fire to crash-land on the slowly expanding space held by the paratroops, until they had packed overwhelming force into it. They then proceeded to follow Student's orders to 'roll up Crete from the west'.

There were still five days of bitter action to be fought before it became evident to Freyberg that his own force was being inexorably whittled away while Student's was being regularly supplied and reinforced. On 26 May Freyberg ordered a withdrawal by all his forces across the mountains to the south coast, and asked

This Junkers Ju 52/3m g4e is typical of the planes that carried German paratroopers over Crete, each carrying 12 soldiers and their equipment. The aircraft flew in tight vics of three at 240kmh (150mph), 55m (180ft) apart, at about 120m (400ft). Speed was reduced to about 160kmh (100mph) for the men to jump. After they were out, four containers full of arms, ammunition and stores were also dropped.

General Sir Archibald Wavell to organise an evacuation from beaches around the village of Sfakia. A commando battalion had been landed, and this formed a beach-head around the village. Into this, over the next few days, the exhausted remains of Freyberg's command made their uncomfortable way.

Above: Some 12,000 British troops were left behind after the evacuation and the Germans carried out house-to-house searches in an attempt to find them. Like the Turks before them, the Germans soon discovered that suppressing Cretan resistance was exceedingly difficult.

Left: HMS York is pictured abandoned at Suda Bay. The Luftwaffe had achieved complete supremacy in the air and inflicted severe losses on the Royal Navy. The short nights made it impossible for seaborne supplies to sustain the defenders so once Maleme airfield had fallen, Crete was doomed.

Death from above
The airborne invasion of Crete: Chronology

The battle for Crete heralded a new era of airborne warfare. German airborne troops captured the island in 11 days, but at such great cost in lives they were never used in large-scale parachute operations again.

1941
April 25th
Hitler issues Führer Directive No. 28 ordering the airborne invasion of Crete, codenamed Operation Mercury. The operation will be led by the commander of German airborne forces, General Kurt Student.

April 26th
Allied 'Ultra' codebreaking staff start to decipher German communications referring to a Cretan operation.

April 30th
Major-General Bernard Freyberg takes command of all Allied forces on the island of Crete.

May 19th
Ultra intelligence provides Freyberg with information that Operation Mercury is to be launched the next day. British fighter aircraft on Crete are withdrawn to Egypt.

May 20th
7.00am
The first German assault troops land on Crete around Khania and Maleme using over 500 Junkers Ju-52 transport aircraft. During the first hours of combat they suffer an average of 50 per cent casualties under extremely heavy Allied fire.

1.30-2.00pm
The second waves of German soldiers take off from airfields on mainland Greece and the Greek islands.

2.00pm
The second waves begin to deploy over Rethymnon and Heraklion. They experience a similar rate of attrition to the earlier assault. By the end of the first day many key German objectives remain outstanding.

May 21st
Point 107, a tactically important hill overlooking Maleme, is captured from the Allies. German support troops from the 100th Gebirgsjäger Regiment attempt to cross to Crete using commandeered fishing boats. They are intercepted, however, by the Royal Navy and only 60 German soldiers survive the subsequent bombardment. A German assault on Heraklion is stopped by 8000 Allied defenders.

May 22nd
An attempt by New Zealand troops to recapture Maleme airfield is repulsed by German defence. The British destroyer *Greyhound* is sunk by German bombers.

May 23rd
British destroyers *Kelly* and

A German Fallschirmjäger dressed in combat gear. He is armed with a handgun – a Steilhandgranate 39 tucked into his belt – while the set of magazine pouches suggest that he has a MP40 submachine gun over his shoulder.

A Junkers Ju-52 is shot down over the northern coastline of Crete. Though losses were extremely heavy for the Germans, they still managed to put down 9530 men on 20 May alone, and a total of 17,530 by 23 May.

Kashmir and cruisers *Gloucester* and *Fiji* are sunk by German dive-bombers.

May 27th
German units occupy the town and airfield of Heraklion. Allied troops are driven back to Galatas in the face of the German build-up around Maleme.

May 30th
Rethymnon finally falls to the Germans after overcoming heavy resistance from Australian units.

May 28th-31st
On the orders of Major-General Freyberg, the Allies execute a gradual withdrawal of troops from Crete. They evacuate mainly by sea from Heraklion in the north and Sphakia in the south. Crete falls into German hands.

International Events

May 19th
Over 18,000 Italian troops surrender to British forces at

A stick of German paratroopers exit from a Ju-52. The design of these parachutes meant that the paras had to exit in a head-first dive to cope with the snapping forces of the parachute opening.

Amba Alagi during the Ethiopian campaign.

May 20th
In Paris the French Resistance leader Gabriel Peri is arrested by the Gestapo. He is executed in December along with 100 other French citizens.

May 22nd
Britain issues a warning to French authorities against actively collaborating with the German occupiers. The Prime Minister threatens military action against any French units or installations put to German service.

May 23rd
Reichsmarschall Hermann Göring outlines proposals for exploiting the economic and agricultural resources of the USSR.

May 24th
The British nation is in mourning after the announcement that HMS *Hood*, pride of the Royal Navy fleet, has been sunk by the German battleship *Bismarck* with the loss of 1413 lives.

May 27
President Roosevelt declares a state of 'national emergency' as World War II escalates, stating 'what started as a European war has developed, as the Nazis always intended it should develop, into a world war for world domination.' The US government prepares itself to adopt a military and economic response to possible German aggression.

The hunt for the *Bismarck*
On the run in the Atlantic

May 1941: the battleship *Bismarck*, pride of Hitler's navy, steams into the North Atlantic to attack the UK's vital convoys.

On 18 May 1941 in company with the new heavy cruiser KMS *Prinz Eugen*, the 41,700 ton battleship KMS *Bismarck* sailed from Gotenhafen (Gydnia) on Operation 'Rheinübung'. It was to be a raid on Atlantic commerce and was well supported by prepositioned auxiliaries. It was to occupy the final 10 days of her short career.

As 11 convoys were at sea or preparing to sail, the British Admiralty was gravely perturbed when, on 21 May, the Germans were reported passing through the Skagerrak. Photo-reconnaissance then confirmed their presence, topping up with fuel oil at Bergen.

Rapid dispositions were made. To reinforce the heavy cruisers HMS *Norfolk* and *Suffolk*, already patrolling the ice-encumbered waters of the Denmark Strait (between Iceland and Greenland), the battle-cruiser HMS *Hood* sailed from Scapa in company with the battleship HMS *Prince of Wales* and six destroyers. Two light cruisers were patrolling the Iceland-Faeroes gap and when, late on 21 May a further flight over Bergen showed both Germans to have left, Admiral Sir John Tovey, commanding the Home Fleet, sailed from Scapa towards the area with the main body of the Home Fleet, which included two capital ships and a carrier.

Into the fogbanks

Weather conditions did not favour aerial reconnaissance and the next sighting of *Bismarck* was by *Suffolk*, entering the narrow gap between the ice-edge and the minefield at the northern end of the strait. Only 11.25km (7 miles) distant, the British cruiser took rapid cover in a nearby fogbank, informing both her consort and the commander-in-chief. Under occasional fire, the two cruisers hung on to the

*The broad beam of the **Bismarck** is instantly apparent. She was a powerful vessel but her design suffered from Germany's long break from naval construction between the wars. Nevertheless, her speed and 8 x 38.1-cm (15-in) guns made her a serious menace to Britain's Atlantic artery.*

enemy throughout the night of 23 May, greatly assisted by their primitive radars. Their performance was copybook, delivering the Germans to the *Hood* group, which established visual contact at 0535 on 24 May.

Vice-Admiral Launcelot Holland wore his flag in an imposing but unmodernised ship whose lack of sufficient horizontal protection rendered it imperative that she engaged a powerful opponent at short range, where flat trajectories would present her thicker vertical armour to major-calibre projectiles. Unfortunately, a necessary change of course during the night had caused Holland to lose bearing and battle was joined at 22,850m (74,967ft), with Vizeadmiral Günther Lütjens in *Bismarck* slightly forward of the beam. In order to close the range, the British ships steered a course that rendered them unable to bring their full armament to bear; an unfavourable situation compounded by the brand-new *Prince of Wales*'s forward turrets suffering continuous failures and *Hood* herself probably firing at the *Prinz*

The Bismarck's raid was designed to disrupt the Atlantic convoys. The plan was sound enough but should have been abandoned after HMS Prince of Wales holed Bismarck's fuel tanks.

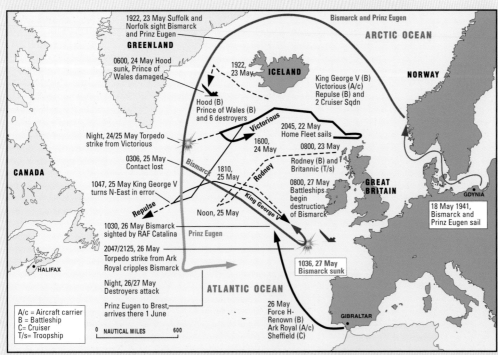

NOWHERE TO HIDE: THE CRUISE OF THE *BISMARCK*

1922, 23 May Suffolk and Norfolk sight Bismarck and Prinz Eugen

0600, 24 May Hood sunk, Prince of Wales damaged

Night, 24/25 May Torpedo strike from Victorious

0306, 25 May Contact lost

1047, 25 May King George V turns N-East in error

1030, 26 May Bismarck sighted by RAF Catalina

2047/2125, 26 May Torpedo strike from Ark Royal cripples Bismarck

Night, 26/27 May Destroyers attack

Prinz Eugen to Brest, arrives there 1 June

Bismarck and Prinz Eugen

ARCTIC OCEAN

GREENLAND

1922, 23 May

ICELAND

NORWAY

King George V (B) Victorious (A/c) Repulse (B) and 2 Cruiser Sqdn

Hood (B) Prince of Wales (B) and 6 destroyers

Victorious

2045, 22 May Home Fleet sails

1600, 24 May

1810, 25 May

0800, 23 May

Rodney (B) and Britannic (T/s)

0800, 27 May Battleships begin destruction of Bismarck

CANADA

Repulse

Noon, 25 May

Prinz Eugen

GREAT BRITAIN

GDYNIA

18 May 1941, Bismarck and Prinz Eugen sail

1036, 27 May Bismarck sunk

HALIFAX

ATLANTIC OCEAN

26 May Force H- Renown (B) Ark Royal (A/c) Sheffield (C)

GIBRALTAR

A/c = Aircraft carrier
B = Battleship
C= Cruiser
T/s= Troopship

0   NAUTICAL MILES   600

Above: **Prinz Eugen** *was a 'Hipper' class heavy cruiser displacing nearly 20,000 tons at full load and armed with 8 x 20.3-cm (8-in) guns. After escaping to Brest she joined* **Scharnhorst** *and* **Gneisenau** *on their celebrated dash up the Channel and back to Germany.*

Left: **HMS** **King George V.** *Launched, like* **Bismarck,** *in February 1939,* **King George V** *was smaller and lighter than the German battleship. Her sister ship* **Prince of Wales** *inflicted enough damage to ruin* **Bismarck's** *commerce-raiding sortie and on 27 May,* **King George V** *and* **HMS** **Rodney** *avenged the loss of the* **Hood.**

Eugen, which had a profile very similar to that of *Bismarck*. The latter, having the advantage of a superior gunnery radar, opened an accurate fire at 0553.

At this range, her salvoes were plunging at a steep angle and the third one found *Hood* after just seven minutes. She blew up in a massive explosion that only three men survived.

Now alone (her destroyers had earlier been detached) *Prince of Wales* fought on, down to ranges of 16,450m (53,970ft). Despite gunnery problems, she hit the *Bismarck* with two 356mm (14in) shells before being obliged to break off the action with increasing damage. Lütjens was sufficiently perturbed to signal his intention to abandon his mission and return to a French port.

Fortunately for the British,

Norfolk and *Suffolk* remained in contact and, as Tovey strove to close the 480km (300 miles) that still separated his HMS *King George V* and HMS *Victorious* from Lütjens, the Admiralty hurriedly arranged reinforcements. From Gibraltar was sailed Force H, with the carrier HMS *Ark Royal*, while battleships, including the 406mm (16in) HMS *Rodney*, were released from their convoys.

Lost touch

During the night of 24/25 May, *Victorious* closed sufficiently to launch a small force of nine radar-equipped torpedo aircraft. The single hit that they achieved did not slow the battleship, while the latter made a successful feint to cover the detachment of *Prinz Eugen*. These irregular manoeuvres succeeded also in causing the tracking

cruisers to finally lose touch, with the result that at 0306 on 25 May all contact with *Bismarck* was lost, with Tovey only 160km (100 miles) short.

Only after 30 hours of anxious search was Lütjens relocated by a Consolidated Catalina of No. 209 Squadron. *Bismarck* was making for Brest, now only 1125km (700 miles) away, and Tovey, still 160km (99.4 miles) distant to the north, needed to slow her in order to be able to force an action. By great good fortune Force H was well placed, and an aircraft from *Ark Royal* established contact before noon on 26 May, the cruiser HMS *Sheffield* being sent ahead to consolidate the sighting. In marginal flying conditions, however, *Ark Royal*'s first strike of 14 torpedo aircraft found and attacked the *Sheffield* in error. She survived nevertheless and acted as a waypoint for a second strike at about 2000. In the conditions a co-ordinated attack was out of the question, individual aircraft dropping their

torpedoes on opportunity between 2047 and 2125. Two further hits were scored, one severely damaging the fugitive's steering gear.

As darkness fell, *Sheffield* vectored-in five destroyers (under Captain Sir Philip Vian in HMS *Cossack*), including the Polish *Piorun*. These probed and tormented their great adversary throughout the night as she steered a course toward sanctuary. Almost miraculously the destroyers sustained little but splinter damage, while scoring two, or possibly three, more torpedo hits.

With the dawn of 27 May, *Bismarck*'s weary gunners could still see a destroyer in each quadrant as nemesis loomed in the shape of Tovey's *King George V*, in company with *Rodney*. Manoeuvring independently, these opened fire at 0848 in gale conditions. By 1015 *Bismarck* was a silent, blazing ruin and was finished off by torpedo from the cruiser HMS *Dorsetshire*. It is a moot point whether gunfire alone could have effected her destruction.

Norfolk *and* **Suffolk** *were both 'County' class cruisers: good sea boats displacing up to 14,000 tons and armed with 8 x 203mm (8in) guns. Their primitive radar sets were of limited value and their crew first spotted* **Bismarck** *visually. Dodging in and out of fog banks they came under fire but escaped damage.*

The hunt for the *Bismarck*
Chronology

The pursuit and destruction of the German pocket battleship *Bismarck* began in the North Sea and ended near the coast of France. Its destruction became a matter of national urgency after the *Bismarck* destroyed the battleship HMS *Hood* with the loss of 1413 lives.

1941
April 2nd
Grand-Admiral Raeder of the German Navy outlines Operation Rheinübung. The objective is for the *Bismarck* and other German surface raiders to sink British merchant shipping in the Atlantic, avoiding engagements with warships if possible.

May 20th
The *Bismarck* and heavy cruiser *Prinz Eugen* leave port and enter the waters of the North Sea.

May 21st
The British Admiralty is alerted to the threat of the German warships. Admiral Sir John Tovey (C-in-C Home Fleet) is given reinforcements in the form of the battle-cruiser *Repulse* and the aircraft carrier *Victorious*.

May 22nd
The battleships *Hood*, *Prince of Wales* and *King George V*, along with seven destroyers and four cruisers, depart from Scapa Flow in search of the German warships.

May 23rd, 7.22pm
The *Bismarck* is spotted by the cruiser *Suffolk*. The *Suffolk*, along with its sister-ship *Norfolk*, shadow the German vessel and report its

*The **Bismarck** fires a full salvo at the ill-fated **HMS** Hood. While having a well-reinforced hull, the **Hood** had weak deck armour. The **Bismarck's** shells were able to cut through this and enter the main ammunition magazine.*

position to the main British battle-squadron under command of Vice-Admiral L.E. Holland.

May 24th
5.52am
British ships begin engaging the *Bismarck* and *Prinz Eugen*.

6.00am
The *Hood*'s ammunition magazine is struck by a salvo from the *Bismarck*. The ship is utterly destroyed in a vast explosion. Only three men survive out of a ship's complement of 1324 men and 95 officers. The *Prince of Wales* is also badly damaged

A dramatic representation of the attack upon the Bismarck. The antiquated Swordfish faced barrages from the Bismarck's 16 105mm (4.1in), 16 37mm (1.4in) and 12 20mm (0.7in) anti-aircraft guns..

in the engagement, and pulls away at 6.13am.

6.01pm
The *Bismarck* has been damaged by the *Prince of Wales* and is leaking oil. Admiral Lütjens, the *Bismarck*'s commander, turns the ship around and begins heading for the French port of St Nazaire.

May 24th
Contact with the *Bismarck* is lost by HMS *Suffolk*.

May 25th
On Admiral Lütjens' orders the *Prinz Eugen* leaves the *Bismarck*.

May 26th
The *Bismarck*'s position is relocated by a Catalina flying boat of Coastal Command roughly 1126km (700 miles) from Brest. British units hunting the *Bismarck* receive reinforcements – *Ark Royal*, *Sheffield* and *Renown* – sailing from Gibraltar.

2.50pm
Swordfish torpedo planes flying from the *Ark Royal* begin the first of a series of strikes against the *Bismarck*.

8.47–9.25pm
The *Bismarck* is struck by two air-launched torpedoes. The second hits the stern, jamming the *Bismarck*'s rudder in a fixed position. With the *Bismarck* now circling helplessly, Allied ships close in for the kill.

May 27th
8.47am
After a period of long-range heavy bombardment from Allied ships, the *Bismarck* comes under close-range fire from the guns of *Rodney* and *King George V*. The *Bismarck* is devastated from bows to stern.

10am
Bismarck falls silent.

10.36am
The *Bismarck* finally sinks. Only 115 survivors are recovered.

International Events 1941
April 4th
Hitler commits himself to declaring war on the US should America enter into hostilities with Japan.

'Force H' sailing off Gibraltar, destined to join the hunt for the Bismarck. In the middle ground can be seen the HMS Ark Royal, commissioned into the Royal Navy in 1938 and having a complement of 38 aircraft.

April 6th
Operation Marita, the German invasion of Greece and Yugoslavia, is launched using 24 divisions of troops, 1200 tanks, and heavy Luftwaffe air support.

April 8th
Up to 30,000 civilians are killed in a German air raid upon Belgrade.

April 27th
Athens falls to German forces as the Allies evacuate over 50,000 troops from the Greek mainland.

May 11th
Former US President Herbert Hoover states his belief that the US must stay out of the European conflict.

May 14th
France. Over 1000 Jews are arrested by French police and given to the Germans for deportation.

May 15th
Allies in North Africa launch Operation Brevity to take the Halfaya Pass from the German forces under Rommel.

May 20th
Reichsmarshall Göring refers to the 'Final Solution' in documentation ordering the banning of Jewish emigration from France and Belgium.

May 20th
German airborne forces begin the invasion of Crete, the largest parachute and airlanding operation of the war to date.

May 27th
Major-General Freyberg, the commander of Allied forces on Crete, orders the evacuation of troops from the island as the German offensive advances across the island.

Panzergruppe Guderian
The drive on Smolensk 1941

The plan is audacious: in just eight weeks the German army will blitzkrieg its way through the Red Army to dictate peace in Moscow.

'When Barbarossa is launched,' declared Hitler, 'the whole world will hold its breath!', and indeed the forces massed along the Soviet frontier from the Arctic Circle to the Black Sea during that early summer of 1941 represented the greatest concentration of military force the world had seen to that date.

Three German army groups had under command 80 infantry divisions, 18 Panzer divisions and 12 motorised divisions, while behind them waited another 21 infantry, two Panzer and one motorised divisions; in reserve: some two million men, 3200 tanks and 10,000 guns. Already in position by mid-June to supply them were enough stores dumps, fuel and ammunition reserves to feed them over a 565 to 645km (350 to 400 mile) advance, and 500,000 lorries waited in massed parks from East Prussia to Romania to rush it forward on demand. To the modern mind the only questionable (indeed alarming) figure to emerge from the tables of statistics among the planning memoranda for Operation 'Barbarossa' is that for 'stabling': 300,000 horses were to play an

apparently essential part in this monumental military exercise.

The disposition of the army groups (and the directions of their advances) were dictated to a large extent by one inescapable geographical factor, namely the Pripet Marshes, a virtually uncrossable swamp nearly 160km (100 miles) from north to south and 480km (300 miles) from east to west, dividing Belorussia from the Ukraine. Because of this, there could be little contact during the first stage of the operation between Army Group South launched from Lublin towards Kiev and the lower reaches of the River Dniepr, and the two groups to the north. These were Army Group Centre aimed first at Smolensk and then (at least in the minds of the military leaders) at Moscow, and Army Group North launched out of East Prussia first towards Lake Peipus and then Leningrad.

Victory in eight weeks

It was in the northern sector that the greater weight of the attack lay: 50 infantry, 13 Panzer and nine motorised divisions between the groups and, of the two, Army Group Centre was the

German soldiers carry out an intensive search on Russian prisoners. If any of the captives were identified as Commissars they would be executed on the spot.

ZHITOMIR: HOUSE-TO-HOUSE FIGHTING

A 10.5-cm (4.1in) gun fires on isolated Soviet troops fighting on 129km (80 miles) west of Kiev. As Guderian and Hoth's Panzer divisions raced north of the Pripet Marshes, vast numbers of Red Army soldiers were left in the Ukraine, exposed to encirclement.

stronger. Under the command of the icily aristocratic Generalfeldmarschall Fedor von Bock were two infantry armies, the 9th and the 4th, and two Panzer formations, Panzergruppe 3 under General Hermann Hoth and Panzergruppe 2 under General Heinz Guderian. These were the armies whose commanders intended to reduce Napoleon's feat of arms of 129 years earlier to historical obscurity, for they planned to reach Moscow in less than eight weeks and to annihilate the Soviet army in the process.

In this hope they were encouraged by Hitler, who had assured them 'We have only to kick in the front door and the whole rotten Russian edifice will come tumbling down!' Guderian's first task was to throw his Panzergruppe across the River Bug on each side of the fortress of Brest-Litovsk, capture the fortress and then drive precipitously forward towards the city of Minsk, curving up to it from the south to meet Hoth's spearheads coming down from the north. Thus would the Soviet forces immediately behind their attack fronts be isolated in a huge cauldron in which, once their supplies had run out, they would have little alternative but to surrender.

Optimism of leaders

This was all achieved in five days of breathtaking exhilaration, which seemed to confirm Hitler's pronouncements and the optimism of the Wehrmacht leaders. On the afternoon of 27 June the leading tanks of the 17th Panzer Division drove into Minsk to meet the spearheads of Hoth's Panzergruppe 3, which had covered 320km (200 miles) in five days and accomplished the first stage of their mission.

Ju 87 Stukas over the USSR, July 1941. Just as in Poland and France, the Stuka dive-bombers proved extremely effective in the USSR. The Soviet fighters were all but driven from the sky by the Luftwaffe, allowing the bombers to wreak havoc on the Red Army, which had no answer to well coordinated tank and airpower.

German infantry of the 4th and 9th Armies trudging stolidly behind the Panzer divisions.

Not surprisingly, arguments arose. Guderian and Hoth were convinced that they must immediately race further ahead, first to Smolensk and then to Moscow, confident that speed would prove the decisive factor in this campaign. And with a burst of insubordination, on 1 July Guderian and Hoth released Panzer units towards the next obstacle, the River Beresina, and were threatened with court martial for so doing by their immediate superior, General Günther von Kluge. On the same day, Guderian's Panzers met for the first time a Soviet T-34 tank, which blocked their advance

yet experienced, for although advanced units of the 29th Motorised Division reached Smolensk on 16 July, fierce fighting still raged behind them and there was as yet no sign of Hoth's Panzergruppe 3 spearheads. For 10 days Panzergruppe 2 had three separate objectives to pursue: to bar the Soviet forces it had bypassed since crossing the Dniepr from escape south or east; to seek contact with Panzergruppe 3 fighting its way down from the north-west; and to widen its hold on the land east of Smolensk (towards Roslavl and the River Desna at Elnya) into a solid bridgehead for the final thrust towards the Germans' great goal, Moscow. But on 29 July Hitler's adjutant, Colonel Schmundt, arrived at Guderian's headquarters, bringing with him Hitler's felicitations and the Oak Leaves to the Knight's Cross (Guderian was only the fifth man in the army to receive them) and also the first hint of changes of plan and emphasis. Moscow was

perhaps not so important after all. The rolling wheatlands of the Ukraine would provide the granary from which the ever-growing Axis armies could be fed and, moreover, down in that direction lay the Bakr oilfields.

Moscow could wait. Guderian for the moment must go no further east.

The war in the East was characterised by ruthless barbarity from the start. Prisoners of war were simply a source of slave labour and civilians suspected of guerrilla activities were slaughtered.

But behind them they had left pockets of Soviet troops who, unlike those enemy forces similarly encircled the year before in France, showed little inclination to lay down their arms and surrender. There were four of these pockets: the fortress at Brest-Litovsk, six divisions around Bialystok, six more at Volkovysk, and another 15 between Novogrudok and Minsk itself. The task of first containing and then destroying and capturing them was assigned, in Hoth's and Guderian's minds, to the

for three hours, knocked out five PzKpfw III tanks and was only removed by an attack from the rear with an 88mm (3.46in) gun. Fortunately no more T-34s were encountered in the area and then, on 3 July, the order came for the next stage of the advance. So from his illicit bridgehead over the Beresina, Guderian launched the 18th Panzer Division towards the River Dniepr, which was reached on 5 July.

The next three weeks were occupied with the hardest fighting Panzergruppe 2 had

Armed with an MP32/40 submachine gun, this NCO wears the basic German army uniform of 1941. He has part of a rubber inner tube around his helmet to add local camouflage. Since victory was anticipated before the autumn no winter clothing was prepared.

Panzergruppe Guderian

Chronology

Guderian, the man who designed Blitzkrieg itself, was to successfully test his theories in the Soviet Union following Operation Barbarossa. His Panzergruppe 2 advanced from the Russian border to Smolensk – a distance of 400 miles (643km) – in little over two months.

1941

June 22nd
German forces invade the Soviet Union in Operation Barbarossa. Guderian's Panzergruppe 2 is part of Army Group Centre, a force tasked with the drive towards Moscow down the line of the Minsk–Smolensk–Moscow highway. While Panzergruppe 2 attacks directly along the highway, General Hoth's Panzergruppe 3 swings south from Grodno making a pincer action against Gorodishche and Minsk.

Below: Five Russian citizens hanged near the town of Velizh, Smolensk region. An estimated 20–25 million Soviet citizens would die in World War II.

June 29th
Panzergruppe 2 and Panzergruppe 3 meet at Minsk. Huge Russian forces have so far been encircled at Brest-Litovsk, Bialystok, Volkovysk, Gorodishche and now Minsk itself, the latter containing 15 divisions of Soviet troops.

July 1st
Guderian and Hoth's forces cross the Berezina River 80km (50 miles) west of Minsk and resume their push towards Vitebsk and Smolensk.

July 3rd
Both Panzergruppe 2 and

Above: A German officer blows the whistle for an attack. Soviet fur hats and felt boots became two of the most popular acquisitions amongst German troops during the harsh Eastern winters.

German soldiers engage in city fighting. The Panzerkampfwagen III medium tank on the right originally had a 50mm (2in) L/42 gun (seen here). However, this proved unable to penetrate the Soviet T-34's sloping armour, so was upgraded to the KwK 39 L/60 with a longer barrel to increase muzzle velocity.

Panzergruppe 3 are absorbed in the German 4th Panzer Army under General Günther von Kluge.

July 9th
All Soviet resistance in the pockets of encirclement collapses, and Minsk falls to the Germans. General Hoth's Panzergruppe 3 assaults northwards towards Vitebsk, while Guderian makes a bold direct drive towards Mogilev and Smolensk itself. On July 10th Guderian crosses the River Dniepr less than 80km (50 miles) from Smolensk.

July 13th
The Soviet Nineteenth and Twentieth Armies retreat into the Smolensk pocket, joining the 16th Army in preparing a defence of the city.

July 16th
Smolensk itself falls to Guderian's 29th Motorised Division. While Hoth's Panzergruppe 3 – which has already taken Vitebsk – assaults towards Yartsevo, Guderian's forces fight off a flanking counter-attack by Marshal Timoshenko's Fourth and Thirteenth Armies along the River Sohz. The counter-attack is not entirely defeated until July 22nd.

July 17th–25th
The strength of Soviet forces in the Smolensk–Vitebsk–Mogilev pocket numbers 25 divisions. Guderian's and Hoth's Panzergruppe encircle the Soviet troops just east of

the city and begin to squeeze inwards. A badly coordinated Russian attempt to break the encirclement of July 22nd fails and the encirclement is completed by July 24th.

July 19th
A directive from the OKW (army high command) orders that after the destruction of the Soviet forces at Smolensk, Panzergruppe 2 and the 2nd Army should divert south to tackle the Russian 5th Army around Kiev. Guderian is bitter about the decision, believing that the attack on Moscow should take priority. Many later argue that Hitler's decision resulted in a failure to take Moscow and began the German road to defeat.

August 5th
All resistance in the Smolensk pocket is finally destroyed or overcome. It is a crushing defeat for the Soviets. The 16th and 20th Armies cease to exist, and 300,000 Soviet soldiers are taken prisoner. Material conquests for the Germans include 3200 tanks and 3100 artillery pieces. These totals were added to gains from the earlier encirclement battles – 300,000 Soviet prisoners, 2500 tanks and nearly 1500 guns.

International Events 1941
June 27th
Stalin and Churchill reach an agreement that the UK and Soviet Union will form an alliance dedicated to the defeat of Hitler.

July 1st
In the USA, all male citizens over 21 are obliged to register for the draft in case of open hostilities.

July 2nd
Japan initiates a period of mass conscription. It brings over one million men into military service, at least half destined to reinforce operations in China.

July 6th
Over 2500 Jews are murdered by Lithuanian militia under German control. Lithuanian Jews and other citizens experience repeated atrocities from SS units.

July 26th
In response to Japanese operations in French Indochina, the UK and US freeze Japanese assets to the value of £33 million. The measure has a massive effect on Japanese imports, reducing

oil imports alone by over 80 per cent.

July 30th
The US gunboat *Tutuila* is bombed by Japanese aircraft, though the Japanese authorities later issue an apology.

Stalin's winter offensive

An expensive lesson

Never having visited the Front himself, Stalin decides on a wholesale offensive from Finland to the Black Sea.

By mid-December some of the effects of the gigantic Soviet mobilisation system were being seen. The Red Army now had more than four million men under arms, though there were not always weapons for them and a large proportion of the soldiers were totally untrained: no matter – they could be fed into battle, pick up arms where they found them and, to use one of Churchill's expressions, 'always take one with them'. And they had one advantage over the German enemy: they were warmly clad, for every Soviet citizen knows about the Russian winter, which was coming as such a shock to the invaders.

On 5 December, on Stalin's instructions, the Red Army went over to the offensive on both the Kalinin and West Fronts in order to push the German Army Group Centre back from Moscow. On the following day they were joined on their left flank by the armies of South-West Front – 15 armies altogether, plus one cavalry corps, and if the Soviet army of those days barely exceeded a German corps in manpower, this first counter-offensive was nonetheless conceived on a grand scale. And because it was attacking forces at the end of lengthy communications and supply lines who were tired, ragged and freezing, the counter-attacks succeeded despite the lack of heavy weapons or armour to support them.

Gradually German armies were levered away from the outskirts of Moscow, the pincers on each side bent back. And if the distances the Red Army advanced during those days were minuscule compared with those of the German army in the summer, this did not affect the fact that the Red Army was going forwards, the Wehrmacht backwards – with inevitable effects upon their morale. On 17 December Stalin issued orders to armies of the Leningrad Front and to the Volkhov and North-West Fronts beside them. They were to drive south-west

The Orel sector, March 1942. German soldiers help civilians out of a bunker during the last phase of Stalin's ill-conceived offensive. They did not know it but Stalin's rigid insistence on attacking was doing to the Red Army what Hitler's 'no retreat' orders had done to the German army.

SS AID POST: WINTER 1941

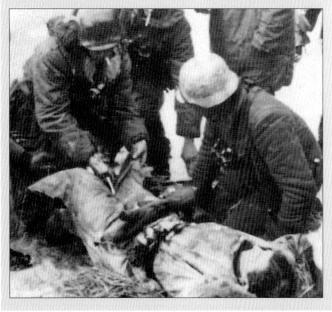

Confident of victory before winter, the German army had pitifully little warm clothing. Boots stuffed with straw and newspaper, and suffering from snow blindness and frostbite, the German troops suffered badly.

against German Army Group North, both to check the encirclement of Peter the Great's city and to prevent a link-up between German and Finnish forces. Stalin also planned to drive a wedge between Army Groups North and Centre with a drive by the 4th Shock Army, aimed at Smolensk.

Far to the south Stalin's directives also launched 20,000 men in 14 transports and a Force Eight gale across nearly 160km (100 miles) of the Black Sea, from Novorossiisk to the Kerch Peninsula, where they landed to pose what General Erich von Manstein admitted was a serious threat to his 11th Army besieging Sevastapol. Then on 5 January, at a suddenly convened meeting of STAVKA (Soviet high command), Stalin announced an all-out offensive along the entire front from the Baltic to the Black Sea.

It was certainly a grandiose plan. The main blow was to be delivered in front of Moscow by the

The Soviets had husbanded the bulk of their T-34/76 tanks in readiness for the winter counter offensive. They had their greatest impact in the counter-attack launched from Moscow that drove the Germans back from the capital. Fast, well-armed and well-armoured, the T-34 had only one serious weakness, its lack of a radio.

armies of the Western, Kalinin and Bryansk Fronts with the left wing of North-Western Front, all against Army Group Centre. Army Group North was to be defeated by the Leningrad Front, the right wing of the North-Western Front and the

Isolated in his Kremlin bunker, Stalin had no understanding of the difficulties faced by front-line Soviet soldiers, who courageously continued with what little weaponry they could find or repair.

Baltic Fleet; Army Group South was to be flung out of the Donbass by the South-Western and Southern Fronts, while the Crimea was to be liberated by the Caucasus Front and the Black Sea Fleet.

General Georgi Zhukov had a number of comments to make on these strategies. At both the northern and southern ends of the proposed offensive line, he claimed, German forces had had time to build and occupy strong defences; in the centre, however, the present pressure on Army Group Centre had not only pushed the Germans back, it had also thrown them into considerable organisational chaos. Here, undoubtedly, lay chances for great Red Army gains should

it be possible to supply them with sufficient reinforcement and re-equipment – but it was certainly not possible to reinforce and resupply the entire length of the front; therefore the proposed actions on the wings should be abandoned, and everything concentrated in the centre. His words fell on deaf ears; Stalin held to his plans.

Grinding to a halt

Zhukov was, of course, right. Stalin by dictatorial decree might be able to produce another three or four armies from the apparently limitless population of the USSR, but that decree would not produce weapons of quality or weight with which to arm them. Nor within days would it provide the training those armies needed to use the weapons with expertise. Nevertheless, attacking across 1600km (1000 miles) of front, they did push the Germans back between 80 and 320km (50 and 200 miles), partially cleared the Kalinin, Moscow, Orel and Kursk regions, and below Kharkov drove in a deep salient (known later as the Izyum Bulge) between Balakeya and Slavyansk that penetrated nearly 130km (80 miles) to reach the banks of the Orel River in the north

and Lozovaya in the south.

But these gains were made almost as much by the willingness of the German forces to go back as by Soviet pressure, and as soon as conditions favoured a stubborn German defence, then Soviet lack of experience and supply shortages compelled a halt to the advance. At times, according to Zhukov, their main purpose in attending STAVKA meetings was literally to wheedle out of Stalin 10 or 16 more anti-tank rifles, a hundred light machine-guns or, even more vital, mortar and artillery shells. At times guns were limited to one or two shells a day – and that when the Red Army was supposed to be conducting a vigorous counter-offensive along a 1600 kilometre front!

A few more small but terribly expensive gains were made, but by March even Stalin had to admit that the winter offensive was over. Until Soviet industry could produce armaments in vast quantities the best that could be expected of the Red Army was that it might hang grimly on and, in doing so, gather experience at all levels. It was a lesson, but a costly one indeed.

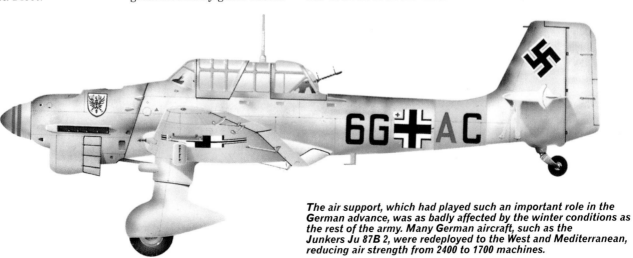

The air support, which had played such an important role in the German advance, was as badly affected by the winter conditions as the rest of the army. Many German aircraft, such as the Junkers Ju 87B 2, were redeployed to the West and Mediterranean, reducing air strength from 2400 to 1700 machines.

Stalin's winter offensive
Chronology

As the Russian winter of 1941–42 set in, the Soviet forces launched a massive counter-attack against the German army assaulting Moscow. It shocked the Germans by its strength and probably saved the Soviet Union from defeat.

1941
December 5th–6th
Soviet forces launch a massive counter-attack against the German Army Group Centre closing in on Moscow. The attack extends over a 805km (500 mile) front and includes over 19 individual armies. The main intention is for the forces of Kalinin Front, West Front and South-West Front to make a pincer manoeuvre against Field Marshal von Bock's Army Group Centre, hopefully encircling and

Women volunteers in Moscow head out to the frontline. Female combatants tended to be used in skilled roles such as snipers, pilots and tank drivers.

destroying the German forces between Smolensk and the Moscow frontline.

December 6th
The Soviet 31st Army pushes 19km (12 miles) into German lines from the start point of Kalinin. Some 17 German motorised divisions are driven into retreat here.

December 9th–13th
Soviet advances on the Kalinin front split Guderian's Panzergruppe 2 from the protection of Kluge's 4th Army.

December 16th
Exhausted by the demands of leadership, Field Marshal von

Bock asks to be replaced as commander of Army Group Centre.

December 17th
Field Marshal von Kluge takes over as commander of Army Group Centre.

1942
January 1st
After three weeks of fighting the Soviet offensive has made significant progress. The South-West Front has advanced nearly 322km (200 miles), while the Kalinin Front has taken back towns and cities such as Vysokovsk, Staritsa and Klin. Soviet forces have not, however, managed to muscle back the 4h Army from the immediate approaches to Moscow.

January 7th
Soviet forces begin a new wave of offensives from the

Kalinin and West Fronts in an attempt to finally complete the encirclement of Army Group Centre.

January 25th–March 21st
Around the end of January the impetus behind the Soviet offensive is running out owing to fatigue and depletion of men and equipment. The Soviet 29th Shock Army closes on the Minsk-Moscow highway but is repelled by the German 9th Army under General Walther Model. In spite of squeezing German forces around Yartsevo into a corridor less than 32km (20 miles) wide, the highway is not cut. Panzergruppe 3 around Smolensk and the 16th Army of Army Group North around Demyansk start to cut deep incisions into the Soviet advances.

April 30th
The spring rains and muds of

A typical Soviet propaganda poster. The propaganda, however, was often based on facts from the Eastern Front, where around 15 million Soviet civilians lost their lives.

March and April restrict offensive movement across all fronts. By April 30th the German forces have managed to stabilise their front along a triangle roughly demarcated by Yartsevo, Vyazma and Olenino. They have held onto the Moscow Highway but lost large areas of territory to the north and south of that line. Moreover, since the start of Operation Barbarossa over one million German soldiers have been lost in action.

International Events
1941
December 7th
The US Pacific Fleet stationed at Pearl Harbor, Hawaii, is attacked by nearly 200 Japanese aircraft flying from six carriers. Sixteen US vessels are sunk, including six battleships. The action brings the US into WWII as Japan commences invasions of many Far East territories.

December 8th
In North Africa the German siege of Tobruk ends. The forces of General Erwin Rommel go into retreat towards Gazala after sustained Allied offensives.

December 19th
Hitler becomes the commander-in-chief of the German Army by his own appointment.

1942
January 9th
Japanese forces continue a powerful advance down through Malaya, forcing the British back over the Slim river and advancing on Singapore.

January 12th
The Malayan capital, Kuala Lumpur, falls to the Japanese.

February 9th-15th
Japanese forces cross the Johore Strait to invade Singapore. After only six days of fighting the British forces on the island surrender and 130,000 British Army and Commonwealth troops pass into captivity. It is the worst defeat in British military history.

March 28th
The German-occupied French port of St Nazaire is wrecked in a British commando raid. The raid involved turning the destroyer HMS *Campbeltown* into an enormous floating bomb and detonating it at the dock gates.

April 18th
Sixteen US warplanes flying from the carrier USS *Hornet* bomb Tokyo. The raid does more psychological than real damage.

A Soviet ski detachment. They are unusually well-armed for Soviet troops, all having the PPSh-41 submachine gun, easily spotted by its 71-round capacity drum magazines.

Death on the Neva
The siege of Leningrad

1 September 1941: the German Army Group North starts to bombard the sprawling city of Leningrad, beginning the worst siege of the war.

Leningrad was one of the primary objectives of the opening phase of Operation 'Barbarossa' in June 1941. The German invasion of the USSR was planned to take place along three main axes, the most northerly of which was the responsibility of Army Group North under the command of Generalfeldmarschall Wilhelm Ritter von Leeb and, paradoxically, such was the success of the opening phase of the campaign that was to cost Germany the war, that in five days Army Group North had covered half the distance to Leningrad.

But at that point a series of massive battles on the Central Front started to divert the impetus away from the north. The reduced Army Group North forces still moved towards the 'Cradle of the Revolution' but at a reduced speed, so that it was not until September that the approaches to the city were in sight. By that time the defenders had sensed their danger and the populace was put to work to construct defences and anti-tank ditches on the approaches.

The Germans themselves assisted this defence by constantly diverting their efforts southwards from their objective as the approaches to Moscow beckoned, but eventually a definite operational plan to take the city was made. The Finns, the reluctant allies of Germany, were coerced into joining the campaign but did little more than cross the Svir river and establish themselves around Lake Ladoga.

The long blockade
By the time the Germans were ready, over one million civilians inside Leningrad had rendered their perimeter into a state fit to defend. When the full German attack took place it almost immediately became bogged down in a myriad of defensive positions, anti-tank obstacles and ditches. The Luftwaffe carried out constant bombing raids, but the German forces were held. Throughout the attack the German local commander, Generaloberst Hermann Hoth, was restricted by the fact that the bulk of his offensive forces were required to take part in operations to the south, against Moscow, but he used these forces at the very time they were requested to move south. Thus Leningrad made

Aboard a Sturmgeschutz, a German assault gun fitted for winter warfare with additional wide tracks. Try as they might, the Germans could not stop the trickle of supplies reaching the city during 1942 and attacks on the perimeter became increasingly costly.

its first major contribution by absorbing forces that might have made all the difference in the battle for Moscow.

The attack on the Leningrad perimeter died out by the middle of September and there began the siege that was to last until the late spring of 1943. It was a rather loose form of siege as the German forces involved could never fully control the whole city boundary and Lake Ladoga could usually be kept open. The Finns did little to assist the Germans, but a city the size of Leningrad requires a great deal of food and other supplies just to exist and these supplies were never forthcoming through the German lines. The civilian population of Leningrad suffered dreadfully. Throughout the winters of 1941/2 and 1942/3 thousands died of cold and hunger to the extent that bodies lay in the streets for days because no one had the strength or time to bury them.

Supply shortage
The front-line soldiers received the bulk of what food and supplies were available, but there was little enough of that and food could only be obtained by small-scale forays through the

CLINGING ON: THE LENINGRAD LIFELINE

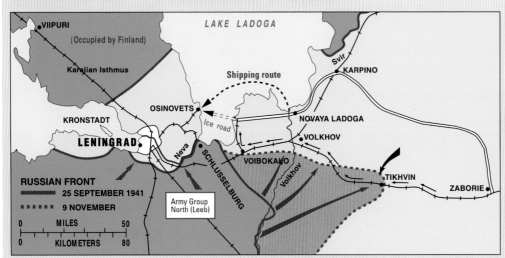

VIIPURI
(Occupied by Finland)
LAKE LADOGA
Karelian Isthmus
Svir
KARPINO
Shipping route
OSINOVETS
KRONSTADT
Ice road
NOVAYA LADOGA
LENINGRAD
Neva
VOLKHOV
SCHLUSSELBURG
VOIBOKALO
RUSSIAN FRONT
Volkhov
25 SEPTEMBER 1941
9 NOVEMBER
TIKHVIN
ZABORIE
Army Group
North (Leeb)
MILES   50
KILOMETERS   80

By clinging tenaciously to the southern shores of Lake Ladoga, the Soviets managed to keep a supply line open to Leningrad. In winter the lake froze solid enough for trucks and even a light railway to pass over. However, under air and artillery bombardment, the winter road over the lake was a dangerous route.

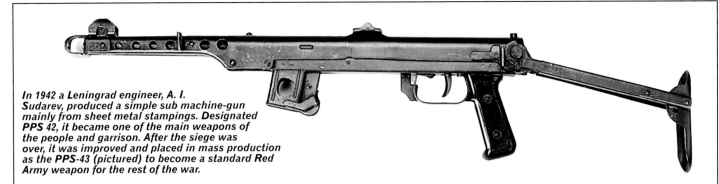

In 1942 a Leningrad engineer, A. I. Sudarev, produced a simple sub machine-gun mainly from sheet metal stampings. Designated *PPS 42*, it became one of the main weapons of the people and garrison. After the siege was over, it was improved and placed in mass production as the *PPS-43* (pictured) to become a standard Red Army weapon for the rest of the war.

Towards the end of the siege, Leningrad had once again become a major source of Soviet armaments. In 1942, tanks completed in this Leningrad tank factory drove out of the gates and straight into action.

loosely-held German lines. Weapons and ammunition supply were a constant headache for the Soviet commanders, who had been allowed to form their own independent Soviet to conduct their own defence, and they used the slender supply lines that came across the Lake Ladoga ice during the winters only for the movement of ammunition and other such material.

Leningrad could supply some of its own defence materials, for it had long been one of the major industrial centres of the USSR. The KV tank factory inside the perimeter continued to build tanks throughout the siege. As they were completed they ran off the lines straight into battle, while machine tools from other factories were used to produce small arms and spares, among them the remarkable 7.62mm (0.3in) PPS-42 which was made more with consideration to what machine tools were available rather than any design refinements.

German retreat

Despite constant artillery bombardment by the Germans and constant small-scale raids, Leningrad held on. By early 1943 the worst was over: the Germans had lost the vital strategic initiative and they fell back to the west leaving the approaches to Leningrad open. Battles still took place along the coastlines to the west of the city, but it had held and the worst siege of the war was over. Leningrad had won through, although at fearful cost.

Many men of the Baltic Fleet served as soldiers during the siege of Leningrad and the ships' guns were employed in defence of the city. Wearing the distinctive striped T-shirt under his quilted combat jacket, this sailor carries a *PPSh-41* sub-machine gun.

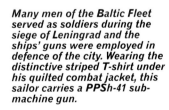

German and Finnish aircraft bombed Leningrad repeatedly but failed to permanently destroy the arms and tank factories within the city. Once supplies could be brought across Lake Ladoga in the winter the anti-aircraft defences took on a new lease of life.

Death on the Neva: Chronology

The siege of Leningrad by Hitler's Army Group North cost the city over one million dead during the 900 days it remained locked in place.

1941

June 22nd
Germany invades the Soviet Union in Operation Barbarossa. Army Group North strikes through Lithuania, Latvia and Estonia before cutting across the Russian border and pushing towards Leningrad.

September 1st
German units close on Leningrad and begin to make initial artillery bombardments of the city.

September 15th
Shlüsselburg, a fortress point to the southeast of Leningrad city, falls to the Germans. The Germans now control

Below: A policeman stares at the victims of a German heavy artillery barrage in Leningrad in the autumn of 1941. By 1942 starvation would be the chief cause of death.

Leningrad's southern perimeter, cutting the city off from the landmass of the Soviet Union. The Karelian isthmus to the north of the city is occupied by Finland. Leningrad is now effectively under siege.

Leningrad citizens at work constructing defences. Stalin had ordered that no citizens or industry should evacuate Leningrad, as that would be seen as an act of defeatism and might, Stalin thought, encourage acts of surrender.

November 9th
The Germans take Tikhvin to the east of Shlüsselburg, a staging post for passing some supplies into Leningrad using boats sailing from Lednevo across Lake Lagoda.

October–December
Starvation begins to take hold

Leningrad was home to some of the finest music houses in Russia. Here a string quartet from the Kirov Opera House entertain Russian troops. The composer Shostakovich was a well-known Leningrad survivor.

amongst the Leningrad population as initial rations run out.

December 10th
Soviet forces retake Tikhvin. A supply route across Lake Lagoda is re-established, but it is extremely precarious. Boat traffic suffers constant German aerial attack and only in deepest winter can vehicular traffic cross the lake when it freezes over.

1942
January–July
850,000 Leningrad citizens are evacuated from the city using the Lagoda crossing.

January 7th
Soviet forces of the Volkhov Front launch a major offensive against German lines between Leningrad and Lake Ilmen in the south near Novgorod.

March
The Soviet offensive is finally crushed by German counter-attacks, and the entire 2nd Shock Army is lost around Novgorod.

July
Hitler issues two directives to Army Group North instructing their operations against Leningrad. The first orders the complete isolation of Leningrad, including the cutting of the Lagoda supply route. The second orders that Leningrad be entirely destroyed using artillery and air power and the whole northern sector of the USSR be occupied.

August 19th–September 30th
A Soviet offensive aims to cut through German lines between Shlüsselburg and Tosno, drive through to Orienbaum in the Gulf of Finland, and link up with Russian forces there. After a costly campaign the Red Army makes no progress and is forced to give up the offensive.

September 25th
Hitler cancels operations for further territorial gains around Leningrad as the winter approaches.

October
The Soviet Leningrad Front forces begin to receive substantial reinforcements and new supplies of matériel, enabling them to build up their offensive strength.

1943
January 12th
The Soviets launch Operation Spark, a massive two-pronged offensive across the entire Volkhov and Leningrad front. The offensive manages to clear a narrow land corridor south of Leningrad, retaking Shlüsselburg on the 19th. Land-transported supplies are thus reopened to Leningrad, though the quantities of food scarcely reach subsistence level for the population. Following the offensive the lines stay almost static for another year.

1944
January 14th
Army Group North – severely depleted by years of combat and constant reductions of strength through redeployment – is overwhelmed by a Soviet offensive involving the entire Volkhov, Leningrad and 2nd Baltic Fronts. During a violent two-week offensive the German Leningrad forces are pushed away from the city.

January 27th
The Leningrad–Moscow railway is reopened and Stalin declares the siege of Leningrad over.

International Events
1941
September 3rd
Nazi security services begin experiments using the Zyklon-B gas as a means for industrial-scale extermination of Jews and other alienated peoples.

October 20th
Operation Typhoon – the German attempt to take Moscow – is cancelled because of severe winter weather and a determined Soviet resistance. The failure of Typhoon possibly saves the Soviet Union from defeat in the entire war.

December 7th
The US Pacific Fleet at Pearl Harbor is almost destroyed by the Japanese First Air Fleet in a surprise bombing assault. War is consequently declared between the US and Japan.

1942
January 20th
A meeting of senior Nazi officials headed by Reinhard Heydrich, head of the Reich Security Main Office, leads to the official adoption of the 'Final Solution', the complete and systematic execution of European Jewry.

May 4th–8th
The Battle of Coral Sea. US and Japanese fleets clash in the first carrier battle of the war. Though the US loses the carrier *Lexington*, the Japanese lose two carriers and huge volumes of aircraft which it could not replace as easily as the US.

November 2nd
Field Marshal Erwin Rommel orders the withdrawal of his troops from El Alamein under the weight of a tremendous Allied offensive led by General Bernard Montgomery.

1944
January 10th–February 9th
The Japanese are ejected from the island of Guadalcanal during a bitter offensive by over 50,000 US troops. It is Japan's first major defeat in a land campaign during WWII.

The Battle of Sevastopol
Conquest of the Crimea

Soviet forces in the eastern Crimea are overwhelmed in May 1942. Only the fortress of Sevastopol still holds out against the invaders.

The Soviet attempt to relieve Sevastopol by landing a force of 20,000 men on the Kerch Peninsula during December 1941 had resulted in the formation of bridgeheads around the town of Kerch and the port Feodosia. There had followed a build-up of strength until by April five Red Army brigades had been formed, consisting of nearly 250,000 men, together with some supporting artillery and 200 tanks. This was a considerable force, but it had been fed in piecemeal and committed to battle in the same unskilful way.

The sheer weight of German men and metal forced the Soviet rifle divisions in Feodosia backwards, then drove through the peninsula waist towards Kerch itself.

The Germans were protected above by Messerschmitt Bf 109s and their way was prepared by screaming dive-bombers. Generaloberst Erich von Manstein's task was also apparently made easier by the inefficiency of the Soviet command, and the constant nagging and wrangling of the STAVKA representative, L. Z. Mekhlis.

Von Manstein's siege train included the largest gun ever built: the 80cm (31.5in) 'schwere Gustav', which fired 7 ton armour-piercing projectiles or 5-ton high explosive shells. Sevastopol's mighty concrete forts were pulverised.

SCHWERE GUSTAV: FORT KILLER

Needless to say, the commanders were among the 86,000 men, including 23,000 wounded, who were evacuated between 15 and 20 May across the Kerch Strait to Taman and Cape Chushka – leaving behind nearly 100,000 men and all the remaining tanks.

Manstein could now turn his attention and the enormous weight of artillery and air power at his command to the reduction of the port of Sevastopol. To defend Sevastopol the Soviet Coastal Army had some 106,000 soldiers, sailors and marines, 600 guns including those in the heavy coastal batteries, about 100 mortars, 38 tanks and, in the airfields within their perimeter, 55 aircraft. Manstein now marshalled against them 204,000 men of 11th Army, 670 guns including those of enormous calibre in a siege train which he had assembled, 450 mortars, 720 tanks (at something of a disadvantage in such limited

It took 2000 men six weeks to prepare Gustav for firing at Sevastopol. The leviathan fired just 48 rounds but all with cataclysmic effect. Nine rounds were fired into Severnaya Bay, through the water, 30.5m (100ft) of sea-bed and into a supposedly invulnerable Soviet magazine.

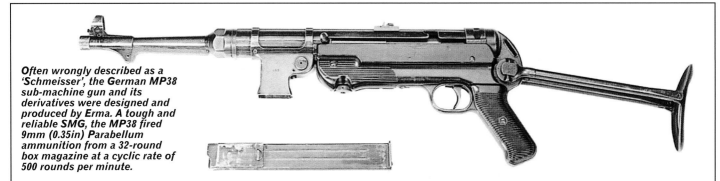

Often wrongly described as a 'Schmeisser', the German MP38 sub-machine gun and its derivatives were designed and produced by Erma. A tough and reliable SMG, the MP38 fired 9mm (0.35in) Parabellum ammunition from a 32-round box magazine at a cyclic rate of 500 rounds per minute.

space) and 600 aircraft.

The siege opened with a five-day barrage from every piece of artillery Manstein's experts could bring into action, and reminded some of the older members of the 11th Army staff of Verdun and St Quentin 25 years before. The shaking of the earth caused by the mortars, not only when their bombs landed but also when they were fired, would have registered quite high on the Richter Scale – and the shelling was augmented by the bombs dropped by the Luftwaffe, flying in to support Eleventh Army from bases as far away as Perekop and even Odessa.

The main blow fell on the Kmaytsjly-Belbek sector and heralded a drive by LIV Corps towards the eastern end of North Bay. All through the first half of June there was the most bitter fighting, the Soviets defending their trenches and holes in the ground with great tenacity.

By the third week of June, Manstein was sufficiently worried by the apparent lack of progress that he fed the 46th Division into the ring around Sevastopol, bringing it in from Kerch, and then begged more formations from the 17th Army upon the Donbass.

But eventually, of course, experience plus guns, mortars and their ammunition won the battle, though

the Red Army and the Red Navy performed miracles in reinforcing Sevastopol. Destroyers, minelayers, minesweepers, torpedo-boats, even submarines were used to ferry men, weapons and ammunition into the besieged port, on occasion the ship's officers being told that there was no chance of them all reaching the shore; they should try to get as near as possible before they were sunk so that at least some of their cargo might be able to swim or wade in, with luck carrying some weapons or stores.

Smoke screen

All the time the huge mortars and guns of Manstein's siege train hurled their massive shells and bombs into the fortress. On 5 June, the huge 80cm (31.5in) gun 'schwere Gustav' began firing its 7-ton shells into the fortress from nearly 30km (19 miles) away and systematically destroyed the main forts and the huge 'Maxim Gorky' Battery during the next three weeks. Gradually, ammunition shortages, smashed artillery, complete lack of air cover or support after 28 June began to take effect, and the German attacking infantry fought their way into the port.

On the night of 28/29 June the Germans managed at last to cross North Bay under cover of a smoke screen, and the following morning other

formations drove in from the Fedyukhin Heights towards Sapun Gora; by the morning of 30 June German troops were fighting inside the town of Sevastopol, taking cover in the ruined buildings they had themselves demolished.

During the next three days a Dunkirk-style evacuation was organised, with every craft that could sail coming in from Novorossiisk and the neighbouring Black Sea ports, some even braving the

Soviet troops advance through a marsh during the botched Soviet counter-attack on the Kerch peninsula. Mekhlis's incompetence lost the Red Army 176,000 men, 3500 guns and 350 tanks. He was demoted to corps commissar.

perils of the Kerch Straits and coming down from the Azov ports. It is not known how many servicemen and women, how many civilians, died in the siege of Sevastopol; but it had lasted

250 days from the time it had first been surrounded by German troops who had driven down into the Crimea. And the last 24 days had been of close hand-to-hand combat and devastating bombardment.

The battle had been by no means without cost to 11th Army, and Generalfeld-marschall von Manstein – awarded his baton with the occupation of Sevastopol and the whole of the Crimea –

found in July that he was commanding an army, if not desanguinated, at least decimated. It was not immediately available for the next stage of the Führer's plans, which had to be left to Sixth Army to the north under its ambitious commander, General Friedrich Paulus. He knew exactly where his fame and, he hoped, his fortune were to be made, and his eyes were firmly fixed upon it: Stalingrad.

Three sailors of the Black Sea Fleet pose for the camera. The naval personnel fought hard in defence of their base and as the end approached some battery garrisons blew themselves to pieces rather than surrender.

The Battle of Sevastopol
Chronology

Sevastopol demonstrated that siege warfare still had a part to play in Hitler's Blitzkrieg. The coastal city was pounded by some of the heaviest artillery pieces ever created, but resisted German occupation for over six months.

1941

September 25th
The Crimea is isolated by the advances of the German Army Group South in southern Russia.

September 26th–November 16th
The German 11th Army under Lieutenant-General von Manstein occupies almost the whole of the Crimea except for Sevastopol and the Kerch peninsula. During this period, however, Major-General I.Y. Petrov and 32,000 soldiers of the Independent Maritime Army occupy the fortress at Sevastopol and build three substantial defensive rings around the city.

December 17th
Manstein launches a major assault against Sevastopol with his 11th Army.

A German heavy mortar fires against Soviet forces landing near Feodosia in the Crimea, February 1942. The gun is a 21cm (8.3in) Mörser 18 capable of firing a 121kg (267lb) HE shell 16,700m (18,270ft).

December 26th
As Manstein's troops cut into the innermost defensive ring at Sevastopol, the Soviets make a substantial amphibious landing of troops near Kerch. Further landings of troops on the 28th leads Soviet forces to secure the Kerch peninsula and Manstein to withdraw from the Sevastopol attack.

1942
January
With the Kerch peninsula secured, the Soviet military creates the Crimea Front under the command of Major-General D.T. Kozlov with a strength of three armies.

April–May
Manstein's forces, previously under-resourced, begin a build-up of forces in preparation for an attempt to clear the Kerch peninsula known as Operation Bustard. Also delivered to German forces are 33 huge siege artillery pieces to be used for smashing Russian defences and resistance in Sevastopol.

May 8th
Manstein's offensive begins and utilises small-unit amphibious assaults around the Black Sea to disrupt the Kerch defence. By May 15th the Kerch peninsula is in German hands and 170,000 Soviet soldiers are taken

Three young Panzergrenadier soldiers. The soldier at the front is decorated with the Iron Cross and the Knight's Cross, decorations which became increasingly commonplace as the Germans fought for survival on the Eastern Front.

A German anti-tank gun crew at Sevastopol. As the war progressed German forces relied increasingly on captured Soviet guns, but this resulted in terrible problems for supplying the correct ammunition to all units.

prisoner. Sevastopol is isolated, though since January the city has been hugely reinforced and contains more than 186,000 Russian troops. Manstein makes plans for Operation Sturgeon, the conquest of Sevastopol.

June 2nd
A huge five-day artillery bombardment of Sevastopol begins, utilising over 600 artillery pieces.

June 6th
The Luftwaffe joins in the bombardment of Sevastopol.

June 7th–11th
At 2.30am on June 7th four divisions of 11th Army begin their assault upon Sevastopol from the north, while on the 11th a major attack by the Romanian Mountain Corps and 30th Army Corps is launched. Both are stopped by vigorous Soviet defence.

June 17th–28th
Manstein renews the assault upon Sevastopol. Soviet artillery observation posts and fortified hill positions fall to Romanian and German units and Axis forces enter the outskirts of the city. By the 18th only one fortification of the original 12 in the city

remains intact and operational.

June 30th
Vice-Admiral F.S. Oktyabrsky, the commander-in-chief of the Black Sea Fleet, begins the evacuation of the Sevastopol garrison by sea and air.

July 1st–2nd
German troops begin the final assault on Sevastopol, capturing the city's airfields, taking the urban centre and pushing the remainder of Soviet forces onto the coast. The evacuation of Russia forces ends on the 2nd.

July 4th
Sevastopol finally falls. The Germans take 90,000 Soviet soldiers prisoner.

International Events 1942

June 4th–7th
US naval forces at Midway inflict a major defeat upon the Japanese Navy in the Battle of Midway. Four Japanese carriers are sunk, a loss from which the Japanese never recover. The US Navy loses the carrier *Yorktown*.

June 10th
Following the assassination of Reinhardt Heydrich, deputy Reich protector of Bohemia and Moravia and head of the Reich Security Main Office, by Czech partisans the Czech village of Lidice is annihilated in reprisal. Over 170 men and boys are shot, and 296 women and children deported to concentration camps. The village itself is burnt to the ground.

June 21st
Field Marshal Rommel's Afrika Korps captures the contested Libyan port of Tobruk, taking over 35,000 Allied soldiers prisoner.

June 25th
Major-General Dwight David Eisenhower is appointed commander-in-chief of US forces in Europe.

July 2nd
British Prime Minister Winston Churchill easily survives a vote of censure in the Commons focused on his conduct of the war. The votes produce 476 against the vote, 25 for, and 30 abstentions.

German troops lay out a Nazi flag. Flags were not only used as ceremonial national emblems. Stretched out on the floor they identified the forces occupying positions to prevent attacks by friendly aircraft.

Gazala and Tobruk
Desert Fox in action

On 26 May 1942, Rommel led the Afrika Korps forward to smash the 8th Army and drive it back to Egypt. However, by the end of this period, the tables had begun to turn, and the outcome would be decided at El Alamein.

Erwin Rommel had first made his name in a daring infantry raid on the Italian front in October 1917, and the same audacity that enabled him to raid deep behind established positions, marked his operations once he became a Panzer officer. His part in the Fall of France in 1940 was again characterised by a deep Panzer raid into the French rear at Avesnes and the subsequent dash to the Channel coast. By 1941 he was in North Africa carrying out a series of armoured operations that constantly defeated numerically superior British and Commonwealth forces, which were unable to adapt to the tactics of tank warfare as carried out by Rommel.

New 'rules'
By May 1942, Rommel had rapidly learned that armoured warfare in the desert entailed using a new set of 'rules'. In the wide open spaces of the unpopulated desert, mobility and firepower took on new meanings. In the desert there was always a flank to be turned, and positional warfare became increasingly meaningless as mobile forces could turn up from any point of the compass.

Warfare initiative
In May 1942 Rommel was ready to begin what was to become one of the classic examples of this particular approach to warfare. In that month he had to hand a total of 561 tanks (333 German and 228 Italian) ready to take on a superior British force which had over 900 tanks and numbers of new anti-tank guns. But Rommel did have several advantages. One was that the British tank force was scattered in small pockets, and another was that the Luftwaffe had a local numerical superiority that was to serve Rommel well in the days ahead. The British were emplaced in a long defensive line south of Gazala, well protected by massive minefields and located mainly in well-defended 'boxes'. They were expecting Rommel to attack

A Commonwealth soldier who escaped from Tobruk chats with a British officer. Many units in the Tobruk garrison fought a successful battle, but there was no leadership to co-ordinate the defence. The 8th Army made no effective attempt to interrupt Rommel's attack.

TOBRUK: THE LINE IN THE SAND

As a strategically important port on the Mediterranean, the capture of Tobruk enabled the Germans to dramatically shorten their logistics tail and open a new Sea Port of Disembarkation (SPOD). Rommel's Panzers previously had to rely on fuel, ammunition and supplies being moved by land from the captured port of Tripoli in modern-day Libya. This was a hard and arduous journey. Long supply lines were vulnerable to attack, and there was always the added risk that they could be overextended if the armoured divisions outran the speed of their supply vehicles. The longer the logistics tail, the more likely this could become.

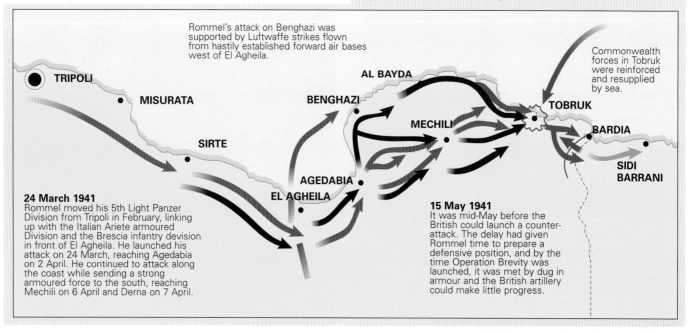

Rommel's attack on Benghazi was supported by Luftwaffe strikes flown from hastily established forward air bases west of El Agheila.

Commonwealth forces in Tobruk were reinforced and resupplied by sea.

TRIPOLI
MISURATA
SIRTE
EL AGHEILA
AGEDABIA
BENGHAZI
AL BAYDA
MECHILI
TOBRUK
BARDIA
SIDI BARRANI

24 March 1941
Rommel moved his 5th Light Panzer Division from Tripoli in February, linking up with the Italian Ariete armoured Division and the Brescia infantry division in front of El Agheila. He launched his attack on 24 March, reaching Agedabia on 2 April. He continued to attack along the coast while sending a strong armoured force to the south, reaching Mechili on 6 April and Derna on 7 April.

15 May 1941
It was mid-May before the British could launch a counter-attack. The delay had given Rommel time to prepare a defensive position, and by the time Operation Brevity was launched, it was met by dug in armour and the British artillery could make little progress.

Right: On 13 June Rommel's surviving armour triumphed again and Lt Gen. Neil Ritchie of the British Army, ordered the Knightsbridge defensive position to be abandoned. XIII Corps was now in dire danger of being cut of from Tobruk, so it too retreated. A series of fierce rearguard actions followed.

Below: At regimental level British armour fought with a new-found professionalism, but senior commanders reacted too slowly and failed to co-ordinate their actions. Rommel led from the front, relying on his fingertip feel for the battle to keep him one step ahead all the time.

and were not disappointed.

Rommel's attack plan was simple and typical of his methods. Using the relatively immobile Italian infantry to pin the British in their defensive line, he moved his main striking forces south. These were made up of the crack Italian Ariete Division, a unit that Rommel was later to state never let him down, and the bulk of the Afrika Korps, made up of the 15th and 23rd Panzer Divisions and the 90th Light Division.

Frontal attack

These moved south around the end of the British defence lines and then moved north as the Italian Trieste Division carried out a frontal attack on the southern portion of the line. Within a few hours Rommel's forces were well to the rear of the static British lines and began to move towards the Knightsbridge Box, a defensive area which became the focal point of the Gazala battle.

As soon as the British became aware of Rommel's

move they started a protracted series of armoured counter-attacks against the attackers. But while the German and Italian units were operating as cohesive formations under central control, the British tank attacks were made by fragmented units operating under various higher tactical controls.

Many of these counter-attacks were made in the traditional British cavalry manner by lines of tanks simply charging towards the Germans, who destroyed them by a combination of tank gun and anti-tank gun fire, including numbers of 37mm (1.46in) and 88mm (3.46in) anti-aircraft towed weapons that accompanied the Panzers into action. These fragmented attacks, included some which had numbers of the new 75mm (2.95in) gun-armed Grant tanks recently arrived in the theatre, did manage some successes, and gradually Rommel's forces diminished in numbers and effectiveness

as supplies of ammunition and fuel were expended. Rommel himself saved this situation by leading a supply column straight through the British minefields and lines on the night of 29 May. He was able to do this mainly because the minefields were not covered by defensive fire and thus Rommel was able to bring forward the fuel to keep his units in motion.

Continuing action

The Gazala battles went on for two weeks in a series of attacks and counter-attacks that gradually threatened to bring both sides to a complete standstill from sheer exhaustion. As a general rule the Germans and Italians were able to keep the overall initiative, as they were able to keep switching the point they wished to attack and were always able to move out to the south when things went against them. The British and Commonwealth troops generally remained static or else fell back

towards their main supply bases in the El Adem and Tobruk areas. From time to time frontal attacks were made against the main line south of Gazala. By mid-June Rommel's supply line was in a precarious state, to the extent that his armoured units were keeping going on captured supplies alone. The Grants, when encountered, were a particular headache for the Germans, who were able to destroy them only by the use of their 88mm (3.46in) anti-aircraft guns, although the 37mm (1.46in) anti-aircraft guns were only marginally less effective.

Tobruk, and its prized port, eventually fell to the Germans, allowing them to shorten their supply lines. Rommel continued to drive east, however, his advance would lead him to the British and Commonwealth defensive lines at Alam Halfa and ultimately to El Alamein, where the desert war would be decided.

Above: Tobruk was now exposed to German attack. It had a strong garrison, but the defences had been neglected and Maj.Gen. Klopper surrendered after just 48 hours of fighting. Some 30,000 bewildered and angry men were captured, including 19,000 British soldiers.

Left: Rommel's attack began on 26 May, concentrating on the southern flank of the British line. The British knew the attack was coming but failed to concentrate, and brigades were beaten one by one by the massed German armour.

Gazala and Tobruk: Chronology

Rommel's Gazala Line offensive initially looked as if it would be defeated by British armoured resistance. Brilliant German defensive tactics, however, sapped the Allied strength and Rommel was able to take Tobruk.

1942
May 26th

Rommel launches his major offensive to take the Gazala Line – a series of British defences running over 80km (50 miles) south from just west of Gazala to Bir Hacheim in the south. In the early afternoon of May 26th the Italian X and XI Corps, known collectively as Group Cruewell, begin a diversionary assault against the northern half of the line.

7.00pm

Rommel attacks around the southern sector of the Gazala Line using the German 15th and 21st Panzer divisions, the 90th Infantry Division and the Italian XX Corps. His aim is to move around the bottom of the Gazala Line at Bir Hacheim, then strike north to the coastline, capturing Tobruk and surrounding the Allies on the Gazala Line.

May 27th

Rommel's troops reach positions just south of Bir Hacheim and begin to swing their attack northwards. The 1st Free French Brigade at Bir Hacheim obstinately holds onto their positions.

May 28th–May 31st

The German Panzer divisions suffer very heavy losses amongst their armour, particularly when attempting to take the Sidra ridge (a section of high ground behind the centre of the Gazala Line near Sidi Muftah). By June 1st nearly 30 per cent of his tanks have been lost. Rommel changes his original plan. He stops the drive to the north, instead circling his forces against the British 150th Brigade around Sidi Muftah and preparing defensive positions in an oval area approximately 16km (10 miles) long and 11km (7 miles) wide.

June 1st–June 6th

The area around Sidi Muftah becomes known as 'The Cauldron'. The 150th Brigade is entirely destroyed with 4000 soldiers captured, and the Allies lose a further 230 tanks attempting to retake the German pocket.

June 10th–11th

The French defenders at Bir Hacheim are finally overcome and put into retreat. On June 11th the Germans break out of the Cauldron. They swing south then east to attack the British 7th Armoured Division around El Adem.

An Allied soldier sets his Bren gun in the bombed window of a Tobruk house, ready to defend the town against an air strike.

June 11th–18th
The Allies are forced into a retreat as Rommel's Afrika Korps attacks northwards towards its original objectives. By June 18th Tobruk is completely surrounded. Tobruk is garrisoned mainly by the 2nd South African Division under General Klopper.

June 20th
Rommel begins his assault against Tobruk, leading with a heavy artillery and air bombardment. By 7.00pm 21st and 15th Panzer Division have cut through Tobruk's perimeter defences and minefields and have entered the town itself.

June 21st
General Klopper surrenders Tobruk to Rommel.

International Events
1942
May 27th
Reinhard Heydrich, deputy Reich protector of Bohemia and Moravia and an architect of the 'Final Solution', is seriously injured in a hand-grenade attack by Czech resistance fighters. He dies of his wounds on June 4th.

June 2nd
The RAF make a 1000-bomber raid against the industrial town of Essen, following up on its earlier 1000-bomber attack against Cologne on May 31st.

June 5th
The United States declares war on Hungary, Romania and Bulgaria.

June 23rd
Auschwitz concentration camp begins the systematic slaughter of Jews using the gas chamber. The first victims to enter the chambers are a group of Parisian Jews.

June 25th
Major-General Dwight D. Eisenhower is appointed commander of US forces in Europe.

June 26th
Yet another 1000-bomber raid by the RAF strikes Germany, this time directed at Bremen

Above: An Allied defensive position in Tobruk town. The Allies expected Rommel's assault to come from the west and southwest. By attacking the town from the southeast, Rommel wrong-footed Tobruk's defenders.

Below: A German soldier observes Allied positions. The desert landscape made life difficult for offensive man-oeuvres, which came to rely on the attrition inflicted by artillery, tank fire and air attack to overcome defences.

Forgotten sacrifice
The Arctic convoys

June 1941: the hard-pressed Royal Navy receives a new and perilous task – convoying vital war supplies to the USSR.

As the rate of Arctic convoys gathered pace in 1941, the German navy detached U-boats from the main campaign in the Atlantic to operations off Norway, where they could operate with the support of the Luftwaffe. The tables were turned from 1944 when bigger convoys included escort carriers.

Hitler's ill-advised assault on the USSR in June 1941 gave the beleaguered British an unlikely and problematical ally. Supplies were needed urgently in the USSR and had to come by sea, adding to the responsibilities of the already overstretched Royal Navy, and only the Soviet Arctic ports could be considered for shipments.

Depending on the season, this demanded a 10- to 15-day passage for convoys, with the route flanked to the east by German-occupied Norway. During winter pack ice forced the route closer towards this hostile coast, with near four months of unbroken darkness and deep gloom affording some cover, but at the expense of weather conditions of unrelenting vileness. With the ice sheet retreating in summer the route could be more distant, but was in permanent daylight and open to virtual round-the-clock attack.

Where the North Atlantic convoys were threatened predominantly by submarines and those operating in the Mediterranean by surface forces and aircraft, the Arctic run was menaced by all of these threats, and as a result the escort system was organised in light of these threats. This soon developed the form of an immediate escort. In the early days this was usually of corvettes and anti-submarine trawlers/whalers; a close cover of free-manoeuvring

MURMANSK: THE CONVOY ROUTES

Summer was the more dangerous time for the convoys as the 24-hour daylight left them open to air attack. On the other hand the ice retreated allowing the ships to sail farther away from the Luftwaffe airfields in Norway. The weather conditions in winter were indescribable but restricted German air and surface ship activity.

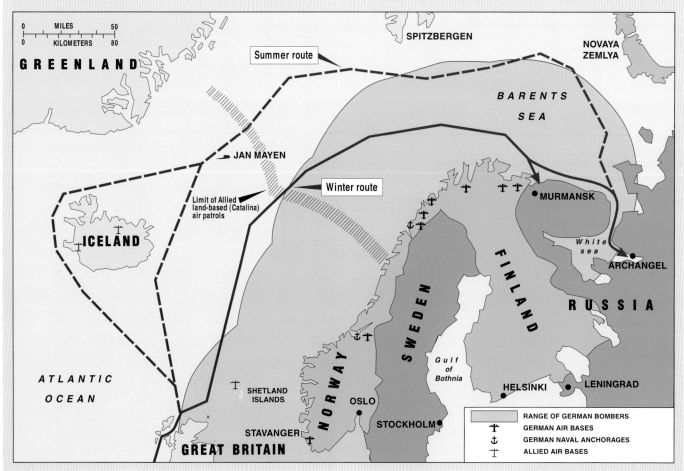

Known to the Luftwaffe as the 'flying clog', the five-man Blohm und Voss Bv 138 reconnaissance flying boat was used to shadow the Arctic convoys.

cruisers with destroyer escort that could rapidly reinforce the convoy on demand; and a distant cover of Home Fleet heavy units to guard against forays by the substantial naval forces built up by the Germans in northern Norway.

Political gesture

On 21 August 1941 the first, unnumbered seven-ship convoy sailed from Iceland for Archangel, arriving without incident 10 days later. This was shortly after the invasion of the USSR, and was a political gesture as much as experiment. The PQ/QP convoy cycle was inaugurated soon after this, the inability of the Germans to interfere allowing escort strength to drop to as little as a cruiser and a pair of destroyers.

With the coming of the dark period the cycle was accelerated, so that by a time early in February 1942 12 north-bound PQs, totalling 93 ships, had been passed with the loss of only one ship to a U-boat. With lengthening daylight in March 1942 things livened up with the passing PQ12 and QP8 narrowly avoiding interception by the newly arrived battleship KMS *Tirpitz* and her destroyers.

Only three weeks later the enemy achieved something like co-ordination and PQ13 lost five ships: two to the very effective Junkers Ju 88

torpedo bomber, two to U-boats and one to a marauding destroyer force. In tackling the latter, the now usual close cover was unfortunate to lose the cruiser HMS *Trinidad* to one of her own rogue torpedoes. Two U-boats were sunk, one rammed by one of the ocean minesweepers that gave such yeoman service.

Unpredictable weather reduced to chance planned interceptions by both sides. Sixteen of PQ14's 24 ships were obliged to return because of ice conditions, but Ju 88s out of Kirkenes sank two of the empty QP10.

Over 260 Luftwaffe aircraft and over 30 U-boats were by now available, and both remaining 'pocket battleships' had been moved north. Despite the daylight lengthening ominously, politics demanded the running of PQ16 in May. It suffered seven losses, six of them to aircraft.

By the end of June, when PQ17 sailed, German surface forces in the north had been reinforced by the battleship *Tirpitz*, a heavy cruiser and all remaining serviceable destroyers. By 1 July eight U-boats were concentrating on the convoy, which was also under continuous aerial surveillance. Only on 4 July, however, did the attack develop and the Admiralty ordered the convoy to scatter,

firmly believing that the *Tirpitz* was out. As it happened she did not sail until the next day and then returned almost immediately. This, however, did not help the convoy, which lost 23 out of its 34 ships to aircraft and submarine as, singly or in small groups, they struggled the last 1300km (810 miles) virtually unescorted.

Formidable escort

Not until September 1942 did the next convoy run, in the form of PQ18. Its 40 ships enjoyed a formidable escort that, at last, included an escort carrier. The Germans mounted a major effort but, though mass air attack sank 10 ships and U-boats a further three, the price was the loss of three U-boats and 27 aircraft.

Subsequently northbound convoys were recoded JW, starting at JW51. This much-delayed operation ran in two parts. Neither suffered loss but the cruiser and the destroyer close cover of JW51B fought a spirited defensive action against superior enemy surface forces on the last day of 1942.

Between February and November 1943 no convoys ran as all escorts were diverted to the Atlantic route, where the U-boat offensive had reached its peak. Then, within the space of nine

weeks, a total of 106 ships passed north in six operations for the loss of just three ships.

From the spring of 1944 the convoys doubled in size and were accompanied by one, or sometimes even two, of the highly utilitarian escort carriers. The aircraft from these made short work of shadowers while ever less experienced U-boat commanders found themselves pitted against 20 destroyers and a battle-hardened support group before being able to penetrate as far as the corvettes of the close escort itself. Not surprisingly, the convoys ran to the close of hostilities with small inconvenience other than from the eternal, remorseless weather.

In all, 1,526 ship movements were involved in 77 convoys to and from the northern ports of the USSR, with, somewhat incredibly, just 98 ships being lost. The overall success of the convoys to and from the northern USSR was attributable to the dedication and perseverance, under the most adverse conditions, of both merchantmen and escorts.

The Soviets never accepted the difficulties involved in sailing the Arctic route and loudly complained about 'British cowardice'. The First Sea Lord was driven to ask the Soviet ambassador how he would like to command the Royal Navy.

Forgotten sacrifice: Chronology

Between August 1941 and May 1945 Allied convoys sailing from the UK injected 4.43 million tons of supplies into the Soviet war effort. The convoy duties were made in constant danger from U-boats and the appalling Arctic weather of the Norwegian and Barents seas.

1941

August 21st

The first Arctic convoy sails for Russia from Scapa Flow in Scotland, taking Hurricane fighters and other war supplies.

1942

March 20th

Convoy PQ13 sets sail for northern Russia, but is intercepted by German U-boats, aircraft and destroyers. Out of 19 ships, five are lost, the heaviest losses to date amongst a single Arctic convoy.

June 27th–July 28th

Convoy PQ17 sails from Reykjavik, Iceland, consisting of 36 ships. During the voyage 34 of the ships are sunk by German U-boats or anti-shipping aircraft, the worst Russian convoy losses of the war.

August–September

Arctic convoys are suspended while shipping is diverted in support of the Allied landings in North Africa.

September 2nd–26th

Convoy PQ18 makes its Russian voyage with 40 ships under increased escort protection by 17 destroyers and the escort carrier *Avenger*. Though the convoy suffers heavy losses –13 ships sunk – the improved escort numbers and tactics provide a greter survival rate than previous convoys.

December 31st

The Battle of the Barents Sea. The convoy JW51B is attacked by the German battleships *Lützow* and *Admiral Hipper* and six German destroyers. Despite being outnumbered, the escort unit of six Allied destroyers under Captain Robert Sherbrooke successfuly defends the convoy, losing two destroyers but protecting the merchantmen. The defeat so enrages Hitler that the commander-in-chief of the German Navy, Admiral Raeder, resigns.

1943

March–August

Arctic convoy traffic is halted because of priorties in the Atlantic theatre and also because the German battle-cruiser *Scharnhorst* has moved into Norwegian waters to join the *Tirpitz* and *Lützow*.

September 22nd

A daring attack on the *Tirpitz* by Royal Navy midget submarines puts the battleship out of action for six months.

November

Russian convoys resume activity throughout November and December.

December 26th

Convoy JW55B is attacked by the *Scharnhorst* and five German destroyers near Bear Island. The battleship is engaged in a running battle by Royal Navy warships and sunk at 7.30pm with the loss of all but 36 of its crew.

A German aerial reconnaissance photograph of convoy PQ17 heading for Murmansk. The letters in convoy titles referred to the departure and destination points, P referring to Iceland and Q north Russia. The numbers were simply indicators of numerical sequence.

1944
April 3rd
The *Tirpitz* is attacked at anchor in Altenfiord by Fleet Air Arm aircraft. Though the sink is not sunk, it is put out of action for another three months.

May–July
Arctic convoy activity is suspended once more as resources are diverted into the Normandy landings operation.

August 15th–29th
Tirpitz suffers further damage during engagements with the escorts of convoy JW59.

November
As Germany edges towards collapse in the war, the Russian convoys enjoy a month without any losses. On November 12th the *Tirpitz* is finally destroyed by an RAF bombing raid over Troms.

May 1945
Having enjoyed a period of almost a year with only eight ships lost, the last Russian convoy, JW67, sails between the Clyde and Kola just after the German surrender.

International Events

1941
June 22nd
Germany invades the Soviet Union in Operation Barbarossa, beginning the largest land war in history.

December 7th
Japan launches a preemptive attack on the US Pacific Fleet at Pearl Harbor, Hawaii. The action brings the US into WWII.

1942
February 15th
The British colony of Singapore falls to the Japanese. It is the worst defeat in the history of the British Army, as over 130,000 Allied soldiers go into captivity.

June 1st
Three Japanese midget submarines attack Sydney harbour in Australia. Though all three vessels are sunk, they in turn sink one merchant vessel and cause considerable psychological

A common sight on the Arctic convoys: one of the escorts heavily iced up, its guns useless until the ice had been chipped off. However the main threat to the safety of the convoys to the Soviet Union lurked under the sea's surface: the U-boats.

anxiety amongst the Australian population about a possible Japanese invasion.

1943
January 31st
The remnants of the encircled German Sixth Army at Stalingrad surrender to Soviet forces having lost 200,000 troops. It is the first major German defeat of the war.

May 13th
The last German forces to remain in North Africa surrender after a successful Allied campaign in Tunisia.

September 3rd
US and British forces invade Italy, committing Germany to open yet another front of operations.

1944
June 6th
Operation Overlord. The Allies open the Second Front with a massive amphibious landing at Normandy, France.

December 28th
The Ardennes offensive, Hitler's last attempt to defeat the Allied advance through Europe, fails with heavy German losses

1945
May 7th
Following the suicide of Adolf Hitler, and with Berlin about to fall to the Russians, Germany surrenders.

August 14th
Japan signs its unconditional surrender following two US atomic bomb attacks on Hiroshima and Nagasaki.

Disaster at Dieppe
No second front

Dawn, 19 August 1942: the biggest cross-Channel raid begins on the town of Dieppe. However, the Germans are ready and waiting.

Operation 'Jubilee', the raid on Dieppe, was the biggest operation of its type carried out during World War II. Ten major military units took part – the larger part of them Canadian. Casualties were heavy, only one formation succeeded in taking its objective, but the operation did succeed in answering a vital question that had been plaguing the Allied planners since Dunkirk, when it had first been realised that in order to defeat Hitler and all for which he stood, an invasion of the French coast would have to be undertaken. The question was: would it be possible to capture a French port during the first days of the invasion?

The attempt to capture Dieppe itself was made by six battalions and an armoured regiment of the 2nd Canadian Division, landing at Puys, Pourville and on the Dieppe beaches between these villages. But on each side of this coastal stretch were batteries of coastal defence guns, which could blow out of the water any ships seen approaching the shore. To deal with this problem two British Commandos were landed – No. 4 on the west to destroy the batteries at Vesterival-sur-Mer and Varengeville, and No. 3 on the east to destroy those at Berneval.

Canadian landings

On 8 August 1942, 252 craft left four English south coast ports, the nine infantry landing ships carrying men of the Essex Scottish and Royal Hamilton Light Infantry to land on the beaches in front of Dieppe Casino; of the South Saskatchewan Regiment and of the Queen's Own Cameron Highlanders of Canada to land at Pourville; and of the Royal Regiment of Canada to land at Puys. The 14th Canadian Army Tank Battalion and the Fusiliers Mont-Royal would land in support of the Dieppe assault, while the Royal Marine 'A' Commando would assist in the capture of headlands that dominated the exposed beaches.

Copybook attack

By 0335 on 19 August the convoys were off their objectives, the men were in their landing craft and an apparently unobserved approach to the shore was in progress. Then a burst of fire on the far left flank revealed that No. 3 Commando had run into enemy shipping off Berneval and within minutes the whole length of the

Although a second line formation, the 302nd German Infantry Division defending the Dieppe sector had fortified its position well and the beach was completely covered by interlocking fields of fire.

enemy defences was alert.

Nevertheless, on the right flank the troops of No. 4 Commando were carrying out a copybook attack. They landed on time, were well ashore and approaching their main target from two directions by 0540, had destroyed a nest of machine-guns by 0607 and at 0630 assaulted the main battery. The charges were placed, the guns blown up and No. 4 Commando was back aboard their craft and on their way home by 0730. At the eastern end, No. 3 Commando had emerged from the fight with the enemy ships badly scat-

MASSACRE: THE FALL OF THE CALGARY REGIMENT

27 Churchill tanks landed on the beach and 12 were knocked out before they had travelled more than a few yards. The others found themselves unable to break into the town and were picked off one by one.

The infantry were supported by the Calgary Regiment of Churchill tanks. But the first wave of armour was late, their CO was killed as soon as his vehicle landed and the tanks found all entries into the town were blocked.

Ultimately a very successful fighter bomber, the Hawker Typhoon first saw action over Dieppe. The results were inauspicious with two aircraft lost when they were attacked in error by Canadian Spitfires. The whole Allied air effort was poorly co-ordinated and failed to provide much help for the ground troops.

tered and only one troop of 17 men and three officers was ashore on time. But they so harassed their target, the Goebbels Battery, with sniper and Bren gun fire that the guns never opened up on the main assault taking place around Dieppe. They also were successfully withdrawn.

But between these two Commando assaults, total disaster had fallen upon the Canadians. Whether the Germans had prior intelligence of Operation 'Jubilee' or not (and there is some evidence that they did), they had obviously anticipated an attempted landing on the Dieppe beaches and had prepared meticulously for it.

Concealed heavy machine-guns swept the approaches and then the barbed wire

German officers examine the interior of a wrecked landing craft. There is some evidence that the Germans were forewarned of the Dieppe assault, but the attack lost the element of surprise anyway when 3 Commando's landing raft ran into a German coastal convoy.

entanglements that ranged along the beaches between the sea and the promenade, and when the desperate survivors of the first landing dived for hollows in the sand and shingle, mortar bombs landed among them with a precision that spoke of careful preparation. Snipers coolly picked off anyone showing leadership, to such an extent that no commanding officer, few company commanders and

fewer senior NCOs survived the morning, and the battle became a series of desperate actions by individuals – most of whom were killed as soon as their purpose was seen – or small groups, quickly isolated.

Caught on the beaches

The attack on Dieppe itself foundered in the shallows and died on the beach. The Essex Scottish and Royal Hamiltons met such a weight of fire that it was a wonder that any of them reached even the prison camps, let alone returned home. Tank landing craft attempting to get in to give support were blasted as they emerged from the smoke, and their tanks hit as soon as the ramps went down. Nevertheless, 27 tanks did reach the shore and six ploughed through the wire to reach the promenade. One climbed the steps of the casino, and three moved along the promenade blazing away at enemy posts until they ran out of ammunition: in the end

all were wrecked and most of their crews were killed.

In ignorance of the true situation, the force commander sent in the reserves of Fusiliers Mont-Royal and Royal Marines: but it was to no avail and these men were virtually thrown away. By 0900 the true situation had been realised and an attempt was made to withdraw. The naval craft raced in and out, desperately trying to lift men off the beaches, but the sacrifices they made were poorly rewarded: when by early afternoon on 19 August the ships finally withdrew to make their sorry way home, they left behind 215 Canadian officers and 3164 men, 279 Royal Navy or Commando officers and 726 British other ranks.

They also brought back the answer to that vital question. It was a resounding 'No!' If a port was necessary in the first days of the great invasion, then the Allies must take one with them.

Disaster at Dieppe: Chronology

Dieppe was an expensive experiment in amphibious warfare. The ill-conceived assault against the German-occupied port cost the Allies 4000 soldiers.

1942

May 20th

Canadian troops of the 2nd Canadian Infantry Division begin training on the Isle of Wight for Operation Rutter, an amphibious assault against the German-occupied French port at Dieppe. Rutter is intended for July 7th.

July 7th

The assault is postponed because of poor weather conditions at sea. Debates follow about whether to cancel the operation entirely. Instead Vice-Admiral Mountbatten maintains the plan under a new name, Operation Jubilee.

August 19th

Operation Jubilee is launched using a force of 4962 Canadian troops, 1000 British soldiers, and 50 US Rangers transported by 237 naval craft.

3.48am

Parts of the landing force are engaged at sea by a German

Above: Canadian troops with a Bren Carrier vehicle wait for their landing craft to take them into Dieppe. Many Allied vehicles landed were unable to negotiate the shingle banks and concrete obstacles on the beaches, and were quickly destroyed.

Below: A German soldier heavily laden with stick grenades inspects the destruction of the Dieppe beaches. The disaster at Dieppe led the Allies to make major revisions in amphibious warfare tactics. Key points to emerge were the need to have effective landing vessels and significant preparatory bombardment, but many still felt that Dieppe had been a useless waste of lives.

convoy several hours prior to the main landings, losing the element of surprise in key sectors along the 10-mile front.

4.30am

Canadian units make flanking attacks against German coastal batteries and positions at Varengeville, Pourville, Puys and Berneval. The landings at Varengeville and Pourville are almost entirely unopposed, and at Berneval a small section of No.3 Commando manage to silence the coastal batteries for around 90 minutes. At Puys units of the Royal Regiment of Canada and the Black Watch take heavy casualties on the beach.

5.20am

The main assault is launched

in the central sector. German units are now in full alert owing to the flanking attacks. As units from the 14th Army Tank Regiment, the Essex Scottish Regiment, and the Royal Hamilton Light Infantry disembark they come under hails of machinegun fire. Armour lands on the beach 15 minutes later, but 15 of the 27 vehicles are either knocked out or cannot cross the shingle sea banks or sea walls.

11.00am–2.00pm
Having suffered appalling casualties and made little progress, Allied forces withdraw from Dieppe. By 2.00pm all surviving soldiers have been evacuated, leaving behind 3367 dead, wounded or prisoner.

International Events 1942

August 15th
Churchill and Stalin meet in Moscow to discuss strategic options for operations in North Africa and for opening a Second Front in mainland Europe.

August 17th
Twelve USAAF Flying Fortress bombers pound the railway marshalling yards at Rouen, France. It was the first raid conducted by US bombers of the war. All aircraft and crew returned safely to bases in England.

August 19th
Australian troops of the Australian 7th Division enter the New Guinea campaign with amphibious landings at Port Moresby.

August 21st
The leader of the French collaborationist government, Marshal Pétain, praises German forces for crushing the Allied Dieppe raid.

August 22nd
Brazil declares war on Germany and Italy. The declaration follows the sinking of several Brazilian merchant vessels by German submarines. Japan was excluded from the declaration.

British commandos remain defiant following the Dieppe raid. The Army Commandos were formed in 1940 from the desire of Winston Churchill for an elite unit capable of small-unit assault operations using the latest weaponry and tactics. At Dieppe, Nos. 3 and 4 Commandos were used, assaulting German coastal battery positions at Berneval and Varengeville respectively.

Operation Torch

US troops come ashore at Arzan, near the port of Oran and Casablanca. It had been hoped that the French would avoid engaging the American units, but every landing was opposed to some degree.

North Africa landings

As Rommel retreated from the El Alamein battlefield he received news that Allied troops had landed at the opposite end of North Africa, in Morocco and Algeria. The Vichy French garrisons fought against the Allied invasion force, but once Hitler sent troops into the unoccupied zone of metropolitan France, the Vichy units ended their loyalty and the way was clear for an Allied pincer movement against the Axis army in North Africa.

Two GIs hitch a lift to the beach on a towed AA gun, in the process keeping their feet and their ammunition dry in the process. As well as troops, thousands of tons of materiel were rapidly landed.

On 8 November 1942, Anglo-American armies were landed on the north coast of Africa between Casablanca and Algiers in an operation which still excites incredulity when its details are examined, even though such enterprises as the Sicily and D-Day landings, the war in Korea, the Six-Day war, the Falklands conflict and Desert Storm have taken place since that time.

A fleet of 102 ships, including 29 transports carrying 35,000 US soldiers with all their impedimenta, had crossed the 6435 km (4000 miles) of the Atlantic to Casablanca; another task-force carrying 39,000 US soldiers and escorted by Royal Naval escorts had left the Clyde on 26 October, passed through the Straits of Gibraltar and landed at Oran, while a third which had left the Clyde at the same time went on to land at Algiers. This third force carried 23,000 British and 10,000 American troops, and some 160 Royal Navy ships had acted as cover down the Atlantic and into the Mediterranean to the 250 merchantmen carrying the forces from the Clyde; only one transport of the entire joint fleet had been lost to enemy action, the men aboard quickly being transferred to landing ships, which took them ashore.

Going ashore

By the end of the first day at Algiers the men were all ashore, despite a brisk resistance from French marines and native troops during the first attempt to storm the port. At Oran the plan to encircle the city had gone well and the troops had all disembarked, but by evening it was becoming evident that the French troops were organizing a strong defence.

At Casablanca, although the landings had all been virtually unopposed – to the surprise of their charismatic commander, Major General George Patton – a measure of confusion had delayed the deployment of Allied troops. By the end of the second day, a combination of poor administration and growing French opposition seemed likely to block expansion of the beach-head.

From the beginning, one of the great imponderables of the entire operation had been the extent of opposition which might be expected from the French. After centuries of Anglo-French antagonism, exacerbated by the destruction of the French fleet by the Royal Navy after the fall of France, plus the attacks on French positions at Dakar and in Syria, it was considered unlikely that even the grim realities of German occupation would persuade the French to lay down their arms and welcome British soldiers as liberators. But the relationships between France and the USA had been close since the days of Lafayette, and many US troops and their commanders expected something more in the manner of brass bands and flag-waving to greet their appearance, than the doubtful approaches and occasional shots which occurred during the first few hours ashore.

Attempts had been made to clarify the situation before

This Messerschmitt Bf 109F-2/Trop of 1./JG 77 was captured by Allied forces after the battle of El Alamein in early November 1942. It was typical of the Bf 109 fighters equipped for service over the African deserts.

Lt Dennis Mayvore Jeram flew this Grumman Martlet Mk II of No. 888 Sqn off the carrier HMS Formidable for the Torch landings. Many British aircraft acquired US-style markings for Torch, it being thought that US forces might otherwise confuse British and French warplanes.

the landings – Major General Mark Clark had been smuggled ashore by British Commandos and had talked to General Mast, commander of the French troops in the Algiers sector – while the chief US diplomatic representative in North Africa, Robert Murphy, had tried sounding out French military opinion throughout the whole theatre. But such investigations must by their very nature be tentative, and security demanded that the Americans gave very little specific information to Frenchmen who might have been attempting to entrap them, and who would in any case remain under German control after investigation.

As a result, the landings came as almost as much of a surprise to Mast and his associates (who genuinely wanted to help as much as they could), as to the remainder of the French forces. These all certainly disliked the German occupation, but they were unsure of where their real responsibilities lay. As a result, their resistance during the first few days was patchy – sometimes fierce, sometimes hesitant, but never prolonged – as a result of their commanders' doubts while they awaited orders from some properly constituted authority.

French loyalties

That authority was vested in Marshal Pétain, but by a piece of astonishing good fortune for the Allies his deputy, Admiral Darlan, was in Algiers visiting his son who had recently contracted poliomyelitis. The admiral's immediate reaction was not promising ('I have known for a long time that the British were stupid, but I always believed the Americans were more intelligent') and his reputation as a collaborator with the Nazis would have made him a most unwelcome ally had he not been so important. By a combination of diplomacy and straightforward bullying, however, Mark Clark persuaded him that his best course of action would be co-operation, and at 1120 on the morning of 10 November, Darlan ordered an end to all French resistance in North Africa.

Generally he was obeyed in Morocco and Algeria, though

the extraordinary rapidity of the German reaction in Tunisia held up matters there – but the whole picture was clarified when the news came in that Hitler's furious reaction to the Anglo-US landings had been to order German troops to move into the Unoccupied Zone of southern France, which they did on 11 November. This, in the opinion of the French command in North Africa, relieved them of their pledge of obedience to Pétain who they judged, quite rightly, would now be acting under some duress.

Allied advances

From then on, the Allied moves went smoothly. By 12 November, British airborne forces had been dropped at Bône and had captured the airfield there, later they had advanced to Souk el Arba, 483km (300 miles) east of Algiers, while the US 503rd Parachute Infantry Regiment had dropped at Youks les Bains nearly 160km (100 miles) to the south and within two days had taken Gafsa airfield inside Tunisia.

Behind them, US troops had shaken out and were moving up, Lieutenant General Kenneth Anderson had landed and taken command of the British First Army, which was commandeering every piece of transport it could as the long slog across North Africa began in earnest.

British troops ride a Valentine tank triumphantly through a Tunisian town. The fighting after Torch lasted into the spring of 1943, by which time the Axis forces were exhausted, but scenes such as this were commonplace among the Allies.

Operation Torch: Chronology

Operation Torch brought the US emphatically into World War II. Though many US military leaders desired an invasion of northern Europe, the US President became convinced that a second front in North Africa was the best immediate policy.

1942

September

After much debate, the final plan for Operation Torch is laid down. Three 'Task Forces' are to land across the northern coastline of Morocco and Algeria. A US Western Task force is to land around Casablanca in Morocco, a US Central Task Force (though transported by the Royal Navy) is destined for Oran in Algeria, and a British Eastern Task Force was to land near Algiers. The eastward advance of these three elements is hoped to squeeze German forces into Tunisia and trap them against the 8th Army advancing from the east.

November 7th

The three Task Forces approach the coast of North Africa and coordinate. The Western Task Force has sailed all the way from Virginia in the US.

November 8th

The landings begin. The US forces of the Western and Central Task Forces meet some heavy opposition from Vichy French units in the region. At Oran 200 US soldiers are killed when French coastal batteries shell their transport ship in the harbour. The British Eastern Task Force, by contrast, lands with the full cooperation of the local French commander, General Mast, though this does not stop them coming under bombardment from French coastal guns.

November 9th

The US Task Forces are still engaging French forces, and there is some heavy fighting for another two days. Ceasefires, however, are starting to take effect throughout Morocco and Algeria.

November 11th

Units of the Eastern Task Force make an amphibious jump from Algiers eastwards to Bougie to capture a vital airfield near Djidjelli. Also on this day, Admiral Jean Francois Darlan, the French Foreign Minister and Vice Premier in the Vichy government, and General Alphonse Juin, commander of French troops in Morocco, order a general ceasefire amongst French troops in Africa.

November 12th

British airborne units make a parachute assault ahead of the main advance at Bône.

The US troops in Operation Torch relied mainly on landing craft such as the LCM (3) to put them ashore. These shallow-draft boats could carry one medium tank or 60-fully armed troops, with a maximum load weight of 52 tons.

US troops advance ashore in North Africa during the Torch landings. Their initial opponents were not the Germans but the 100,000 Vichy French soldiers stationed in Algeria, Morocco and Tunisia, though these ceased hostilities within four days of the landings.

Their objective is again an airfield, and they hold this despite counter-attacks from German paratroopers moved into the area only minutes after the Allied deployment.

November 15th
US paratroopers make a drop at Youks les Bains to seize the airfield.

November 16th
A further British airborne operation captures the last main airfield in the region at Souk el Arba.

November 16th–26th
Allied forces advance into Tunisia against very determined German resistance. On the 17th they capture Béja and on the 18th Sidi Nsir, both on the main road route to Tunis. On November 26th Medjez el Bab – a key staging post for the final assault on Tunis, less than 48km (30 miles) away – falls after six days of heavy fighting.

November 30th
Further Allied advances into North Africa are stopped by the German defence. A line of resistance is established from Sedjenane to Bou Arada which is still in place at the beginning of 1943.

International Events 1942

November 10th
After the Allied victory at El Alamein, British prime minister Winston Churchill declares, 'This is not the end. It is not even the beginning of the end. But it is, perhaps, the end of the beginning.'

November 11th
Following the French ceasefire against the Allied invasion in North Africa, German troops occupy the previously unoccupied regions of France in Operation Anton.

November 12th
Tobruk falls into the hands of the Allies as Rommel retreats westwards across North Africa towards Tunisia.

November 13th
Yet another major German offensive to take Stalingrad ends in costly failure. The Germans do manage to establish a footing on the River Volga, but Russian forces maintain a fanatical level of resistance.

November 15th
US Navy forces in the Pacific beat off a Japanese resupply convoy heading for Guadalcanal. The victory is significant because it cuts the Japanese seaborne supply line to its Guadalcanal garrison.

November 20th
Russian forces on the Stalingrad front encircle the city, surrounding the beleaguered German 6th Army and ensuring its doom.

Drive for the Volga
Looking for oil

One year after the invasion of the Soviet Union, the German army launches its great summer offensive of 1942 with confidence that this would win the war.

On 28 June 1942 the great summer offensive of the Wehrmacht opened with Colonel General Hermann Hoth's 4th Panzer Army sweeping forward to the north of Kursk, while Colonel General Friedrich Paulus's 6th Army, which included 11 infantry divisions and a Panzer corps of its own, drove parallel with it to the south of the city. Their first objective was the Don bend, but 160km (100 miles) beyond lay the prize of Stalingrad and control of the lower Volga and its oil traffic to the industrial centres of the USSR.

Two days later, Army Group A under Field Marshal Wilhelm List burst over the Donets bend and drove towards Proletarskaya, the Caucasus and the oil centres themselves: Maikop, Grozny and Baku.

It seemed at first that the days of easy victory had returned, for whatever Soviet forces were encountered they were swept away with almost contemptuous ease. For the first time in many months the ground favoured the Germans' large-scale, sweeping advances, hundreds of miles of open rolling corn and steppe grass offering perfect country for the massed armour of both Hoth's and Paulus's legions. Indeed, to those who watched the huge motorised squares with Panzers forming the frames, with soft transport and artillery crashing along inside, it seemed that the day of the modern Roman legions had dawned. Their advance was visible from miles away – smoke from

burning villages and dust-clouds as the heavy vehicles rumbled over the fields signalling the implacable progress of a perfectly functioning war machine.

Hoth's Panzers were at Voronezh by 5 July, throwing both the local Red Army command and STAVKA (high command) into turmoil as they tried to foresee which

Bugbear of Allied tank crews, a dreaded 88mm (3.46in) gun serves here as additional field artillery against the retreating Soviets. Unknown to these men, the Red Army's massive reorganization is under way and it is becoming a far more dangerous opponent.

The German plan was to break through over the Don and take the Donets crossings with their armour, encircling vast Soviet forces in the Donets Basin. Now fighting far more effectively than in 1941, the Red Army retreated and just managed to halt the German penetration of the Caucasus.

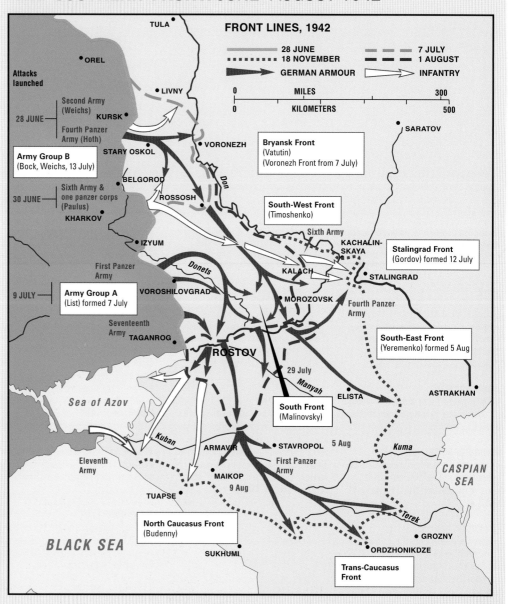

THE SOUTHERN FRONT: JUNE–AUGUST 1942

way this huge offensive would turn. General Nikolai Vatutin was hurriedly ordered to form a new 'Voronezh Front' and was so successful in herding together the remnants of the Red Army divisions swept away to the north by the Panzer army in those first few days, that Field Marshal Fedor von Bock, commanding Army Group South, proposed to swing both Hoth's Panzers and part of Paulus's infantry to the left to deal with Vatutin before driving on towards the main objectives.

Objective: oil

But excitement had gripped the German High Command. Von Bock was summarily dismissed; Paulus was entrusted wholly with the advance and capture of Stalingrad while Hoth's Panzers, instead of leading Paulus's divisions, were to swing southeast, drive down between the Donets and the Don to 'assist in the early passage of the lower Don'. At this time the oil was still the major objective, Stalingrad merely another Soviet city to be despoiled in due course

and one not likely to give the Wehrmacht much trouble.

Hitler was in a happier frame of mind than he had been for months. 'The Russian is finished!' he announced on 20 July.

It continued to look the case for a few weeks yet. The only problems posed in the south were those of traffic control, for the Panzers of both Colonel General Ewald von Kleist and Hoth arrived at the Donets crossing at the same time. A certain amount of acrimony resulted, especially as von Kleist saw not the slightest reason for the change in plans or for the introduction of a rival Panzer commander into the theatre of his own 1st Panzer Army. To demonstrate his own virtuosity, he accele-rated the pace of his advance once across the river, captured Proletarskaya on 29 July, and by 9 August was at Maikop, with another column guarding his left flank at Stavropol. The great prizes of Grozny, Batumi and Baku seemed within grasp.

But for Paulus, matters were not going quite so well. In the 6th Army's progress

German infantry advance through typical farmland during the autumn of 1942 as they seek to push ahead through agricultural areas to reach and take the industrial city of Stalingrad. Even the onset of winter did nothing to abate the fierce fighting. Combat continued through the cellars and wreckage of the ruined city, with no quarter being given by either side.

down the Donets/Don corridor there was little problem for his Panzer corps (under General Gustav von Wietersheim) driving alongside Hoth's corps; but of course the 11 infantry divisions, many of whose formations were on foot, found it difficult to keep up. By the time they had reached Chernyevskaya on the River Chir in the Don bend they were all well strung out, and only the lack of a well-organised Red Army block allowed them to close up to the huge river itself.

Unexpected resistance

Nevertheless, there was some fighting in the bend, and Paulus became more and more convinced that without Hoth's support he would not be able to get the 6th Army across the Don in sufficient strength to take Stalingrad 'on the march', which had been his original ambition. As Hoth's Panzers were doing little but annoying Kleist, OKH (the army high command, responsible since December 1941 for control of operations on the Eastern Front but under Hitler's direct control) agreed that the Panzer army should now hook around to the north east and drive along the south bank of the Don. But unexpected resistance along the River Aksay delayed them, so that from 10 to 19 August Paulus's army waited in the bend, its artillery

massed and ready for the great attack.

The plan was straightforward and conventional. Wietersheim's XIV Panzer Corps would form the northern flank, three of Hoth's Panzer divisions and two motorised divisions would form the southern flank, while nine infantry divisions would fill the centre. They were all across the Don within 24 hours and, to the delight of every German headquarters organisation between Stalingrad and Berlin, Wietersheim's Panzers reported that they had reached the banks of the Volga across the northern suburbs of Stalingrad by the evening of 23 August. It was only a narrow penetration, but support was driving through to bolster the advance, Hoth's Panzers were slowly forcing their way from the south and it seemed that just one more heavy blow would secure triumph.

On the night of 23/24 August, Stalingrad was subjected to an air raid reminiscent of the heaviest London blitz. The bulk of the bombs dropped were incendiary, and the wooden section of the city burned in a holocaust as spectacular as the destruction of the London docks. By morning the pyre rose high into the air, acres of Stalingrad suburbs had been reduced to charred ashes and it was evident to the thoroughly satisfied German observers that only the main factories and stone-built offices remained for the attention of the German artillery.

But during the next few days something else became evident: the Soviet determination to fight every step of the way.

A German machine-gunner presides over a peaceful Volga. The city of Stalingrad was expected to fall like all the others and the 6th Army looked forward to wintering in the captured city. In fact 180,000 civilians were busily fortifying the place and the Red Army was preparing to stand and fight.

Drive for the Volga: Chronology

By 1942 Germany's war effort was beginning to show signs of instability, particularly in relation to its oil supplies. Hitler's offensive in southern Russia aimed to reach and secure the river Don from Voronezh to Stalingrad and capture the oil fields of the Caucasus.

1942

March–April

The plans for Operation Blue – the conquest of the Russian Caucasus – are developed between Hitler and his military leaders. The Führer Directive for the operation is released on April 5th.

May 8th

Operation Blue begins with an offensive by Manstein's

A Russian gun crew fire their 76mm (3in) Model 42 field gun during fighting on the approaches to Stalingrad. The Model 42 was the most prolific artillery piece of WWII and was used as a field gun, tank gun and anti-tank gun.

11th Army to take the Kerch peninsula and the city of Sevastopol in the Crimea.

May 12th–June 27th

Russian forces launch an offensive towards German-occupied Kharkov, a pre-emptive attack intended to spoil an assault by German Army Group South against the Soviet pocket at Izyum. Operation Fridericus – the subsidiary German operation to take Izyum – is launched as a counter-offensive. Kleist's 1st Panzer Army from the north and von Paulus' 6th Army from the south achieve another massive encirclement of Soviet forces around Kharkov. The Soviets lose over

250,000 men at Kharkov and Izyum is taken.

June 28th

German forces begin their main drive for the Volga. The 2nd Army and 4th Panzer Army begin their assault southeast of Kursk and attack towards Voronezh.

June 30th

The 6th Army under von Paulus attacks out towards Belgorod and strikes down the Donets Corridor towards Stalingrad.

July 2nd

Sevastopol falls after a lengthy German siege.

July 6th

Voronezh is taken by the 4th Panzer Army. Meanwhile, the 6th Army has reached the Don and pushes southeast towards Stalingrad.

July 7th

Army Group A is formed, consisting of the 1st Panzer Army and 17th Army positioned between Kharkov and the Sea of Azov under the command of Field Marshal List.

July 9th

Army Group A begins a push out into the Donets Basin, curving out and then south towards Rostov and the Caucasus. The 2nd Army, 4th Panzer Army and 6th Army, formerly Army Group South, are renamed Army Group B commanded by Field Marshal von Bock, then General Maximilian von Weichs from July 13th.

July 13th

Hitler gives von Paulus' 6th Army the capture of Stalingrad as its main operational objective, supposedly to protect Army

Group A from Russian flanking attacks as it drives down into the Caucasus.

July 17th

Hitler reassigns the 4th Panzer Army to the southern drive for the Caucasus instead of the assault on Stalingrad.

July 23rd

Army Group A completes an encirclement of Rostov and takes 83,000 Soviet prisoners. Hitler issues Führer Directive 45 for the continuation of Operation Blue. Part of the directive orders the 6th Army to take and occupy Stalingrad city before driving down the line of the Volga and capturing Astrakhan on the Caspian Sea.

August 23rd

Army Group B finally reaches the Volga to the north of Stalingrad. However, Army Group A's deep push into the Caucasus has been such a success – it captures the first oilfield at Maikop near the Black Sea on 9th August – that around half of the 6th Army's fuel and ammunition has to be diverted to the southern operation. Army Group A, however, is deeply overextended and vulnerable.

September–November

The German offensive slows dramatically. Army Group A makes the best progress. By mid-November it has penetrated the Caucasus as far south as Mt Elbus and Ordzhonikidze. Von Paulus' 6th Army, however, has stalled around Stalingrad, and Hitler makes its clear that the city must fall as a priority before the other Caucasus objectives were given full attention.

International Events 1942

May 26th

A combined German–Italian offensive is launched against the British Gazala Line in Libya.

June 4th–5th

The Battle of Midway is fought in the Pacific, the most decisive naval engagement of the war. Japan loses four aircraft carriers – half of its carrier fleet – which severely curtails the Japanese from mounting offensive naval engagements in the future.

June 21st

Tobruk on the coast of Libya falls to the German forces of Field Marshal Rommel after the successful resolution of his Gazala Line campaign. Over 30,000 British and Commonwealth soldiers are taken prisoner.

August 19th

The German-occupied French port at Dieppe sustains an amphibious assault by 6000 Allied troops, mainly Canadian infantry and British commandos. Around 4000 Allied soldiers are killed or captured and the mission ends in failure.

October 23rd

General Bernard Montgomery launches a huge offensive against German forces around El Alamein, North Africa. The subsequent battle is the turning point in the North African campaign, and begins a long fighting retreat for the soldiers of Field Marshal Erwin Rommel back to Tunisia.

German logistics on the Eastern Front relied heavily upon the occupation of Soviet villages for billeting soldiers. The civilian occupants – usually women, children and old people – would simply be put out into the countryside to survive.

Montgomery's victory
El Alamein

23 October 1942: under the inspired leadership of Lt. General Montgomery, the 8th Army hits back at the Afrika Korps.

The front line at El Alamein was blocked at the northern end by the sea and at the southern end by the Qattara Depression. There was thus no open flank for the attacker to swing around as had happened at all previous desert battles, and as a result no alternative to a frontal assault, similar to those of World War I.

At 2100 on 23 October 1942, the artillery of General Sir Bernard Montgomery's 8th Army opened with a barrage unparalleled in North Africa, and under it the Australian, New Zealand, Scottish and South African infantry of XXX Corps advanced, followed immediately by thousands of engineers clearing 7.3m (24ft) wide paths through minefields in places extending for 2750 m (9022ft). Through these paths the armour of X Corps was intended to pass before fanning out in front of the infantry to protect them from counter-attack by Field Marshal Erwin Rommel's Panzer divisions.

Grim battle

By dawn on 24 October the infantry had in most cases reached their objectives, but traffic jams and accidents had held up the armour, which, when daylight came,

A Kittyhawk fighter-bomber of the RAF takes off to attack the Axis supply lines. Montgomery appreciated the importance of the air battle, pitching his headquarters next to that of the Desert Air Force. By the time of El Alamein, the British enjoyed a 5:3 numerical superiority in the air, and were also beginning to benefit from the arrival of more modern warplanes.

was directly under fire from German artillery. As a result, for nearly eight days a grim battle was fought in the vast dust-bowl between the coast and the Miteirya Ridge, the Australians in the north fighting a series of 'crumbling' battles, in the centre on Kidney Ridge the men of the 2nd Battalion the Rifle Brigade fought the famous 'Snipe' action, and the New Zealanders edged their way up and over Miteirya Ridge itself. Montgomery meanwhile reconsidered his plans, regrouped his armour – including the 7th Armoured Division, brought up from XIII Corps area in the south – and prepared a further armoured thrust.

Operation Supercharge

At 0105 on the morning of 2 November Operation Supercharge was launched. Once again a shattering bombardment opened across the width of the advance, and once again the infantry marched forward with minefield clearance teams immediately behind, their objective the line of the Rahman Track. Close behind the infantry advance came their own support armour, whose task was to thrust forward in the darkness up and over the Aqqaqir Ridge, while behind them the 1st Armoured Division was to crash out through the gap they had made and destroy the Axis forces beyond. Speed and exact timing were essential.

Unfortunately one of the armoured brigades delayed the main thrust for a quarter of an hour; as the main assault climbed the Aqqaqir Ridge, the sun rose behind them, and they moved dramatically from shadow at the foot to full daylight at the crest. Here they met the massed fire of all the remaining German anti-tank guns: in less than 30 minutes 75 of the 94 tanks had been wrecked, over half the crews killed or wounded.

But Rommel was having major troubles of his own. Since the last days of October he had realised that his German-Italian Panzer Army was being ground down by sheer weight and volume of fire, and he had

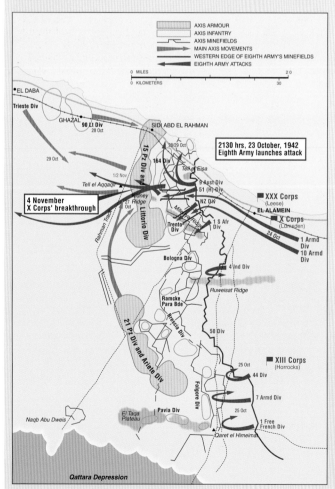

DESERT VICTORY: A CLASSIC SET PIECE

AXIS ARMOUR
AXIS INFANTRY
AXIS MINEFIELDS
MAIN AXIS MOVEMENTS
WESTERN EDGE OF EIGHTH ARMY'S MINEFIELDS
EIGHTH ARMY ATTACKS

0 MILES 20
0 KILOMETERS 30

EL DABA
Trieste Div
GHAZAL
90 Lt Div 28 Oct
SIDI ABD EL RAHMAN
28/29 Oct
29 Oct
15 Pz Div and
164 Div
Tell el Eisa
1/2 Nov
Tell el Aqqaqir
9 Aust Div
51 (H) Div
2130 hrs, 23 October, 1942 Eighth Army launches attack
Kidney Ridge 27 Oct
Rahman Track
Littorio Div
NZ Div
XXX Corps (Leese)
EL ALAMEIN
4 November X Corps' breakthrough
Miteirya Ridge
Trento Div
1 S Afr Div
X Corps (Lumsden)
24 Oct
1 Armd Div
10 Armd Div
Bologna Div
4 Ind Div
Ruweisat Ridge
Ramcke Para Bde
21 Pz Div and Ariete Div
Brescia Div
Trento Div
50 Div
XIII Corps (Horrocks)
25 Oct
44 Div
Folgore Div
7 Armd Div
Naqb Abu Dweis
El Taqa Plateau
Pavia Div
25 Oct
1 Free French Div
Qaret el Himeimat
Qattara Depression

Desert Victory
Unlike the fluid desert battles that preceded it, the front at Alamein was restricted by the sea to the north and the impassable Qattara Depression to the south. Set-piece battles have always been the British army's forte, and Rommel had no chance to display his genius for improvisation in a mobile battle.

This Messerschmitt Bf 110E was based at Berca in late 1942 and carries a 30mm (1.18in) MK 101 cannon providing an anti-tank capability. The British also employed cannon-armed aircraft to attack the thinner top armour of German tanks, equipping Hawker Hurricanes with twin 40mm (1.57in) guns. With both armies dependent on lorry-borne fuel, water and ammunition, control of the air was literally vital.

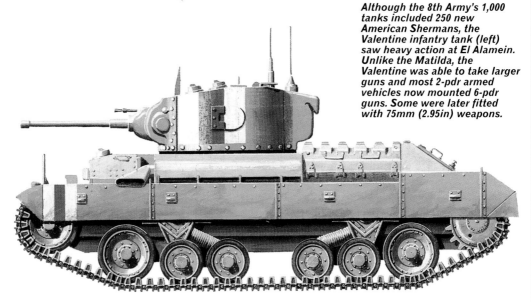

Although the 8th Army's 1,000 tanks included 250 new American Shermans, the Valentine infantry tank (left) saw heavy action at El Alamein. Unlike the Matilda, the Valentine was able to take larger guns and most 2-pdr armed vehicles now mounted 6-pdr guns. Some were later fitted with 75mm (2.95in) weapons.

made plans to disengage them and pull back. But as he began to put these plans into action, an order from Hitler arrived forbidding the slightest retreat and ending 'As to your troops, you can show them no other road than that to victory or death!'

25-pdr field guns provided the bulk of the British field artillery. Until the Battle of El Alamein the 8th Army had usually failed to concentrate its artillery, but this time this branch of the army's strength was co-ordinated masterfully. Over one million rounds were fired during the course of the battle.

If he could neither retreat nor stay where he was, then he must order an advance – in the hope that fortune might favour him as she had in the past and his thrust might hit a weak spot. But there was no weak spot in Montgomery's deployment, and during the rest of the morning and the afternoon of 2 November the Panzer divisions threw themselves against the solid wall of 8th Army artillery, and by the evening had only 35 tanks left between them. This was the action in which the strength of the famous Deutsche Afrika Korps was finally broken.

It was also the day when the Panzer Army defences at El Alamein were first punctured, albeit by but a small force. During the previous night armoured cars of the Royal Dragoons had found their way out of the south-west corner of the salient that had been driven into the original Axis defence line, and threaded their way through and into the rear areas of the defending formations, shooting up quite a number of them on their way.

The great break-out

Their signals convinced Montgomery that the way was open for the great break-out, so during the next 48 hours the main armoured weight of the 8th Army was regrouped. By dawn on 4 November the Argyll and Sutherland Highlanders had penetrated through south of Tel el Aqqaqir to find that the expected DAK defences had gone, that Rommel had decided to disobey his Führer and that the whole Panzer Army was withdrawing – leaving behind a few stragglers, some wrecked artillery and tanks, areas of uncleared mines and a large number of booby-traps. The Battle of El Alamein was over, and all that remained was to organise an effective pursuit.

El Alamein: Chronology

The Battle of El Alamein was a true changing point in Allied fortunes during WWII. It sent Rommel's forces into full and final retreat and began the end of Germany's presence in North Africa.

1942

July 1st–22nd

The first Battle of El Alamein. Rommel's Afrika Korps and three corps of Italian troops assault the Allied defensive line stretching southwards from the Alamein perimeter. By July 3rd the offensive is grinding to a halt with severe Axis losses. Rommel makes several more offensives, but Allied counter-attacks, a collapsing Italian force in the north, and constant Allied reinforcements leads him to abandon the campaign on July 22nd.

August

Winston Churchill makes command changes in North Africa in the hope of injecting more offensive dynamism into the Allied campaign. Auchinleck is replaced with General Harold Alexander as C-in-C Middle East, and Major-General Neil Ritchie with General Bernard Montgomery as commander 8th Army. Rommel's units are reinforced by a German parachute brigade and an Italian division, with tank strength increased to 440 vehicles.

August 30th

The Battle of Alam Halfa begins. Rommel makes a pre-emptive strike against Allied

Right: British infantry advance through German frontal defences at El Alamein. The troops on the ground are using their bodies to flatten the barbed wire while their colleagues make the crossing.

Below: A column of British Army vehicles passes the wreckage of a German Junkers Ju 52 transport aircraft. By the battle of El Alamein, the British had asserted air superiority in the North African theatre, and the Germans had to rely upon tenuous land supply routes.

British anti-tank gunners in action at Alamein. The British Army suffered from poor coordination between anti-tank guns and armoured vehicles, unlike the Germans who in one day destroyed 102 tanks out of the 128 of the 9th Armoured Brigade.

lines at El Alamein. The main attacks are in the far south, aimed at crossing the weak southern sectors of the defences and taking the strategic high ground of the Alam Halfa ridge about 21km (13 miles) behind Allied lines.

2nd September
Rommel is forced to retreat to Bab el Qattara, his start point for the Alam Halfa offensive, after British armoured brigades inflict unacceptable losses on his Panzer formations. The Axis troops now adopt defensive positions and wait for an Allied counter-offensive.

3rd September–23rd October
Montgomery concentrates on building up huge superiority in artillery, armour, airpower and manpower for his coming offensive. Men and tanks come to outnumber the Germans 2:1, while the 8th Army possesses 2311 artillery pieces as opposed to 1219 German weapons.

October 23rd
9.30pm
Over 800 Allied guns pound German forward positions. It is the beginning of Operation Lightfoot, Montgomery's attempt to break through the German defences and put Axis forces in a eastward retreat.

10.00pm
The Allied XXX and X Corps launch powerful armoured thrusts against the German lines in the north, while XIII Corps makes diversionary assaults in the far south against the Italian Folgore and Brescia divisions and the German 21st Panzer Division.

October 25th
Following two days of exhausting mine clearance and combat, four Allied brigades begin to penetrate German lines, but at an appallingly high cost. The northern attack is so sluggish that Montgomery develops a new operation, named 'Supercharge'. Units making

diversionary attacks in the south are pulled up to the north to provide a reinforcing push to the main offensive.

October 26th–November 2nd
Supercharge makes little physical progress, but German and Italian forces are chronically exhausted and depleted by the incessant assaults. On November 2nd Rommel orders his troops to begin withdrawing eastwards along the northern coast as Allied units begin to break through the lines.

November 4th
X Corps pushes completely through the German lines at Tel el Aqqaqir, bringing the Battle of El Alamein to a close.

International Events
1942
August 7th
The US 1st Marine Division makes an amphibious landing on Guadalcanal Island, part of the Solomon Islands chain in

the Pacific. It would take six months of bloody campaigning by US troops and over 6000 casualties to clear the islands.

August 12th-17th
Winston Churchill and Joseph Stalin meet for the first time to discuss strategic options for developing a Second Front in the West.

August 19th
Some 6000 Allied troops, most Canadian, make a disastrous nine-hour amphibious assault against the French port of Dieppe, losing 4000 men dead, wounded or captured in the process.

September 2nd
Nazi security forces begin clearing the Warsaw Ghetto of over 50,000 Jews. The Jews are destined for extermination or concentration camps.

Stalingrad
Death of an army

September 1942: the German 6th Army hammers its way into Stalingrad, but its flanks are guarded only by a thin screen of Rumanian and Italian troops.

By the end of the 6th Army's initial thrust into the city in September 1942, Berlin was already proclaiming the capture of Stalingrad. To Hitler, no loss of life could compensate for his own loss of face if that were not quickly confirmed. To make certain, General Paulus, commander of the 6th Army, must have as many men as could be shipped to him and he must feed them into the cauldron without scruple.

But the Soviet Marshal Georgi Zhukov had a different view. He had plans for the employment of the armies being formed on the east side of the Volga, and they did not include immolation in the devastated city, no matter what the men of the desperate 62nd Army might be suffering. He would feed in just enough men to keep the defence of Stalingrad alive – and dangerous to the besiegers – but the mass of men and arms accumulating under his command had a more strategic purpose.

Attack after attack

By November, the 6th Army had thrown six major attacks against Stalingrad's defenders, who by then were confined along some 8km (5 miles) of the river bank, around the Krasni Oktyabr steelworks and the Barrikady armaments factory. After weeks in that hellish environment, one tortured soul wrote in his diary, 'when night arrives, one of those scorching howling bleeding nights, the dogs plunge into the Volga and swim desperately to gain the other bank. Animals flee this hell; the hardest stones cannot bear it for long; only men endure.'

Zhukov's purpose was revealed on 19 November. At dawn, a thunderous barrage from 2000 guns and Katyusha batteries opened to the north, and all who heard it sensed that a new phase of the battle was about to begin.

Later in the morning another bombardment crashed out, this time in the south – and the 6th Army staff officers suddenly became acutely conscious of the weakness of their flanks. These were held by Rumanian armies whose soldiers and commanders were not so dedicated to the destruction of Soviet Russia as the Germans – nor so well armed, for the bulk of their weapons and vehicles had been captured in France two years before.

Stalingrad's ruined factories served as makeshift but strong fortifications. Here, the defenders of the Red October steel works look on as Red Air Force Sturmoviks pass overhead.

STALINGRAD: BATTLE ON THE VOLGA

After careful preparation the first heavy and concentrated attack on Stalingrad by the German 6th Army took place between 14 and 22 September 1942. The attackers controlled the air, and had a three-to-one advantage in manpower. In nine days of bitter action, Generaloberst Friedrich Paulus' Infantry cleared the bend of the River Tsaritsa and reached the Volga. They captured Stalingrad's Number 1 Railway Station, forcing General Vasili Chuikov to move his 62nd Army headquarters. The advance brought German guns close enough to the main landing stage to jeopardise the nightly passage of ammunition and stores from the main Red army dumps on the east of the river.

Both sides were so prostrated by exhaustion that for a few days a sullen silence fell upon the area, punctuated only by sporadic machine-gun fire and mortar bursts. But it was not long before the fighting again flared up into a battle of attrition among the ruins, in which the side with the larger numbers should win. However, larger numbers do not always count. German losses were far higher than those of the Soviets, reflecting the very different purposes and mentalities controlling each side.

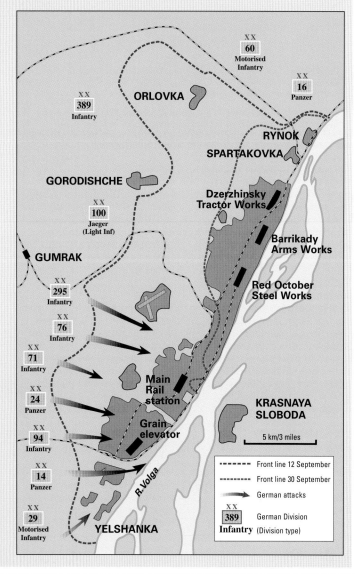

Above: The Germans expected their initial drive on Stalingrad to succeed quickly, but in spite of being forced into a small enclave on the west bank of the Volga, the Red Army continued to resist.

Left: The onset of winter did nothing to abate the fierce fighting. Combat continued through the cellars and wreckage of the ruined city, with no quarter being given by either side.

Three days later, the staff officers knew that their fears had been well-founded. Along 80km (50 miles) in the north and 50km (31 miles) in the south, Zhukov's shock armies had shattered the Axis front, encircling General Paulus and a quarter of a million soldiers of the 6th Army. Now the besiegers were themselves besieged.

At first, in both Berlin and Stalingrad, the view was taken that it was good to have an army of such size behind enemy lines. Its reinforcement and supply was just a problem to be solved. In the meantime, the Red Army had maintained its encirclement, using hundreds of thousands of men and thousands of tanks and guns which might otherwise be put to use elsewhere.

Generalfeldmarschall Erich von Manstein, whose 11th Army had been incorporated into a new Army Group Don, was given the task of correcting the predicament that had arisen as a result of Zhukov's counter-offensive. At first Manstein felt that his best course would be to tempt the Soviet armies westward away from Stalingrad. That way, he could take some of the pressure off the 6th Army which would allow Paulus room and time to organise a break out to meet the tanks of from Generaloberst Hermann Hoth's 4th Panzer Army, driving up from the south.

Relief attack fails

Manstein launched Operation Wintergewitter (Winter Storm) on 21 December. But the attack from the Don at Kotelnikov was blocked on the Myshkova by the 2nd Guards Army, and Paulus and his 6th Army commanders showed little inclination to order a break out.

On 25 December, Christmas Day for the Germans but not for the Russians, Zhukov launched yet another attack. He drove Hoth's army back beyond its starting point around Kotelnikov. German forces to the north were pushed well back beyond both the Chir and the Aksay. In a matter of days, the distances separating the two German fronts had become too great for supplies to get through to Paulus by land.

As the weather worsened, Luftwaffe Generaloberst Wolfram von Richthofen was becoming more and more gloomy about the prospects of air support. Paulus and his army were evidently in some danger – it was clear that Stalingrad was not quite so firmly in German hands as the Berlin propaganda machine had suggested.

As 1943 started the 6th Army began desperately to build dense fortifications around an area some 50km (31 miles) from east to west and 30km (19 miles) from north to south. It was surrounded by 10 Soviet armies, and although some Red Army formations were guarding against the approach of possible German relief columns, the main energies and attentions of the Soviets were directed against the German pocket.

On 8 January General Konstantin Rokossovsky, who had been given the task of destroying the 6th Army, sent in a proposal for its surrender, and when this was rejected, began the last phase of the Battle of Stalingrad. He launched a bombardment from thousands of guns and mortars, supported by the bombers and ground attack aircraft of the 16th Soviet Air Army.

By 17 January the area in German hands had been halved; by the 21st the last German airfield at Gumrak had been captured and the battle was again being fought out in the concrete tombs of Stalingrad – but with the roles reversed. By this time the 6th Army had suffered more than 160,000 casualties, over half caused by cold and malnutrition.

The last act was played as February began. On 31 January the shell of the Central Department Store was captured and Paulus and his staff surrendered – in spite of the fact that Hitler had promoted Paulus to field marshal two days before, on the understanding that no German Field Marshal would never be taken alive. On 2 February the remainder of the army laid down its arms.

Death of the 6th Army

More than half of the 300,000 men trapped in Stalingrad had been killed by the time of the surrender. A fortunate few – some 35,000 – had been evacuated by air, but the surviving 90,000 men were herded to Siberia on foot. Thousands died on the march as a result of cold and starvation, and the rest were condemned to a slow death in the mines and work camps. Many of those still alive in 1945 were never released, and only about 5,000 of the doomed army ever returned to Germany.

The Soviet counter offensive smashed the Axis forces on each side of Stalingrad. Soon they were in full retreat through the sub-zero temperatures, leaving the 6th Army to its fate.

Stalingrad
Chronology

September 1942: the German 6th Army hammers its way into Stalingrad, but its flanks are guarded only by a thin screen of Romanian and Italian troops. After a few titanic months of struggle against the resolute Russian defence, the Russians encircle the city and force its one-time attackers to surrender.

1941

June 22nd
Operation Barbarossa, the German invasion of the Soviet Union, launched.

1942

June 28th
German summer offensive begins in the Kursk sector.

June 30th
German 6th Army begins its offensive in the Belgorod sector.

Russian fighters in Stalingrad. Often Soviet soldiers would be sent into the frontline with no more than five rounds of ammunition, relying on the dead to supply further bullets.

July 6th
Voronezh on the Don captured by German forces.

July 9th
German offensive in Kharkhov sector begins.

July 21st
The German Army crosses the Don at Rostov.

July 23rd
Rostov-on-Don captured by the Germans.

July 26th
Army Group A launches its offensive into the Caucasus.

Stalingrad was utterly devastated. Incendiary raids by the Luftwaffe were so effective that there were almost no flammable materials left in the city, a fact which worked to the Soviet advantage as Germans froze to death in their thousands in winter.

July 28th
Soviet High Command at Stalingrad issues a directive: 'Not one step backwards.'

August 4th
Germans cross the Aksay, and drive on Stalingrad itself.

August 6th
Germans cross the Kuban near Armavir.

August 7th
German 6th Army attacks near Kalach.

August 9th
Krasnodar and Yeysk, a port on the Sea of Azov, are captured by the Germans.

August 14th
Germans cross the Kuban at Krasnodar.

August 19th
6th Army ordered to attack Stalingrad by von Paulus.

August 22nd
German advance into the Caucasus halted.

August 25th
Stalingrad declared to be in a state of siege.

September 1st
German and Romanian troops cross the Kerch Straits and advance into the Taman Peninsula. Bridgehead on the Terek established by the Germans.

September 3rd
German troops attack the centre of Stalingrad.

September 6th
Novorossiysk on the Black Sea captured by the Germans.

September 15th
Russian attack on Voronezh.

September 24th
Germans advance towards Tuapse.

October 6th
Germans capture Malgobek in the Terek salient.

October 9th
Military commanders, rather than political commissars, are given sole authority in the Red Army.

October 14th
Hitler brings the summer offensive to a close, ordering that all German Army Groups must 'consider their present lines springboards for a German offensive in 1943 and hold them at all costs.'

October 18th
German drive on Tuapse halted.

October 25th
Fresh German offensive in the Caucasus.

November 1st
Alagir in the Caucasus captured by the Germans.

November 2nd
Ordzhonikidse in the Caucasus taken by the Germans.

A Russian propaganda poster showing Hitler sending Germans to their graves in Russia.

November 19th
Operation Uranus launched by the Russians, breaking through the Romanian forces north of Stalingrad.

November 20th
Second part of Operation Uranus launched south of Stalingrad. Manstein appointed commander of Army Group Don.

November 22nd
Russian forces meet at Kalach, encircling 6th Army.

November 25th
German airlift to Stalingrad begins.

December 12th
Operation Winter Storm, the attempt by 4th Panzer Army to relieve Stalingrad. Hitler continues to deny 6th Army permission to break out.

December 16th
Russians launch Operation Little Saturn, an offensive aimed at Rostov. Italian 8th Army retreats in disarray. Attack on Tuapse called off by the Germans.

December 21st
Relief attempt for Stalingrad halted on the Myshkova.

December 23rd
All attempts to relieve Stalingrad called off.

December 24th
Russian attack towards Kotelnikovo. Romanians retreat in disorder.

December 28th
German Army Group A receives orders to retreat from the Caucasus.

1943

January 1st
Germans begin retreat from the Terek.

January 5th
Milch ordered to ensure the Stalingrad airlift succeeds.

January 8th
Surrender ultimatum sent to 6th Army.

January 10th
Rokossovsky leads Russian attack to liquidate 'the cauldron'.

January 12th
Hungarian and Italian lines broken by Russian troops on the Don. Germans in Caucasus retreat to the Kuban bridgehead.

January 13th
Germans retreat from Terek to the Nagutskoye-Alexsandrovskoye Line.

January 14th
German Army General Staff propose to strengthen the Eastern Front by conscripting people from the Baltic States for army or police duties.

January 17th
German panzer corps surrounded on the Don.

January 24th
Russian Trans-Caucasian Front halted at Novorossiysk-Krasnodar.

January 25th
6th Army at Stalingrad split in two by Russian attacks. Germans retreat from Armavir and Voronezh.

January 31st
Paulus surrenders in the southern pocket at Stalingrad.

February 2nd
Northern pocket surrenders. The battle for Stalingrad is over.

Kasserine
Desert Fox strikes back

The Afrika Korps seems doomed by 1943, but Rommel launches his desert veterans against the inexperienced Americans.

By the beginning of 1943 the situation of the Axis forces in North Africa appeared far stronger than could have been foreseen two months before when the Battle of El Alamein had begun. Having starved Field Marshal Erwin Rommel of troops when victory seemed in sight, Hitler now poured men and *matériel* into the 'Tunisian bridgehead', apparently in the hope that the Anglo-American forces that had been put ashore in Operation Torch could be held there almost indefinitely. Colonel General

Jürgen von Arnim had nearly 100,000 men and a considerable force of armour at his disposal in the Fifth Panzer Army, and although the line he had to defend stretched some 480km (300 miles) from the Mediterranean down past Gafsa, his opponents had to man the same length – and feed their armies along much longer lines of communication.

Woefully inexperienced

Moreover, the Allied armies were divided into three not particularly co-operative groups. In the northern

As was so often the case, German armour was outnumbered at Kasserine. This PzKpfw IV mounts a 7.5cm (2.95in) L/48 gun and the crew members have attached spare track wherever they can along the hull front. The 10th Panzer Division included a company of Tiger tanks, which were immune to most Allied anti-tank guns.

sector the British 1st Army was massed, its obvious purpose a drive to Bizerta, Tunis and Cape Bon. To its south lay the French, poorly armed as yet, not very well trained and still resentful of the British attacks on Mers el Kébir two years before. Farther south still lay the Americans, who were eager and confident, but woefully inexperienced.

During the last weeks of 1942, von Arnim had moved to strengthen his defences by driving the French out of the Pichon Pass, about 120km (75 miles) south of Tunis and one of the key points along the Eastern Dorsale, the range of mountains which dominates the Tunisian coastal plain. During

Operation Spring Breeze was deliberately aimed at the US II Corps, and Rommel and von Arnim briefly hoped to split the US forces from the British V Corps to the north. Rommel had but 50 tanks left in the Deutsches Afrika Korps as the 21st Panzer Division had been detached to von Arnim's command. But as the assault developed, Rommel had, for one last time, the whole armoured strength of the Axis forces in Africa under his control. He had little fuel and ammunition, but the chance was too good to miss.

ROMMEL'S MOVE: OPERATION 'SPRING BREEZE'

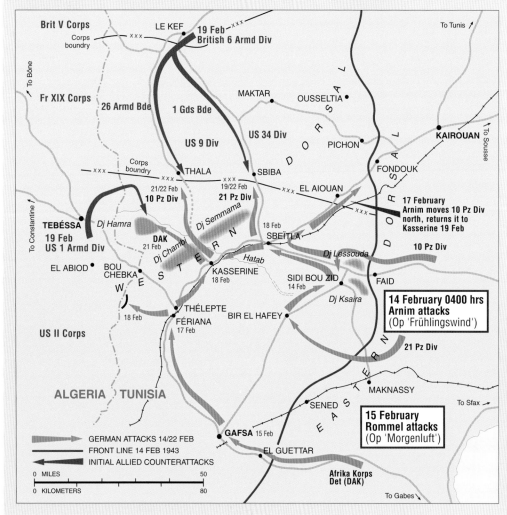

German motorcycle reconnaissance units had swiftly identified the weaknesses in the French positions along the passes, opening the possibility for von Arnim to overrun the vital defensive positions along the border.

January he struck again at the French, driving them out of both the Fondouk and Pont du Fahs defiles, and on the last days of the month he drove them from Faid. The key southern passes of the Eastern Dorsale were now at his command.

Swift action

Meanwhile, to the south, Rommel had completed his withdrawal from El Alamein across Egypt and Libya, his rearguards now occupying the Mareth Line and awaiting the arrival of General Sir Bernard Montgomery's Eighth Army. Rommel could see quite clearly that if he did nothing to prevent it he would soon be squeezed between his new adversaries, the Americans of the US II Corps, and his old foes from Egypt. Swift action might solve the problem, and on 4 February 1943 he suggested that von Arnim's thrusts should be continued past Faid and on down to Sbeitla, while he drove west for Gafsa, on towards Fériana and perhaps, if he could destroy the inexperienced Americans, on to Tébessa and perhaps even to the coast at Bône, thereby splitting the Allied forces irrevocably.

Operation Frühlingswind (spring breeze) opened on 14 February with an expert hook around from Faid to Sidi Bou Zid, which annihilated a US tank battalion, destroyed 44 Shermans, 26 guns and a mass of transport, and isolated 2,000 men on hilltops. Though Rommel was not yet threatening Gafsa, the US general there ordered its evacuation, and that night in heavy rain French and US troops, Arab and French families all mixed together fled in disarray towards Fériana – where the panic engulfed base troops who promptly destroyed papers and materials before joining the exodus north towards Kasserine.

US counter-attack

In an effort to stop the rot the commander of the US 1st Armored Division, Major General Orlando Ward, mounted a counter-attack from Sbeitla – and of 58 Shermans he launched into battle only four emerged, taking his losses in two days to 98 tanks, 29 guns and 57 half-tracks.

Meanwhile Rommel had taken Gafsa and reached Fériana, where he found wholesale flight and panic, botched attempts to destroy fuel and stores, from which his men joyfully salvaged enough to help them well on their way, and sufficient evidence of inexperience and tactical inadequacy to convince him that a bold stroke now would take him at least to Tébessa. Prospects had not been so bright for him since the heady days of the advance to El Alamein.

After a brief conference with his superiors on 18 February, Rommel regrouped and prepared for a drive north towards Le Kef, sending the divisions of his old Afrika Korps through Kasserine and Sbiba, holding his 10th Panzer Division back to exploit whichever of the routes promised the better possibilities.

But by now the British 6th Armoured Division and the US 34th Infantry Division were streaming south to block the gaps torn in the Allied line, and General Sir Harold Alexander, shocked by the confusion he found on visiting the US II Corps headquarters, took command. He issued one simple instruction – there was to be no further withdrawal beyond the passes of the Western Dorsale; Sbiba and Kasserine were to be held.

As the newly arrived forces took up their blocking positions, the panic began to subside. The fleeing columns were channelled into safety and reorganised, and the arrows showing the German advances slowed and then remained stationary. By 22 February, Rommel knew that he must call off the attack as too many Allied reinforcements were flooding down into the line against him, and they were being handled with a much firmer and surer touch.

Operation Frühlingswind was over. It had cost the Allies close to 10,000 men against 2,000 Axis casualties, and it had thoroughly frightened every Allied HQ in North Africa.

Although the Luftwaffe sustained an aggressive defence of eastern Algeria, the Allied ground troops were now supported by a powerful bomber force, which included the B-25 Mitchell medium bomber. This force steadily reduced the German rear area to a shambles.

Kasserine: Chronology

At Kasserine Rommel hoped to split the Allied forces in two and save the Axis presence in North Africa from complete collapse.

1943

January

Field Marshal Rommel and General von Arnim, Supreme Commander of Axis Forces in Tunisia, plan a counter-offensive against the Allied advance into Tunisia. They opt for a strike at the American sector between Gafsa and Kasserine, cutting through Tébessa and reaching Bône on the northern coast. They intended to surround large numbers of Allied troops or force them to retreat eastwards through Algeria.

February 14th
4.00am

Von Arnim's forces attack towards Sidi Bou Zid and Bir el Hafey using 10th Panzer Division and 21st Panzer Division.

February 15th

Rommel launches his attack – Operation Morgenluft – towards Gafsa, Fériana and Thélepte.

February 18th

The two strands of attack meet at Kasserine, having inflicted heavy losses on inexperienced US infantry and armoured troops. The route through the mountains towards Thala and Tébessa –two key objective of the offensive – is through the Kasserine Pass.

February 19th–20th

The mixed US units in the Kasserine Pass are unable to hold up Rommel's penetrating advance. After heavy fighting the Pass is taken by the Germans on the 20th, allowing them to continue the drive up towards Thala and Tébessa. Arnim's troops follow a parallel road towards Sbiba and Le Kef. However, today saw the Allies begin to move units south from Le Kef in preparation for a counter-attack. The British 6th Armoured Brigade advances towards Thala and Sbiba and the US 1st Armored Division attempts to stop the Germans around Tébessa.

February 21st–22nd

Rommel pauses in the Kasserine Pass to await an Allied counter-attack that does not come. By the afternoon he has resumed his

Three US soldiers in a jeep transport a French commercial switchboard in Tunisia. While the driver concentrates on the road, the two other men keep watch on the skies for German strafing aircraft. Dry desert conditions created dustclouds which made vehicles very easy to locate from the air.

march north but the German advance is held at Tébessa, Sbiba and Thala. A German retreat begins on the afternoon of the 22nd after Rommel calls off the offensive with 2000 casualties (despite this figure being far lower than the casualties suffered by the Allies).

February 25th
Kasserine is once again in Allied hands. Rommel turns his attention to the east, where Montgomery's 8th Army is threatening to break through the German defences known as the Mareth Line.

International Events 1943

January 15th
German and Italian occupation forces in Yugoslavia supported by Croatian fascists mount a concerted offensive against Yugoslavian partisans, particularly those marshalled under the communist leader Tito.

January 27th
The US Air Force makes its first air raid over Germany. Wilhelmshaven naval base is hit by 84 Flying Fortresses and seven Liberator bombers.

January 31st
The commander of the German 6th Army at Stalingrad, Field Marshal Friedrich von Paulus, surrenders his remaining force of 91,000 men to the Russians. During the course of the Stalingrad campaign the Germans lost 120,000

German troops man a tripod-mounted MG34 machine gun fitted with long-range sights. In the flat desert terrain such weapons could inflict terrible attrition upon advancing Allied infantry, with a cyclical rate-of-fire of 850rpm and a range of over 1000m (3280ft).

killed. The surrender marks the turning point of German fortunes in the war. On February 3rd Hitler orders three days of national mourning.

February 8th
The embattled city of Kursk is recaptured by Soviet forces of the South-West Front and Voronezh Front after a 160-km (100-mile) advance in little more than a month.

February 9th
President Roosevelt increases the minimum working work in 32 key industries to 48 hours to support preparations for a second front in northern Europe.

February 18th
The German propaganda minister Joseph Goebbels makes a public call for the German public to embrace a

state of 'total war' against the Allies. He is attempting to increase morale after the German defeat at Stalingrad.

February 28th
The German atomic weapon research plant at Vermork, Norway is badly damaged during an attack by Norwegian commandos. Germany's atomic weapon program is set back years by the attack.

Kharkov: Manstein's masterpiece

As the last survivors of the 6th Army hold out in the ruins of Stalingrad, the Red Army stands poised to attack all along the line.

The destruction of the German 6th Army in the frozen hell of Stalingrad during January and February 1943 was followed by an ambitious Soviet offensive intended to force the Germans back on all fronts. It was in some ways a repeat of the winter offensive 12 months earlier: a multi-front assault that was lacking in clear strategic objectives. In formulating his plans, Stalin overestimated the Red Army's capabilities and underestimated the German army's powers of recovery.

The Soviet offensive was to begin with a massive assault into the Ukraine. Three fronts (the Voronezh, South West and South Fronts) were involved. The first was aimed for Kharkov, Kursk and Oboyan. General Nikolai Vatutin's South West Front planned to outflank German forces in the Donbas and pin them against the Sea of Azov. Meanwhile the South Front would advance west along the coast in the direction of Mariupol.

Fourth largest city

The South West Front opened its offensive on 29 January 1943, with four armies and a 'Front Mobile Group', under Lieutenant General M. M. Popov, smashing their way forward. By 2 February, when the Voronezh Front launched its attack to the north, the Third Guards Tank Army was already over the Donets east of Voroshilovgrad. General F. I. Golikov's Voronezh Front enjoyed similar success, its flank armies (40th, 69th and 3rd Tank)

advancing on a line Kursk – Belgorod – Kharkov.

Kharkov was the fourth largest city in the USSR and a major prize. The rapidity of the Soviet advance on Kharkov threatened to cut off II SS Panzer Corps and Army Detachment Lanz, as well as to sever communications between Army Group Centre and the southern German units.

Yawning gap

On 15 February II SS Panzer Corps evacuated the city rather than face encirclement, and a 160km (100 mile) gap yawned in the German front line.

The Red Army was now poised to capture the Dniepr crossings at Zaporozhye, which would cut off the German supply lines to Army Group Don. Vatutin and Golikov were elated at the prospect, while German commanders were wondering when the apparently inexorable Soviet advance could be halted.

But for the Soviet troops on the ground the pressure was telling: their rapid advance had burned out many Soviet formations and divisions were down to a few thousand men. Half the tank strength of the South West

The great Soviet winter offensive, between January and March 1943, started as the last pitiful remnants of the German 6th Army fought on at Stalingrad. The victory on the Volga had imbued the Soviets with fresh confidence and revealed the growing disparity between the German army and the Red Army. The winter offensive recaptured most of the territory lost in 1942.

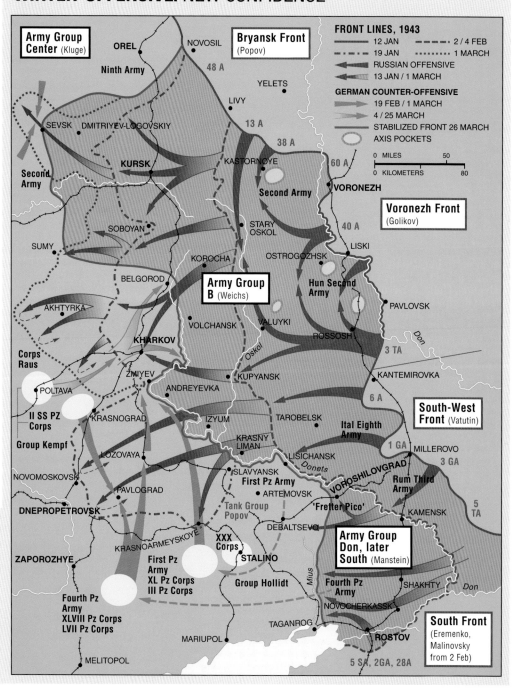

WINTER OFFENSIVE: NEW CONFIDENCE

Front was out of action as a result partly of battle damage, but mainly of mechanical wear and tear. However, the decision was made to continue the offensive: the spring thaw would come soon and would force a temporary halt in operations as the hard, frozen soil turned to liquid mud.

Giving up ground

It may not have been obvious to the exhausted Soviet troops as they advanced westwards against stiffening German resistance, but their enemies were willingly giving up ground. Field Marshal Erich von Manstein persuaded Hitler that mindless adherence to World War I defensive tactics would doom his men to another Stalingrad. By trading ground for time, he argued, he could create a counterstroke, which would regain most of the lost territory and destroy the advancing Soviet forces.

Breakthrough

The Soviet commanders were well served by their intelligence officers, and reconnaissance aircraft observed large concentrations of German armour around Krasnograd and major troop movements near Dnepropetrovsk. Unfortunately the conviction that the Germans were still in retreat led to the assumption that this was simply another rearguard on its way west.

Von Manstein struck on 20 February. SS Panzer troops attacked from Krasnograd while XL Panzer Corps raced north to strike

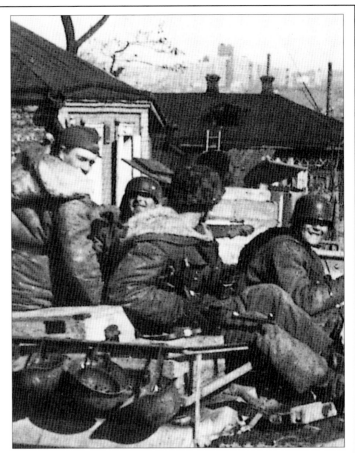

Grinning members of the 2nd SS Panzer Division 'Das Reich' ride on a StuG III 7.5cm (2.95in) assault gun during the recapture of Kharkov in 1943. The snow is thawing but the vehicle still carries widened tracks to reduce ground pressure and improve mobility over snow.

Popov's 'mobile group' of four corps, which had just 25 tanks between them. For several days Soviet units were ordered to continue their offensive until the grim reality of their position filtered through to their senior commanders. Even then many units received no instructions to fall back and were encircled by the Germans. By the end of the month von Manstein's forces had broken through to the Donets.

Snowbound retreat

The flat, wintry landscape was ideal for an armoured offensive and left the retreating Soviets horribly exposed. Visible at up to 20 km (12 miles), Soviet columns could be engaged with artillery as they hurried east. And given the fact that very few tanks had fuel or ammunition, the Soviet formations were unable to resist armoured attack. Many units panicked under the strain and fled with little semblance of military order. Kharkov was recaptured on 15 March and

the front stabilised as the spring thaw imposed its stodgy grip on operations.

Von Manstein's counterattack remains a model example of defensive mechanised warfare. The Germans did not resist the Soviet steamroller, but retreated swiftly until they could mass sufficient forces for a counterstroke and their enemies had outrun their supplies of fuel and ammunition. When the attack was launched, tank commanders were not hampered by rigid instructions from the rear but were allowed to use their *Fingerspitzengefuhl* (fingertip feeling). Bold use of initiative allowed the German forces to react swiftly to changing circumstances and outmanoeuvre larger but more unwieldy Soviet formations. Von Manstein was sufficiently confident of success to begin planning the summer campaign several days before beginning the counter-attack: thus the Battle of Kursk was already taking shape.

The recapture of Kharkov:
II SS Panzer Corps abandoned Kharkov on 15 February to avoid encirclement, but von Manstein's counter-attack recaptured the city a month later. Here SS troops wearing thick winter clothing advance into the city centre.

Kharkov: Chronology

The German defeat at Stalingrad raised Russian hopes of finally putting the invaders into retreat. Manstein's brilliant leadership of Army Group South stunted the Soviet thrusts from the Stalingrad and Trans-Caucasus Fronts and recaptured Kharkov.

1942

December–February 1943
The German defence at Stalingrad collapses, the final surrender coming on February 2nd. The German Army Group Don under Kleist is in danger of being surrounded in the southern Caucasus, so retreats westwards to the Sea of Azov while Manstein's Army Group Don further to the north keeps a corridor open for its retreat. Manstein's own Army Group Don retreats back to Rostov. Stalin, flushed by the success, looks to open a further offensive to crush the German presence in the Caucasus.

January 12th
As Russian forces at Stalingrad near victory, the Soviets launch a fresh offensive aimed at clearing the Caucasus. The offensive is two pronged: Colonel-General Reiter's Bryansk Front and General Golikov's Voronezh Front pushes out from Voronezh and cuts through the German 2nd Army and 2nd Hungarian Army of Army Group B; General Vatutin's South-West Front and General Eremenko's South Front further south launches itself against Manstein's Army Group Don towards Kharkov and Rostov.

February 2nd–5th
On Manstein's urging, Hitler permits Rostov to be abandoned.

February 6th
Manstein returns to Germany for an urgent consultation with Hitler at Rastenburg. He lays out a plan for a German counter-offensive in the Russian south, which is accepted in principle by Hitler.

February 8th
The city of Kursk is retaken by the Russians. It had been previously captured by the Germans in November 1941.

February 12th
The German Army Groups in Russia are renamed. Manstein's Army Group Don becomes Army Group South; Kluge's Army Group B becomes Army Group Centre.

The corpses of SS men lie on the Kharkov battlefield. Because of their well-documented cruelty, SS soldiers were almost never taken prisoner by the Russians, who preferred to execute any such captives on the spot.

Shattered busts of various Soviet political and military leaders – including Marshal Voroshilov, Lenin and Maxim Gorki – form an abstracted tableau in the streets of Kharkov. The busts had been collected by soldiers of the SS Totenkopf ('Death's Head'), and most likely assembled for the purposes of a good propaganda photograph.

February 14th
Rostov falls to the advancing Russians. Vatutin's South-West Front reaches Kharkov.

February 14th–18th
A ferocious street battle breaks out at Kharkov between the Russian troops of the 40th Army and 3rd Tank Army and the elite forces of the I SS Panzer Corps. The sheer weight of Soviet forces, however, eventually over-whelms the Germans, who are forced to relinquish the city on the18th. The Voronezh Front and South-West Front have been chronically depleted by the fighting.

February 17th
Hitler visits Manstein and personally consults with him about the coming counter-offensive in the Caucasus.

February 20th
Manstein performs a massive flanking attack against the Tank Group Popov driving towards Dnepropetrovsk, using his 4th Panzer Army and 1st Panzer Army positioned just north of the Sea of Azov. The II SS Panzer Corps makes a corresponding pincer attack south from Krasnograd.

February 28th
Manstein's southern offensive reaches the banks of the river Donets. Tank Group Popov and huge numbers of Soviet troops from Vatutin's South-West Front are now surrounded west of the river. Other Russian forces are now being pushed back towards Kharkov.

March 7th
The German 4th Panzer Army under General Hoth, including three SS Panzer Divisions, attack hard against the Voronezh Front and begin to retake Kharkov.

March 12th
The German advance reaches the suburbs of Kharkov, and heavy fighting begins in the city once again.

March 14th
The 4th Panzer Army makes a complete encirclement of Kharkov.

March 18th
Kharkov is once again in German hands, finally taken by the Grossdeutschland Division and SS units.

March 18th-26th
The front line stabilises as the Soviet offensive finally peters out. The Soviet occupy a large salient at Kursk which overhangs German positions at Kharkov.

International Events 1943

January 16th
RAF Bomber Command renews its attacks on Berlin after a 14-month reprieve for the German capital.

January 22nd
On Hitler's orders shipbuilding takes second place to tank production in Germany. Increased tank output is required to counter losses of armour on the Eastern Front.

January 23rd
The Libyan capital Tripoli is captured by the British after a 966km (600-mile) advance from El Alamein, pushing back German and Italian forces towards Tunisia.

February 4th
Japanese forces evacuate Guadalcanal after the first successful US land campaign of the war. Around 6000 Japanese soldiers escape the island but leave behind 24,000 dead comrades.

February 20th
US forces in North Africa suffer a heavy defeat by Rommel's forces in the Kasserine Pass, Tunisia.

February 25th
The Kasserine Pass returns to US hands, though the action there has cost the Allies 10,000 casualties.

March 3rd–4th
In the Pacific theatre, US naval aircraft destroy eight Japanese trooper transporters and four destroyers in the Battle of the Bismarck Sea..

Kursk
Eastern turning point

In July 1943, the German army launched its last great offensive in the East. However, the Soviets had deciphered German intentions well in advance.

Above: The German front-line soldiers were aware that they were attacking a well-equipped, numerically superior enemy in prepared postions. Despite the odds, they launched forward with tactical skill.

Left: On 12 July, the Soviet tank armies launched their decisive counter-attack. The Red Army soon regained its lost positions and began to drive the Germans back over their start line.

There was no doubt where the main German blow for 1943 would fall. The fighting of the previous spring had left an outward bulge (salient) in the Red Army lines around Kursk and this was to be the next German objective. Although the German staff planned meticulously, it could not disguise the forthcoming operation, so the Red Army was ideally placed to plan its response.

The Soviets planned for the future blow by moving most of their available armour into the Kursk salient, together with nearly all their artillery and numerous infantry divisions. Much of this investment went not into a forward disposition but into a powerful reserve in the rear ready for a counter-offensive, as the Red Army was already thinking of a huge advance westwards. In the front lines of the Kursk salient whole Soviet armies were deployed, and opposing them were almost equally powerful forces.

German organisation

The German attackers were disposed in two large army groups. To the north of the salient was Army Group Centre based on Generaloberst Walter Model's 9th Army with no fewer than three Panzer corps. To the south was Army Group South base on Generaloberst Hermann Hoth's 4th Army with some of the finest of the available divisions. In all, some 17 Panzer divisions were ready to fall on the Red Army around Kursk. They were equipped with the latest Tiger and Panther tanks. They would also be joined by the new Elefant assault gun with its 88mm (3.46in) armament.

The Red Army prepared thoroughly for the assault. About 20,000 guns of all kinds were massed ready for the

Men from 2nd SS Panzer Division 'Das Reich' question a Soviet prisoner. German commanders became aware the Soviets knew what was coming, but Hitler insisted on sticking to the plan. Many senior officers dreaded the outcome.

KURSK: OPERATION CITADEL

The Soviets anticipated the German blow: strongpoints and interconnecting fire plans abounded, and huge minefields were laid. The Germans prepared to launch their attack in their usual manner, albeit with heavier tanks and improved aircraft. Indeed, the German army's offensive was delayed until the much-vaunted Panther tanks were ready. Their aim was to 'pinch out' the Kursk salient. In response, the Soviets planned to let the Germans wear themselves down against concentrated defences until they could launch their own counter-offensive. The Luftwaffe were kept occupied by numerous dummy airfields in the salient. When the ground battle began, the bulk of Soviet aircraft had survived and pounced on the German armoured columns.

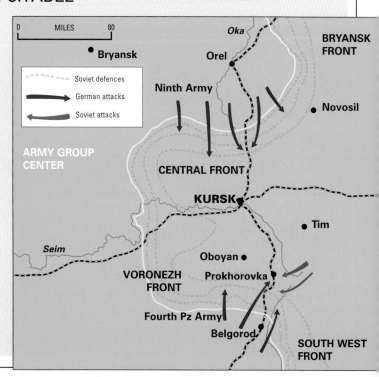

Above: This Fw 190A-5 was based at Kursk in June 1943 and was flown by Hauptmann Fritz Losigkeit, Gruppenkommandeur of III./JG 51, who achieved the majority of his 68 victories flying with JG 51.

Below: The Red Army's plan depended on countless batteries of anti-tank guns firing volleys at individual German tanks such as these. These tactics critically weakened the Panzer divisions.

Widely regarded as the greatest tank battle in history, the mighty Tiger heavy tanks formed the vanguard of German armoured attacks, behind them came the lighter Panzer IIIs and IVs. Formations of up to 200 machines manoeuvred in dense masses on the open steppe.

German attack, and at the front huge defensive lines equipped with various anti-tank weapons stood ready. The defensive belts were very deep, with adequate reserves at the ready.

Partisan movement

Deep in the German rear, partisan bands watched German activities and reported back to Red Army headquarters, and counter-moves were arranged accordingly. Thus it was that as the German forces massed for the attack during the early hours of 5 July 1943, a storm of Soviet artillery fell among them to disrupt and disorganise at a critical moment. The attack had to be postponed for 90 minutes, but eventually it went in to be met by a hail of fire.

The Germans had a qualitative advantage with their new tanks, however this was more theoretical than practical, for the tanks ran directly into a wall of anti-tank fire that stopped them in their tracks. Red Army tank-killer squads then destroyed them by plac-

ing explosive charges in their exhausts or by their fuel tanks. The Elefant assault guns fared particularly badly (nearly all were lost) as they had no defensive machine-guns, and at such close ranges were virtually sitting ducks for the attentions of the tank-killing squads. The Tigers and Panthers managed little better. Many of the prematurely deployed Panthers either broke down or proved to have serious defects. As ever, the Tigers survived well but found they could make little headway against the massed anti-tank guns. By the end of the day the defences of the salient were almost everywhere intact.

Strategic attack

By 12 July the time was right for the counterstroke. It began on the southern flank of the salient when the remaining forces of the 4th Panzer Army massed for another advance. As they moved forward they ran straight into the massed armour of the Soviet 5th Guards Tank Army. It was the

greatest tank battle in history as well over 1500 tanks met head-on in a mighty clash of armour. A huge dust cloud developed in which the tanks of both sides milled and jostled, but this time it was the turn of the Red Army to come out on top. Their tanks and crews had not had to endure over a week of hard combat before they reached the battle, as had been the case for the Germans, and their T-34s were backed up by new armoured vehicles like the SU-85 self-propelled gun, in action for the first time with an 85mm (3.34in) high-velocity gun mounted on a T-34 hull and used as a very effective tank-killer. Another Red Army surprise was the first appearance of the SU-152 Zvierboy (animal hunter), a KV chassis mounting a 152mm (6in) howitzer that was able to shatter German tanks by shell power alone.

By the evening of 12 July the Soviets were in possession of the battlefield as the Germans fell back to the rear to avoid annihilation. The 4th Panzer Army had been virtually destroyed and what was intended to be yet another breakthrough had turned into

yet another major German defeat. A counter-attack duly followed the German withdrawal. Under a huge barrage by over 3,000 artillery pieces the Red Army fell upon the Germans on both flanks of the Kursk salient. Within days it had ceased to exist as the walls of the salient were pushed outward. Soviet air forces were able to gain a mastery of the air which they used to full effect. As the Germans fell back they were constantly harassed by hordes of Ilyushin Il-2s and other strike aircraft.

The long retreat begins

The Kursk fighting did not finally die down until late August, but by that time the Germans had been pushed back far beyond their original start points. Their long retreat to Germany had finally begun, and although they were later to regroup and regain local initiatives, their ultimate defeat was well under way. The Germans were not beaten at Kursk by the Soviet armed forces alone. They were also beaten by the latent energy of the ordinary Soviet people who worked long shifts under desperate conditions for many months in order to arm, clothe and feed the front-line Red Army soldiers, and without them the Soviet armed forces would have been powerless. They provided the energy that finally overcame the power of the German Reich.

The catastrophic losses irrevocably shifted the balance of power in the East and the German army could no longer hold back the Red Army. Hitler could continue to plot, but the 1000-year Reich perished on the steppe near Kursk.

Kursk
Chronology

Operation Citadel was Hitler's attempt to reverse the traumatic German defeat at Stalingrad. It was the largest land battle in history, and ended in a defeat for the Germans which sealed their fate on the Eastern Front.

1943
March–June

Fighting on the Eastern Front slackens off after a winter of offensives. The German high command devise a summer offensive against the Soviet salient at Kursk, occupied by the Soviet Central and Voronezh Fronts. Known as Operation Citadel, the plan is to 'pinch out' the Kursk salient using General Model's 9th Army attacking from the north and General Hoth's 4th Panzer Army attacking from the south, meeting around Kursk.

Rudimentary crosses mark the graves of soldiers killed in the Kursk salient. While the Soviet Union took an estimated one million casualties at Kursk against the German's 700,000, the Red Army was far better placed to replenish its losses and resume the offensive.

April–May

Alongside a huge German build-up of offensive forces, the Soviets pour reinforcements into the Kursk salient.

July 5th

Operation Citadel begins at 4.30am with a German assault into the Kursk salient. The main concentrations of troops, however, are not committed to battle until 5.00am. The delay came from a Russian bombardment of the German assembly areas, Soviet intelligence having informed them of the offensive's time-schedule.

July 6th

Marshal-General Rokossovsky's Central Front counter-attacks against the German offensive in the north, but is unable to prevent the German advance. The German 9th Army's assault, however, meets particularly heavy resistance.

It manages no more than six miles of advance during the entire offensive.

July 7th

The 4th Panzer Army under Hoth in the south of the salient makes good progress, advancing 32km (20 miles) into the salient to Yakovlevo and Pokrovka.

July 10th

Hoth is forced to commit his armoured reserves as the advance slows under tremendous Soviet anti-tank defences and infantry resistance.

July 11th

Two of the Soviet Union's most competent military leaders – Zhukov and Vassilevsky – take direct control of the Kursk battle. Previous tactical decisions had been taken under Stalin himself. The Bryansk Front to the northeast of the Kursk salient makes a flanking

A flight of Ju-57 Stuka dive-bombers seen in action over Belgorod during the battle of Kursk. Kursk is most commonly identified as a tank battle, but it was also a monumental air battle. Over 12,000 Soviet and German aircraft fought, though less than 2000 of them were German.

attack against Model's 9th Army.

July 12th
Hoth's 4th Panzer Army in the south comes under increasing pressure as the Soviets release armour from Konev's Steppe Front for the Kursk counter-offensives. A huge tank battle of more than 1000 vehicles results around Pokrovka. In the north Sokolovsky's West Front begins a offensive into Army Group Centre, aiming towards the rear of the 9th Army.

July 13th–23rd
Sensing impending defeat, Hitler gives the order for Operation Citadel to cease. Fighting continues within the Kursk salient until July 15th. Soviet offensives on both fronts push the German forces back to their start positions by the 23rd. Both German and Soviet forces are hideously slashed by the fighting.

August 3rd
The Voronezh, Steppe, and South-West Fronts begin a major offensive against Army Group South beneath the Kursk salient.

August 5th
The Voronezh Front forces retake Belgorod and maintain the forward thrust of the offensive towards Kharkov.

August 23rd–September 30th
Kharkov falls into the hands of the Soviet advance. The German Army Group South and

Army Group Centre are put into retreat westwards. By the end of September the Soviets have driven the Germans back to the Dniepr and had established five bridgeheads across the river.

International Events 1943

July 10th
US and British forces land on Sicily during Operation Husky.

July 19th
Hitler makes an aggressive appeal to the Italian dictator Benito Mussolini to regain an offensive spirit in the war.

July 19th
The Italian capital, Rome, is bombed by Allied aircraft targeting airfields and rail marshalling yards.

July 22nd
US troops enter Palermo, the Sicilian capital, as German forces are put into retreat across the northern coastline of the island.

July 25th
Mussolini is deposed from office. Marshal Pietro Badoglio takes over as prime minister after the dictator was voted out of power by the Fascist Grand Council. The ejection of Mussolini clears the way for Italy to reject the Axis alliance.

Dejected Russian prisoners at Kursk. The chances of their survival were slim, despite having survived the battle. In 1941 and 1942 alone, it is estimated that around 2.8 million Soviet POWs died in German prison camps from starvation, overwork, execution or exposure. Nazi policy deemed Slavic peoples outside normal conventions of war.

Target for tonight
The night battles over Germany

March 1943: RAF Bomber Command launches a sustained bombing campaign against several major German cities.

Shortly after the 'Torch' landings in North Africa during November 1942, the British and American leaders conferred at Casablanca to determine the future course of the war. One result was a directive, put before Air Chief Marshal Sir Arthur Harris, setting out his bombing priorities, which were 'the progressive destruction... of the German military, industrial and economic system, and the undermining of the morale of the German people to a point where their capacity for armed resistance is fatally weakened'. To begin to achieve this objective RAF Bomber Command was now fairly well equipped, possessing on 4 March 1943 a total of 18 squadrons of Avro Lancasters, 11 of Handley Page Halifaxes, six of Short Stirlings and 15 of Vickers Wellingtons. All of these were operational at night, for a total of 321 Lancasters, 220 Halifaxes, 141 Stirlings and 268 Wellingtons.

The first manifestation of the great night bombing offensive that now broke over Germany and lasted until the end of the war was what came to be known as the Battle of the Ruhr. This started on the night of 5/6 March 1943 with a raid by 442 aircraft against Essen; it was the first full-scale operation in which the navigation and bombing aid 'Oboe' was used successfully.

Six weeks later Bomber

Berlin, the German capital, was subjected to 16 concentrated raids between November 1943 and March 1944, but the great distance to the target and strength of the defences eventually forced Bomber Command to abandon this battle after losing 587 aircraft and 3640 men without crippling the great German city.

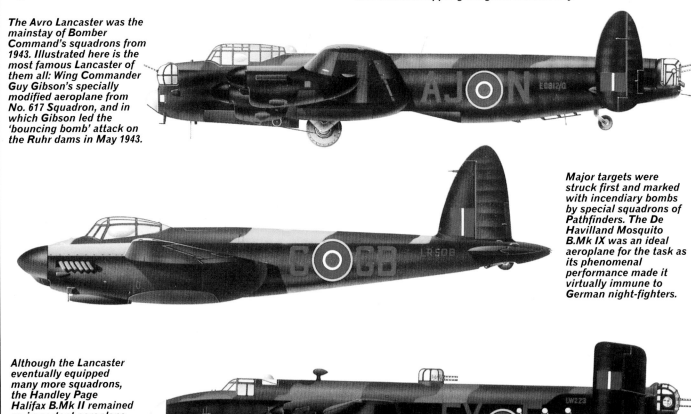

The Avro Lancaster was the mainstay of Bomber Command's squadrons from 1943. Illustrated here is the most famous Lancaster of them all: Wing Commander Guy Gibson's specially modified aeroplane from No. 617 Squadron, and in which Gibson led the 'bouncing bomb' attack on the Ruhr dams in May 1943.

Major targets were struck first and marked with incendiary bombs by special squadrons of Pathfinders. The De Havilland Mosquito B.Mk IX was an ideal aeroplane for the task as its phenomenal performance made it virtually immune to German night-fighters.

Although the Lancaster eventually equipped many more squadrons, the Handley Page Halifax B.Mk II remained an important aeroplane to Bomber Command. Over 6000 Halifaxes were produced in a multitude of versions. This aeroplane flew with No. 78 Squadron.

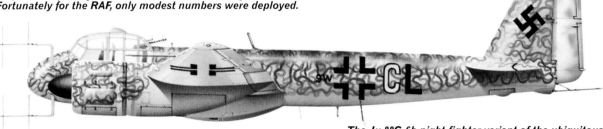

The later years of the Luftwaffe were notable for the appearance of some magnificent aircraft that never realised their true potential as a result of delays caused by political infighting. The Heinkel He 219 Uhu was the best night-fighter of the war: it had outstanding performance, heavy cannon armament and even ejection seats. Fortunately for the RAF, only modest numbers were deployed.

The Ju 88G-6b night-fighter variant of the ubiquitous Junkers Ju 88 multi-role warplane was highly effective. This aeroplane carries a schräge Musik installation of cannon firing obliquely upward and forward, which enabled it to approach British bombers from below and behind, and then inflict fatal damage without warning.

Command carried out one of its most famous raids of all time, Operation Chastise, the attack on 16/17 May by 19 Lancasters of No. 617 Squadron, led by Wing Commander Guy Gibson, against the Möhne, Eder, Sorpe and Schwelme dams, whose hydro-electric stations supplied power to the industrial Ruhr. Dropping special 4196kg (9250lb) 'bouncing' mines, the Lancasters breached the Möhne and Eder dams for the loss of eight aircraft; Gibson survived to be awarded the Victoria Cross for his leadership on the raid.

As new Lancaster and Halifax squadrons continued to join Bomber Command, Harris now determined on the destruction of a single vital city in Germany and on the night of 24/25 July launched 791 heavy bombers against Hamburg. This was the first of four massive raids on the city in 10 days as Operation Gomorrah, carried out in concert with the heavy bombers of the USAAF that attacked the city during daylight hours. Hamburg was chosen not only on account of its importance as an industrial city but also for the manner in which the great port could be distinguished on H2S radar, a blind bombing and navigation aid that had been in use by Bomber Command for some six months ('Oboe' could not be used because of Hamburg's distance from the UK). A vital ingredient in the raids on Hamburg was the first significant use of 'Window' – vast clouds of tinfoil strips dropped by the bombers to saturate enemy radar screens with spurious signals. In the four Bomber Command raids 2630 bombers attacked Hamburg, dropping 8621 tons of bombs which destroyed more than 6000 acres of the port, killed more than 41,800 people and injured over 37,000. The loss of 87 aircraft represented less than three per cent of the aircraft despatched and was well within sustainable limits.

Berlin offensive

The devastating Battle of Hamburg encouraged Harris to open his last great set-piece assault, this time on Berlin itself. On the night of 18/19 November 1943, Bomber Command sent 444 bombers, of which 402 attacked the city, losing nine aircraft, while 325 bombers carried out a simultaneous attack on Mannheim, the first occasion on which two heavy raids were launched on a single night.

The offensive against Berlin continued through the winter of 1943-4, but despite the employment of Bomber Command's specialist Pathfinder Group, No. 8, commanded by Air Commodore D. C. T. Bennett, and the use of sophisticated marking and radio counter-measures techniques, the concentration of damage and accuracy of bombing fell far short of expectations. A total of 16 major raids was launched, involving 9,111 bomber sorties, before the battle ended on 24/25 March 1944. The raids cost the command a total of 587 aircraft and more than 3500 aircrew killed or missing, an unsustainable loss rate of 6.4 per cent. The damage and casualties inflicted were considerably less than at Hamburg, and the Battle of Berlin failed in its purpose of breaking the spirit of the German people.

One other major raid was launched by Bomber Command at this time, 795 four-engined bombers being sent to Nuremberg on 30/31 March 1944. On account of inaccurate weather forecasting, inefficient pathfinding and poor raid planning, the bomber stream disintegrated and suffered heavily from German night-fighter attacks – more than 100 bombers were lost. Worse, Nuremberg was scarcely hit by the bombers.

During the final eight months of the war, Bomber Command returned to Germany in greater strength than ever. Its last target priority was the German oil industry, an industry so completely devastated that it was to be the chronic lack of aviation fuel that finally grounded the once-formidable Luftwaffe.

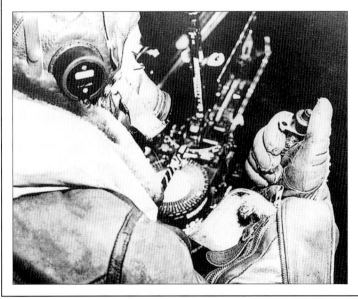

Pressing the button on an Avro Lancaster's bomb sight released the bomb load and marked the halfway point of a mission – it was then time to turn back and head for base.

Target for tonight
Chronology

RAF Bomber Command maintained air raids over Germany from May 1940 to the end of the war. Its later policy of 'area bombing' brought death and destruction to entire German cities, even those which contained no key industrial or military targets.

1940
May 15th–16th
RAF Bomber Command makes its first night assault against Germany. Ninety-nine aircraft bomb industrial targets in the Ruhr, losing one of the aircraft in the process.

August 26th
RAF Bomber Command makes its first raid of the war on Berlin as retaliation against the bombing of London. Eighty-one aircraft take part in the raid.

Frank Wooton's epic picture of Lancasters in action. Sometimes ground fires would produce enough light to project a shadow of the aircraft onto overhead cloud, giving the German AA gunners their aiming point.

October
The Luftwaffe introduces Lichtenstein-radar equipped night fighters (usually Bf-110s) guided to their targets by Würzburg and Freya radar-control stations on the ground. British bombers consequently suffer heavier losses.

December 16th–17th
Mannheim is bombed by 134 British aircraft using area-bombing tactics. The raid is in revenge for recent German bombing attacks on Coventry.

1941
April 1st
Six Wellington bombers hit the German port of Emden, each dropping a single 1814kg (4000lb) bomb.

An industrial target area southwest of Berlin is shattered by bombs from US 8th Air Force Liberators and Flying Fortresses. This target was receiving its second comprehensive bombing in only three days.

April 8th
The German naval base at Kiel is devastated by 229 RAF bombers dropping a total of 40,000 incendiaries.

August 31st
A report released by the British War Cabinet reveals the inaccuracy of British bombing. Only one aircraft in three manages to put its bombs within 8km (5 miles) of the target.

1942
February 14th
A controversial 'Area Bombing Directive' issued by RAF Bomber Command includes German civilian areas as legitimate targets for future air raids.

The Avro Lancaster, workhorse of the RAF bombing campaign over Europe. During the course of the war over 7300 Lancasters flying 157,000 sorties deposited 608,612 tons of high explosive bombs and a staggering 51 million incendiaries onto enemy targets across occupied Europe and Germany.

March
The Lancaster heavy bomber enters service with the RAF, bringing with it a six-ton bombload and an operational range of 2671km (1660 miles).

March 28th–29th
Lübeck is hammered by 234 British bombers using the new 'Gee' electronic navigation system. Another new feature of the raid is that the aircraft drop mainly incendiaries. Twelve British aircraft are lost in the raid.

May 30th–31st
RAF Bomber Command unleashes its first '1000-bomber raid' against Cologne. A force of 1046 aircraft obliterate large areas of the city. The death toll is surprisingly low at around 500, but over 45,000 people are made homeless.

August 1
Specialist 'Pathfinder' units of Mosquito light bombers are formed to mark out targets using incendiaries and flares in advance of a main bomber strike.

September 10th
Dusseldorf is set ablaze when 476 RAF bombers drop 100,000 incendiary devices over the city.

1943
January
British bombers receive the new H2S navigational equipment which provides aircrew with an electronic map of the group beneath them.

July 27th
The second RAF raid on Hamburg in less than a week creates a firestorm which kills 44,600 civilians. The raid is also the first time the RAF have used 'Window', strips of metal foil released from aircraft to interfere with enemy radar.

November 18th–19th
Berlin is bombed. Out of 444 RAF bombers only nine are lost. Sixteen further night attacks are made on the German capital by the beginning of March 1944.

1944
March 30th–31st
RAF Bomber Command suffers its greatest losses in a single raid. Ninety-five bombers are lost and 71 damaged out of 795 aircraft assaulting Nuremberg.

September 23rd–24th
The Dortmund-Ems canal is bombed by 141 British aircraft, 11 using 5443kg (12,000lb) 'Tallboy' bombs, causing massive damage to the canal.

1945
February 13th–14th
The German city of Dresden, containing no important military targets, is utterly destroyed by a raid of 805 British bombers, mostly using incendiary devices. The resulting firestorm caused up to 130,000 deaths and the operation proved extremely controversial at home and abroad.

The Bielefeld viaduct is devastated by 9979kg (22,000lb) Grand Slam bombs dropped from specially adapted Lancasters of the 617 ('Dambuster') Squadron. The Grand Slam is the largest conventional air-dropped munition used in the war.

International Events
1940
July 10th
The Luftwaffe begins attacking British shipping in the English Channel, and soon moves onto attacking RAF airbases around the UK. The Battle of Britain begins.

September 7th
The 'Blitz' bombing of London by the Luftwaffe beings in earnest.

September 17th
Operation Sealion, the proposed German invasion of the UK, is indefinitely postponed because of the Luftwaffe's inability to crush the RAF.

1941
May 10th–11th
London is bombed by 507 German bombers. Following this operation Britain enjoys a respite from German air raids until 1944 as the German air force diverts its resources to the Eastern Front and other theatres.

December 7th
The Japanese Navy demonstrate the superiority of carrier aviation in naval warfare by destroying almost the entire US Pacific Fleet at Pearl Harbor.

1942
August 17th
USAAF bombers flying from the UK make their first daylight raids over Europe, attacking railway marshalling yards in Rouen, France.

1945
March 10th
Up to 80,000 people are killed in Tokyo by US bombing raids dropping 1700 tons of incendiary munitions.

August 6th
The first atomic bomb is dropped on the Japanese city of Hiroshima, killing over 80,000 people.

August 9th
Nagasaki is hit by the second atomic bomb, resulting in 35,000 people dead and 60,000 injured

The Schweinfurt raids
Battle over Germany

August 1943: over 300 B-17 Flying Fortresses raid Schweinfurt, centre of the German ball-bearing industry. But they are unescorted and the Luftwaffe is waiting.

The original plan to cripple the vital German ball-bearing industry centred on Schweinfurt and was called Operation Juggler. It called for the despatch of 150 Boeing B-17Fs of the 4th CBW (Heavy) to bomb the big Messerschmitt factory at Regensburg-Prüfening and then to fly on to bases in North Africa, taking off shortly before the 240 B-17Fs of the 1st CBW, which were to attack Schweinfurt. British and American Supermarine Spitfire and Republic P-47 fighters would provide penetration cover as far as Brussels for the Regensburg raid. This would attract the great majority of enemy fighters into the air too soon to interfere seriously with the main raid on Schweinfurt by forcing them to land and refuel at the critical time as the main force pushed through.

From the outset of the raids, which were launched on 17 August, bad weather destroyed these carefully laid plans. Thick fog over the 4th CBW's bases delayed the Regensburg raiders, but eventually they were ordered off to ensure their arrival over the African bases in daylight. However, being based further inland in the UK, where the fog persisted longer, the 1st

CBW was unable to take off until three-and-a-half hours later, by which time the covering fighters were themselves on the ground refuelling. Furthermore the 4th CBW had attracted the undivided attention of the German defences, losing 24 B-17s (from the 94th, 95th, 96th, 100th, 385th, 388th and 390th Bomb Groups) of the 146 aircraft that crossed the enemy coast.

Aircraft withdrawn

By the time the 1st CBW reached the Belgian coast the German fighters had been re-armed and refuelled, and were again on the alert. Moreover, fighters that had been called from distant sectors of the Reich earlier in the day were now concentrated in the very areas to be covered by the Schweinfurt raiders. As 230 B-17Fs of the 91st, 92nd, 303rd, 305th, 306th, 351st, 379th, 381st and 384th Bomb Groups entered Belgian skies the leading box of 60 bombers was assaulted by successive waves of fighters from JG 26, followed by elements of JG 2, JG 3 and I/JG 5. Before the target was reached and bombed at 1457, this one box had lost 21 aircraft, and seven others had turned for home without bombing. In all, the target was struck by

After the attack in August, Schweinfurt was raided again in October with the loss of another 60 bombers. This Flying Fortress is warming up for the third attack, which was launched the following February, this time with vital support by long-range escort fighters.

183 B-17s despite the persistent attempts by the fighters. By the time the 1st CBW arrived back over its bases it had lost 36 aircraft together with 371 crewmembers; 19 other B-17s were withdrawn from the combat-ready list for lengthy repairs.

Subsequent reconnaissance disclosed that only two of the five vital ball-bearing plants had been significantly damaged (the VKF and KGF facilities); post-war intelligence showed that bearing production was reduced by only 21 per cent, and then for

not more than three weeks.

Indicative of American realisation that the raid had failed in its aim was the absence of any Distinguished Unit Citations (DUCs) among the 1st CBW's groups; by contrast, every one of the 4th CBW's groups that had bombed Regensburg won a DUC.

As combat reports were studied it became all too clear that with the current level of German ability and determination to resist the deep penetration raids, the unescorted daylight raid

Bristling with defensive machine-guns, the Boeing B-17 Flying Fortress received its name in 1935 when the first prototype flew, and it was confidently believed that the firepower of massed bombers was sufficient to beat off attacking fighters without the need for fighter escort. This B-17F is shown in the colours of the 91st Bomb Group, which took part in the disastrous raid on 17 August.

124497

P

LG ★ P

The spectacular contrails left in the wake of the bomber stream made the mass daylight raids a stunning sight but, from the crews' point of view, represented an unwelcome advertisement of their presence. No amount of dashing leather flying kit could keep out the icy chill of 6100m (20,000 ft) and more, and frostbite was a real hazard, particularly to the waist gunners who stood by open hatches. As each attacking fighter was fired on by a multitude of USAAF gunners, the American kill claims sometimes exceeded the entire fighter strength of the Luftwaffe. This, and an exaggerated belief in the effects of the bombing, encouraged the USAAF to press on with the concept of unescorted daylight attacks even though their units had already suffered heavy losses over Schweinfurt.

plan was failing. An immediate outcome was accelerated delivery of the B-17G with increased forward gun armament (in a chin turret); in the longer term the range of the American escort fighters (the Republic P-47 and Lockheed P-38) was progressively increased by the use of larger drop tanks, until eventually these two types were joined by the superlative North American P-51D.

Industry dispersed

Unknown to the Americans at the time, the 17 August raid on Schweinfurt prompted the Germans to start dispersing the ball-bearing industry throughout

Germany. A second heavy raid was launched on 14 October by 420 B-17s and Consolidated B-24s. Once again bad weather interfered and prevented the B-24 element from assembling with the B-17s, and it was accordingly ordered to fly a diversionary feint over the North Sea. Thus it was that no more than 291 B-17s eventually set out for Schweinfurt, the leading 1st Division flying an almost direct route to the target, and the following 3rd Division following a dogleg route in an attempt to confuse the enemy as to its eventual target. The former therefore took the brunt of

the German fighter reaction – the 305th Bomb Group, for instance, losing 14 of its 17 aircraft. Once more 60 American bombers were lost to the Luftwaffe, the majority of them to the pilots of I Jagdkorps. Ironically, on this occasion the bombing results were judged to be excellent – against an industrial target that had largely been moved elsewhere. Even the claims by the American B-17 gunners to have destroyed 288 enemy fighters had eventually to be confirmed as no more than 53 aircraft.

Schweinfurt revisited

The USAAF's 1st Division again raided Schweinfurt on 24 February 1944 when 238 B-17Fs and B-17Gs, this time with long-range fighter escort, took off for the long flight over Germany, losing only 11 of their number. The RAF now took a hand, and on the same night 663 Handley Page Halifaxes and Avro Lancasters dropped

2000 tons of bombs. And on the night of 30/31 March 1944 during the disastrous RAF raid on Nuremberg, more than 100 Halifax and Lancaster crews dropped about 400 tons of bombs in the Schweinfurt area, believing it to be Nuremberg. Further attacks by the 8th Air Force B-17s and B-24s were flown by day on 21 July and 9 October 1944 against Schweinfurt, and the last raid, by medium bombers of the US 9th Army Air Force, took place in April 1945.

While the martyrdom of Schweinfurt assumed the proportions of an American bombing epic, it served well to demonstrate the characteristic flaws in the whole Allied strategic bombing plan: that no decisive result would be achieved through bombing without comprehensively accurate intelligence about the enemy's ability to disperse targets, and without prior winning and retention of air superiority in the enemy's air space.

The Messerschmitt Bf-110 Zerstörer (destroyer) twin-engined heavy fighter had come badly unstuck during the Battle of Britain. However, it survived as a fighter-bomber and was in its element against unescorted heavy bombers until the arrival of long-range Thunderbolt and Mustang escort fighters in 1944 banished it to night operations. Here again it proved successful.

The Schweinfurt raids
Chronology

The USAAF raids against Schweinfurt changed the Allied bombing campaign against Germany. Though they had significant impact on German ball-bearing production, the losses in aircraft ran up to 30 per cent. Following the October 14th raid strategic bombing over Germany itself was suspended for nearly four months.

1943
June
The Allied Combined Chiefs of Staff issue the Pointblank Directive, clarifying the tactics for a combined US and British bomber offensive against Germany. A priority of the directive is the destruction of the German Luftwaffe through targeting air

production facilities or associated industries. Two major targets to emerge from the directive were the ball-bearing factory at Schweinfurt and the aircraft production plant at Regensburg.

August 17th
The first raid against Schweinfurt and Regensburg. The attack plan called for 230 aircraft of the USAAF 1st Bombardment Wing to strike the factories at Schweinfurt,

Above: Pieces of a downed German Messerschmitt fighter go smoking past two Flying Fortresses during the 17 August raid on the Schweinfurt ball-bearing works.

The Schweinfurt raids fell heavily on the town's population of 40,000 inhabitants. The misery of its bombing only stopped in April 1945 when the elements of the US 7th Army occupied the city.

while 146 aircraft of the 4th Bombardment Wing would attack Regensburg. Fighter escort would be provided only up to the border of Germany.

5.30am
The planned take-off time of 5.30am is delayed because of poor weather. This has a major impact on the outcome of the operation, forcing the two wings of aircraft to take off at separate times and so enabling the Germans to respond to the USAAF attacks separately.

6.20am
The 4th Bombardment Wing – which has to fly to North Africa after the raid so needs all available daylight – takes off. By 8.00am it is engaged in violent clashes with German fighters over France, and is constantly attacked throughout its flight to Germany.

11.18am
The 1st Bombardment Wing takes off. The Germans, now thoroughly alerted because of the first flight, send up almost every available fighter – around 250 aircraft.

11.46am–12.09pm
The 4th Bombardment Wing make their attack on Regensburg.

3.00pm
Having already suffered appalling losses, the surviving 1st Bombardment Wing aircraft drop their bombs over Schweinfurt.

4.50pm
The surviving aircraft of the Regensburg force begin landing at bases in North Africa. Twenty-four out of 122 aircraft had been lost.

6.00pm
US aircraft from the Schweinfurt attack begin to land back at their UK bases. Out of 194 aircraft 36 have been shot down.

October 14th
The Schweinfurt raid is repeated using a force of 291 USAAF B-17 bombers of the 13th Bombardment Wing. The US aircraft take off from their UK bases at around 10.00am, Once again they are massively engaged by German fighters, who this time wait until most of the escorts have turned back at the German frontier. The bombing is successful, with around 25 per cent of all German ball-bearing

production put out of action. Yet out of the 291 aircraft which left the UK, 60 do not return, again an unacceptably high ratio of loss. The USAAF consequently suspends all long-range raids into Germany until the 'Big Week' raids of February 1944.

International Events 1943

August 17th
US troops enter the city of Messina, northern Sicily, effectively bringing the Sicilian campaign to an end following the amphibious landings on the south coast on July 10th.

August 18th
New Guinea. Concentrated air attacks by the US Fifth Army Air Force destroy 150 Japanese aircraft at Wewak. The losses give the US almost total air superiority over New Guinea.

August 18th
The RAF bombs the German rocket weapon development centre at Peenemünde, disrupting production and killing over 700 of the centre's staff.

October 12th
Portugal permits the Allies to use Atlantic naval and aviation bases in the Azores. The bases enable Allied anti-U-boat aircraft to patrol target areas previously outside their range.

After the concentration of raids in 1943, the Allied bombers periodically returned to Schweinfurt. Here a raid goes in on 13 April 1944 in a effort to crush attempts to rebuild Schweinfurt's industrial base.

October 13th
US forces battling up Italy cross the Volturno river near Naples.

October 13th
Marshal Badoglio, the Italian leader following the overthrow of Benito Mussolini, announces that Italy is rejecting the Axis alliance and siding with Allies.

Operation Husky
The invasion of Sicily

With North Africa in Allied hands, the invasion of Sicily is a necessary preliminary to an attack on mainland Italy.

Throughout the morning of 9 July 1943 the invasion fleets steamed past Malta, those carrying the US 7th Army being under command of Lieutenant General George Patton on the west of the island, those carrying the British Eighth Army under General Sir Bernard Montgomery on the east. Some 2500 ships and landing craft escorted or carried 160,000 men, 14,000 vehicles, 600 tanks and 1800 guns in what was to that date the largest amphibious operation in history.

Upon reaching the shores of Sicily the armies would storm open beaches, but in order to occupy the entire island they needed to defeat an enemy force of nearly 300,000 men, largely Italian.

On crowded airfields in Tunisia, the engines of 109 American Douglas C-47s and 35 British Armstrong Whitworth Albemarles were warming up and their crews climbing aboard, while behind each plane was linked a Waco or Horsa glider, together packed with the 1500 officers and men of the British 1st Airlanding Brigade. Just before 1900 the aircraft began to take off into clear evening air. But by the time they were approaching Malta for their assembly and turning point the sky had darkened, they were into the centre of a gale and the winds were driving the planes off course and buffeting the gliders.

Turned back

Two hours after the British airborne forces had taken off, another 222 C-47s filled with 3400 American paratroops took off from Tunisian airfields, soon to find themselves in the same chaos as that which engulfed the British brigade. Nearly 40 of the tows of the combined force wisely turned back, but only 54 of the British gliders landed in Sicily, the rest going down into the sea with their 'cargoes' drowned. The American paratroops were dropped into Sicily, but only some 200 were anywhere near their objectives.

The Italian units along the stretch between Cape Passero and Syracuse had

German suspicions of Italian intentions were confirmed early in the campaign for Sicily – Italian privates surrendered while their officers plotted to overthrow Mussolini.

decided that no-one in their senses would attempt a seaborne landing in such weather and had relaxed their attention once the Allied aircraft had flown off, so the first waves of the British assault landed without opposition and swept over the coastal defences almost before their presence was noticed. Belatedly, a few inland artillery units opened fire on the invasion beaches, to be blanketed immediately with shells from one or more of the six battleships (*Nelson*, *Rodney*, *Warspite*, *Valiant*, *Howe* and *King George V*) that had accompanied the force for just this purpose.

Shortly after dawn on 10 July advanced units of the British 5th Division were approaching Cassibile, and by 0800 the town was in their hands. The whole of the British XIII Corps was coming ashore to the south of the division while the 51st (Highland) Division and the 1st Canadian Division of XXX Corps, with Royal Marine Commandos on their western flank, were ashore around the corner of Cape Passero, between the point and Pozzallo.

Over to the west, the US 7th Army had not been quite so fortunate. The coastal defenders had not been asleep along their stretch and the ships and landing craft came under fire from almost the moment of their arrival. Again, fire from the heavy naval guns soon obliterated most of the opposition (much to Patton's astonishment and

HMS Nelson was one of six battleships that led the shore bombardment group of a naval task force comprising 182 warships and 126 landing craft.

Above: A failed British bomber design, the Armstrong Whitworth Albemarle was pressed into service as a transport aeroplane. This is an Albemarle Mk V of the RAF's No. 297 Squadron that towed some of the ill-fated gliders during the Sicily landings. Note the 'invasion stripes' that would regularly adorn Allied aircraft from this time on.

Right: Montgomery's 8th Army, which landed in Sicily, comprised four infantry divisions with two in reserve plus three armoured brigades. The fighting resembled the last stages in Tunisia and the 8th Army was to suffer 9000 casualties as it pressed slowly north.

delight, as he had placed little reliance upon naval assurances) but the pier at Gela, which would have been very useful for a quick build-up, was blown to pieces by demolition charges as two Ranger battalions were actually sailing for it. By 0430 Italian and German aircraft were over the crowded beaches to sink two transports in an awkward position.

Airborne landings

By mid-morning all of the 8th and 7th Armies' forward formations were ashore and probing inland, and the British forces suddenly received an unexpected bonus. If their airborne colleagues were not in exactly the right positions, they had coagulated during darkness into 20 or 30 independent groups and were creating chaos in the country

just behind the landing beaches. Between them they were cutting communications, ambushing lone cars, lorries or even small convoys, attacking crossroad guardposts and on one occasion holding up an entire Italian mobile regiment that had been sent to find out what was happening at Gela.

At the other end of the invasion beaches, however, the tiny part of the British airborne force, just 100 men who had been landed in the correct place, assumed the task of the entire 1500-strong brigade and had rushed and taken the Ponte Grande over the River Cavadonna just south of Syracuse. By mid-afternoon they were in desperate straits. At 1530 a massed assault overran the survivors, but eight managed to escape and, as the British

had removed all the demolition charges while in possession of the bridge, the Italian marines had now to try to emplace some more. Two of the escaping eight therefore took position half way up an overlooking hill and from there sniped at every movement on the bridge, while the remaining six, stumbling with exhaustion, made their way south towards Cassibile. Some 5km (3 miles) along the road they met a mobile column from the 5th Division. They led this column back to the bridge, which fell immediately into British hands again, and by 1700 the column was driving into Syracuse itself.

By the end of the first day

As the Allies prepared to attack, the Germans combined the 7th Air Division (redesignated 1st Parachute Division) with the newly formed 2nd Parachute Division to form a strategic reserve of 30,000 elite troops. These two formations would be a cornerstone of the German defence of Italy.

the British therefore held the coastal strip from Pozzallo around to Syracuse, a vital port that was in their hands and sufficiently undamaged for immediate use, while the US 7th Army held nearly 65km (40 miles) of beach between Scoglitti and Licata. Inland, scattered bands of British and American airborne troops were loose over the southern half of the island, successfully spreading confusion.

Within 10 days Canadian units had reached Enna in the centre of the island, and two days later Patton's troops had not only reached the north coast but had turned west and occupied Palermo, taking prisoner thousands of Italian soldiers who were more than happy to stop fighting, and being welcomed everywhere by delighted Sicilians, to whom quite a number of the American soldiers were related. Very soon it became evident that the bulk of the inhabitants of the Italian mainland felt the same way.

Operation Husky: Chronology

Operation Husky was the Allies' first step back into Axis Europe. The island was heavily defended by the Germans in a 39-day campaign, but the eventual Allied victory bought a jumping off point for the invasion of mainland Italy.

1943

July 10th

Operation Husky, the invasion of Sicily, begins. The invasion force consists of a landing fleet of 2590 ships, and 478,000 British and American troops would be landed by July 13th. The initial assault by 15 Army Group takes place along the southern Sicilian coastline and is preceded by parachute drops at key locations by the British 1st Airborne Division and the US 82nd Airborne Division.

July 11th–12th

The US 1st Infantry Division and US Rangers at Gela are attacked by the Hermann Göring Panzer Division redeployed from Caltagirone. Offshore bombardments from Royal Navy and US Navy ships demolish the attack with over 6000 heavy-calibre shells.

July 13th–14th

Allied airborne troops and commandos are dropped ahead of the main advanced in the east to take bridges over the Simeto river. Though they initially capture their objectives, counter-attacks by German paratroopers drive them out. The Germans hold onto the key Primasole bridge for another three days.

July 14th

The British and US elements of Operation Husky, having landed in separate sectors of the island, meet up at Comiso and Ragusa. Several key airfields are occupied, enhancing the Allies' already significant air superiority.

July 22nd

The Sicilian capital Palermo falls to General George C. Patton's 7th US Army after an arduous advance up the western side of the country.

July 25th

Hitler permits the drawing up of evacuation plans for German forces on Sicily. Such unusual defeatism from Hitler was a result of the overthrow of the Italian dictator Mussolini in Rome.

August 5th

The port of Catania falls to British forces, though the effort of doing so has severely delayed the advance up the eastern coastline.

August 8th–15th

Having advanced from Palermo to San Stefano along the northern coastline, the US 7th Army makes a series of amphibious jumps to outflank German rearguard units as they are pressed back into the northeastern tip of Sicily. The landings take place on the 8th, 11th and 15th of August.

August 11th–12th

Over 100,000 Axis troops are evacuated from Sicily to mainland Italy during the night.

August 17th

Troops of the US 3rd Division enter Messina in the far northeastern tip of Sicily,

A US military policeman looks out on two Landing Ship Tank Mk II (LST 2) off the coast of Sicily. The LSTs were indispensable in Allied amphibious operations. They could carry 18 heavy tanks, 27 lorries or 163 fully armed troops directly onto a beachhead and had a 11,120km (6910-mile) range.

A Sicilian farmer gives directions to a US infantryman. Roughly 150,000 US and British troops were put ashore on the first day of Operation Husky and experienced almost no opposition at the initial landings. The Italian coastal defenders were convinced that a storm during the night would preclude any invasion.

German paratroop units were heavily involved in the German defence of Italy. Though they conducted no major airborne operations after the costly Crete campaign in 1941, as ground troops they ranked amongst Germany's elite, with excellent training and a ferocious ésprit de corps.

signalling the clearance of the island and victory in the Sicilian campaign.

International Events 1943

July 10th
German forces cross the river Don in their drive against Stalingrad and the Caucasus.

July 19th
A directive from Heinrich Himmler orders that all Jews in the General Government sector of Poland are removed by the end of the year. The specific phrase he uses – 'total cleansing' – is a thinly veiled term for extermination.

July 22nd
After listening to vitriolic cross-Atlantic debates between British and US military officials, President Roosevelt decides that an invasion of northern Europe in 1943 is not feasible. The focus continues to be given to the Italian campaign

July 29th
The Canadian government passes legislation which will allow the introduction of conscription for overseas service.

July 31st
Stalin gives orders to the Soviet forces in the Caucasus that they can retreat no longer, and must prefer death to surrender.

August 8th
Three US cruisers and one Australian cruiser are sunk off Savo Island near Guadalcanal by a surprise attack from Japanese naval units. The day before 19,000 US Marines had made an amphibious landing on Guadalcanal and nearby Tulagi.

The Battle of the Atlantic
Defeating the U-boat offensive

The most critical battle of the war takes place not on the European mainland but across thousands of miles of ocean.

Successful prosecution of the war in Europe depended absolutely upon a steady flow of supplies being maintained by convoyed merchantmen plying between the New and Old Worlds. The primary weapon employed by the Germans in their attempts to strangle this flow was the U-boat, and the submarine supremo, Admiral Karl Doenitz, well understood his priorities. Even before his appointment in 1935 he had developed and proved group ('wolf pack') tactics, and went on to define the types of boat best suited to near and distant operations as well as the number required to beat a fully organised convoy system. Even after the Anglo-German Naval Agreement of 1935 had allowed the Germans quite generous limits to submarine construction, the grandiose Z-Plan for surface vessel construction prevented their realisation. As a result, in September 1939, rather than the 300 boats considered necessary, only 56 were complete, of which only 22 were of types capable of ocean service. For a time, losses exceeded commissionings so that, in February 1941, only 22 operational boats remained.

Caught by a Sunderland of the Royal Air Force's No. 422 Squadron, the U-boat U-635 is successfully depth-charged. Aircraft and airborne radar sharply reduced the potential of the U-boats, whose underwater performance was far inferior to their surface capabilities. Some boats took the council of despair and shipped extra anti-aircraft guns, determined to fight it out.

Nicknamed the 'Flying Porcupine' by German pilots, the magnificent Short Sunderland was feared by U-boat crews. The masts along the fuselage are for its radar, and its depth charges are carried internally. RAF Coastal Command began the war just four years old and starved of funds, but it expanded rapidly to play a vital part in the Allies' eventual Atlantic victory.

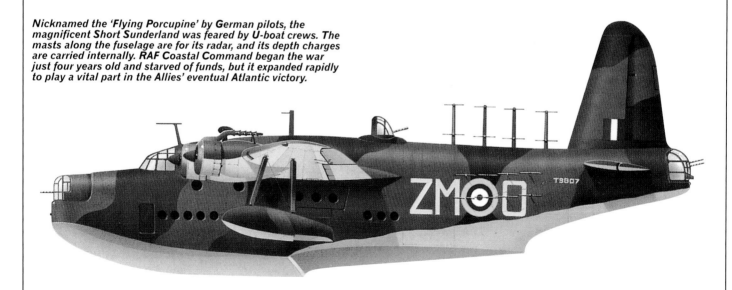

Originally a 26-seat fast airliner, the Focke-Wulf Fw 200 Condor ranged far over the Atlantic searching for convoys and vectoring in the U-boats. The type carried bomb and cannon armament so that it could itself attack shipping: at a radius of 1600 km (1000 miles) from their Bordeaux base, five Condors attacked a convoy in February 1941 and sank five ships.

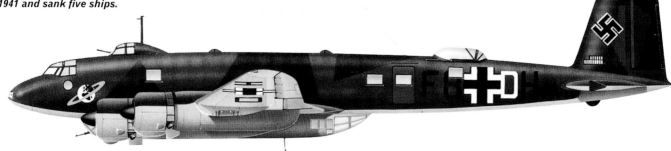

An unrestricted sinking policy was, Doenitz considered, legally justified with merchantmen escorted, armed and given instructions to ram on opportunity. The declared war zone first extended to 20° West, about 800 km (500 miles) west of Ireland. Initially pickings were rich as merchantmen returned individually to the UK, while the major routes from the UK to Halifax and Sydney, Nova Scotia saw convoys escorted through only 15° longitude from either end for lack of suitable escorts. Small numbers at this time prevented the U-boats from attacking in packs, but surface raiders were proving a real threat so that great efforts had to be made to cover convoys with older battleships.

With the fall of France in June 1940 Doenitz could operate his boats from Biscay ports, shortening transit times and effectively increasing numbers on station. Convoys were, therefore, routed north of Ireland while the increasing availability of long-range maritime aircraft encouraged U-boats to work farther to the west. To this time total Allied losses had been a containable 630,000 gross registered tons (grt), but already the 'aces' were beginning to emerge, such as

Hartmann's U-37 returning on 9 June 1940 with a 43,000 grt bag from a 26-day cruise.

The low, plunging platform of a submarine's tower offers a very restricted horizon, but Doenitz's pleas for regular air searches fell largely on deaf ears, while his hopes of an improvement in locating convoys, using Italian boats based at Bordeaux after July 1940, were dashed – the boats were of unsuitable design and national temperaments clashed.

Successful attacks

In January 1941 Doenitz gained control of I/KG40, a Luftwaffe wing equipped with the Focke-Wolf Fw 200 Condor, which could not only sink stragglers but also report convoys to available submarines.

The first successful group attacks on Atlantic convoys occurred in September 1940, with SC2 and HX72 losing a total of 17 ships of nearly 100,000 grt. Assaults were made at night and at the surface, exploiting the U-boats' small profile and favourable surface speed, while rendering the escorts' Asdic (sonar) useless.

Despite Doenitz having written of it before the war, the British had no plans to counter the tactic and U-boat commanders such as Kretschmer, Schepke, Prien

and Kuhnke began to make their names. The escorts' initial response was in powerful illuminants such as 'Snowflake', but the real answer by night lay in the radars that began to become available early in 1941. Further escorts were also being supplemented by more aircraft, while high frequency direction-finding (Huff Duff) sets in the escorts turned Doenitz's reliance on regular radio transmissions from his boats into a weapon that was used against them.

It was a dour struggle, with 1941 seeing the loss of 496 Allied merchantmen of 2.42 million grt in the North Atlantic, a total eclipsed by 1006 ships of 5.47 million grt in 1942. Half a million gross tons per month would have put in sight Doenitz's objective of destroying shipping faster than it could be replaced. He was frustrated by the enormous Allied programmes of emergency construction of standard types, Liberty, Ocean, Fort, etc, and by the German high command's repeated use of his boats for less productive 'side-shows'.

Despite some setbacks, most convoys managed to cross with little incident, and during 1941 close cover became possible for the whole crossing. Further, even as the Allied escorts added to

their experience, the Germans began to lose theirs with the gradual loss of their 'aces'. A sustained air offensive against U-boats in the Bay of Biscay produced an excellent return, the Germans buying increased protection by the development of the *Schnorkel* (snort), but in forcing them to remain submerged this expedient greatly reduced their performance. Having contacted a convoy, submarines were now also likely to find an escort carrier providing local air cover to keep them down, while cruising escort groups quickly reinforced the close escort if trouble threatened.

U-boat decline

March 1943 saw 500,000 grt lost but, from this point, the U-boat offensive went into decline. Between May and August alone, though 98 new boats were commissioned, 123 were lost. Despite the submarine loss rate, total strength remained at well over 400 from mid-1943 until the end of hostilities. But their North Atlantic success rate declined dramatically. The victory in the Battle of the Atlantic was, arguably, the single most important of the war and cost the Allies some 12 million grt, over half their mercantile losses for the complete conflict.

Displacing 1320 tons and armed with a 10.2cm (4in) gun, 'Hedgehog' and 200 depth charges, 'River' class frigates were dedicated escort vessels introduced after the limitations of the 'Flower' class had been revealed. Some 138 'River' class frigates were built during 1942-44, 70 of them in Canadian shipyards.

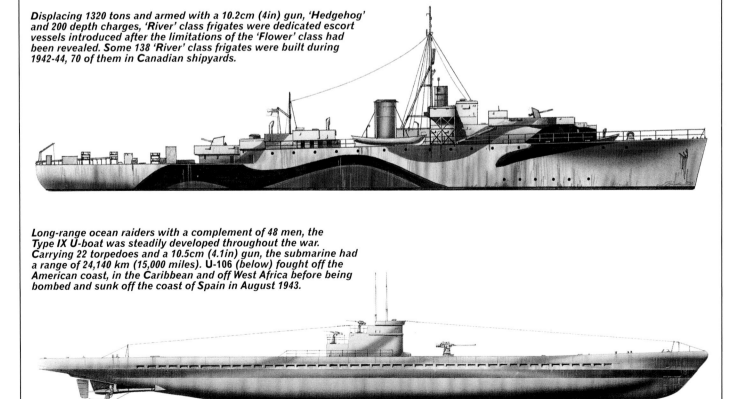

Long-range ocean raiders with a complement of 48 men, the Type IX U-boat was steadily developed throughout the war. Carrying 22 torpedoes and a 10.5cm (4.1in) gun, the submarine had a range of 24,140 km (15,000 miles). U-106 (below) fought off the American coast, in the Caribbean and off West Africa before being bombed and sunk off the coast of Spain in August 1943.

The Battle of the Atlantic
Chronology

The battle between the transatlantic convoys and Germany's U-boat Wolf Packs was one the UK could not afford to lose. If it did, the nation would have effectively been starved into surrender.

1939
September 3rd
The British liner *Athenia* is sunk by *U-30* on its voyage between Glasgow and Montreal with the loss of 112. It is the first U-boat victim of the war.

September 5th
U-boats make the first sinking of a merchant vessel, the *Bosnia*.

September 6th
Merchant vessels make the first transatlantic crossing using the convoy system. The convoy consists of 36 ships set in rows of four ships.

1940
July 6th
France having fallen a month previously, German U-boats begin operating from French coastal bases. The initial base is at Lorient.

August 17th
Hitler orders that the U-boats make a total blockade of the UK, freeing them to attack any merchant vessel approaching or entering British waters.

September 20th
German U-boats begin operating 'Wolf Pack' tactics, using around 20 U-boats to make a mass attacks on single convoys.

October
The rate at which merchant vessels are being sunk peaks at 60,000 tons per month. On October 18th–19th alone six U-boats sink 36 vessels in two convoys.

1941
March 11th
In Washington President Roosevelt signs the Lend-Lease Bill. The Bill sanctions the US government to supply military aid to countries fighting the Axis. Lend-lease depends on keeping open the Atlantic corridors .

April 10th
The US destroyer *Niblack* fires on a U-boat which has entered the US security zone. It is the first US–German engagement of the war.

May 9th
The first Enigma machine is captured from *U-110* by HMS *Bulldog*. The find is crucial, and enables British Ultra codebreakers to crack the German submarine codes by the end of the year.

May 27th
Convoy HX129 crosses the Atlantic, the first to have an escort through its entire voyage.

1942
January
German U-boat fleet grows to 331 vessels, in contrast to 21 operational submarines at the beginning of 1940. Between January and March 216 ships are sunk off the eastern coast of the United States.

May 14th
US finally adopts the convoy system for transatlantic crossings and initiates blackouts along the eastern seaboard.

June
Over 834,000 tons of Allied shipping are sunk, making it the worst single month of the war.

July 19th
All German submarines operating off the east coast of the United States are

Survivors of a sunk German U-boat scramble up nets to board an Allied ship. By the end of the war the efficiency of Allied anti-submarine tactics and weapon resulted in 80 per cent of all operational U-boats being sunk, giving the U-boat crews the highest percentage of fatalities amongst any German arm of service.

repositioned to concentrate on intercepting North Atlantic traffic.

1943
January 14th
The RAF begins bombing U-boat bases at Cherbourg and Lorient in attempt to reduce increasing U-boat activity.

February
The US President orders 250 aircraft to concentrate on anti-U-boat operations in the Atlantic theatre.

May
Allied aircraft are now equipped with 10cm (4in) radar for detecting U-boats, and Allied escort vessels are using improved tactics and weaponry. In this month the U-boat fleet suffers 43 vessels sunk but only sink 34 Allied merchant ships. On May 19th 33 U-boats attack a single convoy but are unable to make a single sinking because of the effective Allied response. On May 24th Dönitz recalls all U-boats from the North Atlantic.

June 1943–May 1945
German U-boats return to the Atlantic in small units to harry British shipping and keep escort vessels from other theatres. Though new technologies are used – such as homing torpedoes and the 'Schnorkel' breathing apparatus – they are unable to make good their losses or severely retard Allied convoys. Following the D-Day landings on June 6th the U-boats also lost their French coastal bases. In April 1945 the US

Survivors of a U-boat attack on a mercy ship carrying 321 British schoolchildren to Canada. In this case no children lost their lives, but other mercy ships were not so fortunate.

Navy sink four submarines off the US east coast, one of the last U-boat actions of the war in the Atlantic theatre.

International Events
1939
The German pocket battleship *Graf Spee* is scuttled after being trapped by Royal Navy vessels in Montevideo harbour, Uruguay.

1940
July 3rd–7th
One French battleship is sunk and two others damaged by a Royal Navy assault force at Oran and Mers-el-Kebir in Algeria. It was feared that the vessels would be operated by the Germans following the fall of France.

A 12,000-ton liner sinks after hitting a German sea mine. Sea mines were exploded by either contact, acoustic or magnetic detonators. They were not only laid by German ships and submarines, but were also air-dropped by long-range aircraft (parachute-retarded sea mines were also dropped on British land targets).

1941
May 27th
The German battleship *Bismarck* is finally destroyed after a five-day combat pursuit by the Royal Navy.

July 21st
The British Navy begins Operation Substance, shipment of supplies from Gibraltar to the besieged island of Malta.

December 7th
The US Pacific Fleet at Pearl Harbor, Hawaii, is decimated by a Japanese aerial attack launched from six carriers. Six battleships are sunk and 10 other vessels badly damaged.

1942
May 2nd–8th
The Battle of Coral Sea in the Pacific results in the sinking of the US carrier *Lexington* while the Japanese also lose a carrier and another two are badly damaged. The Japanese are forced to call off a planned invasion of Papua New Guinea.

June 4th-7th
The Battle of Midway, Pacific. In the decisive naval engagement of the Pacific war, the US Navy destroys four Japanese carriers – half of the total Japanese carrier strength.

The Big Week

Striking at the heart of the Reich

February 1944: imminent landings in France demand air superiority, so the Allied bomber fleets attack German fighter factories in a sustained offensive.

Throughout 1943 the US strategic bomber forces had been developing their daylight offensive with pinpoint attacks against Germany's war-making industries. Some successes had been achieved, but the primary lesson of the 1943 campaign for the daylight bombers remained the inescapable fact that the strength of the German fighter arm was too great to allow the US 8th and 15th Air Forces to maintain a sustained campaign. The advent of long-range escort fighters, had alleviated the situation, but the New Year's Day message to USAAF commanders in Europe issued by General H. H. 'Hap' Arnold, Commanding General of the US Army Air Forces, made the point forcibly: 'It is a conceded fact that Overlord and Anvil [the proposed Allied landings in France] will not be possible unless the German Air Force is destroyed. Therefore my personal message to you – this is a must – is to destroy the enemy air force wherever you find them, in the air, on the ground, and in the factories.'

European commanders were all too aware of the problem, and by November 1943 Operation Argument had been developed as an Anglo-American scheme to address the situation. This was to be a short but sharp round-the-clock offensive

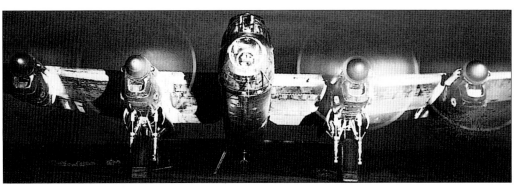

against the German fighter arm: the bombers would strike Germany's fighter production centres, causing decisive damage and in the process tempting up current German fighter assets to be destroyed in large-scale battles with the Allied fighters escorting the bombers. For some months there was no adequate weather 'window' for the offensive, whose purposes were defined on 14 February 1944 as the destruction of the German fighter arm and the industries on which it depended, followed by attacks on the German V-1 sites in France and the Low Countries, and by attacks on Berlin.

Break in the weather

The right weather finally arrived late in February, and on the night of 19/20 February, RAF Bomber Command got the ball rolling with the despatch of 823 four-engined bombers against Leipzig. The fact that

the German night-fighter arm was still in good fettle was attested by the loss of 78 bombers. On the following morning the Americans joined the fray, despatching 1008 Boeing B-17s and Consolidated B-24s against Leipzig, Poznan, Tütow, Halberstadt, Brunswick, Gotha, Oschersleben and a number of smaller targets. The 8th Air Force's bomber fleet was escorted by no fewer than 661 fighters (17 US groups and 16 British squadrons found by the US VIII and IX Fighter Command and RAF Fighter Command), North American P-51s being supplemented by Lockheed P-38s and Republic P-47s all fitted with drop tanks to give them an operational radius of 800km (500 miles) or more.

Lieutenant General Josef Schmid's I Jagdkorps responded in modest strength, launching 362 sorties to meet the 941 bombers that were credited

An Avro Lancaster of RAF Bomber Command lines up to take off on a raid against Germany. With the British attacking during the night and the USAAF bombing by day, the German defences were stretched to the limit.

with attacks. The Americans lost 21 bombers, and the Germans suffered 62 aircraft shot down and another 18 damaged: it was a good start for the American side in what was to become known as 'The Big Week'.

It was now the RAF's turn again, and on the night of 20/21 February Air Chief Marshal Sir Arthur Harris despatched 598 bombers against Stuttgart, suffering 11 losses. The following morning another US bomber fleet began to rise from Major General James Doolittle's 8th Air Force bases in England: 861 four-engined bombers were launched against Brunswick and the airfields or bases at Diepholz, Rheine, Werl,

The 8th Air Force's raids involved formations of bombers several hundred strong. These aerial armadas were marshalled over England by specially painted B-24s, which returned to base once the formation had been assembled and despatched on its way to Germany.

Gütersloh, Münster-Handorf and Achmer. American losses were 16 aircraft, while Colonel General Hans-Jürgen Stumpff's Luftflotte Reich lost 33 fighters of its subordinate formations (I and II Jagdkorps plus the 7.Fliegerdivision). For the next three nights RAF Bomber Command launched only minor operations, in the form of nuisance raids by de Havilland Mosquito twin-engined bombers and mine-laying sorties by four-engined aircraft, and the weight of the offensive thus fell on the American forces.

On 22 February the 8th Air Force was joined by Major General Nathan Twining's 15th Air Force from bases in Italy, and the Americans planned a medium effort against the major Messerschmitt production centre at Regensburg and the ball-bearing factories at Schweinfurt, supported by smaller efforts against Oschersleben, Halberstadt, Aschersleben, Bernburg and Gotha. In the event part of the 8th Air Force's effort was curtailed, and of 44 bombers despatched some 41 were lost, while the 529 American fighters scored 59 German fighters shot down and another 14 damaged.

The weather intervened on 23 February to cause a respite, and on this day Field Marshal Erhard Milch returned from an inspection tour of aircraft production centres to report that 'The situation of our leading production centres is highly

Impeccable formation keeping by B-17s of the 381st Bomb Group. Leaving the surface of the aircraft polished rather than painted gave the bombers a little extra speed through the air and, in any event, camouflage was of little real relevance within the context of a 1000-bomber raid.

Despite Allied bomber raids, German fighter production continued to increase, month by month until 1945. The Messerschmitt Bf 109K was the ultimate production version of this veteran fighter, seen here with the green band denoting its Defence of the Reich role.

The long-ranged North American P-51B Mustang finally tipped the scales against the Luftwaffe. This aeroplane belonged to the 357th Fighter Group of the 8th Air Force, which escorted a bomber formation all the way to Berlin and back in March 1944.

strained, not to use a stronger word.' Milch had anticipated a production rate of 2,000 aircraft per week for February but now conceded that 800 was more likely.

Final raid

Operations resumed on 24 February. The 15th Air Force launched 87 bombers against the Daimler-Benz aero engine factory at Steyr: Major General Joachim Huth's 7.Fliegerdivision responded with vigour and shot down 17 of the bombers. The 8th Air Force sent out 809 four-engined bombers against Schweinfurt, Gotha and Poznan; again the defences responded in strength, with some 48 bombers being shot down. However, the initial part of the attack had been targeted on Schweinfurt and Gotha to the south, drawing the bulk

of German fighter strength in that direction and permitting the northern force to hit Poznan, Tütow and Kriesing against minimal opposition.

On the night of 24/25 February, RAF Bomber Command attacked Schweinfurt with 733 four-engined bombers, of which 33 were lost. And the following morning the final American raid of 'The Big Week' was committed: the 15th Air Force raided the Messerschmitt works at Regensburg while the 8th Air Force tackled Regensburg as well as targets at Augsburg and Forth. Huth was faced with the problem of two bomber streams converging on Regensburg, and decided to pitch his major strength against the southern stream: 33 of the 15th Air Force's 179 unescorted bombers were shot down. The 8th Air Force had supplied an

escort for its 738 bombers, but though the Germans downed 39 bombers, this was a smaller proportion of the overall strength.

The 8th and 15th Air Forces had launched some 3300 bomber sorties, losing 226 bombers. In addition 28 fighters of the VIII, IX and XV Fighter Commands had been lost. But on the other side of the coin the Germans had lost some 290 fighters (plus another 90 damaged) and, importantly, large numbers of their dwindling supply of experienced pilots. Ultimately fighter production was not too severely affected, for decentralisation of production was already under way. But while the Allied fighter forces grew in strength and capability, the German fighter arm had suffered a mortal blow to its skilled manpower.

The Big Week: Chronology

Big Week saw the first 1000-bomber raid conducted by the USAAF. The raid was just one in a week of enormous strikes against German industrial plants throughout Germany.

1944

February 19th–20th
RAF Bomber Commands strikes Leipzig with 823 aircraft, but loses 78.

February 20th
The first day of the 'Big Week' raids. Over 1000 USAAF bombers of the United States Strategic Air Forces in Europe bomb 12 separate targets throughout Germany, including Leipzig visited the previous night by the RAF. The main focus of the raids is industrial facilities, particularly aircraft production sites. Losses are much lower than previous raids on Germany because of the introduction of long-range P- 51 Mustang fighter escorts capable of protecting the bombers throughout their entire mission. Only 21 US aircraft are lost during the raid.

February 21st
The second day of the Big Week sees 900 US bombers attack aircraft production centres at Brunswick. The bombing runs result in heavy damage to the German industrial faculties.

February 22nd
US bombers return en masse to strike at industrial targets throughout Germany. The weather is extremely poor over Europe, resulting in collisions and bombing inaccuracies. Nijmegen in the Netherlands is accidentally bombed, resulting in the death of 200 civilians. In total 41 aircraft are lost during the day's operations.

February 23rd
The bombing operations are halted one day to allow the crews to rest and to effect aircraft repairs.

February 24th
Over 800 US bombers return to Germany for further strikes. A major target is the ball-bearing production facilities at Schweinfurt, previously hit by the US Air Force on October 14th 1943, and bombed today with 266 aircraft. An aircraft factory at Gotha is almost entirely destroyed. Forty-nine aircraft are lost during the day's raids.

A group of Germans queue outside a wine shop in Hamburg, hoping for a rare wine ration. Hamburg suffered appalling punishment from Allied air raids. A series of massive incendiary raids in 1943 killed 40,000 of Hamburg's citizens in firestorms of 1000 degrees Fahrenheit and winds of 241km/h (150mph).

February 24th–25th
RAF Bomber Command follows up on the day's USAAF raids by hitting Schweinfurt with over 730 bombers during the night. The raid makes no significant contribution to the US bombing and 33 British aircraft are shot down.

Flying Fortresses of the US 8th Air Force drop sticks of 454kg (1000lb) high-explosive bombs over the port of Emden, Germany, in October 1943.

International Events 1944

February 22nd
General Hideki Tojo, Japan's premier and leader, sacks the heads of the Japanese Army and Navy. Tojo himself steps into the roles.

February 24th
The Finnish prime minister Risto Ryti makes peace overtures to the Soviet Union.

February 26th–27th
The Finnish capital Helsinki is devastated by a 12-hour air attack from 600 Soviet bombers.

February 29th
US forces in the Pacific gain a foothold on the Admiralty Islands.

February 25th
A US force of 830 bombers finishes Big Week by bombing three main targets: Augsburg, Stuttgart and Regensburg, concentrating mainly on aircraft production factories and other industrial targets.

A group of B-17 Flying Fortresses seen here on a raid over Stuttgart. Because of the lack of fighter escort cover during the early years of the war, US B-17s would fly in large mutually protective box formations, each bringing its 13 12.7mm (0.50in) calibre Browning heavy machine guns to bear on enemy fighters.

February 25th–26th
RAF Bomber Command strikes Augsburg, reinforcing bombing done during the day by the US bombers. The historic city centre suffers massive damage from the 594-aircraft raid.

February 29th
The Red Army officer General Nikolai Vatutin is severely injured in a partisan attack in the Ukraine. His loss as commander of the First Ukrainian Front is a blow to the Soviets, who lose one of their best tacticians. Vatutin dies on April 14th.

Breakthrough at Cassino
Battle for the Monastery

January 1944: the Allied advance on Rome is blocked by the town of Cassino in the Liri valley. Is this the weak link in the seemingly impenetrable Gustav Line?

From the east to the west coasts of Italy the Germans built the Gustav Line. Using some of the most powerful defensive features that nature could supply, they constructed a long line of defensive positions, both man-made and enhanced-natural, that created a major obstacle to the Allied armies driving north through Italy in the winter of 1943/4.

In only one place was there even a remote chance of breaking the line and that was at Cassino in the Liri valley. Even here the town was protected by an artificially swollen river and numerous fortified positions, and overlooked by what became known as Monastery Hill with its Benedictine monastery forming a natural observation post to cover the country for many miles around. Such was the strength of the Gustav Line that even this best chance of Allied success was a veritable fortress for the defence.

If the strength of the Gustav Line were not enough, the Allies had to attack in the middle of the Italian winter, which is a season of rains, cold and poor visibility. Additionally, they were hampered by a long supply line that extended across a large number of river crossings, and over which supplies had to be moved on Bailey or improvised bridging. The Italian campaign was as much an engineer's as an infantryman's campaign.

Frontal attack fails

The first battle took place over a month during January and February 1944. It was very much a frontal attack and it soon stalled. The Allies found themselves attempting to advance directly into a well-organised and stubborn defence. A direct frontal attack across the Liri by an American force in brigade strength turned into a major military disaster, and even when they managed to cross elsewhere the Allies found themselves faced with an almost sheer climb to the crest of Monte Cassino.

The Gustav Line was held by a variety of formations including two Panzer divisions. These Panzers could do little to influence the fighting directly for the terrain was just as hostile to them as it was to the Allies, so the tanks were frequently used as pillboxes, often dug into strong buildings to

The pulverised monastery after the German evacuation of May 1944. General Freyberg's request for the air attack remains controversial but the 4th Indian Division, which attacked on 15 February, was sure it contained German artillery observers if not weapon positions.

provide added protection. The Germans also used a new ploy in the form of simplified Panther tank turrets set into steel boxes dug into specially chosen defensive positions. Most of these were inland from Cassino, up in the mountains, but where they were situated the Allies soon learned that there was no way through. Prominent in the German defence of Cassino was the Luftwaffe's 1st Parachute Division, devoid of parachutes since the invasion of Crete and fighting as infantry.

It was these paratroops who were in the thick of the fighting during the 2nd

The second attack on Cassino was preceded by a massive barrage, and 455 bombers levelled the Benedictine monastery. The 4th Indian Division failed to make any real progress, suffering heavy losses from hidden machine-gun posts on Monastery Hill.

Battle, which opened in mid-February. This started with an attack on the monastery itself, which was utterly destroyed by precision bombing. Unfortunately for the Allies this proved to be a major mistake, for all it achieved was to turn the monastery from a strong position into an impregnable fortress. The German paratroops promptly moved into the debris, which they found to be an ideal defensive position, and there they remained. The rest of the battle evolved into a fierce round of infantry attacks met with strong defensive fire, and even hand-to-hand fighting in some areas. What advances were made were later lost in the usual German counterattacks.

There followed a lull, mainly imposed by the weather, which changed from bad to worse, preventing any operations. The 3rd Battle started on 15 March with a

A view from in front of Cassino graphically demonstrates the importance of Monte Cassino. Both sides had agreed with the Vatican not to attack this international religious centre. This is one of the last views of the monastery before it was destroyed.

strengthened to the point where 23 German divisions faced 28 Allied divisions, a ratio very much in favour of the defence. The only way the Allies could really force their way through was to mass an attacking force at one point and ram their way through. Thus the pattern for the 4th Battle was set. The Allies rearranged their forces to obtain a local superiority, and when the attack started early in May it was made by several divisions in place of the brigade-sized grouping that had been used earlier.

Tanks in the town

By the time the attacks started the winter was long past and the infantry moved forward into the dust of an Italian summer. As usual the attack got under way with fire from massed artillery, over 1600 guns in all, and as usual the Germans fought back as stubbornly as ever. But this time the Allies were attacking in overwhelming strength. In the mountains the French broke through the defences, and at Cassino itself the Polish II Corps surged forward to take the monastery. With the monastery taken the whole of the Gustav Line had been penetrated, for the old military adage that a mountain line is turned once it is penetrated at any point held just as true for the Gustav Line as for any other. With the Cassino ridge in Allied hands the way through to Rome was cleared. From 19 May onwards the Allies could once more resume their advance north and Rome was duly taken in early June.

The battles for Cassino had lasted for five months. When it was over the town of Cassino resembled one of the villages on the Western Front of World War I. Whole areas around the town were shattered and the monastery itself was a heap of ruins. Between them the Allies and the Germans had suffered over 50,000 casualties, many of whom were never found; the British alone lost over 4000 men 'missing'.

Only with armour in close support and with ferocious artillery preparation could the Allies force their way into the town. Here, an M4 Sherman advances over the remains of part of Cassino with the German-held hills in the background.

major aerial attack on the town of Cassino itself. In this bombing attack every structure in the town was either demolished or damaged in some way, and the waiting attackers believed that no-one could be left alive in the inferno. But as is often the case enough defenders did survive, and these also lived through the artillery bombardment that followed the bombers. They managed to put up their usual spirited defence and delayed the bulk of the Allied attacks apart from one small operation in which a feature known as Castle Hill was taken. This hill was directly under Monastery Hill, and throughout that night the Germans made several attempts to retake the hill together with the old castle on the summit. In some of the most ferocious combat of all the Cassino actions the Germans were

held off, but at a fearful cost.

This 3rd Battle was noteworthy as it was the first time the Allies had attempted to use tanks. The Shermans and Stuarts of the 2nd New Zealand Division managed to find a way through the rubble of the town itself and started to climb towards the summit. They could not get far without infantry support and had to turn back, but at last a foothold on Monte Cassino ridge had been made. Farther inland the *goumiers* of General Alphonse Juin's French Corps were making steady but unspectacular progress through the mountains using time-honoured tactics and mule-carried supplies.

The 3rd Battle eventually came to a halt after only a week. Once again the defence had held, mainly because by that time it had been

German airborne troops captured during the unsuccessful assault on Cassino during 15 February 1944. Their gallant and skilful defence of Monte Cassino was an extraordinary achievement.

Breakthrough at Cassino
Chronology

Monte Cassino dominated the Liri Valley, the route the US 5th Army needed to take to capture Rome. The battle to take Cassino became a killing ground for Allied and Axis alike.

The Benedictine monastery at Monte Cassino. The monastery was founded in 530 AD and stored one of the most important religious art collections in Europe, a collection almost entirely destroyed by the Allied bombing raids in 1944.

1944
January 11th
Units of the French Expeditionary Corps attack the outer defences around Cassino with some success. They and the US IV Corps reach the River Rapido by January 16th.

January 17th–February 10th
First major US offensive to take Cassino. US II Corps crosses the Rapido and begins a assault up the Liri valley. Monte Calvario, a salient point 1km (0.6 miles) from Cassino is captured by the US troops, but they are ejected shortly afterwards by an attack from elite German paratroopers.

February 11th
US 34th and 36th (Texas) divisions and the 4th Indian Division suffer terrible casualties, including the loss of the entire US 142nd Regiment, during large-scale attacks against Calvario, Cassino town and Monte Cassino. The Allies retreat and prepare for a second offensive.

February 15th
As preparation for a second offensive, 229 Allied bombers devastate the ancient Benedictine monastery atop Monte Cassino, believing incorrectly that the Germans were using it as a defensive position. The ruins of the monastery actually provide excellent defensive positions which the German forces, previously on the mountain slopes, subsequently occupy.

February 15th–18th
The second major attempt to take Cassino is launched following the preliminary bombardment. The 2nd New Zealand Division has Cassino railway station as its objective, whereas the 4th Indian Division is attempting to take Monastery Hill and Monte Calvario. Both suffer terrible casualties from the well-emplaced German resistance and the attacks fail.

February 19th–March 14th
Appalling weather sets in over the Cassino area, and further Allied offensives are put on hold.

March 15th–22nd
The Allies try once more to take Cassino. Over 600 Allied bombers hammer the town while Allied artillery pours 196,000 shells into German positions. The 4th Indian Division, 2nd New Zealand Division and 78th British Division renew the offensive using large amounts of armour. Some significant gains are made – including the capture of positions on Monte Cassino itself – but by the 22nd further attacks are called off because of the losses in manpower and tanks.

March 23rd–May 10th
The Allies take a six-week respite from offensive campaigning.

May 11th–18th
The fourth, and final, offensive against Cassino. A 2000-gun artillery barrage smashes the already ruined town before the British 13th Corps, Polish II Corps and the US 5th Army make a general assault against the Cassino front. Cassino town falls to the British. The Poles take Monte Calvario and eventually Monte Cassino itself (suffering 3500 casualties in the process), the German paratrooper defenders having withdrawn on the 17th.

International Events
1944
January 27th
An offensive by the Soviet Volkhov Front around Leningrad manages to break the German siege nearly three years after the siege of the city began.

January 31st
US forces make major amphibious landings on the Japanese-occupied Marshall Islands.

February 9th
Voices of concern are raised in the UK concerning the morality of RAF Bomber Command's strategic policy. Figures such as the Bishop of Chichester, Dr George Bell, question whether fire-bombing civilian areas compromises the Allies' ethical position against fascism and does little to hasten the end of the war.

February 19th–25th
Allied air forces pound strategic targets throughout Germany in a six-day period known as 'Big Week'. Over 1000 bombers performed 3800 sorties.

March 9th
General Orde Wingate's Chindit force makes an air landing 322km (200 miles) behind Japanese lines in Burma in Operation Thursday.

March 19th
Germany occupies Hungary to allay fears that the country will capitulate as the Allies approach its borders.

May 9th
The German siege of Sevastopol in the Crimea is lifted by a Soviet offensive.

Two German soldiers are led away to captivity through Cassino town amidst scenes of total devastation. Monte Cassino was finally taken by soldiers of Polish II Corps commanded by General Wladyslaw Anders, but they suffered around 25 per cent casualties to dislodge elite German parachute soldiers.

The Anzio landings
A 'stranded whale'

The Italian campaign seems deadlocked, so the Allies launch another amphibious landing at Anzio, 32km (20 miles) south-east of Rome.

By January 1944 the Allied armies in Italy had closed up to the Gustav Line, Monte Cassino looming menacingly over Lieutenant General Mark Clark's US 5th Army and the British 8th Army (now under Lieutenant General Sir Oliver Leese) edging its way along the Adriatic coast towards Ortona. Rome, which had seemed so easily within reach three months before, was still beyond grasp, and the succession of frontal attacks that had been necessary to push the Allied armies this far up the Italian peninsula were taking their toll not only of men but also of morale.

Something new was necessary, and Winston Churchill felt he knew what: a hook by sea around the Germans' defences, the hurling ashore of a fierce assault force, which would rampage across the German lines of communication and supply. In order to pin down as large a proportion of the German army as possible, both the 5th and 8th Armies would mount wide attacks on the main defences of the Gustav Line and, if surprise could be achieved and time given for the really powerful force to be landed, this latter could

break out rapidly and smash its way across the western half of the peninsula.

On the afternoon of 21 January 1943, 243 ships of all sizes sailed from the Bay of Naples and under clear skies made for the beaches on each side of Anzio and neighbouring Nettuno. Allied aircraft had pounded German airfields for days before and did so still, keeping the Luftwaffe on the ground, while naval bombardments kept the attention of Field Marshal Albert Kesselring and his subordinate commanders fixed on other points. By midnight the first ships were off the beaches, the landing craft were loaded and moved off and, to everybody's astonishment, there was no sign of opposition anywhere. By the evening of 22 January, 90 per cent of the assault force – some 45,000 men and 3000 vehicles – were ashore, the British units on the left already holding the line of the River Moletta, and the American units on the right holding the line of the Mussolini Canal. Hardly a man had been lost and hardly a hostile shot had been heard. To those poised and ready for the break-out it seemed that first the Alban

DUKW amphibious truck transports run the gauntlet of German artillery as they deliver supplies to the beleaguered troops in the Anzio beach-head. The landing achieved complete surprise, but then the vacillating Allied commanders failed to use this advantage.

Hills and then Rome were theirs for the taking.

Caution and bitterness

Unfortunately they were commanded by the wrong men. Clark, commanding the 5th Army from which the force had been taken, was still cautious after the bitterness of the Salerno battle, and Major General John P. Lucas, commanding the Anzio assault force, VI Corps, was neither enthusiastic about the project nor, it seems, anything else. Of his 54th birthday that month he wrote 'I am afraid I feel every year of it!' This was no man to direct an operation that depended upon imagination, eagerness and a willingness to take risks.

The result was that when the forward units had reached their first objectives

they were told not to advance further but to await 'consolidation' – which certainly took place. By 28 January 70,000 men were in the beach-head, together with 27,000 tons of stores, 508 guns and 237 tanks – but no orders to move out and begin the 'rampage' had been issued: no orders, it seemed, but to await enemy attack.

Against so expert and imaginative an enemy as Kesselring and the men under his command, this was courting disaster. The landing had taken the German command completely by surprise and shock overwhelmed them for a few hours. But though surprise remained, the shock gave way to professional contempt for the lamentable waste of opportunity the Allied commanders were exhibiting. Very quickly Panzer and Panzergrenadier divisions were moving into place to put a band of steel around the Anzio beach-head.

Within a week, eight German divisions had taken position and their artillery was shelling the entire area. This artillery eventually included 'Anzio Annie', the pair of 280mm (11.02in) K5E

Armed with an 88mm (3.46in) gun in a fixed barbette, the PzJg Tiger, a type otherwise known as the Elefant, was a tank destroyer with excellent offensive capability but poor protection except for its armour. This knocked-out machine was abandoned as the Germans retreated.

railway guns which hurled 255kg (562lb) shells into Anzio from the Alban Hills, 32km (20 miles) away. At first Kesselring's intention was to destroy the beach-head entirely, but if the Allied commanders were unable to break out they did possess the means and the determination to remain where they were. Fierce battles of thrust and counterthrust were fought, at one moment a German penetration seemed likely to reach the beaches and cut the beach-head in two, but a counter-attack halted the drive and during the next few days it was thrown back to its starting point.

Even though both sides soon accepted the reality of the stalemate, the bitter fighting went on day after day, and the weather made conditions worse. Something of a lull began in early March – though the killing went on with little pause – and through the rest of that month, all of April and most of May a grim war of attrition was fought out, reminiscent of battles on the

The most sustained effort to push the Allied forces back into the sea began on 3 February. On the 16th of that month, the *LXXVI Panzer Corps* locked horns with the *US 45th Division*, the Germans' two *Panzergrenadier* and one *Panzer* division including a battalion each of *Panther* medium and *Tiger* heavy tanks.

One of the factors that distinguished **German** ground troops in World War **II** was the ability to extemporize swiftly and efficiently to create defensive positions wherever the opportunity offered.

Western Front in 1917. Then in May the Allies launched their big offensive on the Gustav Line, Monte Cassino was taken by Polish troops on 17 May and on 25 May, four months after the original Anzio landings, patrols met up north of Terracina, linking the main body of the 5th Army with VI Corps.

In no way can the story be presented as an Allied success. Churchill probably summed it up best: 'We thought we had hurled a wild cat ashore. All we got was a stranded whale!'

It had been a long time since the German army could parade a haul of prisoners before the camera. Here the column of POWs is marched past the monument to Victor Emmanuel II. Note the soldier on the right making the only protest possible in the circumstances.

The Anzio landings: Chronology

The Allied landings at Anzio were intended to break the bloody deadlock of the Italian campaign. The opposite happened, with the Allied forces pinned into a narrow beachhead taking heavy casualties from German counter-attacks.

1944

January 22nd

Operation Shingle is launched by the US VI Corps commanded by Major-General John Lucas. The landings are concentrated on a 24km 15-mile stretch of Italian coastline 48km (30 miles) south of Rome, and centred on Anzio-Nettuno. The landings are virtually unopposed. By 12 midnight over 36,000 Allied troops and 3069 vehicles have been landed on the Anzio beachhead for the cost of only 13 soldiers killed and 97 wounded.

January 23rd

Instead of pushing out into the interior, Lucas fatally decides to consolidate the Anzio beachhead. He maintains his positions for two days, allowing the Germans to build up counter-attack forces. Colonel-General von Mackensen is sent to take over the newly created German 14th Army headquartered less than 48km (30 miles) west of Rome. Through various improvisations, von Mackensen creates four divisions of combat troops, the number steadily increasing through reinforcement and redistribution of units. The Luftwaffe begins heavy air attacks.

January 28th

Von Mackensen redeploys several German units to bring six divisions to bear on Anzio The US 1st Armored Division captures the town of Aprilia 16km (10 miles) north of the Anzio beachhead, but suffers defeats elsewhere at Cisterna. Field Marshall Kesselring, supreme commander-in-chief in Italy, receives a directive from Hitler instructing him 'to hang on until the last enemy soldier has been exterminated or driven back into the seaí.

January 30th

Allied casualties now number over 5000.

January 31st

Von Mackensen has eight divisions at his disposal to resist the Allies at Anzio.

February 12th

Winston Churchill writes to Sir Harold Alexander, commander-in-chief of all Allied forces in Italy, complaining that 'I expected to see a wild cat roaring into the mountains – and what do I find? A whale wallowing on the beaches!'

February 16th–20th

Pushed on by the Führer's

British and US soldiers greet each other at the Anzio beachhead. Only 13 soldiers were lost during the initial landings at Anzio, killed by land mines, out of 50,000 Allied troops put ashore.

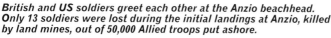

A British officer looks out over the Italian front. The Italian terrain proved as much an obstacle to the Allied advance as the German resistance. Italy is a defender's country, with large mountain chains, narrow coastal strips, and a multitude of river systems providing natural defensive positions at frequent intervals.

earlier directive to Kesselring, von Mackensen launches a substantial counter-attack against the Anzio forces, pushing the Allied lines back nearly six km (four miles). The Allies, however, used timely Ultra intelligence and massive firepower to successfully defend the Anzio perimeter. The Germans suffer nearly 5500 casualties.

February 22nd
Major-General John Lucas is replaced by Major-General Lucius Truscott.

February 29th
Von Mackensen calls off all offensive activity against Anzio owing to unsustainable losses. For almost three months the battle settles into a bloody stalemate, the Germans resorting more to siege tactics.

May 23rd
Following Allied successes further south on the Cassino front, the US VI Corps manages to break out of Anzio and push outwards into the Alban hills.

May 25th
The US VI Corps joins up with the US II Corps advancing up the Italian mainland and begin the drive towards Rome.

International Events 1944

January 27th
Soviet units break through the German defences surrounding Leningrad. Stalin declares the end of the 900-day siege.

January 30th
US forces in the Pacific begin Operation Flintlock, the operation to take the Marshall Islands back from the Japanese. Some 85,000 troops are put ashore in an amphibious landing on Majuro Atoll.

February 15th
The 700-year-old Benedictine monastery at Monte Cassino, Italy, is obliterated by Allied bombing. The Allies believed

British soldiers flatten themselves in a trench as protection from German bombardment. By 3 February the Germans had thrown a ring of over 70,000 men around Anzio and began to pour tank and artillery fire into a claustrophobic Allied space. Only massive Allied firepower broke the deadlock.

the Germans were using the mountaintop monastery as a strategic position.

March 4th
US bombers join British aircraft for bombing raids against Berlin. They enjoy round-trip escort by Lightning and P-51 Mustang aircraft, which can make the 1931km (1200-mile) journey by using underwing auxiliary fuel tanks.

March 8th–11th
British and US forces in Burma make substantial gains against Japanese in several offensives. The Japanese reply with Operation U-Go in northern Burma aimed at capturing the logistical and communications centre at Imphal.

March 30th
Hitler sacks field marshals von Manstein and von Kleist in anger at Russian advances

in the Ukraine. Von Manstein in particular resisted Hitler's credo that the German soldiers should never retreat in battle.

April 6th
The Japanese U-Go offensive is stopped at Imphal.

May 18th
The German-held monastery at Monte Cassino finally falls to the Allies at appalling cost to both defenders and attackers.

May 31st
Allied bombers begin preparatory bombardment of targets along the French coastline as the date for the Normandy landings approaches.

Their job done in delivering US Army gliderborne infantry into the Normandy 'air head', glider pilots head back to England two days after the landings. The airborne assault was designed to prevent the Germans from reinforcing their units along the coast. On the day the three airborne divisions and the intensive onslaught prevented any concerted counter-attack.

D-Day
The Normandy landings

6 June 1944: the largest amphibious invasion force ever assembled attacks Hitler's 'Atlantic Wall' in the Normandy region of northern France.

In the spring of 1944 Adolf Hitler knew that the war would be decided in France. To a conference of senior generals at his retreat of Berchtesgaden he observed: 'The whole outcome of the war depends on each man fighting in the West, and that means the fate of the Reich itself...' Casualties on the Eastern Front were then far exceeding Germany's ability to find replacements, and the Reich's industrial centres were under increasingly effective attack from Allied bombers. If the Allied invasion of France were to fail, however, Germany might have the breathing space to counterattack the Soviets and deploy the advanced submarines and 'V' weapons that Hitler hoped would regain him the initiative.

Allied deception plan

The German high command was convinced that the Allied landing would take place in the Pas de Calais area: this was nearer both to the British ports and the German frontier than any other stretch of coastline. That the Germans continued to believe this even after the Normandy landings had begun was primarily due to an exceptionally well orchestrated misinformation campaign. Whereas the real invasion armies assembled in great secrecy all along the south coast, the air waves above Kent hummed with the radio traffic of the non-existent 'US 1st Army Group'. Fake ammunition dumps, dummy positions and the presence of the famed Lieutenant General George Patton all added to the effect.

The exact timing of the Allied invasion depended on correct meteorological conditions: above all, a low tide at dawn, which would expose the underwater defences laid along the beaches. This dictated either 17 May or 5/6 June 1944, and in the end General Dwight D. Eisenhower ordered the attack for 5 June, but had to postpone for 24 hours as a result of poor weather conditions.

The invasion was spearheaded by the largest airborne assault yet undertaken: nearly 20,000 men landed by parachute or glider. The US 82nd and 101st Airborne Divisions dropped to seize vital ground inland from 'Utah' beach while the British 6th Airborne Division was dropped to capture the crossings over the River Orne and Caen Canal on the eastern flank of the invasion beaches.

Assault from the air

The airborne landings were chaotic: the Americans were scattered over a wide area and in the early hours of the morning small groups of paratroopers fought a series of confused actions. The vital crossroads at Ste Mère Eglise were taken, but the two US divisions failed to link up and remained badly scattered until 7 June. The British landing was more successful and took most of its objectives before dawn.

The landings from the sea began at 0630 on the beach codenamed 'Utah'. Preceded by a heavy air and naval bombardment, the American troops swept ashore 1830 m (6000ft) away from their intended beach and met the lightest opposition of all five invasion beaches. The surprised defenders were quickly overcome and the remainder of the day was spent in bringing supplies and men ashore while the leading elements began to push inland to reach the American paratroops.

At 'Omaha' the American landing was hampered by a choppy sea and was opposed by the German 352nd Division, which made a determined effort to throw the invaders back into the sea. By nightfall Major General Leonard Gerow's V Corps was still only clinging to the beach, cut off from 'Utah' by flooded estuaries and from the British 'Gold'

Fitted with propellers and a collapsible flotation screen, which could be raised above the turret to provide buoyancy, Sherman DD (Duplex Drive) tanks swam ashore with the first wave of troops. It was a hazardous business in which a number of tanks were flooded and sank, but their close support of the infantry was vital.

beach by the stubborn German presence in the fishing port of Port-en-Bessin. This was finally taken by the Royal Marines on 8 June.

In the Allied centre the landings at 'Gold' faced similar problems with the surf but encountered much lighter opposition, and by midday the British 50th Division was pressing inland. Bayeux was liberated on 8 June and was spared the battering that was needed to free most other towns in Normandy. On 'Juno' the Canadians were 9.6 km (6 miles) inland by the end of the day although short of the

very ambitious objectives set for them. Their attempts to move on the next day were frustrated by a savage counter-attack by the SS Panzer Division 'Hitler Jugend'.

More obstacles

The easternmost landing at 'Sword' beach was strongly opposed. The troops encountered far more obstacles and fortifications than they had been led to expect, mainly because their briefing photographs were nearly a year out of date. They were the only Allied forces to face a major German counter-

attack on 6 June, when the 21st Panzer Division launched a vigorous assault at the gap between British and Canadian forces. However, the Panzers were beaten off and the leading troops were within 4.8 km (3 miles) of Caen.

On 7 June Allied attacks all along the coast linked the five invasion beaches to form an 80km (50 mile) front which no subsequent German attack seriously threatened to breach. Field Marshal Erwin Rommel, commanding Army Group B, had been proved right: the armoured reserve was held

back too far and too late to defeat the invasion, and Hitler's inflexible grip on operational planning had effectively paralysed the German response to the landings. Some 156,000 Allied troops landed on D-Day, and at a cost of 9000 casualties they had fatally wounded the Third Reich.

Photographed from a captured German position, the awesome scale of the Allied amphibious assault becomes apparent. Barrage balloons provide passive protection from a Luftwaffe that was scarcely given a chance to intervene thanks to the overwhelming power of the Allied air forces.

D-Day: Chronology

The D-Day landings on 6 June 1944 opened the Second Front in Europe. In a single amphibious operation over 132,000 Allied soldiers were landed on the beaches of Normandy.

1944

May 17th

Eisenhower, the supreme commander of Allied forces in Europe, sets the date for the D-Day landings – Operation Overlord – as June 5th.

April 1st-June 5th

Allied bombers make 200,000 sorties against key targets in western France, including railway yards, roads, bridges, radar sites and military positions in preparation for the D-Day landings.

June 4th

The Normandy landings are postponed for 24 hours because of bad weather.

June 5th

British meteorologists promise a break in the weather for June 6th. Eisenhower orders the offensive to go. Over 6000 naval vessels begin to leave ports from around the southern coastline of the UK.

A soldier from the US 82nd Airborne Division helps a French family at Eglise sur Mer two days after the Normandy landings. Many French and Belgian civilians were displaced by Allied air raids in the build up to the landings.

June 6th
Midnight–6.30am

Allied airborne operations begin over Normandy in advance of the main amphibious landing. The US 82nd and 101st Airborne Divisions are dropped into the Cotentin peninsula, while the 6th British Airborne Brigade are dropped on the eastern flank of the landing zone around Benouville. The US landings are heavily scattered and achieve few of their original objectives. The unintended dispersion of the paras, however, throws immense confusion into the German response to the invasion. By 00.30am the British had seized their primary objectives – the bridges over the Orne River and Caen Canal. Subsequent British operations destroyed the German coastal battery at Merville and blew up five bridges over the river Dives. In the immediate hours before the landings Allied naval vessels pound the landing zones with heavy fire.

6.30am

US forces make the first landings in German-occupied France at two beaches codenamed Utah and Omaha. At Utah, navigational problems puts the landing force of the US 4th Infantry Division 2000yds away from its intended landing point. This actually works to the benefit of the US troops, who avoid heavy German defences at Les-Dunes-de-Varreville. The Utah landings take only 300 casualties. The Omaha beach landings are heavily resisted by the veteran

Citizens of London digest the newspapers reporting on the D-Day landings. Prior to the landings, Allied troops in the UK were confined to isolated camps with no outside contact to prevent invasion plans leaking out.

German 352nd Division, and the 1st US Infantry Division takes 2400 casualties. Nevertheless, it manages to retain the beachhead.

7.25am
British and Canadian forces go ashore at Gold and Sword beaches. The Gold beach landings are a great success, and the British 50th Division subsequently pushes six miles inland. At Sword beach heavier resistance is faced by the British 3rd Division, but by 8.00am most German defences in the area have been suppressed.

7.55am
The Canadian 3rd Infantry Division goes ashore at Juno beach. Around 30 per cent of the landing craft are destroyed on the approach by rough seas, underwater defences and mines. Heavy German resistance builds up as the foothold is expanded, and the Canadians take major casualties as they advance out of the beachhead.

10.00am
The British advance out from Gold beach takes La Rivière.

11.00am
The town of Bernières is taken by the Canadian forces from Juno beach.

12.00 Midday
Units of the US 4th Infantry Division advancing out from Utah beach make contact with paratroopers from the 101st Airborne Division around the town of Pouppeville.

1.00pm
British and French Commandos from the landings at Sword beach link up with British airborne troops holding the bridges over the Orne.

4.00pm-8.00pm
A German counter-attack by the 21st Panzer Division towards Sword beach is stopped by Allied armour and air strikes, despite reaching the beach itself. The Canadian 3rd Infantry Division links up with the British 50th Division from Gold beach to form the largest Allied-occupied area of D-Day.

Midnight
D-Day concludes with varied gains. The largest bridgeheads are in the British and Canadian sectors. The Gold and Juno landings result in a pocket 10km (6.2 miles) deep by 15km (9 miles) long on the French coast, while the Sword beachhead is roughly 10km (6.2 miles) square and has been unable to join up with the Juno forces. The US landing zones fared less well. The Omaha beach force held positions at Vierville sur Mer, St-Laurent sur Mer, and Colleville, creating a beachhead about 2km (1.2 miles) deep and 7km (4.3 miles) long. Utah beach forces, supported by US airborne troops ended D-Day with scattered possessions reaching 10km (6.2 miles) inland, including Ste Mère Eglise, the first town to be liberated in France.

International Events 1944

June 4th
The US 5th Army under Lieutenant-General Mark Clark enters Rome. German troops left the city prior to the US arrival.

June 4th
The US destroyer *Chatelain* retrieves further Enigma codes and previously unseen Zaunkönig acoustic homing torpedoes from the damaged U-boat *U-505* off the coast of Sierra Leone, Africa.

June 7th
US forces advancing through New Guinea capture Mokmer airfield on Biak.

June 10th
Russian forces around Leningrad launch an offensive against Finnish units in the Karelian isthmus.

June 10th
Units of the 2nd SS Das Reich Panzer Division massacre 642 people in the French village of Oradour-sur-Glâne.

An English port fills up with Allied ships and logistics just prior to the D-Day landings. During the D-Day landings some 59 Allied ships were sunk by U-boats, coastal artillery, German surface vessels and air attack, a tiny fraction of over 7000 craft used for the assault.

Unstoppable Red Army
The destruction of Army Group Centre

June 1944: three years after the German invasion of the USSR and a massive rebuilding effort, the Soviets launch their greatest offensive of the war.

On 22 June 1944, three years to the day after Barbarossa had been launched, the great Soviet summer offensive opened. From Velikiye Luki in the north around a huge arc to Kovel below the Pripet Marshes, the artillery of four Red Army fronts – 15 armies in all – crashed out, while the aircraft of four air armies flew overhead, and the infantry and tanks – increased over normal establishment by more than 60 per cent – moved out of their concentration areas into the attack. Their objective was the obliteration of the German Army Group Centre, which consisted of three infantry armies and one Panzer army under Field Marshal Ernst Busch (altogether over one million men with 1000 Panzers and 1400 aircraft), smash through their defences and force back the Finnish and German armies to the north, and the Hungarian, Romanian and German armies to the south. This was the onslaught that would clear the invader from the soil of 'Mother Russia'.

Defences captured

Within a week the three main bastions of the German defences had been cut off and then captured. There were Vitebsk in the north, by converging attacks from one army of General I. Kh. Bagramyan's 1st Baltic Front above and one of General I. D. Chernyakovsky's 3rd Belorussian Front below; Mogilev, by two armies of General G. F. Zakharov's 2nd Belorussian Front; and Bobruisk, by the armies of

Marshal K. K. Rokossovsky's 1st Belorussian Front, which moved massively but secretly over countless small rivers and lakes at night, then attacked out of marshy ground that their opponents had considered impassable.

Parts of two Panzer corps were cut off and bombed into disintegration, and then Rokossovsky's armies took Bobruisk with 24,000 prisoners.

Great momentum

By 4 July both Zakharov's and Chernyakovsky's men had driven forward nearly 240km (150 miles) leaving behind them only one small pocket of German resistance, which surrendered on 11 July; Rokossovsky's 28th Army was approaching Pinsk and, except in the north around Daugavpils (Dvinsk), the Germans were back over the old pre-war Soviet–Polish border.

The momentum never flagged. Everywhere the

> The Germans' Army Group Centre was overwhelmed by an offensive of staggering proportions. The co-ordination of this five-Front offensive revealed the new power and confidence of a Red Army that was now unstoppable.

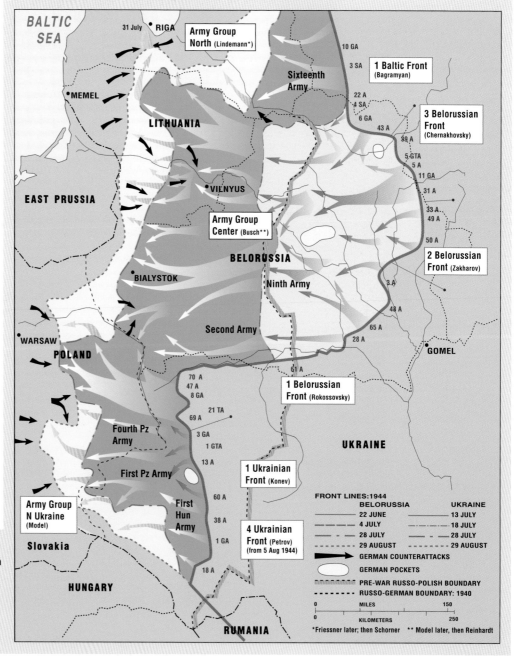

STAGGERING OFFENSIVE: ON TO BERLIN!

Despite a savage counter-insurgency campaign conducted by the most barbaric of the SS units, the German rear areas were subjected to concerted attack by the powerful Soviet Partisan movement.

the end of August had reached the borders of East Prussia, while farther north Bagramyan's Baltic Front armies crossed into both Latvia and Lithuania, and sent an armoured raid up to the Gulf of Riga.

Brest-Litovsk fell to Rokossovsky on 28 July and soon afterwards his forces had reached the Bug north of Warsaw, while on his left General V. I. Chuikov's 8th Guards Army had stormed

and fire-power began to tell, that the defences cracked. Forty thousand Germans were surrounded near Brody, Rokossovsky's right-hand army drove straight to the Vistula, crossed it and formed a bridgehead at Sandomir, one tank army flanked Lwow to the north and another was thrown into an assault that captured the city on 27 July; Przemysl fell, then Mielec at one end of the front and Nadvornaya at the

Germans were in full retreat, though they turned and struck back ferociously at times. Nevertheless armies of the 1st Baltic Front forced the Dvina and took Polotsk within days; the armies of Chernyakovsky and Zakharov – having already cut off 105,000 Germans as they crossed the Beresina – drove on towards Vilnyus and

Bialystok, taking the latter at the end of the month and causing Colonel General Heinz Guderian, the newly appointed Chief of the General Staff, to note caustically in his diary, 'Army Group Centre has now ceased to exist.'

Immediately north, Chernyakovsky's right flank drove on from Vilnyus to Kaunas in Lithuania and by

With the capture of Tukums on the Gulf of Riga during 31 July, Army Group North was completely cut off. A counter-attack by the 5th and 14th Panzer Divisions opened a narrow corridor on 21 August but it could not be held for ever. The Baltic republics were doomed.

Tank-riding infantry – Soviet tactics had improved but the infantry support for Soviet armour usually had to ride on the tanks themselves.

out of Kovel in mid-July, captured Lublin and reached the Vistula, which they crossed on 2 August.

Driving forward

Marshal I. Koniev's armies on the Ukrainian Front had not been embroiled at the start of the offensive, but on 13 July they drove forwards against very strong resistance from Army Group North Ukraine (for this was where the German army had strongly expected the Soviet onslaught) and it was not until two more tank armies had been brought up from reserve on 16 July, and this tremendous weight of men

southern end.

By the end of August the Carpathian Mountains had been reached along their main length and the Polish border was now behind the leading positions of the Red Army, which had now closed up to the old borders with Czechoslovakia and with Hungary. In two months the Soviet troops had advanced 725km (450 miles) – at great cost to themselves in manpower and equipment but also inflicting enormous losses on their foes – and now the time had come again to reorganise the supply lines for the next advance.

The strength of Soviet heavy industry had grown enormously during 1943. Not only did the Germans face superior numbers of T-34 medium tanks, but the Red Army was now able to field heavier armour such as the IS-2 heavy tank, the first tank to mount a 122mm (4.8in) gun. Its thick armour was impervious to most anti-tank weapons.

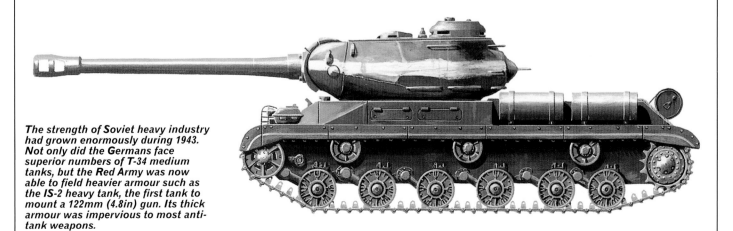

Unstoppable Red Army
Chronology

By April 1944 the Red Army had driven German forces from the south of Russia back into southern Poland. Further north, the German Army Group Centre retained a large bulge of Soviet territory reaching out only 80km (50 miles) short of Smolensk. On June 23rd the Soviets began the operation to crush this salient.

May
Operation Bagration – a crushing offensive against Army Group Centre (commanded by General Busch) in Belorussia – is conceived and planned in the Soviet High Command. The operation name is given on May 20th and the launch date is June 22nd.

June 19th–23rd
Army Group Centre suffers from very heavy partisan activity in its rear lines in the run-up to Bagration. Over 40,000 separate acts of explosive sabotage impair German transportation networks, communications and logistics.

June 22nd
Operation Bagration begins. Under the supreme command of Zhukov, the 1st Baltic Front and the 1st, 2nd and 3rd Belorussian Fronts comprising some 1.2 million troops, launch a four-pronged assault towards Minsk, the capital of Belorussia. Simultaneously, the 1st Baltic Front north of the Minsk offensive attacks against Army Group North towards Riga, Lithuania. Vitebsk is taken early on by the 1st Baltic Front and 3rd Belorussian Front in a pincer action, trapping and destroying much of the 3rd Panzer Army.

June 26th
Hitler permits the German 9th Army, savaged from the early Soviet assaults, to withdraw to the river Berezina east of Minsk and avoid being encircled by the 1st and 2nd Belorussian Fronts.

June 23rd
The 4th Army in positions northeast of Minsk are encircled by the 1st and 3rd Belorussian Fronts. By June 30th the Germans have lost over 200,000 men in the fighting.

June 28th
Field Marshal Busch, the commander of Army Group Centre, is replaced by one of Hitler's favourite tacticians, General Model.

June 29th
Bobruysk in the southern sector of Army Group Centre is taken by the Russians, clearing the way for the 1st and 2nd Belorussian Fronts to close the pincers around Minsk with the 3rd Belorussian Front.

July 4th
Minsk falls to the Belorussian Fronts. The 4th Army has lost over 130,000 soldiers out of a force of 165,000, and total German dead by this point amounts to around 400,000.

July 5th–11th
The remnants of the 4th Army steadily surrender or are killed attempting to break out of the Soviet encirclement. The 9th Army is completely crushed by constant Soviet onslaughts.

Captured Germans are marched through the streets of Kiev, December 1943. The Soviet advance into Germany precipitated one of the biggest refugee crises in history as 12 million East Prussians and eastern Germans fled west.

Soviet infantry and T-34 tanks move on the offensive. By 1944 Soviet industry was producing well over 1000 tanks per month. An incredible 35,120 T-34s were produced during the war, accounting for 68 per cent of total Soviet wartime tank production.

July 13th
Soviet forces capture Vilnius, Lithuania. At the same time the Soviet 1st Ukrainian Front and 4th Ukrainian Front begin their major offensive against German Army Group North Ukraine. The primary aim of the offensive is to take Lvov and push on into southern Poland.

July 17th
Moscow formally celebrates the expulsion of German forces from White Russia. Over 57,000 captive German soldiers are marched through the streets of the capital. Army Group Centre has effectively ceased to exist except on paper.

July 27th
Lvov is finally captured by the Ukrainian Fronts after two weeks of bitter fighting.

July 28th
Having pushed past Minsk, the 1st Belorussian Front takes Brest-Litovsk on the Russian-Polish border.

August
The Soviets continue to advance eastwards until over-extended supply lines force a halt. From the original start lines of Bagration, the Belorussian and 1st Baltic Fronts make advances of 724km (450 miles). August ends with the Soviet frontline pushed hard up against the Warsaw suburbs in Poland, cutting through East Prussia, and running up to Riga in Latvia.

International Events 1944

June 19th–20th
In the Battle of the Philippine Sea US fighters shoot down 242 Japanese aircraft, losing only 29 in the action. The slaughter of Japanese pilots put paid to the Japanese plans to destroy the US carrier aviation during the US invasion of the Marianas Islands.

June 27th
Cherbourg is liberated from the Germans by the US VI Corps advancing up the Contentin peninsula, France.

July 8th
British and Canadian troops fighting out from Normandy, France, enter the heavily defended city of Caen. Despite having been pounded by RAF bombing raids and Royal Navy artillery, the German defenders of Caen contest every street.

July 17th
Field Marshal Erwin Rommel is severely injured when his staff car is strafed by an RAF fighter in Normandy.

July 24th
Soviet forces liberate the Majdenek concentration camp in Poland, revealing the true horror of the Nazi camps from the first time.

August 1st
Pacific. US forces capture Tinian in the Marianas Islands from the Japanese after a costly nine-day battle.

August 15th
Further amphibious landings in France are made by the US 7th Army at Cannes. The landings meet only minimal resistance.

August 25th
Paris is liberated by the Allies.

Normandy breakout

The Normandy *bocage* favoured German infantry defenders more than Allied armour. Even so, a breakout had to be achieved.

At the end of June 1944 there were many worried men in Whitehall and Washington. These were men whose attention had been concentrated upon the liberation of Europe, and who now suspected that their plans were going awry. On 6 June the Allies had stormed ashore in Normandy, and had secured such apparent success as to raise the hopes and banish all doubts. Now the hopes were lower, the doubts back and growing.

However, there was an exception among these Allied leaders – the man in command of the formations engaged in the fighting. Gen. Sir Bernard Montgomery's confidence provided balm to those who believed in him and was a source of deep annoyance to the many who did not. As early as 11 June, Montgomery had stated that his objective was to draw the greatest possible weight of enemy forces on to the eastern end of the bridgehead, towards Dempsey's forces aimed at Caen. This would weaken the opposition in front of Bradley's forces until the time came when they could break out, first to occupy the Cotentin peninsula, then to cross the Selune river just south of Avranches and release the US 3rd Army, under Lt Gen. George Patton. They would flood out to the west and take the whole of Brittany and the vital ports of Brest, Lorient and

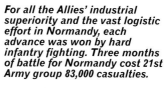

For all the Allies' industrial superiority and the vast logistic effort in Normandy, each advance was won by hard infantry fighting. Three months of battle for Normandy cost 21st Army group 83,000 casualties.

St Nazaire.

Patton's position before 1 August had been somewhat equivocal, for the US VIII Corps under Maj. Gen. Troy Middleton was really a part of Patton's 3rd Army but had been loaned to Bradley's 1st Army for the invasion. This was the corps on the western flank of Cobra which had swept down the coast to take Avranches and cross the Selune. On 28 July Bradley had asked Patton to assume responsibility for VIII Corps area as 'Deputy Army Commander', despite the fact that Patton was not meant to be in Europe and was officially commander of the 3rd Army.

Left: The liberation of Caen. The heavy bomber raid on Caen remains one of the most controversial actions of the Normandy campaign. Here, a British armoured car halts in front of a gigantic bomb crater in the remains of the town.

On 1 August all this changed. Patton was now in undisputed command of four corps (VIII, XIII, XV and XX) containing eight infantry and four armoured divisions. This was under operation orders issued before D-Day, and confirmed by Montgomery on 27 July and by Bradley that morning; his first task was to liberate Brittany and its ports as quickly as possible.

Destination Paris

Instructing the armoured divisions of Middleton's VIII Corps to race straight for Brest, Vannes and Lorient, he turned away from the Atlantic. He directed his attention eastward to the gap between Chartres and Orléans, over 160km (100 miles) away, beyond which lay the Seine and Paris; and Patton purposed to be the first Allied commander to reach the French capital.

By now, XV Corps under Maj. Gen. Haislip was forming south of the Avranches gap to hold enemy pressure off the hinge of Middleton's corps and to protect its left flank. However, as the divisions came up, they faced

Festooned with local camouflage, British Cromwell tanks east of the Orne await the order to advance. Attacking on a narrow front during Operation Goodwood, the British armoured forces were unable to break through the extensive German defences.

east, away from Brittany and towards the heart of France.

Haislip's XV Corps moved first and by 8 August was across the Mayenne and had reached Le Mans; Walker moved on 7 August, took Angers on 11 August, racing forward to cover Haislip's flank towards the Chartres/ Orléans gap, moving at 25–32km (16–20 miles) per day.

There now occurred a slight check on the onward rush. Eyes other than Montgomery's and Patton's were watching strategic developments, and whatever the Wehrmacht generals might prescribe, Hitler was still in command. His eyes were on that narrow gap between Mortain and Avranches, through which all Patton's supplies must be fed. On 4 August, four Panzer divisions of Gen. Paul Hausser's 7th Army struck eastwards through Mortain and were 11.3km (7 miles) on towards Avranches before they were stopped, as Bradley, now commanding the 12th Army Group, sensed the danger and threw in two corps from the US 1st Army.

German strength

There was bitter fighting, but Avranches remained inviolate. Now, two German armies and a Panzergruppe (nearly 100,000 men) were concentrated west of a line running south from Falaise to Alencon, while Dempsey's British and Canadians were a few miles north of Falaise and Haislip's tanks were at Le Mans. It needed no great imagination to see what would happen if they met, and Montgomery was playing it cool when he said 'If we can close the gap completely, we shall have put the enemy in the most awkward predicament.'

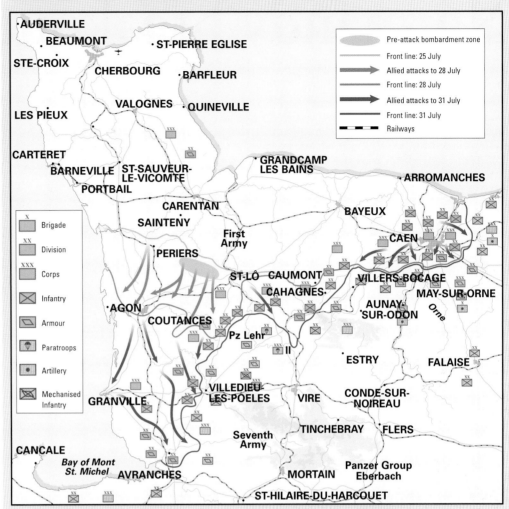

ASSAULT ON FRANCE: OPERATION COBRA

Legend:
- Pre-attack bombardment zone
- Front line: 25 July
- Allied attacks to 28 July
- Front line: 28 July
- Allied attacks to 31 July
- Front line: 31 July
- Railways

Symbols:
- X Brigade
- XX Division
- XXX Corps
- Infantry
- Armour
- Paratroops
- Artillery
- Mechanised Infantry

In 21 days, Patton's 3rd Army had advanced eastward from Avranches 320km (200 miles) to the Seine, and westward 240km (150 miles) to Brest. The Americans succeeded in liberating some 116,550 km² (45,000 square miles) of France, and played a significant part in the destruction of the immense German forces trapped in the Falaise pocket. This was a considerable military achievement by any standards and, in terms of logistics, a classic.

The Falaise Gap was not closed with total effectiveness, though the destruction of German equipment and their loss of some 60,000 men was a severe blow; however, Haislip's XV Corps did reach Argentan on 13 August and could probably have gone on to Falaise had not demarcation lines and poor liaison prevented it.

To the south of them Walker's XX Corps had, by 16 August, reached Chartres, while Patton had fed in his fourth corps (XII Corps under Maj. Gen. Manton S. Eddy) even farther out on the right flank to take Orléans. Around 485km (300 miles) now separated the farthest-flung divisions of Patton's 3rd Army (Middleton's men at Brest and Eddy's at Orléans) and the gap was to widen even further. Haislip's men left Dreux on 16 August and reached Mantes-Gassicourt on 19 August; Walker's XX Corps left Chartres on 16 August to reach Melun and Fontainebleau on 20 August (thus XV and XX Corps cut the Seine both above and below Paris almost simultaneously); and Eddy's XII Corps drove into Sens from Orléans on the afternoon of 21 August.

The Allied advance was often hampered by the desperate resistance of a handful of German troops. A few well-concealed snipers could mean that it took hours, and many casualties, to clear a French village.

Normandy breakout
Chronology

At the beginning of July 1944 the Allied offensive in Normandy was being held by a resolute German defence about 48km (30 miles) inland. Several key Allied operations levered them out of Normandy and almost destroyed the German Army Group B in the Falaise pocket. Thereafter, the Allies could strike towards Paris.

1944

July 7th
British forces renew their attempt to take Caen, this time after the town has been carpet-bombed by the RAF.

July 13th
British and Canadian soldiers enter the outskirts of Caen, but are stopped by surprisingly heavy improvised resistance from the Germans.

July 18th
US forces gradually bring the much-contested town of St Lô under their control. St Lô provides a jumping-off point for assaults out of the southern sector of the Contentin peninsula.

July 18th–20th
The British 2nd Army launches Operation Goodwood. British armoured units strike around the north of Caen and attempt to meet up with the 2nd Canadian Division moving around the south. Goodwood is aimed to capture Caen and move on to Falaise. Though it achieves the former it only advances 8km (5 miles) towards Falaise before the operation is halted on July 20th.

July 24th
The US forces in the Contentin peninsula launch Operation Cobra, an attempt to break through German lines and clear the Allied path through to Avranches at the base of the peninsula

July 30th
The 1st US Army takes Avranches and holds onto it against counter-attack from the German 7th Army.

August 1st
US 3rd Army under General George S. Patton attacks through the Avranches gap and drives for the Loire and into Brittany.

August 4th
German troops of XXX Corps in Brittany, unable to hold up Patton's advance, withdraws into the coastal ports and turn them into siege positions.

August 7th
A German counter-attack towards Avranches captures Mortain and drives about 11km (7 miles) towards Avranches before being halted by Allied artillery and tank-busting air strikes.

August 7th–10th
The 1st Canadian Army commits itself to a major offensive south of Caen, advancing several miles towards Falaise.

August 8th
General Omar Bradley, commander of the 12th US Army, proposes a plan to Montgomery designed to trap 21 divisions of German soldiers in the Falaise-Argentan 'pocket' between Montgomery's 21st Army Group driving south from the Caen front, and Patton's 3rd Army swinging eastwards from Avranches. The plan is accepted.

August 10th–13th
Having reached Le Mans on August 8th, Patton swings his 3rd Army north, reaching Argentan on August 13th.

August 14th
Large sections of the US 3rd Army, at Patton's request, break away from Falaise and begin the drive eastwards towards Chartres and Paris.

August 16th
The Canadians reach Falaise after an arduous week of fighting. German forces around Falaise are finally given Hitler's permission to withdraw out of the steadily closing trap. Away from Falaise, the US 3rd Army reaches Chartres.

August 19th
One division of the US XV Corps crosses the Seine river at Mantes Grassicourt.

August 20th
The open end of the Falaise pocket is closed by US and Canadian forces. Most of the German forces in Normandy are now trapped in an area 9 by 11 km (5.5 by 6.8 miles).

August 22nd
The surviving Germans trapped in the Falaise pocket surrender. Up to 50,000 are taken prisoner and 10,000 have been killed.

August 25th
Paris is reached and liberated by the Allies. Patton's forces secure further bridgeheads on the Seine at Louviers and Elbeuf.

Caen's central railway station, devastated by Allied bombing raids. Over 6000 tons of Allied bombs were dropped on Caen, resulting in the deaths of 5000 civilians. The raids probably hindered more than helped the Allies, filling the streets with tons of rubble and debris.

General George C. Marshall, US Chief of Staff, shakes hands with Brigadier-General Charles de Gaulle, leader of the Free French forces, following the liberation of Paris. De Gaulle walked down the Champs Elysées on 26 August 1944 to a rapturous reception from the Parisian population.

International Events
1944

July 3rd
Minsk is recaptured by Russian forces during the massive offensive in Belorussia codenamed Operation Bagration. The German Army Group Centre is decimated by Bagration in enormous encirclement manoeuvres.

July 20th
Adolf Hitler is injured by a suitcase bomb in an attempted assassination at his HQ in Rastenburg, East Prussia. The bomb had been planted beneath a table in a conference room by Count Claus von Stauffenberg, an aristocratic Wehrmacht officer appalled by German atrocities on the Eastern Front.

July 21st
US forces in the Pacific land on Guam, the southernmost

A group of female 'Axis collaborationists' are rounded up in Cherbourg, have their heads shaved and are publicly humiliated. Such women would effectively become aliens within their own country.

island of the Japanese-occupied Marianas.

July 31st
The Soviet Army draws within 19km (12 miles) of Warsaw. It does not take the city, however, leaving the

Germans to crush a rising of the Polish Home Army in the city who are attempting to take control of Warsaw before the Soviets arrive.

August 10th
Hitler diverts the entire

contingent of Luftwaffe fighter aircraft to the Western Front. Allied air superiority there has stripped the German Army of its armoured advantage.

Death of a city
The Warsaw rising

With the Red Army's guns audible in the distance, the Polish underground rises against the apparently retreating Germans.

During July 1944 the Red Army had swept forward through Belorussia, at times advancing a remarkable 40km (25 miles) per day. By the end of the month the Soviets had taken Brest-Litovsk, to the south of Warsaw they had crossed the Vistula between Magnuszew and Pulawy, and to the northeast they were fighting for the town of Wolomin, less than 16km (10 miles) away. On the evening of 31 July rumours swept Poland's capital that Soviet units were already fighting in the suburbs around Praga on the eastern side of the Vistula.

The Polish Home Army had been in existence as a clandestine force almost since the city had fallen in the late summer of 1939. In Warsaw itself the army consisted of some 38,000 soldiers – 4000 of them women. But there were arms

With metal plates mounted on their sides to protect them against infantry anti-tank rockets, two Sturmgeschütz assault guns lead a German attack on a Polish strongpoint. Against such odds it is remarkable that the Poles managed to hold out for two months.

for only 25 per cent of them, ammunition for a maximum of seven days' fighting, no artillery, no tanks, few vehicles of any sort and, of course, no air force. But they were inspired by the age-old patriotic fire of the Poles, consumed by hatred of the German occupiers – and at this particular moment anxious that when the Soviets entered the city the Poles would be in a position to welcome them as 'master in their own home'. The Polish Home Army and its leaders were loyal to the London-based Polish government in exile, not to the Polish communists led from Moscow.

During the third week of July it had seemed that the Germans had decided to evacuate Warsaw. German stores, workshops, military commands, police and army units were all pulled out, only the military traffic feeding the remaining Vistula river bridgeheads still remaining in evidence. Then Hitler commanded a halt to retreat, Colonel General Heinz Guderian was placed in command, German units flooded back, two SS Panzer divisions and a parachute division closed up to the

In the Old Town, August 1944: a German infantryman watches from the rubble of a building as a Hetzer tank destroyer enters the street. The Poles had enough small arms for about a quarter of their force, and the shortage of anti-tank weapons was even more desperate.

south of the city, and wall posters, street address systems and police patrols all exhorted the Poles to rally to the defence of their capital against the Bolshevik invaders.

Old Town captured

But by this time the decisions had been taken. General Tadeusz Komorowski, codenamed 'Bor', had issued his orders, and at 1700 on 1 August the Polish Home Army in Warsaw struck against the Nazis. The element of surprise helped them, as did the fact that some of the German units and patrols were still in the process of establishing themselves. During that night the Old Town, the City Centre, Powisle along the river between the Poniatowski and Kierbedzia Bridges, Zoliborz in the north, and Mokotow, Sielce and Czerniakow in the south, were all taken over by the Poles while large areas

between became the scene of heavy fighting.

For the next two days the battles in the streets continued, although German strongpoints proved impregnable to the light infantry weapons (and rapidly decreasing stock of ammunition) that were all which the Poles had – though they were buoyed up all the time by the sound of heavy fighting only a few miles away on the other side of the river. They were sure they could hold out until the Red Army arrived.

Then on 3 August the sounds of battle faded, and on 4 August they stopped altogether and the Red air force disappeared from the skies above Warsaw. The Polish Home Army realised it was on its own.

Both Winston Churchill and Franklin D. Roosevelt were appalled. Urgent representations to Stalin were at first ignored, then countered with the announcement that as the Poles had not

The mounting of an anti tank gun with limited traverse on an obsolete tank chassis produced a mobile armoured, anti-tank platform that was much cheaper than a tank. The Germans were one of the first armies to deploy tank destroyers: the Hetzer (pictured) was a 75mm (2.95in) PaK 39 gun on the chassis of the old Panzer 38(t).

As the Germans overran each position any prisoners were usually shot or driven in front of the tanks as a shield for the next assault.

consulted him about their revolt he could take no responsibility for it; anyway, after the enormous efforts of the Red Army throughout July in reaching the Vistula, it was now so exhausted that it could mount no more attacks until rested and resupplied. He also refused permission for American or British aircraft to land on Soviet soil should they attempt to drop ammunition or food into Warsaw and then lack the fuel to return to the Allied lines. It was quite evident that Stalin did not wish any except those he nominated to be 'masters in their own home'.

It is a tribute to Polish valour and endurance that they held out for so long. Hitler's fury at the Polish revolt was such that he ordered the extermination of all of them and the destruction of Warsaw, then handed the execution of his commands to Reichsführer-SS Heinrich Himmler. Reinforcements were rushed to the city by road and rail – police, infantry, a brigade of criminals especially recruited from jails, two brigades of Soviet troops who had defected to the Nazis, all under SS Gruppenführer Erich von dem Bach-Zelewski, an expert in fighting partisan movements.

Burned alive

Aided by tanks, cannon, flamethrowers and Luftwaffe dive-bombers, the Germans inevitably beat the Poles back from their positions. For some time the Poles kept communications going through the sewers. Their spirits were cast down by the lack of outside help, but their determination stayed alive appeared above the city and dropped food and arms: but 'dropped' was literally true, for no parachutes were used so most of the weapons were smashed on landing. It was perhaps the cruellest – certainly the most cynical – of Stalin's reactions to the Polish attempt to preserve some form of democracy.

After two months an armistice was agreed on 2 October and the Home Army laid down its weapons. It is estimated that some 150,000 Poles died during the Rising and German losses are given as 26,000. When the survivors had been marched away and the city completely evacuated, von dem Bach-

Deportation or immediate extinction in the gas chambers awaited the survivors of the battle for Warsaw. The Soviet attack towards the city came too late and their bridgehead over the Vistula, which included pro-communist Polish troops, was overrun.

due to the reports reaching them of German atrocities being committed all around them. Prisoners were shot; doctors, nurses and civilians in the hospitals murdered; and the wounded soaked in petrol and burned alive. Until 16 September no help came to them at all from the Red Army, sitting but 16km (10 miles) away to the east. On that day Soviet aircraft Zelewski's units began their systematic destruction, blowing up or burning whole areas, removing any valuables worth taking to the Reich. When it was complete they turned their faces eastwards again, where the Red Army was now ready to recommence its advance towards Berlin.

Women members of the Jewish resistance. The anti-Semitic policies of the pre-war Polish government were nothing compared with the 'final solution' engineered by the Nazis. The Jewish underground had nothing to lose by 1944 and as the battle progressed, the whole Polish resistance fought with the courage of despair.

Death of a city: Chronology

The Warsaw rising in August 1944 had two aims. First, eject the German occupiers of the city as the Axis headed for defeat. Second, stop the advancing Soviets taking over political control when they arrived at Warsaw's gates.

1944

July

The commander-in-chief of the Polish Home Army, Lieutenant-General Komorowski, makes plans for a rising in Warsaw. On July 26th the Polish Government-in-Exile asks the UK for assistance in the action, though there is little practical help that the British can give apart from provide arms drops on the perimeter of the city. Because of Soviet designs on the city, there will be little help from Stalin.

August 1st

As the Soviet 1st Belorussian Front, 2nd Belorussian Front and 1st Ukrainian Front approach within 32km (20 miles) of Warsaw, Komorowski gives the order for the rising to begin. The Poles have about

German prisoners from a telephone exchange are marched to temporary captivity by their Polish captors.

37,000 men on their side, most poorly armed.

August 1st–20th

Hitler, enraged at the rising, begins to pour German units into the city, building up a force of 21,300 soldiers by August 20th. The German forces are under SS command.

August 4th

The Polish Home Army, outgunned and outclassed by the Germans, appeals directly to the Allies for assistance.

August 11th

The Pope himself implores the Allies to intervene quickly in the Warsaw rising. He expresses deep concerns that the Russians are holding back from entering the city because they want the Germans to crush the uprising and leave the political road open. The Russians are now 19km (12 miles) from the Warsaw suburbs.

US bombers drop weapons containers over Warsaw, the parachutes opening out in the slipstream. Because the Soviets almost entirely denied the other Allies use of their air fields, the attempts to resupply the Warsaw uprising were extremely limited.

August 16th

Stalin formally refuses to supply aid to the Polish Home Army and other partisan units in Warsaw. He describes the rising as a 'reckless, appalling adventure' and berates the Polish insurgents

German soldiers fire a salute over the graves of comrades killed during the Warsaw uprising. The Red Army entered Warsaw from the east on 17 October, just over two weeks after the collapse of the uprising which the Soviets had watched only 19km (12 miles) from the Warsaw suburbs.

for not informing the Soviets of their intentions. Soviet troops are now only 9.6km (6 miles) away from Warsaw at Ossow.

August 20th
The Polish forces in Warsaw are by now broken up into three isolated regions of the city, and the Germans begin a move towards a final counter-offensive.

August 25th
German forces begin a major counter-offensive against the Warsaw insurgents. The operation is conceived and commanded by SS Obergruppenführer Erich von dem Bach-Zelewski.

September 16th
Stalin makes a pathetic airdrop of arms – two machine guns and 50 pistols – to the Warsaw insurgents. The nominal contribution comes after constant pressure from the British and Americans to assist the Polish action.

September 18th
A single flight of US B-17 bombers on a resupply mission to Warsaw are allowed to refuel at Poltava, a Soviet conquest, before proceeding with their mission. Apart from this incident,

Stalin refuses British and US aircraft flying from Foggia, Italy, to use Soviet forward air bases. The B-17s drop their supplies to the Poles on September 25th, but the containers fall straight into German hands.

September 16th–21st
A force of soldiers from the 1st Polish Army fighting under the Soviets attempts to reach and assist the Warsaw insurgents, crossing the Vistula towards the outskirts of the city but being beaten off by a heavy German defence. The commander of the Poles, Lieutenant-Colonel Zygmunt Berling, is stripped of his command of the Army, for going against the Soviet orders.

September 30th
All parts of Warsaw except sectors of the Central District are now in the hands of German forces.

October 2nd
Komorowski orders the remaining insurgents in Warsaw to surrender to the Germans. Nearly 250,000 of the city's inhabitants would die in the aftermath of the

rising, victims of Nazi reprisals or deportations to the concentration camp at Pruszkow.

International Events

August 1st–16th
Allied forces begin their breakout from Normandy, the US 3rd Army cutting south through the Avranches gap, while British, Canadian and US forces further push German units out into a pocket between Falaise and Argentan.

August 1st
US forces capture Tinian in the Marianas Islands.

August 10th
Guam falls to the US forces in the Pacific, bringing all of the Marianas Islands under US control.

August 21st
Over 50,000 German soldiers fall into Allied hands in France after being encircled in the 'Falaise pocket'. Another 10,000 soldiers had been killed during Operation Totalize, the action to cut off

the Germans in the Falaise-Argentan region.

August 25th
Paris is liberated by the advancing Allies.

September 11th
US forces begin to cross into Germany around Trier and advance towards Aachen.

September 17th
The Allies launch Operation Market Garden, an attempt to capture a series of key bridges across the Lower Rhine using British and US airborne forces ahead of the main Allied advance.

Operation Market Garden:

The Battle for Arnhem

In September 1944 the Allies staged the greatest airborne assault of the war, taking vital bridges on the road to Germany.

On 17 September 1944 south-east England witnessed the assembly of the greatest airborne armada of all time. From 22 airfields, over 1500 aircraft climbed into the air. As the fighter and bomber units sped away on their protection or distraction tasks, Dakota transports and Stirling bombers, converted for troop-carrying, formed up for their journeys to Holland.

One stream made for their dropping zone at Eindhoven; these held the men and equipment of the US 101st Airborne Division. The second, larger, stream carried the US 82nd Airborne Division towards the area between Grave and Nijmegen, and the Air Landing Brigade and one Parachute Brigade of the British 1st Airborne Division (commanded by Maj. Gen. Urquhart) to landing grounds 16km (10 miles) to the west of Arnhem and its vital Neder Rijn bridge.

The bridge and four other bridges to the south at Nijmegen, Grave, Veghel and Eindhoven were the objectives for these airborne forces. Farther to the south waited forward troops of the British 2nd Army, poised to hurl forward along the Eindhoven-

MARKET GARDEN: ASSAULT ON THE BRIDGES

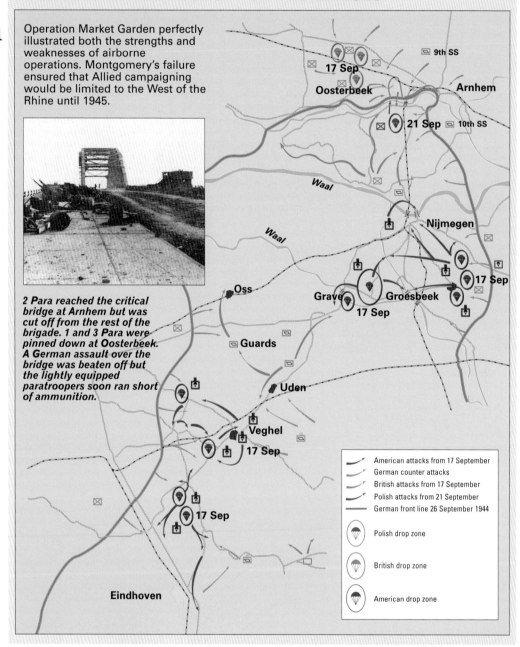

Operation Market Garden perfectly illustrated both the strengths and weaknesses of airborne operations. Montgomery's failure ensured that Allied campaigning would be limited to the West of the Rhine until 1945.

2 Para reached the critical bridge at Arnhem but was cut off from the rest of the brigade. 1 and 3 Para were pinned down at Oosterbeek. A German assault over the bridge was beaten off but the lightly equipped paratroopers soon ran short of ammunition.

American attacks from 17 September
German counter attacks
British attacks from 17 September
Polish attacks from 21 September
German front line 26 September 1944

Polish drop zone

British drop zone

American drop zone

Arnhem road and across all the canals and rivers between, outflanking the German defences of the Siegfried Line. They would thus form, in the words of Field Marshal Montgomery, "a springboard for a powerful full-blooded thrust to the heart of Germany".

What Allied planners had not appreciated was that the Germans were using the area to rest first-line divisions. In addition to local forces, the lightly armed paratroops would come up against the 9th and 10th SS Panzer Divisions and the headquarters of Generalfeldmarschall Model's Army Group 'B'.

Twelve converted British bombers and six American C-47s carried the Pathfinder company, which completed its work by the time 149 Dakotas carrying the men of 1st Parachute Brigade arrived over Dropping Zone X. This was also the case for Landing Zones S and Z, where 254 Horsa and 38 Hamilcar gliders of the Air Landing Brigade and Urquhart's headquarters were released. From the entire force only five gliders were hit or the tows cut during the journeys, and only 35 were lost.

Heading for the bridge

Nevertheless, the first troop movements were slow to begin. It was 1530 before Lt Col Frost had assembled the men of his 2nd Parachute Battalion and led them off on their 13km (8 mile) march to the Arnhem Bridge.

Halfway to Arnhem, Frost was about to detach one company to capture the rail bridge over the Neder Rijn when a loud explosion revealed that the bridge had been blown. The British paratroops pressed on, although it was dark by the time Frost and his men reached Arnhem Bridge.

Meanwhile, Urquhart was facing another severe difficulty: his signal sets were not working. In order to find out what was happening, Urquhart set out after his paratroops by jeep.

He found Frost's HQ close to the Rhine bank, then turned back towards Oosterbeek. There, Urquhart found Lt Col Fitch's 3rd

Hampered by defective radio sets and the absence of tactical air support, the paratroops could only hold on and hope for a XXX Corps breakthrough.

Battalion (heavily engaged with German troops) and the commander of 1st Parachute Brigade, Brigadier Lathbury.

It was now evident that Panzer units were coming into position between 3rd Battalion and Arnhem, as they were also between Lt Col Dobie's 1st Parachute Battalion working its way along the railway running into Arnhem from the west.

German units were being fed into the gap between Frost's men at the bridge and all possible reinforcements. Even when the 4th Parachute Brigade under Brigadier Hackett arrived the following afternoon, it could only fight its way forward to join the remnants of 1st and 3rd Battalions. Over the next two days, the separate battles raged with ever-increasing ferocity, the advantage moving to the Germans due to dwindling British numbers and ammunition.

By 20 September it was all

over at the bridge. Frost had been wounded, the Germans had shelled every building the paratroops had occupied, and the Panzers moved inexorably across the bridge. German infantry closed in to take the few survivors prisoner.

Rescue attempt

Spirits were raised briefly on 22 September, when the Polish 1st Airborne Brigade under Gen. Sosabowski was dropped just south of the river, but the ferries had been destroyed and every attempt by the Poles to go to the rescue of the British came under fire from both banks.

The men had been told that they would be relieved within four days; in the event they were on their own for nine days. Three battalions of the 43rd Division reached the southern bank of the river,

and men of the 5th Dorsets crossed to bring help to the paratroops still holding on, and the following afternoon their evacuation was organized.

That night XXX Corps artillery put down a devastating curtain of fire around the perimeter. The glider pilots of the Air Landing Brigade taped out an escape route and guided their comrades down to the bank where British and Canadian engineers waited in assault boats which had been rushed up from Nijmegen.

Market Garden was a good idea defeated by lack of information of enemy dispositions around Arnhem, by the weather which had contributed to XXX Corps' delay, and by mistaken planning which had dropped 1st Airborne Division too far from its objective.

British Army cameramen of the Parachute Brigade share food with a Dutch woman at Oosterbeek. The Dutch underground smuggled many British soldiers to Allied lines after Market Garden's failure.

Below: The British glider landings of 17 September entailed considerable risk but were the only way of providing lightly-armed airborne soldiers with anti-tank guns, jeeps and heavy supplies.

Bottom: Dutch SS battalions offered light resistance, but opposition was stiffened by Panzer troops. Arnhem was the HQ of Field Marshal Model, who improvised a defence until reinforcements arrived.

Operation Market Garden
Chronology

Operation Market Garden was the Allied attempt to establish a bridgehead across the lower Rhine at Arnhem, and expedite the advance into Germany. The furthest airborne operation at Arnhem, however, was too far for Allied reinforcements to reach and relieve.

1944

September 10th

The supreme commander of Allied forces in Europe, General Eisenhower, gives his approval to Operation Market Garden, conceived and designed by Field Marshal Montgomery. An airborne deployment is intended to capture key bridges at Eindhoven, Veghel, Grave, Nijmegen and Arnhem, and hold them until the British XXX Corps, advancing 152km (95 miles) up from the Meuse-Escaut canal, can relieve them.

British paratroopers and Dutch civilians meet around Arnhem. The British Parachute Regiment was formed in 1941 in response to German successes in using parachute deployments over western Europe and the Balkans.

September 17th

Operation Market Garden is launched using the British 1st Airborne Division, the US 82nd Airborne Division, and the US 101st Airborne Division. Parachute drops take place near Eindhoven, Veghel, Grave and Oosterbeek. The US landings around Eindhoven and Veghel (US 101st Airborne Division) and Grave (US 82nd Airborne Division) are successful and all bridge objectives are captured, but the British landing near Arnhem runs into heavy resistance from the 9th and 10th SS Panzer Divisions which are refitting in the area. The 2nd Battalion manages to capture the bridge at Arnhem, but is immediately cut off and surrounded by German forces.

US troops of the 82nd Airborne Division aboard a C-47 transport aircraft in England, heavily burdened with parachutes, radios and weapons, wait to be transported to their drop zone in Holland. Each C-47 Skytrain could carry a total of 27 fully armed paratroopers.

September 18th

The British XXX Corps links up with the 101st Airborne at Eindhoven and Veghel after tortuous progress up the main Eindhoven road under intense German resistance.

September 19th

British XXX Corps joins the US 82nd Airborne Division at Grave at 8.20am.

German prisoners captured a few minutes after British gliders had landed outside Arnhem on 17 September 1944. After recovering from the initial shock of the landing, the Germans resisted strongly.

September 20th
Reinforced by the British XXX Corps, the US 82nd Airborne makes assaults against the bridge over the river Waal at Nijmegen, even sending a battalion across the river in small assault boats. Once Nijmegen bridge is taken, a delay prevents the XXX Corps commencing its advance towards Arnhem for another 24 hours.

September 21st
Under major German counter-attacks the British paras at Arnhem relinquish their hold on Arnhem bridge and begin a vigorous fight for survival in Arnhem town. The XXX Corps advance is held up by German artillery and anti-tank defences just north of Nijmegen.

September 22nd
The Polish Parachute Brigade drops just south of Arnhem in support of the British 1st Airborne Division.

September 25th
Survivors of the 1st Airborne Division at Arnhem make a retreat across the Neder Rijn river in an attempt to reach the XXX Corps still short of the city. Just over 2200 men manage to escape, leaving behind them 6000 prisoners and 1000 dead.

September 27th
The remaining British and Polish troops in Arnhem surrender to the Germans. US forces beneath Arnhem continue to hold the front against the Germans, suffering over 3500 casualties during the next two months of fighting.

International Events 1944

September 17th
Adolf Hitler suffers a mild heart attack.

September 19th
The UK Prime Minster Winston Churchill and US President Franklin Roosevelt reach agreements about the use of atomic power after a three-day conference. The agreements include the possibility of dropping an atomic weapon on Japan.

September 21st
The Italian town of Rimini falls to Canadian and Greek forces after a month of combat.

September 22nd
Soviet forces under Marshal Govorov capture the Estonian capital, Tallinn. The victory is important as Tallinn provided a final seaward escape route for the retreating German Army Group North.

September 22nd
US Navy carrier aircraft make their first-day raid on the Philippines, bombing Japanese airfields at Luzon and near Manila.

September 24th
Soviet forces advancing from Czechoslovakia push some 32km (20 miles) into German-occupied Poland.

The last Blitzkrieg
The Ardennes offensive

16 December 1944: to the astonishment of the Allies, the Germans launch a major offensive through the apparently impenetrable Ardennes forest.

By mid-December 1944 the main bulk of the Allied forces was concentrated (as were the attentions of the Allied high command) towards both ends of the Western Front. In the north the Anglo-Canadian armies had at last cleared Antwerp and opened the Scheldt estuary, and the US First and Ninth Armies were set to close up to the lower Rhine and threaten the vital Roer dams. In the south Lieutenant General George Patton's US Third Army, after its spectacular drive across France, was poised to sweep through the equally important Saar region towards the Rhine at Mannheim.

Between the two powerful groupings were strung out some 80,000 American troops along 145km (90 miles) of front, the bulk of them consisting of Major General Troy Middleton's VIII Corps, which had been brought across from Brittany, backed by one armoured division, the 9th, which had but lately arrived in the area and had not yet seen action. They were there because this part of the front, the Ardennes section, was a quiet part, covered in the front by the sparsely settled German Schnee Eifel, and behind by the steep wooded hills and foaming trout streams that had always been regarded as unsuitable for open warfare.

'Wacht am Rhein'

The Americans were thus considerably shaken when at 0530 on the morning of 16 December they were suddenly deluged by the heaviest artillery bombardment that even the veterans among them had experienced, and when they peered out into the pre-dawn murk, they found themselves overrun by German shock troops surging forward through their positions, followed closely by powerful Panzer and Panzergrenadier units, many of them bearing the jagged double streak of the Waffen-SS.

Even as the fighting in the Falaise Gap had been ending, Hitler had announced that by November a force of some 25 divisions

The overcast skies deprived the Allies of close air support, and made the role of the artillery doubly important. The M7 105mm (4.13in) self-propelled gun was the first fully tracked self-propelled gun introduced by the US Army and was widely used by British forces.

must be prepared to launch a huge counter-offensive against the Anglo-American armies; and to the astonishment of the German high command that force had come into existence, conjured from every corner of German life: rear-area administrative echelons, 16-year-old boys, civil servants, small shopkeepers, university students and the scourings of the prisons had all been swept into the armed services.

Thus had been formed three German armies, and they were, by mid-December, marshalled under an exemplary cloak of secrecy and subterfuge opposite the US VIII Corps. In the north were poised the units of the Sixth SS Panzer Army under SS-Oberstgruppenführer Sepp Dietrich, erstwhile commander of Hitler's personal bodyguard in the streetfighting days and later of the crack 'Liebstandarte Adolf Hitler'. In the middle section of the attack front waited the Fifth Panzer Army under the trusted army General Hasso von Manteuffel. And on the southern flank of the attack to form the 'hard shoulder' against any possible northward countermove by formations of the US Third Army was the Seventh Army under the dogged but unimaginative General Erich Brandenberger.

Altogether some 200,000 men would take part in Operation Wacht am Rhein (Watch on the Rhine), and in addition to those more or less conventional fighting divisions, there waited in the rear 1250 paratroops under Colonel von der Heydte, a veteran of Crete, to drop in front of the main assault, seize bridges and crossroads, and attack any headquarter organisations they could find. Moreover, to help them spread alarm and despondency, the famous raiding commander SS-Sturmbannführer Otto Skorzeny commanded a special force of volunteers driving American vehicles and wearing American uniforms, a ploy that would result in their being shot if they fell into Allied hands.

The objective for this surreptitiously assembled force was Antwerp, plus the splitting of the Allied armies threatening the German frontier, the annihilation of the Anglo-Canadian armies and the US First and Ninth Armies alongside them by starvation as their main supply port was captured, and an immense morale boost for the German public together with such a shock to the Allies that the consequent bickering between them would wreck their future strategic planning for

Sgt Manfred Pernass, aged 23, faces a US firing squad after being captured in American uniform. The US rear areas were raided by English-speaking German troops in Allied uniforms under the command of the redoubtable Otto Skorzeny.

Adopted by the US Army in 1932, the .30 calibre M1 Garand was the first self-loading rifle to enter military service as a standard weapon. Fed by an eight-round clip, it was robust and reliable.

The German Gewehr 43 7.92-mm (0.31in) rifle was a self-loading weapon that fired full-power rifle rounds but was only in limited service on the Western Front. A telescopic sight mount was fitted as standard and many were used as sniper rifles.

Very heavily armoured and carrying an 8.8cm (3.46in) gun, the King Tiger was the most powerful German tank of World War II. This tank was captured on the Stavelot road after German logistic arrangements had broken down and the dejected crew surrendered.

weeks and possibly months.

Leading elements of the 1st SS Panzer Division under their ruthless leader, Colonel Joachim Peiper, swept through a gap in American lines to Honsfeld in the north, captured a large petrol dump at Büllingen and then caught American troops on the move at Malmédy crossroads before racing on towards Stavelot. Unfortunately for all parties concerned, his men, inured to the bitter fighting on the Eastern Front, shot down 19 American prisoners at Honsfeld, 50 at Büllingen and nearly 100 at Malmédy, a piece of barbarism that defeated itself; when rumour of the massacres swept through the embattled American positions it produced feelings of both fury and desperation and caused even the greenest units, sometimes commanded by only junior NCOs, to fight with a committed ferocity that baulked the important German thrust to the south.

One of von Manteuffel's spearheads had success similar to Peiper's, but without that ruthlessness, and reached the village of Auw just in front of the vital road junction of St Vith, but here it ran into the tank destroyers and main artillery of an American infantry division, which held them, forcing the main drive of von Manteuffel's army south into the gap between St Vith and the other vital road junction, Bastogne.

And it was here that the attentions of both attackers and defenders became concentrated. It was Lieutenant General Omar Bradley's 12th Army Group which caught the offensive in its central section, and at first Bradley wrote it off as merely a spoiling attack to disrupt the First Army's threat to the Roer in the north and the Third Army's to the Saar in the south; but he soon realised that it was more than that. On 19 December he ordered Lieutenant General Courtney Hodges in the north to swing some of his First Army divisions back to hold a flank

and then drive down to St Vith, and Patton to do the same in the south and send his crack 4th Armored Division up to relieve Bastogne: with an efficiency that compels the greatest admiration Patton swung the bulk of his army through 90° in 48 hours.

In the meantime, General Dwight D. Eisenhower had released his reserves and they sped to the two vital points in every truck and jeep they could find: the 82nd and 101st Airborne Divisions, recovered from their recent battles at Nijmegen and Eindhoven, raced north from Patton's lines, the 101st dropping off to begin its famous stand at Bastogne and the 82nd passing on to St Vith. The battle now was becoming one of mobility, and that game the Americans knew how to play.

Panthers in the snow

As von Manteuffel's spearheads probed farther west (they never crossed the Meuse, though the 11th Panzer Division nearly reached Dinant), US tank

destroyers and artillery shored up the flanks of the penetration while their infantry fought doggedly forward into the gaps or held on grimly in isolated positions. For most of the time, moreover, they fought without air cover, for the weather favoured the Germans for days on end. But by 25 December, after some of the bitterest fighting seen in Europe, the sting had been drawn from the German onslaught: von Manteuffel mounted a last desperate attack on Bastogne, but it was beaten off and on the following day Patton's tanks arrived to break the siege.

Meanwhile, Field Marshal Montgomery had taken command of the northern flank and in order to 'tidy up the battlefield' he authorised a withdrawal from the St Vith salient, and brought the British 29th Armoured Brigade down on the US right flank to hold the deepest penetration. When on the following day the whole of the US 2nd Armored Division came down to join them, Hitler's last offensive in the west was brought to a halt.

The GIs in the front line displayed a dogged courage in resisting the German onslaught. Hot food was essential but not always possible during the battle. This photograph was taken early in January 1944 after the Germans had been pushed back onto the retreat.

The last Blitzkrieg
Chronology

The Ardennes campaign was Hitler's ill-conceived plan to break the Allied advance on the Western front and rescue Germany from defeat. The aim of the offensive was to cut through the Allied frontline in the Ardennes and drive through to Antwerp. Hitler hoped that the offensive would split the British and US forces in northern Europe, and deprive them of crucial supplies through Antwerp.

1944

December 16th
Four German armies – the 15th, 6th SS, 5th Panzer, and 7th – assault the US VIII Corps between Bastogne and Aachen. Good progress is made in the centre of the attack, but in the north the US 2nd and 99th Divisions hold the German advances at Elsenborn and Malmédy.

December 16th–23rd
Crucially for the progress of the offensive, the weather in this period is extremely poor with low cloud cover. This prevents Allied air forces utilising their air supremacy against the German offensive.

December 17th
Soldiers of the 6th SS Panzer Army massacre 87 US prisoners of war at Malmédy under the direct orders of Colonel Joachim Peiper.

December 19th
Two regiments of the US 106th Division are encircled in the Schnee Eifel region. Over 6000 men are forced to surrender. Elsewhere, however, US forces make a valiant resistance and even go on the counter-offensive. The town of Stavelot on the northern flank of the offensive was lost to the Germans on the 17th, but recaptured on the 19th.

Tanks of the 9th US Army struggle with the appalling climate conditions of northern Europe in winter. Hitler deliberately selected winter as the moment for the Ardennes offensive because the Allies would not be expecting an offensive under such conditions.

Troops of the 6th Panzer Army advance during Operation Wacht am Rhein. In total the Germans managed to muster 950 tanks for the Ardennes offensive.

Generals of the 101st Airborne Division review the positions of their division at Bastogne. The 101st went down in history for holding onto Bastogne for a week while completely encircled by five German divisions.

December 19th
At a conference of Allied tacticians – including Eisenhower, Bradley and Patton – the decision is taken to transfer six US divisions from the Saar front to attack the southern flank of the German offensive between Bastogne and Echternach.

December 20th
The US 101st Airborne Division along with the US 19th and 10th Armored Divisions are completely encircled by the German XLVII Panzer Corps at Bastogne. Montgomery is given command of the Allies' northern defence and Bradley command of the southern defence.

December 22nd
The German offensive is developing chronically over-exposed flanks. Rundstedt suggests to Hitler that the offensive is cancelled, but Hitler refuses the suggestion.

December 23rd
The weather clears over the Ardennes. Allied ground-attack aircraft and bombers

immediately unleash heavy firepower on the German infantry and armour. Over 2000 sorties are flown on December 23rd alone. Air supply flights to Bastogne maintain the Allies' siege defence there.

December 25th
The 2nd Panzer Division under Lieutenant-General von Lauchert reaches the furthest point of advance near Dinant, 97km (60 miles) from the start line of the offensive. Here it is stopped by the British 29th Armoured Brigade and the American 2nd Armored Division. On Christmas Day it loses over 3500 men and 400 vehicles, including 81 tanks.

December 26th
Bastogne is finally relieved by the Allies as the US 4th Armored Division cuts a narrow path through to the town.

December 28th
The Ardennes offensive has been hammered on all fronts, with huge losses in men in armour and chronic shortages of supplies, particularly

vehicle fuel. In ambiguous terms Hitler calls off the offensive, declaring himself satisfied with the progress made to date. He does not, however, withdraw his forces and leaves them to perform a futile defensive action.

February 7th
All gains made by German forces during the Ardennes offensive have been reversed with the loss of 82,000 German soldiers and 77,000 US casualties.

International Events 1944
December 16th
Over 560 people are killed by a V2 rocket in Antwerp after the missile struck a cinema containing 1200 people.

December 20th
British troops rescue 350 British military personnel

from Greek ELAS communist fighters at Kifissia near Athens. Though Greece has been liberated from the Germans, nationalist and communist forces are locked in a violent power struggle.

December 24th
In reprisal for an attack by the French resistance, German SS units kill all adult males in the village of Bande.

December 25th
Japanese forces begin to pull out of the Philippine island of Luzon after heavy US attacks and the collapse of Japanese naval supply routes.

December 31st
The provisional government of Hungary, set up under Soviet control on December 22nd, declares war on Germany.

Storming into Germany

The Battle of the Rhine

March 1945: the Allied armies are poised along the banks of the Rhine river, the last barrier protecting the Reich itself.

In February 1945 the task for the Canadian army in the north, the British army next to it, the four US armies stretching down to Strasbourg and the French army in the Vosges, was to cross the Roer, Our and Saar rivers and reach the Rhine.

By 21 February, Goch, Cleve and Calcar were in British and Canadian hands, and to the south the US Ninth Army could launch Operation Grenade and fling bridges across the Roer opposite Mönchen Gladbach, which they took on 1 March. Five days later Cologne was in American hands and on 7 March, to the astonishment of the Allies and to Hitler's inexpressible fury, the Remagen Bridge over the Rhine had been taken, apparently undamaged, and was in use by the US First Army. Fortunately auxiliary bridges were thrown across, both up- and down-stream from Remagen, during the days that followed. This meant that when on 17 March, weakened by bombing and heavy usage, the whole bridge fell sideways into the Rhine – taking 28 US engineers to their deaths – at least the disaster did not cut off the bridgehead on the east bank from all supplies.

By 24 March over 150,000 more German soldiers found themselves in Allied PoW camps, and a large but unknown number had been killed. By the end of the month the west bank of the Rhine from the Channel to the Swiss border was in Allied hands, and thus the Allies were now only 485km (300 miles) from Berlin.

On the night of 23 March 1945 Field Marshal Sir Bernard Montgomery's 21st Army Group began crossing under a barrage from all of the artillery weapons that had been assembled. The first troops went across in Buffaloes with numbers of DD Shermans and other special vehicles in train. Air support was so intense that Wesel itself was confidently bombed by RAF Bomber Command when Allied troops were only a few hundred yards away. This not only cleared Wesel of the enemy but prevented the Germans from moving through the town to counter-attack.

Intense fire

The Allies did not have it all their own way. The mud was so bad in places that not even the Buffaloes could make much forward progress, with the result that some of the second assault waves, crossing in boats, came under intense fire and took heavy casualties.

The main assault arrived at about midday when the

Men of the Dorset Regiment cross the Rhine in their amphibious tracked personnel carrier, known as a Buffalo. Although lightly armoured and petrol-engined, the Buffalo was highly successful. If light resistance was encountered, the type's availability in numbers allowed the attackers to expand the bridgehead quickly.

first of the Allied airborne forces came into sight. What became known as the 'armada of the air' flew over the Rhine to disgorge two divisions of parachute troops who seemed at times to make the sky dark with their numbers. They were soon followed by glider tugs that unleashed their charges to land in an area known as the

Diersfordter Wald and another known as the Mehr-Hamminkeln. These glider troops did not land unscathed. Despite all efforts of the Allied air forces to neutralise flak sites near the landing points, some guns escaped to concentrate their fire power on the gliders, and about one quarter of all glider pilots involved became casualties in this operation. The numbers that did land safely were such that the airborne forces and the troops that had made the river crossings were able to join up, often well in advance of the anticipated times. By nightfall the Rhine bridgeheads were secure and despite some localised German counter attacks they were across the river to stay.

American crossings

Attempts to cross by the American armies along the more southern stretches of the Rhine, although mounted by fewer men with smaller resources, were just as successful. One had occurred the day before the 21st Army Group launched the main crossing – south of Mainz between Nierstein and Oppenheim by an assault regiment of the US 5th

The final result may have been inevitable and German resistance weakening, but the infantry still had to fight their way forward. The last battles on the west bank of the Rhine involved bitter fighting in close country. Thick mud made it a very disagreeable business.

BREWING UP: MARCH 1945

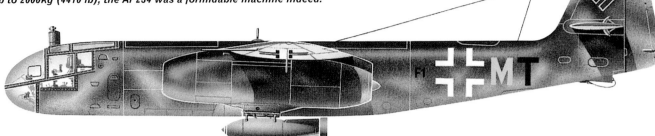

The bridge at Remagen was subjected to the first all-jet bombing raids in history as Arado Ar 234 aircraft swooped out of the low clouds escorted by Messerschmitt Me 262 jet fighters. The single-seat Ar 234 was also used for high-speed reconnaissance flights over the UK. With a top speed of 740kmh (460mph) and a bomb load of up to 2000kg (4410 lb), the Ar 234 was a formidable machine indeed.

Division – part of XII Corps of the Third Army – under command, needless to say, of Lieutenant General George S. Patton.

The divisional commander, Major General Leroy Irwin, made some small protest about the shortness of time

artillery support of a group that later complained that it could find little in the way of worthwhile targets. The first Americans to land captured seven German soldiers who promptly volunteered to paddle their assault boat back for them, and although

them. By the evening of 23 March the entire 5th Division was across the river, a bridgehead formed and awaiting the arrival of an armoured division already on the west bank.

During the next few days crossings were made at Boppard and St Goar, Worms and Mainz, and by the end of the month Darmstadt and Wiesbaden were in US hands and armoured columns were driving for Frankfurt-am-Main and Aschaffenburg beyond; farther south, the French had put an Algerian division across near Germersheim. Now a huge Allied bridge-head could be formed from Bonn down to Mannheim, from which would be launched the last Western offensive designed to meet the Soviets on the Elbe and split Germany in two. The main objective for the US 12th Army Group would be the industrial region of Leipzig and Dresden.

The Luftwaffe was ordered to make up for the army's failure to demolish the Remagen bridge, and mounted a series of intense bombing raids. Here, two M3 half-tracks armed with quadruple .50 cal machine guns wait, in the March drizzle, for German attackers.

he was given for preparation, but in the face of Patton's urgency he sent the first wave of assault boats across the 360m (1180-ft) wide river just before midnight, under a brilliant moon and the

later waves ran into sporadic machine-gun fire the regiment was across before midnight and moving towards the east-bank villages, with support regiments flooding across behind

German infantryman 1945: Although facing overwhelming odds, the German army fought with incredible professionalism into the spring of 1945, long after defeat had become wholly inevitable. This SS trooper has a fully automatic 7.92mm (0.31in) Sturmgewehr 44, the ancestor of modern assault rifles.

Drive northwards

To the north, the Anglo-Canadian 21st Army Group was to drive north towards Hamburg, its left flank (the Canadians) clearing Holland of the Germans and then driving along the coast through Emden and Wilhelmshaven, its right flank (US Ninth Army) curving around the Ruhr to meet Lieutenant General Courtney Hodges's US First Army formations at Lippstadt, thus encircling Field Marshal Walter Model's Army Group B in the Ruhr. After Hamburg the British would

reach the Elbe down as far as Magdeburg, and send other forces up into Schleswig-Holstein and the Baltic.

There was some argument as to the desirability of 21st Army Group racing for Berlin, but General Dwight D. Eisenhower, solidly supported by Roosevelt, felt that the German capital was in easier reach of the Soviets who – Roosevelt was sure – would prove both co-operative and amenable in regard to post-war European responsibilities. Stalin would doubtless have been amused had he learned of the arguments.

Frankenthal, 26 March 1945: men of the 3rd Division's 7th Infantry Regiment arrive on the east bank during the US Seventh Army's assault over the Rhine. The subsequent advance towards Saxony dictated the position occupied by US troops after World War II.

Storming into Germany
Chronology

By January 1945 the Red Army stood on the Vistula, having driven German forces out of Soviet territory. The next stage was the push into Germany itself and reach the Oder less than 80km (50 miles) from Berlin.

1945

January 6th
British Prime Minister Winston Churchill sends a telegram to Joseph Stalin requesting that the Soviet offensive into Germany is launched within January to aid the Allied advance in the West. The offensive was originally planned for January 20th, but Stalin brings forward the launch date to January 12th.

January 12th–14th
Soviet forces launch a huge offensive – the biggest of WWII – against the German Army Group A and Army Group Centre in East Prussia and Poland. The main Soviet thrust is made by the 1st, 2nd and 3rd Belorussian Fronts, the 1st Baltic Front and the 1st Ukrainian Front. The front of attack runs from the coast of Lithuania down to the Balkans.

January 14th
The Soviet assault makes tremendous advances in the first days and begins to press against the defences of East Prussia.

January 16th
Hitler issues orders to transfer the Grossdeutschland Panzer Corps from Army Group Centre to Army Group A. His intention is to make a flanking attack against the Soviet drive on Poznan, but all it achieves is depriving East Prussia of much needed defensive manpower.

January 17th
Warsaw is taken by the Soviet 47th Army after a major encirclement operation. Further north, the Soviet forces are already fighting in East Prussia, moving strongly towards the coastline from Danzig to Königsberg.

January 20th
In a futile attempt to stem the tide of the Soviet advance, Hitler transfers the 6th SS Panzer Army from the Ardennes to Budapest, Hungary.

January 22nd
Konev's 1st Ukrainian Front reaches the Oder and crosses it at Steinau.

January 25th
Hitler renames his forces. Army Group Centre becomes Army Group North. Army Group A is renamed Army Group Centre. A new Army Group, Vistula, is created and charged with the defence of Pomerania and northern Poland.

February 1st
The advance to Berlin of Marshal Zhukov's 1st Belorussian Front is stalled by a determined German resistance at Krustin.

February 3rd
Zhukov's 1st Belorussian Front joins Konev's forces on the Oder, though Küstrin

German civilian labourers watch flights of Allied aircraft heading to bomb targets east of the Rhine in March 1945. Air combat continued over Germany until the very end of hostilities in Europe.

remains in German hands. The Russian front on the river now extends from Zehden, 80km (50 miles) south of Stettin, down to the Czech border.

February 5th
Russian forces begin crossing the Oder and pushing deeper into German territory.

February 15th
Breslau is encircled by Soviet troops, though the city will hold out against the Soviets until the end of the war.

February 22nd
Poznan on the Warsaw–Berlin main axis falls to the 1st Belorussian Front after German forces held out in an isolated pocket behind the main Russian advance.

February 24th
Lower Silesia is now in the hands of Konevís 1st Ukrainian Front.

March 16th
The Soviet 2nd and 3rd Ukrainian Fronts begin their assault along the Danube through Hungary and into Austria towards Vienna.

March 31st
By now the Soviet frontline has pushed deeply into

Germany. It runs along the Oder from Stettin in Pomerania to Küstrin only 80km (50 miles) from Berlin itself and down to Görlitz about 96km (60 miles) east of Dresden. The Soviets prepare themselves for the final assault on Berlin.

International Events 1945

January 15th
Allied forces in western Europe begin a counter-attack following the collapse of the German Ardennes offensive.

January 27th
The Soviet forces advancing through Poland liberate the Auschwitz concentration camp.

February 11th
A meeting of President Roosevelt, Joseph Stalin and Winston Churchill in Yalta, Crimea, decides on how a defeated Germany will be divided and governed. The UK, US, Soviet Union and France are each to govern separate zones of occupation.

February 16th
Pacific theatre. US forces make landings on the island of Corregidor during the advance through the Philippines.

British troops enter the town of Brünen in Germany after crossing the Rhine river. The Allies in the West crossed the Elbe and closed to within 100km (60 miles) of Berlin before being ordered to stop so that the Soviets alone could take Berlin.

March 6th
Hitler launches a futile operation to recapture Budapest from Soviet forces. Operation Spring Awakening uses two Panzer armies attacking from around Lake Balaton and Lake Valencei, hoping for an encirclement of Soviet troops in the city.

March 7th
US troops of the US 1st Army cross the Rhine at Remagen after capturing the Ludendorff railway bridge, one of the few intact bridges across the river.

A pontoon bridge stretches across the Rhine. Bridges had to be laid at all sections of the Rhine except at Remagen, where soldiers of the US First Army captured the Rhine bridge there intact, to the fury of Adolf Hitler.

Battle for Budapest

A city under siege

Although Heinz Guderian, the German Chief of Staff, planned to defend the line of the Oder river against the coming Soviet onslaught, Hitler disagreed, and ordered the relief of Budapest, held by the Red Army since the end of 1944.

On Boxing Day, 1944 the combined forces of the Red Army's 2nd and 3rd Ukrainian Fronts (army groups), commanded respectively by Marshal Rodin Malinovsky and General F. I. Tolbukhin, had surrounded the Hungarian capital of Budapest. The 2nd Ukrainian Front covered the northern approaches and the 3rd those to the south.

Rapid advance

The success of operations in Poland and the collapse of the Axis states of Bulgaria, Romania and now Hungary in November had presented STAVKA, the Soviet high command, with a unique opportunity to advance rapidly into the Balkans.

The Soviet forces had entered Hungary in October but their first thrust against Budapest had been repelled. When on 29 December the Soviets sent two officers carrying a white flag to negotiate a surrender, men of the German garrison shot them dead.

The Hungarians had lost the will for war and wanted out, but German troops were in the country and Hitler had decreed that Budapest, a 'satellite capital', should be held as a 'fortress'. The German forces in Hungary were commanded by General Johannes Friessner.

It was not only a good defensive position but in the area were German divisions that included the army's 13th and Feldherrnhalle Panzer Divisions and two Waffen-SS cavalry divisions, the Florian Geyer and 22nd SS-Freiwilligen-Kavallerie-Division Maria Theresa.

Maria Theresa had been raised from two regiments of Hungarian *Volksdeutsche* and SS Cavalry Regiment Nr 17 (former SS-Reiter Regiment Nr 3) in Hungary during the spring of 1944. The men of Maria Theresa would fight with distinction and the division's 37-year old Sturmbannführer Anton 'Toni' Ameiser would win the Ritterkreuz (knight's cross) after the fighting in November 1944.

The units in Budapest were under command of the elderly General Pfeffer-Wildenbruch, who sited them between Buda, on the west bank of the Danube dominated by the Gelerthey Heights and Palace Hill, and Pest where solidly built government buildings and factories were easily fortified.

Breakout opportunity

As the Germans held on in the city, a counter-attack by the IV SS Panzer Corps under General Herbert Gille and comprising the 3rd Totenkopf and 5th Wiking SS Panzer Divisions, on 24 January reached Budapest airport within 25 km (15 miles) of the city's southern

Hitler decided that preserving Germany's hold on the last surviving oilfields in Hungary was more important than blocking the Red Army's route to Berlin, and ordered the holding of Budapest.

suburbs. Hitler had ordered them away from the defence of Warsaw. Although this attack presented an opportunity for a breakout, Hitler nonetheless demanded that the city be defended to the last man.

Though Tolbukhin's 3rd Ukrainian Front was under

The only hope for Budapest's defenders was that the SS-led relief column could get through. Its leader 'Sepp' Dietrich (left) had little strategic skill, but he was a hard fighter, who looked after his men and brought out their best as fighting troops.

Soviet soldiers had captured Budapest by 12 February. Dietrich eventually ordered his men to head west to surrender to US forces, rather than to the Soviets who would have likely shot SS men out of hand.

severe pressure on the west bank of the Danube, on the eastern side Malinovsky's troops penetrated the Pest suburbs and artillery and Katyusha rockets began to bombard German positions in Buda.

On 12 January, the Soviet forces formed a special Budapest Group Corps to spearhead the attacks. As the corps' tanks drove for the city centre, the Germans fought street by street and even house by house. It took six days for Malinovsky's formations to take Pest, but it cost the Germans 35,000 killed and 62,000 captured.

By the beginning of February, the defenders' rations had been reduced to 75 grams (0.17lb) of bread a day, but they fought on in the rubble and sewers of the city.

Attack on Buda
Tolbukhin was still fending off German armoured thrusts as the 2nd Ukrainian Front mounted an attack on Buda. Here the German troops were well dug in with commanding positions and

held out for a further 13 days before capitulating. Malinovsky took a further 30,000 prisoners. On a bitter night on 11 February some 16,000 German troops, who were the remnants of the garrison, attempted to break out to the north-west. Before they left, wounded survivors pleaded to be killed rather than fall captive to the Soviet forces. Most of the break-out group were surrounded and killed and only 800 reached safety, among them 170 men from Florian Geyer. Their commanding officer, 34-year old Joachim Rumohr, committed suicide during the sortie, just after he had been wounded.

Hitler's insistence on holding the Hungarian plain and Budapest in order to maintain control of vital oilfields compromised the flanks of the Reich and since it squandered troops and equipment, ironically accelerated the fall of Vienna and Berlin in April 1945. The commentators on Radio Moscow recognised this when they broadcast on 13 February 'a major obstacle has been removed and the way to Vienna is open.'

Seizing control
The Germans' final attempt to seize control of the city witnessed 'Sepp' Dietrich's Sixth SS Panzer Army launch an attack. However, Dietrich faced an impossible

task. The Soviets already held the city, Dietrich could only call upon six operational tanks and the Red Army captured the Hungarian oilfields on 2 April. Hitler was enraged; rather than calling the Sixth Panzer Army back to defend Berlin, he rebuked these, the most loyal of all his followers, and Dietrich therefore led his men west to surrender to the advancing US Army.

By the time Dietrich's Sixth Panzer Army, with its small force of King Tiger heavy tanks, had been deployed to relieve Budapest, there was nothing his depleted SS formations could do to overcome the massive Soviet advantage in manpower and weapons.

Battle for Budapest: Chronology

The battle for Budapest has been described as the 'Stalingrad of the SS'. Hitler abandoned several divisions to the city's defence as the noose tightened around the Third Reich.

1944

March 19th
Germany begins the occupation of Hungary as Soviet forces advance towards the Danube plain. Hungary is also Germany's second largest oil importer, and is alarmed at statements by Admiral Horthy, the Hungarian regent, that he will surrender to the Allies when they cross the Hungarian border.

March 27th
Massive German reinforcements are poured into Hungary as the Soviet advance approaches the border.

September
The Red Army forces its way across the Hungarian border and begins to meet fanatical German resistance.

October 18th
Mindful of the German strength in Hungary, Soviet authorities order General Tolbulkin to redirect his 3rd Ukrainian Front from Yugoslavia to Hungary.

October 29th
Marshal Malinovsky's Second Ukrainian Front launches a major offensive towards Budapest. Stalin has given him direct orders to capture the city.

November 4th
The Soviet offensive against Budapest reaches the outer suburbs of the city. There they are stopped by four German

Above: A Soviet heavy field gun fires at German positions during the battle for Budapest. It took the Soviets over three months to crush German resistance in the city.

Below: Soviet tanks surge forward in an attack on Budapest, covered by a machine gun team. The machine gun is the venerable, but reliable 7.62mm Maxim M1910 on the wheeled Sokolov mount.

Above: A Soviet field gun crew in the streets of Budapest. Fighting for the city was a prolonged affair, with the German and Hungarian defenders desperately holding out for their relief.

divisions: the 13th Panzer Division, the 8th and 22nd SS Cavalry Divisions, the SS Panzergrenadier-Division Feldherrnhalle. In addition the Hungarian army has provided its I Corps.

November 11th
Soviet forces assaulting Budapest are decisively halted by ferocious German resistance.

December 26th
Budapest is entirely surrounded by the Soviets. The battle for the city now settles into a siege.

1945
January 18th
The Germans make a counter-attack in an attempt to break the Budapest siege. The IV Panzer Corps is sent from Army Group Centre to join the III Panzer in a direct assault against the Soviet encirclement. At the same time Pest in the east of the city falls to Malinovsky's Second Ukrainian Front.

January 24th
IV Panzer Corps closes to within 25 km (15 miles) of the German defences in the south of the city. Hitler, however, refuses to allow the defenders of Budapest to break out, insisting instead that Budapest itself is relieved. The counter-offensive peters out over the subsequent three weeks and leaves the Budapest garrison to their fate.

February 13th
Malinovsky conquers Buda after a bloody battle and takes over 30,000 Axis prisoners.

February 16th
The last pockets of German and Hungarian resistance in central Budapest are overwhelmed by a final Soviet assault, resulting in the deaths of another 10,000 Axis soldiers.

International Events
1944
October 14th
The illustrious German tactician Field Marshal Erwin Rommel commits suicide by taking poison. The suicide comes after he is implicated in the assassination attempt against Hitler led by Colonel Claus Graf Schenk von Stauffenberg.

November 28th
The British government releases documents showing the full extent of the UK's war production output to date. Totals include 25,000 tanks, 102,600 aircraft and 4.5 million tons of shipping.

December 16th
German forces in western Europe mount the last major offensive of the war through the Ardennes forest. Operation Wacht am Rhine makes good initial progress towards its final objective – Antwerp – but is steadily crushed over the next six weeks by Allied counter-attacks and air assaults.

1945
January 12th
Over two million men of the Soviet Army begin a huge offensive through Poland and East Prussia, driving into Germany itself.

January 27th
Advancing Soviet forces liberate the Auschwitz extermination camp, and witness the full horror of Hitler's 'Final Solution'.

February 13th–14th
Over 50,000 German citizens in Dresden die in a huge fire-bombing raid by 805 RAF bombers. The individual fires coalesced into a huge firestorm with blast-furnace temperatures and hurricane-force winds.

Air war over Europe, 1945

Allies supreme

By March 1945, the Anglo-American allies were across the Rhine river: in the east Hitler's armies faced massed Soviet strength on the Oder–Neisse line, while in the south battles were fought in Hungary. The Luftwaffe fought on bravely, but its days were seriously numbered.

Following the Ardennes offensive of December 1944, the Allied air forces in the West had ceased their efforts to crush the Luftwaffe: the Germans' disastrous Operation Bodenplatte on 1 January 1945, along with their huge losses in air battles against the US 8th Air Force, had already done much of the job. Thereafter, the wholesale movement of fighter and close-support aircraft to the Oder front left only a small force to counter Allied air supremacy. In March 1945, fewer than 1100 German aircraft remained with units in the west, but these included jet reconnaissance units, with Ar 234B-1 and Me 262A-1a aircraft, as well as units with the latest Fw 190D-9 and Bf 109K-4 fighters to cover the jet operations. Arado Ar 234B-1 Blitz and Me 262A-2a bombers were also in service, while the defence of the Reich was entrusted to the Fw 190, Bf 109, Me 163 rocket fighter and Me 262A-1a. Many of the latter carried R4M air-to-air rockets.

Jet interceptions

Throughout February and March 1945, Allied strategic bombing operations over the Reich continued without serious hindrance from the Luftwaffe. The largest number of jets encountered to date came on 3 March 1945, when JG 7 put up 30 or more against US B-17s. Reactions of 50 or more jets became the norm throughout the next three weeks in the Hamburg–Berlin–Brunswick sector. On 4 April 1945, the jets shot down five bombers and a de Havilland Mosquito.

An isolated action by German fighters on 7 April has gone down in folklore: this was the last-ditch operation by Fw 190s and Bf 109s of the so-called Sonderkommando Elbe. The pilots of SdKdo Elbe were instructed to ram the US bombers that they intercepted, but, despite the pilots' bravery, only eight US 'heavies' were brought down.

In April 1945, RAF Bomber Command attained its peak strength of 1609 bombers. With the issue no longer in doubt, however, the RAF effort dwindled, and in April 8822 (51 failed to return) night and 5001 (22 failed to return) day sorties were flown. The 'heavies' of the 8th Air Force flew 19 missions in April 1945 (17,437 effective sorties), losing 108 B-17Gs and B-24s: the 8th Air Force's fighters flew 12,771 sorties, losing 99 aircraft. The fighters now roamed as far afield as Prague and Munich.

Hitler's lost offensive

In the wake of the Ardennes offensive in the West, the Soviets started their drive to the Oder and Neisse rivers on the Reich's eastern borders. As the Soviets drove on to reach the lower Oder at Küstrin, only 84 km (52 miles) from the capital of the Reich, by 31 January 1945, the German forces were hamstrung by the decisions of the Führer which, without exception, were founded on insanity. One major decision was to concentrate remaining German forces in the south to relieve Budapest and to secure the oilfields at Nagykanizsa in Hungary, rather than to stem the rout in front of Berlin.

Bf 109G-10s and K-4s bolstered Hungarian fighter units, while close-support was provided by Ju 87D-5s, Ar 66s and Fiat CR.42s. Nevertheless, the offensive failed, leading Hitler to withdraw his forces, but not to the critical Oder front. Instead, he sent them to Hungary to take part in the 'Spring Awakening' offensive scheduled for 6 March 1945.

Hit by a recurrence of bad weather, the offensive got off to a bad start, and again the Germans were forced to withdraw. The front in Hungary now erupted, with the Soviets advancing into Austria. After a bitter battle, the city of Vienna fell on 13 April 1945.

Battle of Berlin

Late in April, when the Anglo-American allies and the Soviets joined forces on the Elbe, Germany was divided in two. The Allies made the extraordinary decision not to drive all out for Berlin, however, so it was left to the Soviet forces to take the prize.

Heavy bomber operations continued almost to the end of the war. Here ground crew can be seen clearing snow and ice ready for Lancaster operations early in 1945.

The Me 163 was one of the more successful of the extreme measures tried by the Germans to repel the Allied bombers. Although it was the fastest aeroplane of the war, the Me 163 interceptor was tricky to handle in the air and on the ground.

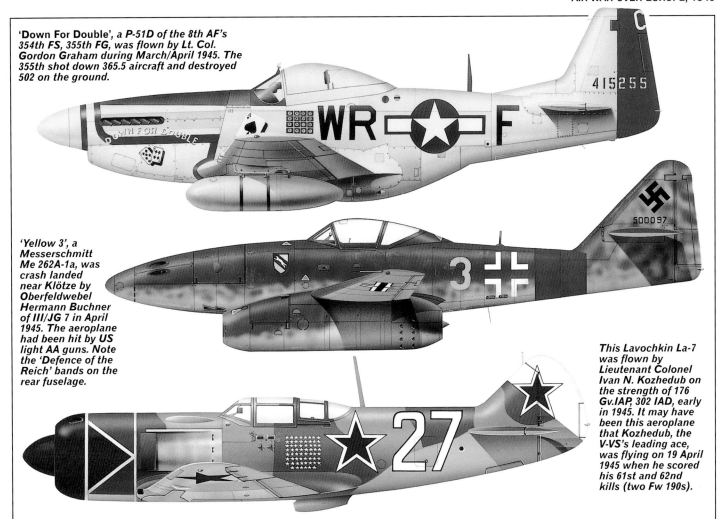

'Down For Double', a P-51D of the 8th AF's 354th FS, 355th FG, was flown by Lt. Col. Gordon Graham during March/April 1945. The 355th shot down 365.5 aircraft and destroyed 502 on the ground.

'Yellow 3', a Messerschmitt Me 262A-1a, was crash landed near Klötze by Oberfeldwebel Hermann Buchner of III/JG 7 in April 1945. The aeroplane had been hit by US light AA guns. Note the 'Defence of the Reich' bands on the rear fuselage.

This Lavochkin La-7 was flown by Lieutenant Colonel Ivan N. Kozhedub on the strength of 176 Gv.IAP, 302 IAD, early in 1945. It may have been this aeroplane that Kozhedub, the V-VS's leading ace, was flying on 19 April 1945 when he scored his 61st and 62nd kills (two Fw 190s).

The air defence of Berlin's eastern approaches was entrusted to over 1850 fighters and close-support aircraft which, although short of fuel, represented a very formidable force.

Against this force, the V-VS (Soviet air force) mustered some 7500 combat aircraft. For the assault on Berlin, which began at dawn on 16 April 1945, air support along each of the Soviet front was bolstered by Petlyakov P-8, Tupolev Tu-2 and Ilyushin Il-4 long-range bombers. Fighter and ground-attack strengths were based on the Yakovlev Yak-3, Yak-7B and Yak-9DD, and Lavochkin La-5FN and La-7 fighters, along with Il-2m/3 Shturmoviks, Pe-2, Tu-2 and Polikarpov Po-2 day and night bombers, and recon-naissance aircraft. On the night before the offensive, thick fog prevented any close-support effort of the scale planned, but on 16 April, the heavy bombers attacked the roads at Münchenberg, Fürstenwalde, Buckow and Heinersdorf. A major air battle took place over Berlin on 18 April, when radar vectored the Yak-3s of the 43rd IAP onto a formation of 35 or more

Junkers Ju 88s. But by 20 April, the Oder defences had been broken, despite an all-out effort of some 1000 sorties per day by the Luftwaffe.

The final days

A German counter-attack in the Först-Muskau sector on 16 April was routed with the help of Shturmovik attack aircraft escorted by 50 or more Yak-9s and La-7s. The fighting now became increas-ingly savage. Another German counter-attack in the Cottbus-Spremberg area was held despite an effort by 100 or more Fw 190F-8s and Ju 87Ds. Son-2A radars vectored the 6th Gv.IAK into

battle, and this unit claimed 56 German aircraft destroyed over the 4th Tank Army during the day. On 20 April the Soviets completed the encirclement of Berlin by striking across the Oder. On 28 April Lieutenant Colonel V. G. Gromov and his wing-man, 2nd Lieutenant Yu. T. Dyachenko, of the 515th IAP (193rd IAD) landed their Yak-7Bs on Berlin-Tempelhof's runways, while other units were already operating from nearby Schönefeld. During the battle for the Reichstag parliament

buildings on 30 April 1945, deep in the Führerbunker, Adolf Hitler committed suicide: on the morning of the following day the Red Banner was flying from the upper-most pinnacle of Berlin's Reichstag.

Surrender

The unconditional surrender was signed at 0141 on 7 May 1945, and between this time and the official laying down of arms at 0001 on 9 May 1945, combats with Fw 190s and Bf 109s continued. But the war in Europe was over.

Along with the RAF's Typhoon, the P-47 became the nemesis of Germany's communications. The rail network, the German forces' primary means of moving their forces and supplies, was badly hit.

Air war over Europe, 1945

Chronology

By 1945 the Luftwaffe was a shadow of its former strength. A last minute introduction of new fighter technologies could not save the German air force from complete destruction.

1945

January 1st
The Luftwaffe launch Operation Bodenplatte. Over 1000 German fighters and bomber attack Allied air bases in Europe and manage to destroy 156 aircraft. It is a Pyrrhic victory, however, as 277 German aircraft are destroyed in air-to-air combat, some by German flak batteries mistaking the German aircraft for the Allies.

January 30th
USAAF P-38s conduct strafing operations against German air defences in Austria.

Berlin after its obliteration by Allied bombing. Over 1.5 million people were homeless in the city. A terrible statistic is that one out of seven buildings destroyed in Germany by Allied bombing raids was in Berlin.

February 3rd
Over 1150 US bombers pound Berlin. They have a fighter escort of 900 aircraft, almost the entire strength of the Luftwaffe's western air units by this stage of the war.

February 9th
Nearly 2000 USAAF bombers, escorted by 871 fighters, hit oil targets throughout Germany. The Luftwaffe's air defence of these targets results in the loss of another 80 aircraft.

March 3rd
German air units send up 30 of the latest jet fighters against the Allied bombers.

Though individually superior to Allied aircraft, the jets are too few in number and their operational time too short to have a significant impact upon operations.

March 8th
Indicative of the chronic depletion in Luftwaffe strength by this month of the war, 1353 Allied bombers and 326 escort fighters hit benzol plants, an oil plant and rail targets in Germany with no losses whatsoever.

March 21st
Over 1000 Allied bombers and fighters conduct raids against German jet-fighter bases.

Around 60 assorted Luftwaffe aircraft are destroyed for USAAF losses of seven B-17s and nine P-51 Mustangs.

April 7th
A series of USAAF bombing raids across Germany is met by a Luftwaffe force of over 100 conventional fighters and 50 jet fighters. Despite the jet presence, the German pilots are hopelessly outnumbered by 898 US fighters and around 100 of the defenders are lost, including several jets.

April 16th
Soviet air forces begin their air campaign to coincide with the battle for Berlin. Although the Luftwaffe can field 1850 aircraft, it is dwarfed by a total Soviet air strength over the city of 7500 combat aircraft.

April 18th
A flight of 35+ Junkers Ju 88s suffers heavy losses at the hands of a massed flight of Soviet Yak-3s over Berlin.

April 28th
Soviet combat aircraft begin to land on the Berlin-Templehof airfield after the almost complete destruction of the Luftwaffe defence.

May 5th
A German Siebel 204 is shot down by RAF fighters over Hamburg. It is the last Luftwaffe aircraft to be shot down during the war.

A traumatised German civilian makes her way through the rubble and debris of a city destroyed by Allied airstrikes. Following the bombing campaign, most German cities had no gas, electricity or water.

International Events 1945

January 31st
The US Army executes Private Eddie Slovik for desertion. It is the first execution on the charge of desertion in the US Army for 80 years.

Flying Fortresses in combat over Germany. By 1945 the use of forward air bases in France and almost total air superiority meant that 1000-bomber raids became relatively commonplace, particularly against Berlin and other major industrial targets.

February 13th
Off the embattled Pacific island of Iwo Jima, Japanese kamikaze aircraft sink the US carrier *Bismarck Sea* and damage the carrier *Saratoga*.

March 5th
In Germany, boys of 16 years old are called up to serve in the *Volkssturm* and fight in the defence of Berlin.

March 21st
An RAF bombing error over the Danish city of Copenhagen results in the destruction of a school, killing 86 children and 17 teachers.

April 6th
US forces in the Pacific land on the island of Okinawa, and begin one of the bloodiest battles in US history.

Battle for Berlin
The fall of the Reich

Berlin, April 1945: the Red Army batters its way into the Nazi capital against a motley army of teenagers, pensioners and desperate SS men.

On 1 April 1945 Marshals Georgi Zhukov and Ivan Koniev arrived in Moscow for a briefing on the subject of the Battle for Berlin. Stalin informed them that the devious and conniving Western Allies were planning a swift Berlin operation with the sole object of capturing the city before the Red Army could arrive – an announcement that, not surprisingly in view of the recent achievements of the Red Army, incensed them both.

They had expected to mount the attack on Berlin in early May, but in these special circumstances they would accelerate all preparations and be ready to move well before the Anglo-Americans could get themselves solidly inside German territory. Which of the two fronts – Zhukov's 1st Belorussian or Koniev's 1st Ukrainian – should have the task, and the honour, of driving straight for Berlin? The wily Georgian gave an ambiguous answer by drawing on their planning map a demarcation line between their commands, which ended short of Berlin at Lübben, 30 km (18.6 miles) to the south east.

German defences

Unorganised and half-trained though they might be, the bulk of the German formations defending Berlin against the Red Army nevertheless fought at first with a blind ferocity and a blistering efficiency. They demonstrated again that the epitome of high morale in

An IS-2 heavy tank parks triumphantly in the 'lair of the Fascist Beast' as the Soviet press described Berlin. As German resistance collapsed the Red Army embarked on an orgy of rape and murder.

BERLIN: LAST DAYS OF THE REICH

When the last offensive of the Red Army was launched, its aims were to advance to the Elbe and to annihilate all organised German resistance that stood in its way, including the capture of Berlin and the reduction of its garrison. For this purpose the Marshals Zhukov and Koniev had some 1,640,000 men under their command, with 41,600 guns and mortars, 6300 tanks, and the support of three air armies holding 8400 aircraft.

Hitler's last defenders

To oppose them were seven Panzer and 65 infantry divisions in some sort of order, and 100 or so independent battalions. These were either remnants of obliterated divisions or formed from old men, children, the sick, criminals and the simple-minded, collected together by SS teams sent out from the Chancellery bunkers – in which Hitler and his demented entourage were living out their last fantasies – with orders to conjure yet another army from the wreckage of the Reich.

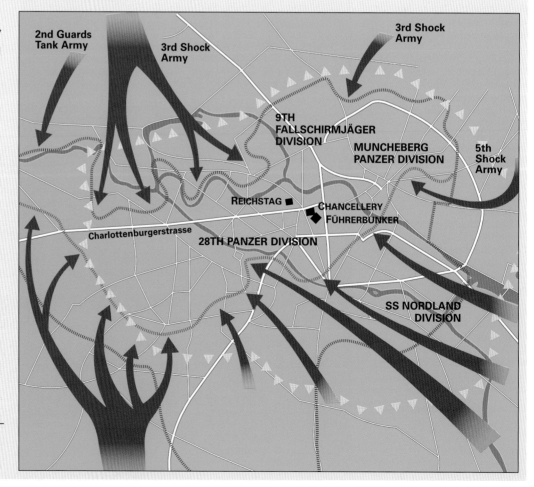

Mounting a 152mm (6in) gun in a heavily armoured box, the ISU-152 was crudely built, uncomfortable to fight from, and only the command vehicles had radios. However, it was also immensely powerful and was available in very large numbers.

Several Soviet tank corps were used to isolate Berlin and then to drive vigorously for Tempelhof airfield, which was Hitler's last escape route. The Soviets were not to know that the Führer had decided to stay and die in the capital of his Thousand Year Reich.

combat is that shown by the 'cornered rat' – a reason it so often survives.

But there would be no escape for the Germans now. At dawn on 16 April a tremendous artillery and air bombardment opened up along the Oder and Neisse rivers and out of the Soviet bridgeheads stormed the first waves of shock troops. It took Zhukov's northern thrust two days to smash through some 6.5km (4 miles) to reach the Seelow Heights, and his southern thrust to advance 13km (8 miles). At that point they had seen no sign of a crack in the German defences. Koniev's troops, however, were not so strongly opposed and they advanced 13 km on the first day. On 18 April Koniev ordered two tank armies to fight their way to the north west and into the Berlin suburbs.

Race for the city

Perhaps inspired by competition, Zhukov now drove his infantry and tank armies forward with ruthless vigour, and by 19 April both his thrusts had advanced 30km (18 miles) on a front almost 65km (40 miles) in width. On 21 April General Ivan Chuikov reported that his 8th Guards Army, which he had brought all the way from Stalingrad, was in the south

eastern suburbs.

Koniev now devoted the bulk of his endeavour west towards the Elbe. By 20 April two of his tank armies had reached Luckenwald – thus splitting the German Army Group 'Centre' from Berlin and the defences in the north – and then drove two more armies given to him by STAVKA up towards Potsdam where on 25 April they linked up with one of Zhukov's guard tanks that had come around the north of Berlin. Thus the city, its inhabitants and its 200,000-man garrison were surrounded.

Germany divided

On the same day, units of the 5th Guards Army reached the Elbe at Torgau and within minutes were exchanging drinks, hats, buttons and photographs with Americans of the US 1st Army. The scenes of triumphant comradeship and co-operation which followed were repeated up and down the central axis of Germany, as soldiers who had fought westwards from Stalingrad met those who had fought eastwards from Normandy. During the brief period in which they were allowed to fraternise they learned to recognise each others qualities. It is a tragedy that the

friendships made then were not allowed to continue.

Surrender talks

On 1 May, Chuikov, now well inside the Berlin city centre, was approached by Generaloberst Hans Krebs – Chief of the German General Staff – with three other officers bearing white flags intent on negotiating a surrender. With almost unbelievable effrontery the German general opened the conversation with the remark:

'Today, is the first of May, a great holiday for our two nations.'

Considering the outrages carried out in his own country by the fellow nationals of the man addressing him, Chuikov's reply was a model of restraint:

'We have a great holiday today. How are things with you over there, it is less easy to say!'

But the first moves towards an official end to hostilities in Europe had

been made.

The unconditional surrender of Berlin occurred on 2 May. On 7 May the 'Unconditional surrender of Germany to the Western Allies and to Russia' was agreed, signed by General Jodl for the defeated, and Generals Bedell Smith and Suslaparov for the victors. The war in Europe was at an end.

Hitler had committed suicide on 30 April, having first made a will leaving the leadership of his country to Admiral Doenitz, spoken briefly to every member of his personal staff, married and then poisoned his mistress Eva Braun and poisoned his dog. Afterwards, the bodies of all three were burned.

A man of enormous but demonic gifts, he had lifted his country from a position of weakness and chaos to unparalleled power, and then dropped her back into chaos again – all in the space of 12 years.

Despite the fearsome odds, few German units disintegrated and most fought on to the bitter end. The formidable discipline and professionalism of the German army was never demonstrated more clearly than in the dying moments of the Nazi regime.

Battle for Berlin
Chronology

The battle for Berlin was the last traumatic episode in the European war. Russian casualties alone numbered 305,000 by the time the city fell.

1945

April 16th

A massive Soviet bombardment begins to pound the German capital and surrounding areas. The Russian guns are positioned almost wheel-to-wheel at a density of 295 per kilometre of front. The bombardment launches the final offensive to take Berlin by Zhukov's 1st Belorussian Front and Koniev's 1st Ukrainian Front.

April 20th

Russian forces break through German defences on the Oder and push on towards Berlin itself. Meanwhile, Hitler celebrates his 56th birthday by decorating a group of Hitler Youth in the Chancellery gardens.

Below: Soviet soldiers storm Berlin's Reichstag building. The Red Army suffered 300,000 casualties in taking the city, in spite of outnumbering the Germans by 2.5 million troops to one million German defenders.

April 21st

Armoured units of Zhukov's 1st Belorussian Front enter the northern suburbs of Berlin.

April 22nd

Stalin gives final directives to Koniev and Zhukov for the final assault on the Berlin centre. Koniev must stop at lines running through the Anhalter railway station only 100m (328ft) from the Reichstag, while Zhukov had the final honour of taking the administrative centre of the capital.

April 23rd

The Russians advance into the Berlin suburbs on all fronts.

Right: A Soviet tank soldier dances to celebrate the victory in Berlin. The honour of taking the capital ultimately rested with Marshal Zhukov, who made an enemy of Stalin by stealing the public limelight.

An SS (indicated by the double lightning flashes on the number plate) SdKfz 251 half-track and its crew lie dead in the streets of Berlin. The SS numbered nearly one million men at its height, but by the end of the war almost one in three SS soldiers were dead.

April 24th
From the west of Berlin the German 12th Army under General Wenck begins a relief counter-offensive. The RAF bombs it heavily, retarding its progress.

April 25th
Zhukov's 1st Belorussian Front, attacking around the north of Berlin, meets west of the city with Koniev's 1st Ukrainian Front striking up from the south. Berlin is now completely encircled by Soviet forces, trapping 30,000 soldiers and two million civilians. All roads leading west out of the city are severed.

April 26th
Berlin's final defensive lines are broken by the twin thrusts of two Soviet fronts. Russian troops cross the Spree river and close in on the Unter den Linden, which leads to the Reichstag, Brandenburg Gate, and the Chancellery.

April 27th
General Wenck's 12th Army is stopped by the Russian

defence around Berlin only 24km (15 miles) from the city. The Germans soldiers still within the city defend a strip of land only 16km (10 miles) long and 4.8km (3 miles) wide.

April 30th
The Reichstag, centre of German administration, falls to the Soviets. Hitler commits suicide in his bunker along with his partner Eva Braun. The two bodies are incinerated in the Chancellery gardens to stop them falling into Soviet hands.

May 1st
All contested areas around the Chancellery are pounded with a huge Soviet artillery barrage. Joseph Goebbels, the Nazi propaganda minister, commits suicide with his wife and six children.

May 2nd
German units begin to surrender and fighting finally ceases in Berlin.

May 5th–11th
The 1st, 2nd and 3rd Ukrainian Fronts begin a major assault to take Prague, Czechoslovakia. German forces within the city put up four days of resistance. The city is liberated on May 11th, and the last outpost of the Third Reich collapses.

May 7th
The German unconditional surrender is signed by General Alfred Jodl, bringing the European war to an end

May 8th
Remaining German forces in East Prussia surrender. Koniev's 1st Ukrainian Front reaches Dresden.

May 9th
The remnants of Army Group North (formerly Army Group Centre) surrender along the Bay of Danzig. Army Group Centre had been pushed back to the Polish and East Prussian coastline by a dual thrust from the 2nd Belorussian Front attacking out from around Warsaw, and the 1st Baltic and 3rd Belorussian Front moving downwards from Lithuania.

International Events 1945

April 17th
British Army units inspect the horrific conditions at the Belsen concentration camp. British medical teams attempt to save some 30,000 survivors of the camp, most riddled with dysentery and typhus.

April 27th
US and Soviet forces link up on the Elbe at Torgau.

April 29th
German forces in Italy make an unconditional surrender to the Allies.

May 1st
Australian soldiers of the 26th Infantry Brigade land on Tarakan, east Borneo, beginning the campaign to retake the Dutch East Indies from Japanese occupation.

May 3rd
General Sir William Slim's 14th Army takes the Burmese capital Rangoon from the Japanese.

THE WAR IN THE PACIFIC

Pearl Harbor
Day of infamy

On Sunday 7 December 1941 the US Pacific Fleet lay peacefully at anchor unaware that 183 hostile Japanese aircraft were approaching.

The USS Nevada *lies burning: A modernised World War I dreadnought, the* Nevada *had improved underwater protection but this did her little good at Pearl Harbor.*

Rich in ambition but poor in natural resources, Japan had long planned the creation of a so-called Greater East Asia Co-Prosperity Sphere, and the straits of the European colonial powers by 1941 stimulated it to occupy part of French Indo-China in July 1941. In response the US, the UK and the Netherlands Indies staged a potentially crippling embargo on oil exports to Japan which, from this point, saw war as inevitable. It was to take the form of a rapid conquest to the defined limits of the Sphere, followed by bargaining with the Western powers from a position of strength and before their superior industrial capacity could be brought to bear, obliging them to accept the status quo as a condition for peace.

Far East threat

The Far Eastern forces of the warring European powers had been drastically thinned, but the US Navy's Pacific Fleet, based in Hawaii, was a major threat and would react strongly to any violation of American territory. It needed to be eliminated – a requirement simplified by its being concentrated within Pearl Harbor. British strikes against Oran, and more particularly Taranto, had confirmed the results of exercises already conducted by the Japanese of the feasibility of causing great damage with little loss. Japan had set a precedent in 1904 for attacking without the formalities of declaring war. All the ingredients were there for a pre-emptive attack on Pearl Harbor.

The commander-in-chief of the Combined Fleet, Admiral Isoroku Yamamoto, entrusted the attack to Vice-Admiral Chuichi Nagumo, with the six largest of Japan's 10 carriers. Between them they could stow about 450 aircraft, equally divided between torpedo bombers,

dive-bombers and fighters. Reconnaissance was largely the province of the specially developed long-range Aichi E13A ('Jake') floatplanes, carried by the escorting battleships and cruisers, particularly the *Tone* and *Chikuma*, modified to carry six each. By this means the strike capacity of the carriers was considerably enhanced. Special shallow-running 450mm (17.7in) torpedoes and 800kg (1764lb) armour-piercing (AP) bombs modified

from 356mm (14in) shells were developed and exhaustively tested. No less than 27

submarines, some carrying midget submarines, were sailed to the area of Hawaii

PEARL HARBOR: AIR POWER VICTORY

Using a 'strike package' of 350 aircraft, the Japanese launched two waves of air attacks early in the morning to devastate the US Pacific Fleet. The first wave, striking at 0755, included a collection of high-level bombers, dive bombers and torpedo bombers protected by fighters; attacking airfields, naval depots and shipping. The bomber force flew in from the north, moving south and then turning west to east to attack Pearl Harbor. This wave was followed by a second attack at 0854. On this occasion, torpedo bombers

made straight for Pearl Harbor, while the fighter force divided itself between military airfields. On this occasion, no dive bombers were deployed, however, a second wave of heavy bombers was used flying towards the entrance to Pearl Harbor. The aircraft followed a southerly attack route, but with the formation breaking shortly before hitting the north-easterly coast of the island. As well as the shipping, the airfields of Wheeler, Bellows, Hickam and Ewa were devastated in the onslaught.

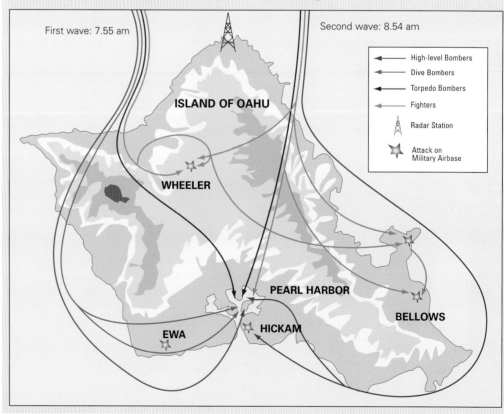

First wave: 7.55 am

Second wave: 8.54 am

High-level Bombers	
Dive Bombers	
Torpedo Bombers	
Fighters	
Radar Station	
Attack on Military Airbase	

ISLAND OF OAHU

WHEELER

PEARL HARBOR

BELLOWS

EWA

HICKAM

Left: *A spectacular explosion rocks the* **USS S**haw, *a destroyer, after it is hit in the first wave of Japanese bombardment. Two other destroyers were sunk.*

Below: *A Nakajima Naval Type 97 carrier-borne attack-bomber takes off from the deck of a Japanese carrier on the lookout for* **US** Navy *shipping during the attack on Pearl Harbor.*

during November 1941, though they were destined to play little part in the action. Nagumo's force, having assembled in the Kurils in great secrecy, sailed on 26 November. At easy speed, with refuelling tankers in company, the force took a circuitous route through the desolate and deserted northern Pacific. Concealed by continuous thick weather it arrived totally undetected at its launch point, 440km (275 miles) due north of Hawaii early on Sunday, 7 December.

At first light floatplanes had confirmed the composition of the American fleet at Pearl Harbor and that no ships were at sea in the flightpath, but that the most desired targets, the American carriers, were absent. (Of the three carriers in the Pacific, USS *Enterprise* and *Lexington* were at sea delivering Marine Corps aircraft to Wake and Midway, while USS *Saratoga* was at San Diego.)

So poor was the weather that Nagumo began launching early, at 0530, the 51 dive-bombers, 49 high-level bombers, 40 torpedo aircraft and 43 fighters being formed up by 0615. This prompt start inadvertently saw the raid being delivered ahead of the declaration of war, instead of a nominal 30 minutes afterward, as had been planned.

Clear weather was found over the islands and, in the exhilaration of the moment and despite all planning, all types of aircraft attacked simultaneously.

Element of surprise

At 0755 all six US airfields were dive-bombed, then strafed to complete the job and prevent any fighters taking off. Simultaneously, achieving complete surprise, the remaining 132 aircraft fell on the fleet, virtually without opposition. Seven battleships were moored off Ford Island in what was termed 'Battleship Row', an eighth (*Pennsylvania*) being in dock in the Navy Yard. These were the victims and, within minutes, the *West Virginia* had absorbed seven torpedoes. It was still settling in the shallow water when, at 0810, the next in line (*Arizona*) was shattered by a devastating explosion as the eighth AP bomb to hit it penetrated to a magazine. USS *Oklahoma* took five torpedoes and was already on its way to capsizing while the two that had struck the *California* were also to eventually put it on the bottom. *Nevada*, hit by one torpedo, got under way but beached itself when bombed by the second wave. Only *Maryland* and *Tennessee* escaped with moderate damage. Some damage was caused to ships in the Navy Yard: two destroyers were sunk in dock and a third, the *Shaw*, exploded spectacularly.

Secondary attack

The second wave of 167 Japanese aircraft arrived at about 0900 and added to the general level of damage while meeting a higher level of resistance. Nagumo did not mount a third strike. Uncertain of the whereabouts of the American carriers, nervous of the number of bombers known to be stationed on the island and informed by the returning second wave that most of the target area was, in any case, obliterated by dense palls of smoke, he pulled away to the north and was never sighted by the Americans.

Significant victory

For the loss of 29 aircraft Nagumo had secured a significant, but not decisive, victory. In addition to the damage to the fleet, nearly 200 US aircraft had been destroyed, mostly on the ground. A foolish oversight in planning had left undamaged the extensive tank farms, the dockyard installations and the submarine base. Pearl Harbor was still functioning and the carriers were still intact. Of equal importance, the Americans were fired with a dreadful resolve to avenge the 2403 lives that had been lost.

Left: **USS** West Virginia *and* Tennessee *lie side by side in the chaos of the aftermath.* Tennessee *escaped serious damage, but* **West Virginia** *was sunk after seven torpedo hits.*

Below: *A force of 490 Japanese aircraft had devastated the* **US** *battleship fleet by midday. However, the original goal of destroying the* **US** *Navy's aircraft carriers eluded Vice Admiral Nagumo.*

Pearl Harbor
Chronology

December 7th, 1941: a day of 'infamy', when aircraft from the Japanese battle fleet attacked the main American base on Hawaii without official prior warning, bringing the United States into World War II. The American fleet is severely depleted, but fortuitously its carriers are not in port at the time.

1941
November 26th
The Japanese main fleet leaves home waters for Hawaii.

December 6th
Washington DC – US President Franklin Roosevelt makes a final appeal to the Emperor of Japan for peace. There is no reply. Late this same day, the US code-breaking service begins intercepting a 14-part Japanese message and deciphers the first 13 parts, passing them on to the President and Secretary of State. The Americans believe a Japanese attack is imminent, most likely

The Seattle Daily Times announces that war has been declared on Japan.

somewhere in Southeast Asia.

December 7th
Washington DC – The last part of the Japanese message, stating that diplomatic relations with the US are to be broken off, reaches Washington in the morning and is decoded at approximately 9am. About an hour later, another Japanese message is intercepted. It instructs the Japanese embassy to deliver the main message to the Americans at 1pm. The Americans realise this time corresponds with early morning time in Pearl Harbor, which is several hours behind. The US War Department then

In Hawaiian tradition, American sailors honour casualties of the Japanese attack on N.A.S. Kaneohe. The men were buried on 8 December and this ceremony took place a few months later.

sends out an alert but uses a commercial telegraph because radio contact with Hawaii is broken.

Hawaii – The Japanese attack force under the command of Admiral Nagumo, consisting of six carriers with 423 planes, is about to attack.

6:00am
The first attack wave of 183 Japanese planes takes off from the carriers located 230 miles north of Oahu and heads for the US Pacific Fleet at Pearl Harbor.

7:02am
Two Army operators at Oahu's northern shore radar station detect the Japanese air attack approaching and contact a junior officer who disregards their reports, thinking they are American B-17 planes.

7:15am
Second attack wave of 167 planes takes off from the Japanese carriers and heads for Pearl Harbor.

WAR EXTRA

WAR DECLARED!
U. S. FLEET SAILS!
BATTLESHIP BOMBED
2ND RAID ON HONOLULU!

America's Best Evening Newspaper

The Seattle Daily Times

3RD SUNDAY EXTRA!

PRICE FIVE CENTS

SEATTLE, WASHINGTON, MONDAY, DECEMBER 8, 1941.

The American fleet lies stricken in Pearl Harbor, with five battleships sunk and another three damaged. Over 2400 servicemen and civilians were killed in the attack. Such was the scale of the surprise, the Japanese lost only 27 aircraft and five midget submarines. Most of the American loss of life occurred on board the USS Arizona, which was sunk by a single bomb.

7:53am

The first Japanese assault wave, with 51 'Val' dive bombers, 40 'Kate' torpedo bombers, 50 high level bombers and 43 'Zero' fighters, commences the attack with flight commander, Mitsuo Fuchida, announcing that total surprise had been achieved with the battle cry: 'Tora! Tora! Tora!' The first attack wave targets airfields and battleships. The second wave targets other ships and shipyard facilities. The air raid lasts until 9:45am. Eight battleships are damaged, with five sunk. Three light cruisers, three destroyers and three smaller vessels are lost along with 188 aircraft. The Japanese lose 27 planes and five midget submarines which attempted to penetrate the inner Harbor and launch torpedoes. The casualty list includes 2335 servicemen and 68 civilians killed, with 1178 wounded. Included are 1104 men aboard the battleship USS *Arizona* killed after a 1760-pound air bomb penetrated into the forward magazine causing catastrophic explosions.

2:30pm (Washington time)

Japanese diplomats present their war declaration – late – to Secretary of State, Cordell Hull in Washington.

December 8th

The United States and Britain declare war on Japan with President Roosevelt calling December 7, 'a date which will live in infamy...'

December 11th

Germany and Italy declare war on the United States. The European and Southeast Asian wars have now become a global conflict with the Axis powers.

Expansion in the Pacific
The Indian Ocean raid

After the attack on Pearl Harbor, the 1st Air Fleet of the Imperial Japanese navy went on to demonstrate its strike power and the superb skills of its fliers against new targets – most notably against the Royal Navy.

The shock effect of Japan's Pearl Harbor strike remains so great that it is widely overlooked that Vice Admiral Chuichi Nagumo's 1st Air Fleet went on within a few months to essay a similar exercise on the British. Four of his six fast carriers engaged in a preliminary warm-up on 19 February 1942 against Darwin and Broome in north-western Australia. For the loss of two aircraft the Japanese sank 12 assorted ships of the combined ABDA (Australian, British, Dutch and American) forces, and spent a leisurely, and largely uncontested, hour reducing the base facilities and much of the town.

By late February 1942, the Japanese had gained most of their objectives in the East Indies, Malaya and the Philippines and, with land-based air power well established, the 1st Air Fleet carriers had a month's well-earned rest before sailing for the Indian Ocean on 26 March.

An Allied agreement of about this time defined the Indian Ocean west of the Malayan peninsula as a British zone of responsibility, but the Royal Navy could muster only a scratch force for its protection. Admiral Sir James Somerville had a force, powerful on paper, built round five battleships and three carriers. Only two of the carriers were modern,

however, and four of the battleships were 'R' class units, too much outclassed by the Japanese to be of more than sacrificial value. Sensibly, Somerville formed two separate forces, the older ships based in East Africa and the remainder in Ceylon and the secret facility at Addu Atoll, 965km (600 miles) away in the southern Maldives.

Intelligence reports indicating strongly a Japanese strike against Ceylon on or about 1 April 1942,

Right: Following its success at Pearl Harbor, the 1st Air Fleet struck at northern Australia, causing serious damage at Darwin. The conquest of the East Indies now freed the fleet to enter the Indian Ocean to attack British possessions there.

HMS Dorsetshire burns following a 90-aircraft attack. In company with HMS Cornwall, the ship was hurrying to meet the force led by the British commander-in-chief, Admiral Somerville, when spotted by a cruiser-launched Aichi E13A 'Jake' floatplane.

Somerville kept his still-complete force well to the west by day, when he considered himself at greatest disadvantage, steaming eastward by night onto the expected Japanese approach.

Although correct in essence, Somerville's intelligence was badly wrong with respect to time.

By the evening of 2 April, the British force needed to fuel and provision and had to return to Addu, except for the heavy cruisers HMS *Cornwall* and HMS *Dorsetshire*, the old carrier HMS *Hermes* and the destroyer HMS *Vampire*. Because of other commitments, these were sent on to Ceylon.

Air search

Barely had Somerville reached Addu, on the evening of 4 April, than an air search spotted Nagumo less than 645km (400 miles) south-east of the island. Caught flat-footed, the British sailed immediately, although with no hope of forestalling the attack. Ceylon, uncovered, sailed the two cruisers to meet Somerville and braced itself for the onslaught.

As at Pearl Harbor, the Japanese picked a Sunday before breakfast for the raid, and shore-based radar tracked the force of 126 aircraft as they made for the target, Colombo. Being protected by organized AA defences and the RAF, the harbour was not cleared of

shipping. As it happened, the 40 or more fighters that met the Japanese lost half their number without managing to break up the attack. But after the 30-minute attack, which cost the Japanese seven aircraft, the port still functioned.

Unfortunately, just before mid-day, an Aichi E13A 'Jake' floatplane from the cruiser *Tone* sighted the two hurrying cruisers. For over three hours the aircraft dogged their heels until it had vectored in a 90-aircraft strike. Lacking any air cover, the two British ships were swamped and sunk within 20 minutes, with the loss of over 400 lives.

Seeking to redress the balance, Somerville steered to intercept Nagumo at dawn on 6 April. The victorious Japanese did not oblige, probably fortunately for the British, who would almost certainly have been worsted.

Japan victorious

To exploit the likely panic resulting from the Colombo attack, Nagumo had formed a separate raiding force, centred on the smaller carrier *Ryujo* which was, in any case, too slow to operate as part of the main group.

This force had sailed on 1 April from newly occupied Burma and had divided into three divisions to mop up mercantile traffic on the Orissa coast. In the space of 10 days the surface warships, backed by submarines and

the *Ryujo*'s 48 aircraft, accounted for 28 merchant ships totalling 145,000 tons and had bombed a couple of ports for good measure.

The *Ryujo* group disengaged on 7 April, but the British were allowed no respite for, on the afternoon of the following day, Nagumo was again spotted by a Ceylon-based PBY, some 725km (450 miles) to the east. Again, Somerville was at Addu, having just detached his older ships for the less hazardous waters of East Africa. The Japanese course suggested either Trincomalee or Madras and, with no hope of a naval interception, the ports were cleared. Some 15 hours after the PBY's sighting report, 85 aircraft hit Trincomalee. They found no shipping and few targets ashore, but again roughly handled the RAF. Nine British bombers became the first to attack the Japanese carriers, but suffered dearly for little return.

A 'Jake' from the *Haruna* found the *Hermes* close inshore. The carrier sailed when the harbour was cleared, carried no fighters and was prevented by communications problems from calling up shore-based air cover. No less than 85 escorted dive-bombers saturated her with bombs. Within minutes, having absorbed an estimated 40 250kg (551 lb) projectiles, she capsized and sank. One destroyer and two tankers followed her.

Admiral Nagumo recovered his aircraft and turned for home. He had succeeded in defeating the British as soundly as he had the Americans and, for the moment, the seas beyond the Japanese western defence perimeter were secure. Although the Japanese never again penetrated the Indian Ocean in such strength, the scale of their activities had guaranteed that a counter-offensive would be a long time coming.

Darwin was the main supply base for the hastily cobbled together ABDA naval force, and one of the 12 vessels sunk or destroyed on 19 February was the **Neptune,** *an ammunition ship.*

Above: HMS Cornwall *founders following the strike by Nagumo's aircraft. After spotting the British cruisers, the E13A from the heavy cruiser* Tone *shadowed the ship for three hours until the massive air strike could be vectored in to attack them.*

Left: Admiral Chuichi Nagumo was to lead the 1st Koku Kantai (1st Air Fleet) of the Imperial Japanese navy's Combined Fleet through six months of the most stunning naval action the world has seen, from the attack on Pearl Harbor to the climactic Battle of Midway.

Expansion in the Pacific
Chronology

The Japanese Pacific offensive following Pearl Harbor matched the brilliance of the German blitzkrieg in the West. By August 1942 Japan had captured territories to a range of 3200km (2000 miles) from the homeland.

1941
December 7th
The US Pacific Fleet at Pearl Harbor is devastated by an Japanese air attack launched from a Japanese Carrier Strike Force of six carriers.

December 10th
Two large Japanese detachments land on the northern coastline of Luzon at Aparri, Gonzago and Vigan. Both advance southwards capturing the airfields at

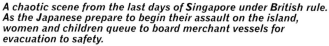

A chaotic scene from the last days of Singapore under British rule. As the Japanese prepare to begin their assault on the island, women and children queue to board merchant vessels for evacuation to safety.

Tuguegarao and Laoag on December 12th.

December 22nd
The Japanese 48th Division lands on Luzon at Lingayen Bay. On December 25th the division begins a strong southwards drive towards the Philippines capital Manila, pushing US forces before them.

December 23rd
General Douglas MacArthur orders US forces on Luzon to withdraw into the Bataan Peninsula as the Japanese advance on Manila from the north. Two further Japanese landings south of MacArthur's troops prevent the US forces withdrawing south.

December 23rd
A Japanese invasion force under Rear-Admiral Kajioka Sadamichi occupies Wake island. The small garrison on the island had resisted Japanese assault since

December 7th, and had killed over 1000 Japanese troops and sunk four warships with its coastal guns.

December 27th
Manila falls to the Japanese as US forces make a desperate fighting retreat into the Bataan Peninsula.

1942
January 9th
Japanese forces begin their main assault into the Bataan peninsula, taking the US troops' initial line of defences on January 23rd.

January 11th
The Malayan capital, Kuala Lumpur, falls to the Japanese 5th Division which has advanced 300 miles down the mainland.

January 15th
The Japanese Southern Army invades Burma at Victoria Point. They proceed to

Japanese troops cheer another victory of the imperial Blitzkrieg in the Pacific. Here they celebrate the capture of a US position on Bataan in April 1942, all US forces on the peninsula surrendering on April 9th and thousands of Allies going into captivity.

advance northwards against a weak British defence, making the 370km (230 miles) to Tavoy in only four days.

January 11th–February 14th
Three separate Japanese assault forces invade the Dutch East Indies. By mid February the Japanese control Borneo, Sarawak and Celebes.

February 15th
Singapore surrenders to the Japanese and over 60,000 Allied troops are taken prisoner-of-war. The Japanese had suffered little more than 2000 casualties during the whole campaign to take the island.

February 19th
Twelve Allied ships are sunk in Darwin and Broome, north-western Australia, when attacked in an hour-long raid by forces of the Japanese 1st Air Fleet.

February 19th–March 8th
Bali, Timor and Java become further Japanese conquests, completing the occupation of the Dutch East Indies.

March 8th
Rangoon, Burma, falls to the Japanese offensive, though the British Burma Army garrison just manages to escape encirclement. On the same day Japanese forces invade New Guinea, though naval defeats later on at Coral Sea and Midway means that they never conquer the country.

April 1st
A force of Japanese warships centred on the carrier *Ryujo* enters the Bay of Bengal. Its mission is to interdict Allied merchant vessels in the Indian Ocean.

April 9th
US forces in the Bataan Peninsula finally surrender after three months of heavy fighting.

April 3rd
Five Japanese carriers constituting Admiral Chuichi Nagumo's 1st Air Fleet enter the Indian Ocean, sailing for Ceylon.

April 4th
The British naval force protecting the Indian Ocean – a fleet of five battleships and three carriers under command of Admiral Sir James Somerville – receives a warning that Japanese carriers are less than 645km (400 miles) from at Ceylon. Somerville sails a force to intercept the Japanese

April 6th
Over 120 Japanese strike aircraft surprise and strike British ships in and around Colombo harbour, Ceylon. Twenty-six Allied aircraft are shot down and three ships sunk, the cruisers *Dorsetshire* and *Cornwall,* and the destroyer *Tenedos*.

April 9th
Eighty-five Japanese aircraft from Nagumo's carriers attack the airfield and dockyards at Trincomalee, Ceylon. British intelligence had forewarned of the attack, and the Japanese find few targets and lose five aircraft. However, Japanese aircraft locate the British carrier *Hermes* and assorted escorts sailing for Ceylon. The *Hermes* is sunk in a massive air raid along with four other Allied vessels.

May 5th–6th
The Japanese take Corregidor island in the neck of Manila Bay after a two-day campaign.

May 15th
Japanese forces in Burma reach the northern borders with India and China, adding another country to their list of conquests.

May–August 1942
The Japanese expand their conquests throughout the Pacific island chains, acquiring the Caroline Islands, Gilbert Islands, Marshall Islands, Marianas Islands and much of the Solomons and reaching the high tide of their conquests. By this stage of the war, however, the Japanese navy had been effectively defeated by the US Navy and the US armed forces were beginning campaigns to take back Papua New Guinea and the Solomon Islands.

International Events
1941
December 22nd
The Arcadia Conference in Washington sees the US President Franklin Roosevelt and the British Prime Minister Winston Churchill agreed that the defeat of Germany remains the Allied priority in spite of the entry of Japan into the war.

1942
January 20th
The 'Final Solution' for the extermination of European Jews is formalised during a conference at Wannsee, Berlin, headed by the deputy head of the SS, Reinhard Heydrich.

February 14th
A controversial 'Area Bombing Directive' issued by RAF Bomber Command includes German civilian areas as legitimate targets for future air raids.

May 30th
The city of Cologne, Germany, receives the first 1000-bomber raid of RAF Bomber Command.

June 28th
The Germans finally break the Russian defences at Sevastopol, taking 90,000 troops prisoner and securing the German hold over the Kerch peninsula, Crimea.

August 23rd
Advancing German forces on the Eastern Front reach the river Volga, but start to experience ferocious resistance around the city of Stalingrad.

Admiral Isoroku Yamamoto, commander-in-chief of the Japanese navy from 1939. Yamamoto was responsible for planning the attack on Pearl Harbor in December 1941, though he was actually opposed to war with the United States. He was killed in April 1943 when US fighters shot down his aircraft near Bougainville.

Coral Sea
Carriers in action

Japan threatens New Guinea, and a new kind of sea battle is in prospect, in which the triumphant Imperial Japanese navy suffers its first setback.

To further their intentions of cutting the lines of communication between the USA and Australia, Japan in April 1942 mounted Operation MO to capture the southern New Guinea town of Port Moresby by seaborne landing and to establish a seaplane reconnaissance base on Tulagi, farther to the east in the Solomons. Where a small force would suffice to take the undefended Tulagi, the dozen transports of the Port Moresby group were covered by an escort that included the new light carrier *Shoho*. As the move was fully expected to attract elements of the US Navy, Vice-Admiral Takeo Takagi was to double the Solomons chain with the two big carriers *Shokaku* and *Zuikaku* and take them from the rear.

Codebreaker success
Even at this early stage of the war, however, the Americans could decode sufficient enemy intercepts to gauge Admiral Isoroku Yamamoto's intentions and CINCPAC (Admiral Chester Nimitz) despatched Rear Admiral Frank Fletcher's Task Force 17 to the area. Built on the carriers USS *Lexington* and *Yorktown*, this force was already in the Coral Sea on 3 May when news came of the landing on Tulagi. *Yorktown* diverted to conduct three separate air strikes during 4 May, which caused little damage but advertised Fletcher's presence to Takagi. The latter could not get into strike range until 5 May, however, by which time *Yorktown* had rejoined her partner farther to the south.

While neither carrier force could locate the other during the 5/6 May, the Port Moresby group, which had departed Rabaul on 4 May, was located, reported and attacked by Allied land-based aircraft. Reacting on cue, Fletcher moved across the Coral Sea to attack it further. Early on 7 May both carrier forces staged air searches. Takagi located the American oiler *Neosho* and her single destroyer escort. Reporting the tanker as a carrier, the pilot brought down a full-scale air attack from the Japanese carriers which, while it caused the eventual loss of the two ships, almost certainly saved Fletcher from discovery at a critical juncture. As it happened, the Americans had located elements of the Port Moresby group and as these, too, were wrongly reported as including two carriers, Fletcher launched two-thirds of his air strength at what he believed to be Takagi.

Knowing themselves to have been located, the Japanese temporarily reversed the course of the transports. As a result the full force of the American attack fell upon the luckless *Shoho*, which could muster only 21 aircraft in total. Engaged herself in launching aircraft, she could offer little resistance: the combined gunfire of the group kept the *Lexington*'s aircraft at a distance but those of the *Yorktown*, following immediately behind at 1025, bore through the flak and overwhelmed her.

Carrier battle begins
Within the space of 10 minutes *Shoho* was hit by 13 454kg (1000lb) bombs, possibly seven torpedoes and a crashing Douglas SBD, and sank, shattered. Only three aircraft were lost in this first example of carrier-against-carrier warfare, but Fletcher had been fortunate in remaining undiscovered while his main strength was thus diverted. Recovering his victorious aircraft, Fletcher retired under the cover of heavy frontal cloud. Surprised by *Shoho*'s loss, the Japanese deferred the

Capable of 394 km/h (245 mph) and with a range of 1770km (1100miles), the SBD was the most effective American strike aeroplane at the Battles of the Coral Sea and Midway.

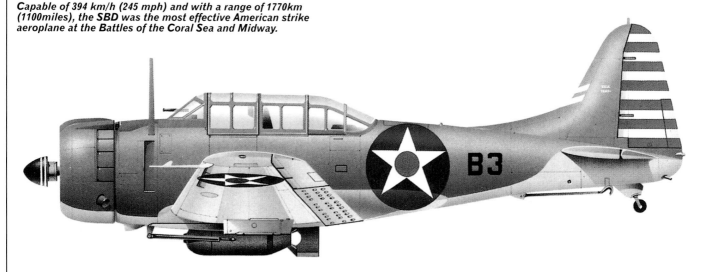

Codenamed 'Kate' by the Allies, the Nakajima B5N was the best torpedo-bomber in the world in 1942. Its only weakness was the poor defensive armament of just one 7.7-mm (0.3-in) machine-gun in the rear of the cockpit.

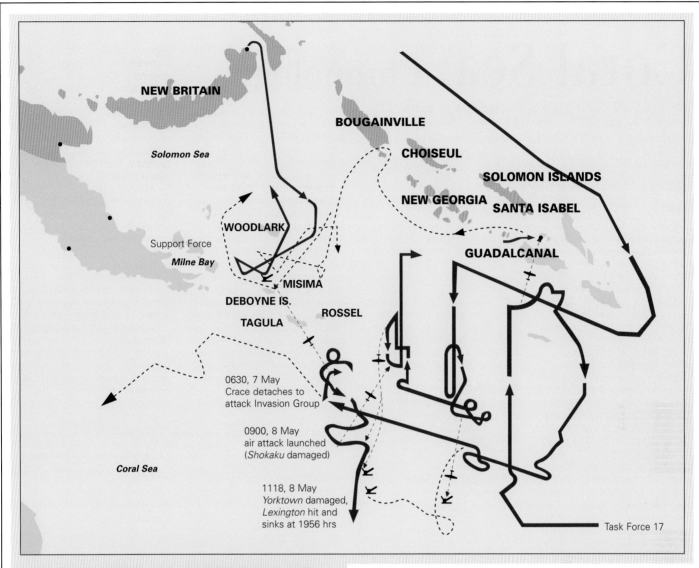

Map labels:
NEW BRITAIN
Solomon Sea
BOUGAINVILLE
CHOISEUL
SOLOMON ISLANDS
NEW GEORGIA
SANTA ISABEL
WOODLARK
Support Force
Milne Bay
GUADALCANAL
MISIMA
DEBOYNE IS.
ROSSEL
TAGULA

0630, 7 May
Crace detaches to
attack Invasion Group

0900, 8 May
air attack launched
(*Shokaku* damaged)

Coral Sea

1118, 8 May
Yorktown damaged,
Lexington hit and
sinks at 1956 hrs

Task Force 17

THE COLLAPSE OF OPERATION MO

The Japanese amphibious assault on Port Moresby was abandoned after the sinking of *Shoho* removed its fighter cover. In the subsequent exchange of air strikes the Japanese lost 86 aircraft which prevented *Shokaku* and *Zuikaku* fighting at Midway, where these big carriers could have made all the difference and prevented US victory.

progress of their transports still further.

Dawn on 8 May saw the two carrier groups only 320km (200 miles) apart. By 0720 each had located the other and each launched an air strike at a maximum strength. By this time it was Takagi concealed beneath murky weather but he was found by *Yorktown*'s aircraft at about 1030. The still inexperienced Douglas TBD crews wasted their torpedoes by releasing at too great a range and at the wrong bearing to take account of the speed of the Japanese. The dive-bombers succeeded in hitting *Shokaku* twice, one hit forward damaging the flightdeck to the extent that she could not launch further aircraft. Most of *Lexington*'s aircraft failed even to find the Japanese but one that did arrive score a further bomb hit at about 1140.

In the meantime, the mixed 69-plane Japanese strike had been detected by Fletcher's radar but arrived as the defensive fighter screen was being changed. A bomb went deep into the *Yorktown* at 1120, damaged her but failed to put her out of action.

Synchronised bombing

Simultaneously, *Lexington* was attacked by a small group of torpedo bombers which, coming from either bow, succeeded in hitting her twice. A synchronised dive-bombing attack also scored two hits. Her elevators were jammed in the raised position, though initially the flightdeck could still be used. Unfortunately, her Avgas system had been badly shaken, releasing highly explosive vapour. At about noon came the first of a series of gas explosions that were to wrack the great ship, causing fires that became uncontrollable. All possible aircraft were flown to *Yorktown* and the ship abandoned at 1700, later to be sunk by torpedo.

The effect of the Coral Sea action was to oblige the Japanese to abandon their seaborne invasion of Port Moresby. Any further attempts were out of the question because of the imminent fleet operation against Midway. The presence of Takagi's two big carriers at the latter action might have proved decisive, but the MO operation caused their absence.

A Dauntless flown by Lt Powers of Yorktown *scored a direct hit on* Shokaku *at the cost of both crew members' lives. The carrier survived, but she lost most of her air group at Coral Sea.*

Coral Sea: Chronology

The Battle of Coral Sea was the first naval battle decided by aircraft carriers in history. Though technically a win for the Japanese, the losses they suffered during the action would help the US to victory in the later Battle of Midway and prevented a Japanese invasion of Australia.

1942
May 3rd
Japanese forces make an amphibious landing at the island of Tulagi in the Solomons group and establish a base for sea planes and shipping. A Japanese Carrier Striking Force meanwhile sails around the Solomons in search of US carrier units. It hopes to make a flanking attack against US forces seeking to disrupt a Japanese Invasion Group destined for Port Moresby in New Guinea. US Navy and Allied forces in the area are aware of the Japanese plan through Ultra intelligence.

May 4th
Aircraft from the carrier *Yorktown* south of Guadalcanal attack Japanese shipping and land positions at Tulagi at 6.30am, sinking several minor vessels. The Port Moresby Invasion Group leaves its base at Rabaul in New Britain. It is under the protection of a two-carrier Covering Group commanded by Rear-Admiral Goto.

May 5th–6th
In conditions of poor weather the US and Japanese carriers fail to locate each other south of the Solomons.

May 7th
Task Force 44, a mixture of Allied cruisers and destroyers under command of Rear-Admiral Crace, Royal Navy, heads to attack the Japanese invasion convoy. They are spotted by Japanese reconnaissance aircraft and bombed through the day, never making the intercept with the invasion force. In the far south of Allied operations, the US destroyers *Neosho* and *Sims* are lost to a Japanese air attack after it confused them for the main Allied fleet. The Allies, however, detect the Japanese Covering Group. Attacks by aircraft from the *Lexington* and *Yorktown* sink the Japanese carrier *Shoho*.

May 7th–8th
The Japanese Invasion Group destined for Port Morseby aborts the mission and heads back for New Britain. On the night of the 7th/8th, 27 aircraft are launched from the Japanese Carrier Strike Force. They cannot locate the Allies, however, and only six return home safely.

May 8th
The Japanese Carrier Striking Force and the US carrier groups (known as Task Force 11 and Task Force 17) locate each other shortly after daybreak.

9.25am
Air strikes are launched from the rival carriers.

May 1942. US Navy Douglas SBD Dauntless dive bombers and Douglas TBD Devastator torpedo bombers prepare to take off from the deck of the USS Yorktown during the battle of Coral Sea. Devastators would soon be replaced by the Grumman TBF Avenger.

11.40am
The Japanese carrier *Shokaku* is badly damaged during US bombing runs.

2.47pm
A huge explosion rocks the *Lexington* after a Japanese torpedo strike blows her gasoline tanks in the generator room. The carrier cannot be saved.

6.00pm
Almost all the crew of the *Lexington* have been evacuated to other ships. At 6.10pm the ship is scuttled and finally sunk.

May 9th
Vice-Admiral Takagi, the commander of the Carrier Striking Force, is ordered back to engage the US carriers despite a chronic depletion of aircraft. The two fleets do not locate each other and the Battle of Coral Sea ends.

International Events 1942
May 5th
The RAF implement a new radio-jamming technology in action. It reduces the accuracy of German bombing runs by over 30 per cent.

May 6th
Allied forces on the Philippine island of Corregidor surrender to the Japanese. Over 12,000 prisoners enter Japanese prison camps.

May 6th
Chinese forces under General Chiang Kai-shek begin a large offensive against Japanese troops in several cities, including Shanghai and Nanking.

May 8th
In London the War Cabinet orders a renewed push in the desert war of North Africa after a 643km (400-mile) advance by Rommel's forces from El Agheila on the Libyan coast to Cyrenaica.

Crew from the doomed US carrier Lexington are helped aboard another US Navy ship. Despite the loss of the carrier to Japanese carrier aircraft, nearly 3000 crew were rescued.

The US carrier Bon Homme Richard (CV-31) is launched on 29 April 1944. The carrier went on to serve in the Pacific, assisting in the bombing of mainland Japan towards the very end of the war.

The Battle of Midway

Decision in the Pacific

On 4 June 1942 the Imperial Japanese Navy tried to lure the Americans into a colossal ambush at Midway. It was a battle of move and counter-move, the main participants never being within 161km (100 miles) of each other.

Like Admiral Jellicoe's Grand Fleet in World War I, the Imperial Japanese Navy was nurtured on the concept of the 'great decisive battle', and Admiral Isoroku Yamamoto devised the 'MI' operation to bring this about. Landings were first to be undertaken in the Aleutians, drawing US strength north in counter-attack. Once this was committed, the strategic US outpost of Midway Island was to be taken. Only 1850km (1150 miles) from Hawaii, it would pose a threat that Admiral Chester Nimitz, commander-in-chief Pacific, could not ignore. His weakened fleet would be thrown into the island's recovery but would be 'bushwhacked' by the Japanese in full strength. The plan was flawed both by its complexity and by its instigators not realising that the US could largely divine their intentions by decoding radio intercepts.

US carrier power

US carrier strength was currently at a low ebb. Of the four decks in the Pacific, only USS *Enterprise* and *Hornet* of Vice Admiral William Halsey's Task Force 16 were at Pearl Harbor (recently returned from launching Doolittle's famous B-25 raid on Tokyo). USS *Yorktown* arrived with bomb damage from the Coral Sea on 27 May but was docked and repaired sufficiently for action in a remarkable three days. The newly-repaired USS *Saratoga* was still on the western seaboard and was never to arrive in time.

The Japanese committed 162 ships to 'MI' organised in 13 separate groups. Of these, aircraft from the carriers *Junyo* and *Ryujo* began their attack on Attu in the Aleutians on 3 June, but the US was not drawn. Planned Japanese reconnaissance by both flying-boat and submarine in the Midway area had failed, but US aircraft from the island located elements of the enemy invasion force in the forenoon of 4 June while they were yet nearly 1125km (700 miles) distant to the west. Still unsighted was the Japanese spearhead, Vice Admiral Chuichi Nagumo's seasoned carrier group less the two decks unavailable following the Coral Sea action. Some 480km (300 miles) astern of these was the main battle fleet, with Yamamoto himself

In the wake of the battle, the shattered Japanese carrier force retreated westward, leaving the crippled 'Mogami'-class cruisers Mogami *and* Mikuma *to make for the safety of Wake Island.*

MIDWAY: DEFEAT FOR NAGUMO'S CARRIERS

Together with Coral Sea, the Battle of Midway highlighted the new prominence of the aircraft carrier in the war at sea. Vice Admiral Chuichi Nagumo's First Carrier Striking Force comprised the carriers *Akagi*, *Kaga*, *Hiryu* and *Soryu*, joined later by the Second Fleet with two battleships, five cruisers, eight destroyers and one small carrier. Facing Nagumo was Rear Admiral Fletcher's Task Force 17, comprising the carrier *Yorktown*, two cruisers and five destroyers; and Rear Admiral Spruance's Task Force 16 with the carriers *Enterprise* and *Hornet*, six cruisers and nine destroyers. Thanks to superior intelligence, the US Navy dive-bombers were able to strike at the heart of the Imperial Japanese Navy, and claim the destruction of all four aircraft carriers within the IJN's First Carrier Striking Force.

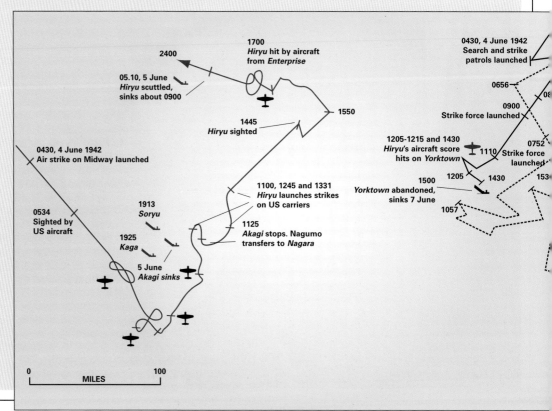

USS Yorktown *darkens the sky with its anti-aircraft barrage while a Japanese torpedo-bomber roars past. Hit by three bombs,* Yorktown *was crippled.*

Below right: Excellent damage control had Yorktown *back in action before the second Japanese air strike from* Hiryu *that delivered two fatal torpedo hits. Listing ominously,* Yorktown *had to be abandoned. A Japanese submarine finally sank the carrier the next day.*

in the battleship *Yamato*, ready to fall upon the Americans once they were committed. As a catalyst, the Midway Operation Force was advancing some 965km (600 miles) to the south.

Element of surprise

USS *Enterprise* and *Hornet* (commanded by Rear Admiral Raymond Spruance in the absence of an indisposed Halsey) were in company with Rear Admiral Frank Fletcher's *Yorktown* (a potentially problematic division of responsibility) and waiting, unsuspected, in a position about 565km (350 miles) north-east of the island. Admiral Yamamoto, the would-be ambusher, was about to be ambushed in turn.

At 0430 on 4 June, Vice Admiral Nagumo launched the first strike of 72 bombers and 36 fighters against the island. He was approximately 385km (240 miles) from target and continued to close at high speed.

As a powerful defensive screen of fighters circled above to take care of a return attack from Midway, nearly 100 aircraft were armed with armour-piercing bombs and torpedoes to deal with the US ships as they approached.

Air attack

At 0530 Nagumo's force was sighted by a Midway-based Consolidated PBY and the island's whole air complement was scrambled. With the Japanese carriers now

pinpointed, Spruance moved in. Between 0630 and 0700 the enemy aircraft succeeded in damaging the island's facilities against a stout defence but signalled that a second strike would be required.

Counter-move

However, Nagumo had already found himself with 67 aircraft lost or damaged, the whereabouts of US carriers (if any) yet unknown, and the remaining four decks involved in the operation widely dispersed in the complexity of Yamamoto's plan. Any unease that Nagumo may have experienced was relieved somewhat by the total lack of success enjoyed by those Midway-based aircraft that had attacked him. Their strength, however, convinced him of the wisdom of a follow-up strike against the island and, in the continuing absence of reports of any US fleet movement, the remain-

ing aircraft aboard were ordered to be rearmed with blast bombs, and were struck below for the purpose.

At 0800, however, Spruance and Fletcher had launched a 151-aircraft strike. This was still en route when, at last, a Japanese reconnaissance floatplane found the Americans. Its signal provoked something akin to panic at Nagumo's end, with the aircraft aboard having to be rearmed yet again. Despite this, the Japanese fighter cover was highly effective. While many of *Hornet*'s aircraft failed to find the target, a combined attack by 41 Douglas TBDs at 1018 lost 35 aircraft. It did, however, bring down the fighters to sea level so that the following 49 dive-bombers had it all their own way. *Akagi, Kaga* and *Soryu*, closely grouped, took two, four and three heavy bomb hits respectively. Littered with fuelled aircraft and two sets of munitions, all were soon fiercely ablaze

and out of the action, later to sink. *Hiryu* was distant from the remainder and escaped for the moment, launching dive-bombers in return. These found *Yorktown* as it was recovering its own victorious aircraft and, though roughly handled by its fighter screen, hit the carrier three times. Ablaze, it came to a halt at about 1220 but then managed to yet again get under way. Only 200km (125 miles) now separated the forces, and a second *Hiryu* strike put two torpedoes into it at about 1445. Abandoned, it refused to sink and was taken in tow.

The last strike

Again *Enterprise* and *Hornet* sent off their weary, surviving aircrews. Forty Douglas SBDs found *Hiryu* about the same business. Four bombs removed most of its forward flight deck and four near misses shook the hull. Completely gutted, it was later scuttled.

Only the eventual loss of USS *Yorktown*, to submarine torpedoes while still in tow, marred the completeness of the US victory. Eleven battleships had been present but the action hinged on, and was decided completely by, aircraft-carriers. The over-confident Japanese had been halted. Within six months of Pearl Harbor four of the six culprit carriers were on the bottom of the Pacific, and the enemy had been obliged to abandon its plans to isolate Australia.

Several TBF-1 Avengers were still on Midway Island when the Japanese attacked. Six of them joined the air strike launched from the island that was massacred by Japanese fighters and naval gunfire. They were all lost and scored no hits. This particular aircraft was to have joined Hornet *as one of the first of the type to go to sea, but was one of the fateful six to attack the Japanese fleet.*

The Battle of Midway
Chronology

The Battle of Midway signalled the high tide of Japanese forces in the Pacific. Following the destruction of half of its carrier fleet, Japanese forces were forced to switch to the defensive.

1942
May 25th–28th
Almost the entire Japanese fleet sails from Japan and the Marianas Islands destined for Midway in the central Pacific. The fleet is divided into four groups. The Northern Task Force heads for the Aleutian Islands far north of Midway, intending to draw US forces away from Midway, while three other Japanese Task Forces sail to Midway to occupy the island itself. The Task Forces destined for Midway are the Midway Occupation Force, a Main Striking Force and the First Carrier Striking Force containing four aircraft carriers.

June 3rd
The Northern Force begins its attacks on the Aleutian islands, and during the month of June the islands of Kiska and Attu are occupied. The US commander-in-chief Pacific Fleet, Admiral Nimitz, had received prior intelligence about the Aleutian diversion and so kept his main forces – including the three carriers *Enterprise*, *Hornet* and *Yorktown* – in the Midway area.

June 4th
4.30am
Midway island is bombed by aircraft from Vice-Admiral Nagumo's First Carrier Striking Force. US aircraft flying from Midway suffer heavy losses, but impose an important delay on Nagumo's plans by forcing his aircraft to return and rearm for a second strike at the island.

7.28am
The crew of a Japanese reconnaissance aircraft informs Nagumo that 10 US ships are positioned roughly

A Japanese Nakajima B5N 'Kate' is cut down by anti-aircraft fire from the USS Yorktown. *The B5N accounted for three US carrier sinkings during the Pacific campaign. By 1943, however, US fighters found it an easy target – its single rear-mounted machine gun was totally inadequate for air defence.*

320km (200 miles) northeast of the Japanese Midway forces. Nagumo is not told, however, what type of ships they are.

7.52am
Torpedo planes and dive-bombers take off from the decks of the USS *Enterprise* and *Hornet*.

8.20am
Nagumo is informed that an aircraft carrier has been spotted amongst the US naval forces. The information is a

shock to Nagumo, who believed that no US carriers were in the Midway area.

8.37am
The Japanese aircraft from the second strike at Midway begin returning to their carriers for refuelling and rearming.

9.00am
The *Yorktown* launches its complement of aircraft. Some 150 US aircraft are committed to the attack on Nagumo's carrier force.

9.30am–10.00am
US torpedo aircraft from the *Enterprise* and *Hornet* begin their first strikes against the Japanese carriers, carriers packed with refuelling and rearming bombers and fighters. All of the US Devastator aircraft are shot down by Japanese Zero fighters in only six minutes. Nagumo also changed the course of his Carrier Striking Force at 9.18am, and the first US dive-bombers cannot find their target. By 10.00am the Japanese force appears to

have survived the US air assault intact.

10.25am
A dive-bomber group containing 37 Dauntless aircraft from the *Enterprise* catches the Japanese carriers by surprise and begins a stunning attack. Within only five minutes three Japanese carriers *Kaga, Soryu* and *Akagi* are destroyed as bombs explode amongst the ammunition, aviation fuel and aircraft on the decks.

Midday-2.30pm
Aircraft from the Japanese carrier *Hiryu* make retaliatory strikes against the *Yorktown*, severely crippling the vessel.

3.00pm
The *Yorktown* is abandoned by its crew. The damaged ship is sunk two days later by a Japanese submarine.

5.00pm
The *Hiryu* is turned into an inferno after being struck by five bombs from *Enterprise* dive-bombers. The ship is scuttled the next day.

International Events 1942

May 31st
Over 1000 RAF bombers obliterate the city of Cologne, Germany. The damage caused has left nearly 50,000 people homeless.

May 31st
Soviet forces around Kharkov are encircled by a massive Germany counteroffensive named Operation Fridericus. Nearly 250,000 Soviet troops are doomed to either death or imprisonment.

June 3rd
Coal-mining in the UK becomes an entirely government-run business to ensure the smooth flow of coal supplies to the war effort.

June 4th
The head of the Reich Security Main Office, Reinhard Heydrich, dies of wounds incurred eight days earlier following a grenade attack by Czech partisans.

June 6th
North Africa. A major offensive by Rommel aimed at breaking through the Allied Gazala Line fails, the German and Italian forces having suffered unsustainable losses.

Crew members of the USS Yorktown *work hard to repair damage incurred at the Battle of Midway. Midway was to see* Yorktown *sent to the bottom of the Pacific. Fire crews brought most of the onboard blazes under control, but the ignition of escaping gas vapour in a huge explosion sealed the ship's fate.*

Battle of Guadalcanal

All for an airfield

7 August 1942:19,000 US Marines land on the island of Guadalcanal at the start of the USA's first counter-offensive in the Pacific theatre.

In 1942 the Solomon Islands suddenly became a key strategic position in the developing war in the South Pacific. In Japanese hands they would threaten the supply routes between the USA and Australia, in Allied hands they would form first a shield for the build-up of Allied strength in Australia, second an essential springboard for an Allied offensive to drive the Japanese back to their own islands.

By May the Japanese had already installed a sizeable garrison at the magnificent anchorage of Tulagi on the small Florida Island at the eastern end of the Solomons, and at the end of that month they began ferrying troops across the Nggela Channel to the larger island of Guadalcanal. Soon reports were reaching General Douglas MacArthur from the team of Australian 'coast-watchers' that the Japanese were constructing an airfield near Lunga Point and the village of Kukum, and the danger of Japanese

The fighting on Guadalcanal presaged the type of combat the Americans would encounter as they stormed across the islands groups of the Pacific: short-range and brutal in hostile conditions.

bombers being able to operate from there against Allied shipping, and even against the Australian mainland, became obvious.

Successful landing

On 7 August, somewhat to the surprise of all concerned, a force of 19,000 US Marines under Major General Alexander Vandegrift was landed successfully at both Lunga Point and Tulagi, and by the evening the Marines had chased the 2200 Japanese construction workers off into the jungle, while 36 hours later the 1500 Japanese soldiers at Tulagi had also been eliminated. By 8 August the airfield was being completed by US engineers and had been rechristened Henderson Field, and by 20 August the

first Grumman F4F Wildcat fighters and Douglas SBD Dauntless dive-bombers had landed.

But before that, of course, the Japanese had reacted. The Battle of Savo Island had severely weakened Allied naval strength, and the withdrawal of Rear Admiral Richmond Turner's force had left the Marines very short of materials with which to build strong defences; fortunately, there was quite a lot of Japanese material around, which was put to good use.

This was proved on 18 August when a Japanese force of some 6000 troops commanded by Colonel Ichiki, who was under the

impression that only 2000 US Marines had been landed, attacked Henderson Field and ran into a deadly storm of fire which quickly wiped his command from the face of the earth. Thereafter, Japanese attacks were a trifle less reckless, but the Imperial command never seemed able accurately to foresee the US Marines' strength on the island.

Every battle of the 'Slot', from each phase of the Battle of the Eastern Solomons, through the Battles of Cape Esperance and the Santa Cruz Islands to the last engagements which the Japanese called the Naval Battle of Guadalcanal, was fought to take more Japanese troops to the island in order to regain control of Henderson Field. The Tokyo Express had brought in another 8000 men by 13 September – and over 1200 of them were killed that night on Bloody Ridge.

A month later, after Cape Esperance, the Japanese strength had risen to 22,000 troops on the island – but there were now 23,000 Marines with another 4500 on Tulagi, for it was far easier for the Allies to reinforce from Australia than for the Japanese from their own homeland, or even from Luzon. Bombardment of Henderson Field by the heavy guns of two Japanese

US MARINE

In overall terms the men of the US Marine Corps, which in World War II was committed only in the Pacific theatre, were superior to their Japanese opponents in terms of physique and training, were well equipped and supplied, and enjoyed the benefits of the high levels of morale and self-confidence that came with the USMC's position as an elite force within the US military. One of the most important features of the USMC in World War II was its readiness to adapt swiftly and readily to the conditions in which its formations found themselves, and this is evident in the kit and equipment of this Marine. Fighting on a jungle island such as Guadalcanal, beset by high temperature, rainfall and humidity, demand the use of lightweight, camouflaged uniform, while the short ranges at which combat typically took place in the island campaigns of the Pacific war placed emphasis on short-range firepower. This was provided by the 7.62mm (0.3in) Carbine M1 with a 15- or 30-round magazine.

Their nature made most Pacific islands unsuitable for heavier armour, but the 37mm (1.45in) guns of light tanks were adequate for tasks such as bunker-busting.

battlecruisers set fire to fuel stocks, destroyed over half the aircraft there and so thoroughly ploughed up the field that the bombers had to return to Australia for a time. But the land attack on the field was beaten off yet again at the end of October with Japanese losses running into thousands, while the Marines, fighting from well-sited and well-dug defensive positions and gaining experience with every hour, lost only a few hundred. American medical teams were now saving a large proportion of the wounded and most of the large numbers of sick.

Abandoned offensive

On the night of 14/15 November, when seven of the transports Rear Admiral Raizo Tanaka was trying to bring down the Slot were sunk, only 4000 of the 11,000 Japanese troops sent to Guadalcanal arrived, and as they went into action the Americans abandoned the defensive which they had held so successfully for nearly

Digging in was difficult in groves of palm trees, but fallen trees provided good defensive positions and the trunks could be used to create extemporized defensive positions.

four months and went over to the offensive. During the last days of the month the Marines enlarged their perimeter so that in the early days of December there was space for the 25th Infantry Division, the 2nd Marine Division and the 'Americal' Division – XIV Corps under Major General Alexander Patch – to come in and relieve Vandegrift's gallant but now tired 1st Marine Division. Quickly Patch organized for a drive out, to clear the Japanese from the island.

But by now Imperial Japanese Headquarters was beginning to count the cost. Since 7 August losses totalled 65 naval craft and more than 800 aircraft; as for men, the calculations were difficult to make. It was apparent that while there were over 50,000 American troops on Guadalcanal, well supplied and well fed, whatever number of survivors of Lieutenant General Harukichi Hyakutake's 17th Army remained were on one-third of normal rations

and so weakened by hunger and disease that a new offensive was beyond them.

On 4 January 1943 the reality was accepted in Tokyo and the orders went out. Between 1 and 9 February destroyers of the 'Tokyo Express' came back to Guadalcanal for the last time, and successfully evacuated 11,000 men – whose rearguard had tenaciously kept back the American advance for the required time, and who left only their dead on the beaches.

Battle of Guadalcanal
Chronology

The Japanese defeat on Guadalcanal had numerous benefits for the Allies. It deprived the Japanese of an important airbase for operations over the Solomons and put a severe dent in the morale and self-belief of Japanese forces.

1942
July
Information reaches the Allies that the Japanese are constructing an air strip – later known as Henderson Field – on the island of Guadalcanal in the Solomon Islands. The news forces the US forces in the Pacific to bring forward plans for an invasion of the Solomons.

August 7th–8th
Landings are made on Guadalcanal, Tulagi and Gavutu in the Solomons by units of the 1st Marine Division. The Guadalcanal landing is virtually unopposed and the US troops are able to march straight to a deserted Henderson airfield and capture it.

August 8th
Major sea battles develop off the Solomons as the Japanese begin to respond to the US invasion. The US troops at Henderson Field consolidate the airfield under heavy bombardment from Japanese naval aircraft. The neighbouring islands of Tulagi and Gavutu are now in Allied hands.

August 18th
Japanese troops land at Taivu 32km (20 miles) to the east of Henderson Field as part of a counter-offensive.

August 20th
Henderson Field receives its first contingent of US fighter aircraft – 31 aircraft in total. The aircraft provide the Henderson garrison and the US ships off the Solomons with a vital source of air cover.

August 21st–22nd
Henderson Field and US positions on the Tenaru come under attack by a regiment of Japanese troops. The Japanese troops cannot break the US Marine defence, and are themselves surrounded and wiped out. The Japanese commander – Colonel Ichiki – commits suicide.

August 23rd–24th
The Japanese navy lose an aircraft carrier during the Battle of the Eastern Solomons.

September 7th–8th
US Marine Raiders launch a surprise amphibious assault against Japanese coastal positions at Taivu, gathering intelligence and destroying Japanese stores.

The Japanese defeat on Guadalcanal was the first major land defeat of the war for the Japanese. US forces learnt a great deal about tropical warfare, including the supremacy of sheer firepower in jungle combat conditions.

Two US Marines proudly display a captured Japanese flag. The campaign provided a salutary lesson about the amount of logistics and manpower required to clear major islands in the Pacific. Upwards of 100,000 US troops were used to clear Guadalcanal, and even small bunkers could take a US battalion half an hour to clear.

September 12th–14th
The Japanese launch their biggest offensive against the US soldiers on Guadalcanal using the Japanese 35th Brigade, 6000 soldiers in total. Though the attack comes within only 0.8km (0.5 miles) of Henderson airstrip, it is beaten off leaving 1200 Japanese dead on the battlefield.

September 15th–October 10th
The Japanese build up reinforcements to the west of Henderson Field and ship them to Tenaro less than 32km (20 miles) from the US perimeter.

October 23rd
Japanese forces under General Maruyama attack from the south with a strength of around 20,000 men of the 17th Army and 2nd Division.

October 26th
The Japanese offensive is called off after sustaining 3500 casualties.

November–January 1943
A stalemate exists between Japanese and US forces on Guadalcanal, with little significant campaigning taking place on either side. US forces grow to 58,000 strong on the island, while the Japanese posses only 20,000. During January the Japanese decide that their costs on Guadalcanal have been too high and they begin to withdraw westwards from January 17th.

1943
February 1st–7th
Around 11,000 Japanese soldiers are evacuated from Guadalcanal at Tenaro, and the island falls into US hands.

International Events
1942
August 23rd
On the Eastern Front the Luftwaffe bombs Stalingrad in a raid using over 600 aircraft.

October 23rd
North Africa. The Battle of El Alamein begins with a huge artillery bombardment and a surge of 195,000 Allied troops.

November 8th–11th
Operation Torch. Over 100,000 US and British troops are landed in Morocco and Algeria to open a second front in North Africa.

December 2nd
US scientists make progress towards developing an atomic weapon successfully making a chain reaction split of uranium atoms.

1943
January 13th
The Kokoda Trail – the vital route across New Guinea between Owen Stanley Range and Port Moresby – is taken by US and Australian soldiers.

January 14th–23rd
The Casablanca conference brings together the UK Prime Minister Winston Churchill and the US President Franklin Roosevelt to discuss the strategic development of WWII.

February 2nd
The German 6th Army at Stalingrad surrenders. Over 90,000 German soldiers enter into Soviet captivity, though only 5000 will survive the experience.

Solomons: The sea battles

As the troops slug it out on Guadalcanal, powerful naval forces converge on what becomes known as 'Iron Bottom Sound'.

The American landings on Guadalcanal marked the first stage in a long Pacific struggle. The Marine landings were soon to come under pressure from the sea, as the Imperial Japanese navy threw its weight behind attempts to defeat the invasion. The virtual annihilation of an Allied cruiser force off Savo Island showed up American inexperience as well as Japanese mastery of night fighting at sea. Fortunately for the landing ships, Vice Admiral Gunichi Mikawa's powerful cruisers left the scene for fear of being found by the American carrier force on the next day. The four cruisers which sank to the bottom of 'Iron Bottom Sound' were the first of many vessels to be lost in these crowded waters.

Tokyo Express

Although the Japanese controlled the 'Slot' (the passage down the centre of the Solomons chain) by night, American air power commanded it by day. The campaign became a series of moves and counter-moves, with the Japanese sending resupply convoys racing down the Slot in what became known as the 'Tokyo Express' with the Americans attacking them during the day from the air. The Japanese navy tried to get the American carriers within striking range of a combined fleet force under the command of Vice Admiral Chuichi Nagumo of Pearl Harbor fame. In the battle of the Eastern Solomons (22-25 August 1942), on 23 August, the Japanese light carrier *Ryujo*

Hornet's *list is evident on the afternoon of 26 October.* **Enterprise** *avoided sharing the* **Hornet's** *fate by darting into a convenient rain squall when the Japanese air attack arrived during the morning.*

After being commissioned in March 1942 South Dakota went straight to the Pacific theatre. Displacing 44,374 tons at full load, and armed with nine 406-mm (16-in) guns, she was more than a match for the modernized World War I battle-cruisers she would face off Guadalcanal.

was sunk while USS *Enterprise* was put out of action. Later, USS *Saratoga* was torpedoed and sidelined for months, while on 14 September the submarine *I-19* torpedoed USS *Wasp*. The ship exploded after fires raged out of control all day. Meanwhile, the Japanese were pressing their convoys forward in support of their starving troops on Guadal-canal. A convoy was attacked by Rear Admiral Norman Scott's force of two heavy cruisers, two light cruisers and destroyers off Cape Esperance on the night of 11-12 October. Scott was not aware of the Japanese

distant escort of three heavy cruisers, but the Japanese were just as surprised when contact was made. In a confused night action the Americans got the better of the Japanese, but at the cost of allowing the convoy through.

Bombardment

The Japanese upped the stakes considerably two nights later, when the Marine positions around Henderson Field on Guadalcanal were hammered by the heavy fire of the battleships *Kirishima* and *Hiei*, the only US Navy challenge being made by four PT boats. The next night heavy cruisers moved down the coast, lobbing 752 203mm (8in) shells into the Marine positions.

Without more naval support Major General Alexander Vandegrift's forces on Guadalcanal would not be able to beat the Japanese. Fortunately, the fire-eating Vice Admiral William Halsey had taken

command in the South West Pacific, and he saw his duty to support the Marines, even if it meant risking his carriers. This is what Admiral Isoroku Yamamoto and the combined fleet expected, and Yamamoto decided to move his own carriers south to finish off American naval power in the Pacific.

On 25 October US aircraft spotted a Japanese force of three carriers, with a fourth on its way down the Slot. After a typical carrier battle off the Santa Cruz Islands (the main combatants never setting eyes upon each other), the Japanese light carrier *Zuiho* had been sunk and the large carrier *Zuikaku* damaged. On the American side USS *Hornet* was abandoned after a torpedo strike, and the long suffering *Enterprise* was hit. Damage was slight, however, and she was operational within hours. The Japanese were convinced that they had sunk her and the *Hornet*, together with a

battleship and a number of escorts. They knew about the *Hornet*, because they had come across the abandoned hulk burning fiercely. The ship which had launched the first strike against the Japanese homeland was eventually sent to the bottom by Japanese torpedoes early on the morning of 27 October.

Tactical victory

Tactically, the Japanese had won a victory. Strategically, the Americans had delayed the enemy enough so that, when the final combined assault on Guadalcanal came, the Marines and the US Navy had more than an even chance of securing the USA's first major campaign victory of the war against the Japanese forces.

Manoeuvring hard to avoid the potentially lethal attentions of a Nakajima B5N 'Kate' torpedo bomber, the battleship USS South Dakota fights back with 127mm (5in) anti-aircraft guns. At Santa Cruz she claimed 26 Japanese aircraft brought down.

Solomons: Chronology

The US land campaign on Guadalcanal brought the Japanese and US Navy into four heavy clashes off the coasts of the Solomon islands.

1942

August 8th

A large unit of Japanese warships – seven cruisers and one destroyer – sail from Rabaul to attack US Navy transport ships and other vessels off Savo Island.

August 9th

During the early hours the Japanese cruiser force sink four Allied cruisers – three US cruisers: *Vicennes, Quincy* and *Astoria*, and one Australian cruiser: the *Canberra*. The success of the Japanese action is in part due to the skill of the Japanese Navy in night-fighting, but the US transport ships are not hit in the battle.

August 23rd

The Japanese Navy attempts to transfer supplies to Guadalcanal. The supply ships are well-protected by combat units containing three aircraft carriers: *Ryujo, Zuikaku* and *Shokaku*.

August 23rd–24th

The Japanese supply convoy is spotted twice by US Navy aircraft on patrol. The US carriers *Saratoga, Enterprise* and *Wasp* of Task Force 61 set course to intercept, moving to positions east of the island Malaita.

3.15pm

The *Shokaku* is damaged by *Enterprise's* aircraft.

3.50pm

The *Ryujo* is sunk by a major strike from the *Enterprise's* dive-bombers and torpedo aircraft.

4.41pm

The *Enterprise* is hit by bombs from the Japanese carrier aircraft and damaged, though not put out of operation.

5.40pm

The Japanese seaplane carrier *Chitose* is hit.

August 25th

Two Japanese transport ships are sunk as they continue to head for the Solomon Islands. The sinking of the *Jintsu* and *Kinryu Maru* ends what is known as the Battle of the Eastern Solomons. In terms of naval aviation losses the US achieve a victory: 90 Japanese planes destroyed for 20 US aircraft.

October 11th

The Battle of Cape Esperance begins. A US force of cruisers and destroyers under Rear-Admiral Norman Scott ambushes a Japanese supply convoy, protected by a cruiser squadron, attempting to pass down between the Eastern and Western Solomons.

11.32pm

The engagement begins after earlier US opportunities were missed because radar contacts were not reported properly throughout Scott's force. The destroyer USS *Duncan* opens fire, followed at 11.46pm by the USS *Helena*. Shortly afterwards the cruiser *Fubuki* is sunk and the *Furutaka* and *Aoba* hit and damaged.

12.00 Midnight–00.40am

The Japanese turn and retreat, and the action finishes at 00.30am. The US cruiser *Boise* has been damaged in the action. The Japanese cruiser *Furutaka* sinks at 00.40am.

October 25th

The Battle of Santa Cruz. Japanese naval vessels sail to positions off Guadalcanal to support a Japanese offensive on the island against Henderson Field. The force is spotted by US PBY Catalina aircraft and US Task Forces 16 and 17 are sent to intercept. These include the carriers *Hornet* and *Enterprise,* and the battleship *South Dakota.* An air assault launched from the carriers cannot find the Japanese ships.

The USS Indiana *opens fire. The* Indiana *operated in a support role during the Solomons campaign, as well as providing surface protection for the carriers* Enterprise *and* Saratoga*. Only two other battleships –* USS Washington *and* USS South Dakota *– were in the theatre at the time.*

October 26th
2.50am
A Catalina flying boat makes a bombing run against carriers of Admiral Nagumo Chuichi's Carrier Group. The attack misses.

5.00am
The *Enterprise* sends out a search-and-strike group of 22 Dauntless dive-bombers. All but two of the bombers are seen off by Japanese fighters, the remaining two crippling the carrier *Zuiho* at 7.40am.

7.25am-8.15am
The *Enterprise* and *Hornet* launch a full strike of 72 aircraft to attack the Japanese carrier force. During this time the Japanese carriers also launch a major air strike consisting of 110 aircraft. The Japanese and US aircraft subsequently meet each other in mid air.

9.15am
The *Hornet* is severely damaged by a Japanese air attack, hit with six bombs and two torpedoes. The crew begin to abandon ship, the evacuation complete by around 11.40am.

9.18am
The already damaged *Zuiho* is hit by four more bombs and is effectively destroyed.

9.30am
The Japanese carrier *Shokaku* is bombed and severely damaged.

10.15am
The *Enterprise* has its flight deck and forward elevator damaged by Japanese dive bombers. The US commander Admiral Kinkaid orders the US ships to withdraw from the action.

October 27th
The wreck of the *Hornet* sinks after being torpedoed by Japanese destroyers.

International Events 1942

August 8th
Six German agents are executed in the US by electric chair. Eight agents in total had been landed in Long Island and Florida on sabotage missions.

Ordnancemen of the USS Enterprise load a 227kg (500lb) high-explosive bomb aboard a Douglas SBD Dauntless dive bomber. The aircraft was subsequently launched on bombing strikes against Japanese land targets on Guadalcanal, close air support being key to the success of the US land campaign in the Solomons.

August 9th
German forces advancing into the Caucasus capture the Krasnodar and Maikop oilfields only to find that they have been destroyed by retreating Soviet soldiers.

August 20th
Over 4000 Allied troops – mostly Canadian – are killed or captured out of a force of 6000 which attacked the German-occupied French port at Dieppe. The major amphibious assault, codenamed Operation Jubilee, was intended to test German coastal defences in preparation for the opening of a second front in Europe.

October 14th
The German forces at Stalingrad launch another massive offensive to try and take the city. Despite using five divisions of infantry and armour the offensive does not overcome the fanatical Soviet resistance.

October 23rd
A huge US amphibious landing force sets sail from Virginia destined for Morocco. It is part of the Allied landings in Morocco and Algeria codenamed Operation Torch, designed to produce a second front in the North African campaign.

October 31st
British forces at the battle of El Alamein finally break through the German lines and put German and Italian units into retreat.

Kokoda Trail

New Guinea 1942–43

The Battle of the Coral Sea ended Japanese naval plans for an amphibious invasion of Port Moresby. Now it was the turn of the Japanese army.

The Australians counter-attacked in September 1942, driving the Japanese from Uberi. Japanese supplies had to cross the mountains while the Australians were only 48km (30 miles) from base.

While the main drive of the great Japanese offensive during the months following Pearl Harbor had been to the south-west of the home islands, on each side of a central axis aimed at Singapore, the Japanese commanders also appreciated that in the end they would have to defend themselves from American forces from the east. They had therefore consolidated control of the island chains to the south – the Marianas, the Carolines and especially the island and harbour of Truk. As early as 23 January 1942 they had put a small force ashore at Kavieng in New Ireland, then one at Rabaul on New Britain, where their force of 5000 quickly overcame the 1400 Australian troops garrisoned there.

Making preparations

In early March Japanese troops landed unopposed at Lae and Salamaua in Huon Bay on the north coast of New Guinea, and busied themselves for several weeks building up stores and work-shops for a possible further advance to the south. Because they were subjected to so little interference – even while they built a fair-sized airfield of obvious tactical importance – and as they soon heard that a large fleet was sailing from the Carolines to capture Port Moresby, they remained fairly confident that their progress to the south would be comparatively easy. Their greatest problem was the difficult terrain.

The defeat of the Japanese invasion force at the Battle of the Coral Sea put an end to such comfortable assump-tions, however, but not to plans for the capture of Port Moresby: as the Imperial Navy had failed to reach the place, then the Japanese army would do so. But the necessary reorganisation took time, and meanwhile

the Australian presence in the area increased.

Already Australian commandos – independent companies – had been harassing the Japanese perimeters, and in April they were joined by another company. Shortly afterwards two Australian brigades

WAR IN THE CLOUDS: ACROSS THE OWEN STANLEYS

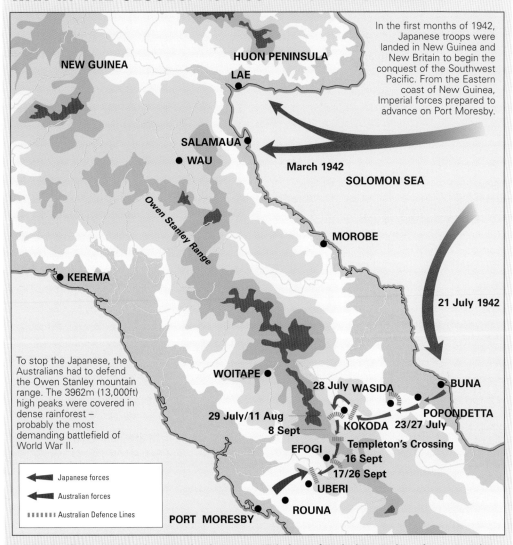

In the first months of 1942, Japanese troops were landed in New Guinea and New Britain to begin the conquest of the Southwest Pacific. From the Eastern coast of New Guinea, Imperial forces prepared to advance on Port Moresby.

NEW GUINEA

HUON PENINSULA
LAE

SALAMAUA
WAU

March 1942

SOLOMON SEA

Owen Stanley Range

MOROBE

KEREMA

21 July 1942

To stop the Japanese, the Australians had to defend the Owen Stanley mountain range. The 3962m (13,000ft) high peaks were covered in dense rainforest – probably the most demanding battlefield of World War II.

WOITAPE

28 July WASIDA   BUNA

29 July/11 Aug   POPONDETTA
8 Sept   KOKODA 23/27 July

Templeton's Crossing

EFOGI   16 Sept

17/26 Sept

UBERI

ROUNA

PORT MORESBY

→ Japanese forces
→ Australian forces
▪▪▪▪▪ Australian Defence Lines

Landing at Buna on 21 July 1942, the Japanese 17th Army fought its way into the mountains at Kokoda within a week. Over the next three weeks the Japanese Army continued to push the Australians back, overcoming a series of savagely fought rearguard actions. However, the further the Japanese got from the coast, the more uncertain were their supply lines. By contrast, the Australians were only 48km (30 miles) from their main supply base. As a result, when the Australian 7th Division counter-attacked at Uberi on 23 September the Japanese could not respond.

The Japanese 14th Army made rapid progress towards Kokoda, but stiffening opposition, Allied airpower and restricted supplies soon began to have a major effect.

arrived at Port Moresby, another was sent to Milne Bay on the eastern tip of the peninsula and two battalions were ordered to push up and over the Owen Stanley Range along the Kokoda Trail to try to reach Buna on the north coast. There they were to construct an airfield from which the Japanese positions along the coast could be attacked.

Not surprisingly, the Japanese reacted swiftly and in some strength. On 21 July 2000 men went ashore at Buna (the Australian battalions were still on their way); by the end of the month 13,500 men of Lieutenant-General Harukichi Hyakutake's 17th Army had followed them, driven south along the trail sweeping up the independent companies as they went, almost effortlessly driving back the two battalions as well, and by 27 July

had arrived at Kokoda. But the iron law of logistics was coming into play: the Japanese were nearly 160km (100 miles) of appalling going from their bases; the Australians were only 50km (32 miles) from theirs.

The Japanese advance was stopped by 25 August, but on the following day the second prong of the Japanese attack formed with a landing of nearly 2000 men at Milne Bay. But their intelligence was at fault for they had expected to find only two or three companies of Australian infantry there. Instead they found nearly two brigades (the first had been reinforced), two fighter squadrons and batteries of well sited artillery. After five days of fierce fighting the Japanese did reach the edge of the airfield but they were gradually driven back, their casualties mounting implacably and on 6 September the survivors were evacuated.

Back over the Trail

The Australians were also making ground on the Kokoda Trail. Slowly but relentlessly they began to force the Japanese back up the 'golden stairs' from Uberi. The 'stairs' were formed by steps some 25 to 45cm (10 to 18 in) in height, the front edge of the step consisting of a small log held by stakes, with little behind it but mud and water. They rose 365m (1200 ft) in the first 5km (3.2 miles)!

Native 'Angels'

For the Australians the physical exhaustion of just climbing the 'stairs' was almost insupportable, and were it not for the Melanesian porters who carried everything (and almost everyone) with a loyalty and enthusiasm which astounded all who saw it – the job would have taken 10 times longer. By early October the leading Australian brigade had

Left: The Japanese army had proved its mastery of the jungle in the Philippines and Malaya. But the rugged mountains of New Guinea were to present a challenge that even it was not prepared to take on.

Right: The Australians, some of the best infantry in World War II, had managed finally to stop the Japanese push on their homeland. They sustained nearly 6000 casualties in action, but many more Japanese died – in battle, from disease and from starvation.

The Australians relied heavily on local porters to carry everything from ammunition and food, to the wounded. These so-called 'fuzzy-wuzzy angels' alone seemed able to cope with the backbreaking labour of climbing the Kokoda Trail.

reached Templeton's Crossing at the ridge of the Owen Stanley Range. Hunger must have played its part in the Japanese defeat, for evidence of cannibalism was found.

Anzac victory

The Australians retook Kokoda on 2 November 1942 and reopened the airfield there from which they could be well supported by Allied airpower all the way to Buna. An attempt by the Japanese to stand on the Kumusi river was thwarted by flank attacks from fresh Australian and American

troops, and their final stand at Buna came to an end on 21 January 1943.

The New Guinea campaign cost the Japanese over 12,000 men, the Australian battle casualties amounted to 5700 and the American figure was 2800 – but at least three times as many had succumbed to tropical hazards from malaria to sheer heat exhaustion.

But the Allies had proved that they could fight and beat the Japanese, even in such appalling conditions – so long as they had air supremacy.

The savage series of rearguard actions over the Owen Stanleys was a harsh classroom for the Australians, but they learned the lessons of jungle fighting quickly.

Kokoda Trail
Chronology

The Kokoda Trail, running across the width of Papua's southern peninsula, provided an ideal route to the Papuan capital, Port Moresby, for Japanese invasion forces in March 1942.

1942

March 8th
Two battalions of Japanese troops are landed in New Guinea at Lae and Salamaua in New Guinea.

July 21st–22nd
Units of the Japanese 18th Army commanded by Major-General Horii land on Papua's southern peninsula around Buna at the eastern entrance to the Kokoda Trail. They begin to advance westwards toward the capital, Port Moresby.

The use of local labour was essential to Allied logistics in many campaigns. Here an Australian private lights the pipe of a man carrying supplies during the New Guinea campaign of 1943.

July 22nd–14th August
Horii's forces push back Allied units consisting of Australian and US infantry and the locally raised Papuan Infantry Regiment. By August 14th the Japanese are moving across the mountainous Owen Stanley Range running down the centre of the peninsula, take Kokoda at the half-way point of the trail and reach Isurava only 100km (60 miles) away from Port Moresby.

August 25th–26th
Japanese Special Naval Landing forces make an amphibious landing at Milne Bay in the far south of Papua, intending to open another front in the Papuan campaign. However, Allied Ultra intelligence had already

Australian infantry on the Kokoda trail. Typical kit for an Australian soldier during the campaign could reach 27kg (60lb), and the khaki uniforms were ill-suited to damp jungle conditions. Heat exhaustion took hundreds of casualties.

revealed the invasion plans. The Japanese landing is met in force by troops of the 18th Australian Brigade and held at the beachhead.

August 29th
The Japanese Milne Bay operation receives reinforcements with another 600 troops (2000 had originally landed).

August 30th
General Douglas MacArthur asserts the need for greater military resources to be given to the Papuan defence, otherwise the island will be lost.

A line of native carriers begin to ascend a New Guinea mountain. The Allied forces on the Kokoda trail were forced to scale thickly jungled mountain ridges 2100m (6800ft) above sea level

September 4th
Having lost 1000 men, the Japanese at Milne Bay begin to evacuate the beachhead, unable to move Allied resistance.

September 26th
The Japanese advance along the Kokoda Trail grinds to a halt, chronically short of supplies and with many casualties. The Australians hold the offensive just west of Toribaiwa. Steadily the Japanese are put into retreat back across the Trail.

October
Troops of the 32nd US Division are landed between Pongani and Wanigela on the eastern coast of Papua, just beneath the eastern end of the Kokoda Trail.

November
The Japanese are by now back within defended positions at Buna, Gona and Sanananda. From mid-November US troops from the south and Australian troops from the west assault the Japanese positions and attempt to clear the Kokoda Trail.

December 9th
Gona is captured by Australian forces.

December 14th–January 1943
Buna falls to US forces by January 2nd 1943, and by the end of January Sananada is also taken. The Allies have now successfully retaken the entire Kokoda Trail, losing 3000 men for Japanese losses of 12,000.

International Events
1942
August 7th
US forces land on Guadalcanal, beginning a bloody battle to recapture the island and take possession of the vital Henderson Field.

August 15th
Some 500 Jewish families are executed by German soldiers in Zagrodski, Poland.

September 15th
The US carrier *Wasp* is torpedoed and sunk by a Japanese submarine near Guadalcanal.

September 23rd
In the US, the government passes the responsibility for the development of the atomic bomb over to the military.

October 3rd
German security forces in Poland complete the liquidation of Warsaw's Jews. Over 310,000 Jews from the ghetto have been 'relocated' to death camps.

October 20th
The premier of Vichy France, Pierre Laval, makes a public plea for 100,000 French workers to go to Germany to support the Axis war effort.

October 24th
In Italy, Genoa and Milan are hit by RAF bombing raids, the first raids of the war on Italy in which RAF bombers fly from the UK mainland.

November 11th
Following the Allied landings in Tunisia on November 8th-11th, German troops in France move into the previously unoccupied area of Vichy France, fearing an invasion into France from the south or French collaboration with the Allies.

November 25th
The Luftwaffe begins a futile four-month airlift mission to maintain the besieged 6th Army in Stalingrad.

November 27th
French naval personnel scuttle over 40 ships at Toulon to prevent the French fleet being captured and put to German use. The scuttled ships include two battleship, 29 destroyers and two submarines.

1943
January 1st
Soviet forces begin major encirclement offensives in the Caucasus as the German resistance in Stalingrad moves towards collapse.

Bloody Tarawa: Battle for the Gilberts

Girded by a coral reef, the tiny atoll of Tarawa looks like paradise in the Pacific. But its coral rock is honeycombed with tunnels manned by 5000 Japanese.

The American advance on Japan from 1943 to 1945 was to follow two major axes, that through the Solomons, New Guinea and the Philippines being paralleled by another through the myriad atolls of Micronesia. Of the latter, the Marshalls were strategically the most important, but had been steadily fortified since the commencement of a Japanese mandate following World War I. As little was known about the Marshalls and, indeed, to protect the rear of the advance, the Gilbert Islands to the south-eastward had first to be secured. Thorough air reconnaissance showed that the islands of Tarawa (with an airfield) and Makin (with a seaplane base but suitable for an airfield) were the key points. Both islands were, therefore, assaulted simultaneously on 20 November 1943.

Diversionary attack

In support was Vice Admiral Raymond Spruance's recently constituted 5th Fleet, whose five modern battleships covered six fleet and five light carriers, with 700 aircraft. These were largely diversionary but had the effect of drawing the main Japanese fleet forward from its base at Truk in the Carolines to Eniwetok in the Marshalls. Though now only 1125km (700 miles) from Makin, and including six battleships in its strength, this fleet was of little practical use as its carriers had been obliged to return to Japan to work up with new air complements following the detachment of their aircraft for the defence of Rabaul. Only the Pearl Harbor veteran *Zuikaku* remained, and then only with a scratch air group aboard. The Japanese commander was thus unable to attack, and sent half of his available 18 submarines south to pick off targets of opportunity.

The capture of Makin

Makin was known to be lightly held but, as significant Japanese air bases existed at Mili and Jaluit, less than an hour's flying time distant, almost disproportionately large forces were used to secure the island rapidly and start construction of an airfield.

Few true amphibious ships of any consequence were available and troops went ashore at the western end of the island in LCVPs lowered from attack transports and LVTs (amphibious tractors) from the two available LSTs. As they ran in, a 20-minute aerial bombardment by carrier aircraft was followed by a pounding from some old battleships, together with cruisers and destroyers. It was fortunate that there was negligible resistance, for the water over the skirting reef was far more shallow than had been expected and, in the face of mounting congestion, the transports had to move close in to the shore as a means of speeding things up. At about 1000, when the beach-head was reported as secured, a second assault was being carried out from the lagoon side of the island, one of many that fringed the atoll like an irregular necklace.

Again the assault was on a small scale, further LCTs being followed by tank-laden LCMs from one of the only two LSDs available in the theatre. Only 800 Japanese were ashore, less than half of them combat troops. Their skilful and stubborn resistance, however, kept 6500 marines at bay for three days until there came the classic signal 'Makin taken'.

Where Makin is a skinny tongue of coral only some 13km (8 miles) in length, Tarawa, some 120km (75 miles) distant, is even smaller, its area measured only in acres and nowhere more than 3 m (10 ft) above sea level. The island was

A Marine squad leader directs the fire of his men against a Japanese strongpoint. The Japanese defensive positions were carefully sited to provide mutually supporting fire, and this inflicted heavy losses on the Marines as they fought their way forward from the beaches.

*Above: Admiral Hill and his command staff observe the bombardment from the battleship **USS** Maryland. It seemed impossible for anything to survive the firepower of the US Navy gunline off Tarawa, but the Japanese had dug well and deep.*

Left: The coral surrounding Tarawa stands out clearly. It was a severe natural obstacle, no boat could cross the last 460m (1510ft) or so, and the Marines had no choice but to wade in and hope they could suppress most of the defensive fire.

almost totally covered by its airfield, which was defended by nearly 5000 seasoned troops, well dug in. Here the Americans put ashore only 5000 Marines who, with their LVTs, suffered dreadfully as they floundered over the ragged coral heads which extended up to 500m (1640ft) offshore. Many drowned through the weight of their equipment as they were wounded or simply fell over. It took another three days of hand-to-hand fighting to secure the island, with the opposing side too closely engaged for warships to have a lot of influence beyond destroyers pounding enemy base areas. By the end of 23 November no Japanese remained alive, and the airfield was operating under new ownership. Tarawa was to be the yardstick for many landings to come and much was learned. Of the enemy, only 150 had been captured alive, while the Americans had suffered about 3400 casualties, including 990 dead.

The success of the US operations was a result largely of the Japanese inability to strike effectively at the naval support groups upon which so much depended. US carrier-based air power suppressed the meagre Japanese air strength but, even so, a comparatively minor counter-attack on the evening of the first day succeeded in putting a torpedo into the light carrier USS *Independence*, which had to be withdrawn. The larger carriers were just beginning to mount radar-equipped night-fighter patrols, in good time to defeat the new Japanese tactic of nocturnal torpedo bomber attacks using markers placed by reconnaissance floatplanes.

Worse, the length of events ashore obliged the fleet to dally longer than had been anticipated and, after 22 November, Japanese submarines began to arrive. While four of the eight were sunk (a catastrophic loss) one (*1-175*) torpedoed the escort carrier USS *Liscombe Bay* early on the 24th. The result cruelly exposed the relaxed standards adopted as an expediency to produce the CVEs in large numbers.

Loss of life

The torpedo struck amidships and splinters pierced the unprotected bulkheads of the bomb stowage. In a catastrophic explosion the entire after end of the little carrier was destroyed, the flight deck then collapsing. So great was the force of the blast that the old battleship USS *New Mexico*, a mile away, was showered with fragments. Two-thirds of the carrier's 900-odd crew lost their lives.

The beaches on 23 November 1943: an M4 Sherman tank and a cluster of Marines who failed to make it ashore. The sight of dead Marines bobbing up and down in the surf was seared into the minds of many men who fought at Tarawa.

Bloody Tarawa
Chronology

Tarawa demonstrated what lay in store for US forces beginning to reclaim Japan's Pacific island conquests. Tarawa atoll's main island, Betio, was only 2740m (3000yds) long by 550m (600yds) wide, but over 5000 men would die on it in three days of fighting.

1943

November
US invasion forces head for Betio – the main island of the Tarawa atoll. The island is garrisoned by 4500 elite Japanese soldiers and features heavy defensive armament. The US force contains 35,000 US Marines and US Army infantry soldiers of the 37th Infantry Division.

November 13th–20th
Tarawa and Makin in the Gilbert Islands are subjected to a heavy US naval and air bombardment.

**November 20th
9.10am**
US Marine units begin to go ashore on Betio at its south-western corner. They run into extreme resistance. Casualties in some US waves run at 50 per cent even before stepping onto the beach. Following the introduction of US armour onto the beach the US troops gain a stronger foothold, and by the end of the day three US Marine battalions are ashore.

November 21st
US Marines and US Army troops land on Makin, another

A US Marine injured in a Japanese air raid on Tarawa awaits medical treatment. The 1056 US deaths on the tiny Pacific atoll created much controversy in the US, but forged better US amphibious tactics.

US assault troops transfer from a Landing Ship, Infantry (LSI) to a small assault boat prior to an amphibious landing. An LSI could carry up to 1000 combat troops, the assault boats up to 60 men.

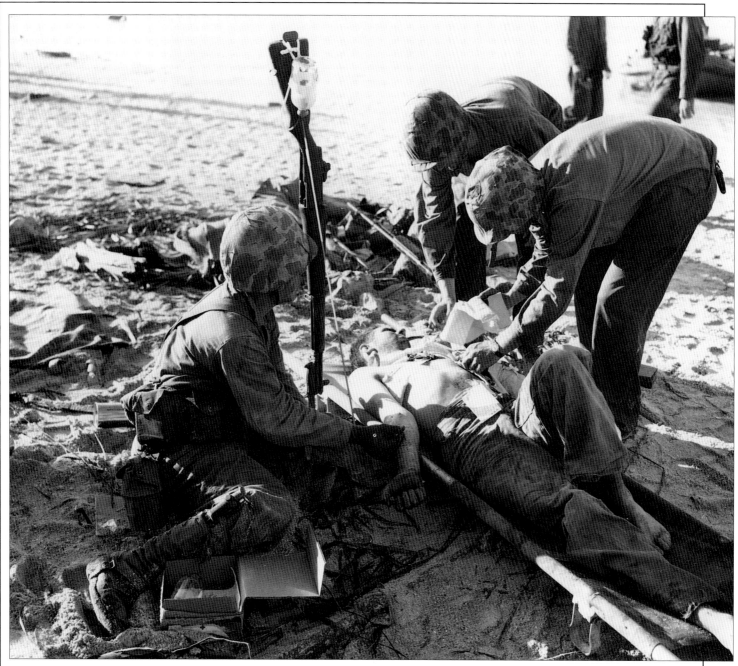

A badly wounded US Marine on Tarawa receives a life-saving blood transfusion on the beach, a plasma flask hanging from the stock of an upended rifle. The US discovery in 1939 that blood plasma could substitute for whole blood in a transfusion revolutionised combat medicine.

island in the Gilberts. They take it comparatively easily, though all but one of the 800-man Japanese garrison is killed in the action. US losses are 66 men dead. The island of Apamama is also taken – its 22-man Japanese garrison simply committed suicide.

November 21st–22nd

The US Marines begin to inch their way inland against a blistering Japanese defence. Progress in slow – every Japanese bunker and position has to be completely destroyed to maintain the advance – but the central and western parts of the island are secured by around 8.00pm.

November 22nd–23rd

Night sees the Japanese forces launch a major counter-attack from the east of the island. The attack is suicidal, and the cost of the human-wave assaults is 300–500 dead by daybreak of November 23rd. At 1.05pm the remaining Japanese forces confined to the northwestern edge of Betio are finally destroyed, bringing the island and the Gilbert chain into US hands.

International Events 1943

November 15th

Nazi extermination policies towards the Jews are extended to Gypsies. Heinrich Himmler, the head of the SS, gives the order today for all gypsies to be sent to concentration camps.

November 16th

US 8th Army Air Force bombers attack the German heavy water production plant at Vermork, Norway. The plant is a vital centre for Germany's production of an atomic weapon.

November 19th

RAF Bomber Command begins heavy air raids on the German capital, Berlin. Four large attacks are launched in the first week alone.

November 22nd

The British 8th Army advancing north through Italy manages to secure five bridgeheads on the northern bank of the Sangro river.

November 22nd

Brazil announces it will send a force of 60,000 men to the European theatre. Subsequently some 25,000 soldiers of the Brazilian Expeditionary Force fight in the Italian campaign.

Imphal and Kohima
Victory of the forgotten army

March 1944: On the grounds that attack is often the best form of defence, the Japanese 15th Army attacks in Burma.

The events which led to the battle for Kohima began on the night of 7 March 1944 when Lieutenant General Renya Mutaguchi, commanding the Japanese 15th Army, launched Operation U-go, throwing his divisions across the Chindwin river in an attack dubbed 'The March on Delhi'. The first stage of this was to be the capture of the vast stores and administration centre which the British had built up at Imphal.

Diversionary attacks were launched to the south of Imphal, but apart from the main assault on the depot the most important step was the move by the 31st Division under Lieutenant General Sato, which crossed the Chindwin on 15 March and drove towards the small settlment of Kohima with its Naga village, its *maidan* on which the detachment of Assam Rifles drilled, its reinforcement camp where soldiers returning from leave or hospital awaited their next move forward, its District Commissioner's bungalow with its terraced garden and tennis court, and its vital tactical position commanding the only road along which British reinforcements and supplies could reach Imphal from the railheads in Manipur.

Hasty British defence

They found facing them a hastily-organised defence perimeter manned at that moment by some 1500 men, mostly of the 4th Royal West Kents augmented by men of the Assam Rifles (streaming back from forward positions where they had been both observing and attempting to delay Sato's advance) and the faithful, tenacious and extraordinarily courageous Naga villagers. One vital British formation of which the first Japanese arrivals remained for some time in ignorance, however, was a battery of 94mm (3.74in) howitzers sited on the reverse slope of a hill at Jotsoma 3.2km (2 miles) to the west of Kohima, manned by Indian gunners of the 161st Indian Brigade.

PRIVATE SOLDIER
14TH ARMY

Fighting in the most appalling terrain and climate against a savage and ruthless enemy, the soldiers of the 14th Army endured the toughest campaign of the war. Initially dressed in the khaki drill uniform worn in the Middle East, by 1943 British and Commonwealth troops wore a jungle green uniform of cellular material. Webbing was often daubed with black patches to improve camouflage.

Japanese troops cross the River Chindwin on elephants at the start of their 'U-Go' offensive. At the end of this bitter battle, half the Japanese soldiers who attacked were dead.

Royal Garwhal rifles patrol forward. The Japanese 15th Army fought with ferocious courage; to defeat such fanatical opposition was a great achievement for British and Commonwealth forces.

Within hours of arrival the men of the Japanese 58th Regiment were giving proof of their ferocity, and the Royal West Kents of their stubbornness. The Japanese swept around Kohima from the Naga village to Jail Hill and on the night of 6 April succeeded in taking two more of the features inside the defence perimeter, known as D.I.S. and F.S.D. But their attacking units were annihilated on the next morning by the counter-attack of the Royal West Kents.

Japanese formations as they assembled, accompanied the waves all the way forward to the defences, and harried the survivors as soon as they were ordered back.

And on the following day reinforcements for the hard-pressed British got through to Jotsoma and began planning to blast their way through the last 3.2km (2 miles). This was to prove appallingly difficult and a necessary delay of 24 hours almost fatal, for during that night the Japanese blasted F.S.D. with every shell and

In a suitably flat jungle clearing, ground crew load rockets on to Hawker Hurricanes. The Japanese air force had been defeated in Burma, allowing British ground forces to be re-supplied by air.

Mahrattas attacking a Japanese position – Indian troops contributed the bulk of British and Commonwealth manpower in the Burma campaign.

The West Yorkshires at Kohima – US-built M3 Lee tanks in close support of an infantry attack; the 37mm (1.45in) gun in the turret tracks to the left while the sponson-mounted 75mm (2.95in) gun sweeps forward and right.

However, by now more and more of Sato's 12,000 infantry and their gunners were coming up, and he himself was confident of success within 48 hours, though seven days later this confidence was waning. On the night of 13 April massed attacks by wave after wave of assault troops foundered on the rock of the stubborn infantry defence, aided by astonishingly accurate fire from the howitzers at Jotsoma. These broke up

mortar bomb they could fire; the perimeter began to disintegrate, and the F.S.D. position and neighbouring Kukri Piquet were lost.

But at 0800 on 18 April, the British at Jotsoma and the surrounding area replied with a devastating bombardment of the same kind and under its protection the relief of the original garrison was carried out.

The battle was by no means over. On the British side, brigades of the 2nd

Division were pouring down the road from Dimapur, while on the Japanese side more and more of Sato's 31st Division were being deployed, and as there was physically not enough room in the Kohima area for two whole divisions to operate, encircling moves were attempted by both sides through the appallingly difficult country around Kohima. This was such that a rate of movement of 1.6km (1 mile) per day against no enemy opposition came to be accepted as the norm, and when on 27 April torrential rain began falling, movement became almost impossible and diarrhoea and dysentery took an even greater toll than bullets and shrapnel.

And all the time, on the central Kohima Ridge, the kernel of the battle was being fought. The Durhams fought off an attack on Garrison Hill which cost Sato such high casualties that he ordered night attacks to cease, and he sent a caustic signal to Mutaguchi complaining of the time the latter was taking to capture Imphal, and also of the total lack of support or supplies coming through to him at Kohima.

Towards the Bungalow

By the end of April the 2nd Dorsetshires had begun fighting their way into Kohima towards the District Commissioner's bungalow, and reached the edge of the tennis court. This now became the scene of an almost Pyrrhic conflict.

The opposing forces were separated by less than 22m (72ft), but the Japanese had

got there earlier and, great diggers always, had burrowed deep into the terrace which rose at the far end, and also under a big water-tank that dominated the area. No-one could move across the open area in daylight, and Dimapur stores were astonished by the continual demands for gym shoes for night patrolling! But though these proved effective, the battle dragged on with ever-increasing ferocity and it was not until the middle of May, when a single tank managed the tortuous route up the District Commissioner's drive and began blasting the Japanese bunkers, that the British could claim 'the first set'.

By the end of May Sato knew that he could not take Kohima, and further sacrifice was pointless. After an angry exchange of signals with Mutaguchi, he sent off his last angry jibe ('The tactical ability of 15th Army Staff lies below that of cadets.'), closed down his radio and ordered his men to retire.

This the Japanese soldiers reluctantly did, desperately fighting off the clutches of the now all-encircling British and firing off the last of their mortar bombs and shells. And the story of their agonising walk back to the Chindwin, living on grass and roots, their clothing and boots in tatters, using canes or their broken rifles as crutches, is an epic of endurance and courage which no soldier will ever decry, certainly not the equally valorous men who fought them.

Imphal and Kohima
Chronology

In early 1944, Japanese forces were rightly concerned about the Allies launching an offensive into central Burma from positions across the border in India. The pre-emptive Japanese invasion of India in March 1944 struck towards Imphal and Kohima, supply points from General Slim's Fourteenth Army.

1944

February 4th

The Japanese 55th Division attacks into the Arakan against the British XV Corps, intending to draw British reserves into action and so keep them away from the major offensive towards

A Chinese soldier receives instruction in the operation of the US M1 Garand rifle from an Australian infantryman in Burma, 1944.

Imphal. Despite the British positions at Sinzweya being entirely surrounded, they were never overcome and would cost the Japanese over 5000 casualties in the coming weeks.

March 7th

The main Japanese Imphal offensive begins, codenamed Operation U-Go. The Japanese 33rd Division begins a two-pronged push towards

Imphal from the south towards Tiddim and Tamu.

March 9th–13th

The 17th Indian Division at Tiddim are put into retreat as the Japanese offensive threatens to encircle them. By contrast, the more northerly advance takes Tamu but is stopped short of Imphal by a vigorous defence of the 20th Indian Division at Shenan Saddle.

March 15th–16th

Two more Japanese offensives are launched as part of U-Go. The Japanese 15th Division advances directly towards Imphal, while the Japanese 31st Division heads by three routes towards Kohima.

March 19th

Imphal starts to receive British reinforcements in the form of the 5th and 7th Divisions.

April 4th–7th

Kohima and Imphal are reached, cut off, and effectively put under siege by the Japanese 31st Division and 15th Division respectively.

April 7th

The British XXXIII Corps begins its relief operations toward Kohima and Imphal.

April 12th

Japanese forces cut the main Kohima–Imphal road. The Allies in these two locations are now entirely dependent on

Local tribesmen set to work clearing the Imphal–Kohima road. The road was severed by the Japanese by April 12th, though the Allies managed to circumvent the supply problem by using air drops to provide all essential materials to the besieged Allied units.

air supply from the RAF's 3rd Tactical Air Force to maintain their perilous defence.

April 14th
The British 5th Brigade from Dimapur overcomes a Japanese road block near Zubza on the westerly Kohima trail and relieves the besieged 161st Indian Brigade.

April 18th
The 5th Brigade begins to attack the Japanese defences around Kohima.

April 26th
The Allies begin a major offensive to clear Kohima of all Japanese resistance. The 4th Brigade attacks from the south and the 5th Brigade from the north, while other elements of the 5th Brigade and the 161st Indian Brigade maintain pressure on the centre.

May–June 3rd
The Kohima battle is fought hard with offensive and counter-offensive. Elements of the Japanese 31st Division begin to withdraw under the weight of the Allied advance on May 31st. Gradually the

Indian and British troops overcome Japanese defences around Naga village and the hills overlooking Kohima in the west. By June 3rd Kohima is once more back in Allied hands. The British 2nd Division (of which the 5th Brigade was part) now turns southwards toward Imphal.

June 3rd–22nd
As the British 2nd Division continue their advance to Imphal, the IV Corps defending inside Imphal itself fight on against constant Japanese offensives. Casualties are extremely heavy on both sides. The British, however, have the advantage of an efficient airdrop lifeline and over 10,000 additional troops are moved in to bolster the defence.

June 22nd
The British 2nd Division and 5th Indian Division meet up with elements of IV Corps at Milestone 107 near Kangpopki, 24km (15 miles) north of the British defensive perimeter around Imphal. Also on this day, the Imphal-Dimapur supply route is

reopened. The Japanese are steadily put on the defensive

July 18th
Japanese force withdraw from Imphal to the Chindwin, the losses from the entire U-Go campaign numbering 65,000 men.

International Events 1944

March 15th
A massive Allied bombing attack and artillery bombardment devastates the Italian town of Cassino. Over 770 bombers dropped 1750 tons of bombs on the town, before artillery fired nearly 200,000 shells into German positions.

March 19th
German forces occupy Hungary to protect Germany's south-eastern flank.

April 8th
Soviet forces advancing into the Balkans enter Romania in force, having made preliminary crossings on April 2nd.

April 29th
German torpedo boats attack a US training exercise in the English Channel and kill 638 US servicemen. The exercise was part of preparations for the D-Day landings.

May 18th
Monte Cassino finally falls to Allied forces in Italy, opening the way for the drive to Rome up the Liri valley.

June 4th
Rome is occupied by the Allies, German occupation forces having withdrawn.

June 17th
US forces storm the Marianas Islands, landing first on Saipan occupied by 32,000 Japanese soldiers.

The Great Marianas Turkey Shoot

19 June 1944: The Japanese navy fights to defend the Mariana Islands in what is destined to be the last of the great carrier battles of the Pacific war.

On 15 June 1944 (just nine days after the Normandy landings) a 535-ship American invasion force hit Saipan in the Marianas, following a nine-day passage from the Marshalls. This major step in the leapfrogging reconquest of the central Pacific was possible only through the massive concentration of air power that could be applied by the US carrier fleet.

The operation provoked the powerful response from the Japanese that the Americans had been seeking. Almost all remaining enemy surface strength had been regrouped, as the 1st Mobile Fleet, around five fleet and four light carriers, overall command being exercised by Vice Admiral Jisaburo

Ozawa, successor to Nagumo in command of the Imperial navy's strike force. Ozawa's 430 carrier aircraft were to be supplemented by 540 more based on a ring of island airstrips so that, if the Americans could be brought to battle within this perimeter, his aircraft would enjoy an effectively doubled range, refuelling at either end and attacking the invaders on either leg of the return trip.

In every respect except enhanced range, however, the Japanese were inferior. Task Force 58 (overall command by

5th Fleet under Admiral Raymond Spruance, but tactically controlled by Vice Admiral Marc Mitscher) had seven fleet and eight light carriers, with 900 aircraft and aircrew of superior training, backed by escort carriers with replacements.

Tactically, any action was necessarily influenced by the facts that Spruance was tied to the defence of Saipan, and that the easterly trade winds allowed the Japanese to launch their aircraft while proceeding toward the island while the Americans would be obliged to reverse course. Spruance, cannily, had reduced the odds by a week's war of attrition against Ozawa's shore-based aircraft and airstrips.

Leaving the Philippines on 15 June the Japanese fleet

progressed steadily, but its position was accurately reported by US submarines. But, in turn, Ozawa's longer-ranged aircraft had found Spruance. TF58 was operating in four fast-carrier groups, spaced on 20km (12.5 mile) centres, protected some 24km (15 miles) to the west by Vice Admiral Willis Lee's surface battle group (including seven battleships) disposed as an AA barrier.

On the morning of 19 June TF58 was still occupied with softening-up the islands when, at 0830 (and still not sighted) Ozawa launched a 69-aircraft strike from 480km (300 mile) range, its aircraft being ordered to attack and refuel ashore before returning. Fortunately, Lee detected them by radar at 240km (150 miles), allowing time to scramble a large force of Grumman F6F Hellcats which destroyed 45 attackers for the loss of one of their own.

For this sacrifice the Japanese near-missed three ships and hit the battleship USS *South Dakota* with one bomb.

Just half an hour behind the first enemy wave came a second and more powerful wave, comprising 110 aircraft. The Americans, fully prepared in depth, cut down a further 79, for which frightful price a further near-miss was conceded.

The recent introduction of proximity-fused ammunition greatly boosted the effectiveness of the American AA fire.

While Ozawa was still beyond Mitscher's aircraft range, he was still attended by submarines. At 0910 the

Taiho was hit by a single torpedo from USS *Albacore*, and three hours later the Pearl Harbor veteran, *Shokaku*, was rocked by four from USS *Cavalla*. Neither carrier seemed in danger of sinking, but at 1510 and 1530 respectively they were destroyed by massive explosions caused by fuel vapour leaking from ruptured lines.

Ozawa's third strike of 42 aircraft was launched at 1000 and bypassed Lee's gunline but, in seeking to attack from the north, missed Mitscher almost completely and achieved nothing for the loss of seven aircraft. A fourth, and last, force of 82 aircraft left Ozawa's decks at 1130. Most again never found their

An F6F Hellcat, the standard US Navy fighter plane. The strength of the US fighter force above the Task Force cut each Japanese attack to pieces. Ozawa could not believe the number of losses.

target but only nine returned, 49 being shot down by Hellcats over Guam or written-off trying to land on its churned airstrips.

Incredibly, the Japanese admiral seemed unaware of the scale of his losses and believed inflatedly optimistic reports from his returning pilots. With barely 100 aircraft aboard, but still not pinpointed by American reconnaissance aircraft, Ozawa pulled back to the westward to refuel overnight and resume the battle on the following morning. He was, in fact, already beaten, having sustained on 19 June a total of 346 lost aircraft against 30 American losses. Scarce wonder that the latter termed it the 'Great Marianas Turkey Shoot'.

From 1430 Mitscher had steamed in the opposite direction in order to recover his own aircraft, and only at 2000 did Spruance allow

The attack on Saipan was preceded by airstrikes on many other potential targets, misleading the Japanese.

three of his four carrier groups to turn westward in pursuit of the Japanese. Save for his reluctance to retire and concede defeat Ozawa would have got clear but finally, at 1540 on 20 June, he was discovered at a daunting 445-km. (275-mile) range by a Grumman TBF Avenger from USS *Enterprise*. It was late on, but Mitscher, grabbing his chance, had 210 aircraft aloft in ten minutes, following them at high speed to reduce the length of their return flight as far as possible.

The strike came in hard and, despite 20 losses to a withering AA barrage, put two torpedoes into the carrier *Hiyo* (which like the others, exploded and sank), hit the final Pearl Harbor

survivor, *Zuikaku*, and the light carrier *Chiyoda* with bombs, and mortally injured two fleet oilers. The 85-strong fighter cover meanwhile downed an estimated 65 Japanese in their defence.

With dry tanks and overtaken by darkness, 80 American aircraft had to ditch short of their carriers although many of the crews were rescued by flying boats the next day. Controversy will continue to rage over whether the cautious Spruance and Mitscher should have taken a chance on Saipan and gone allout for Ozawa's annihilation. The latter, although thoroughly beaten by virtue of inferior aircrew, had fought an excellent tactical battle. Nevertheless, the American victory in the Philippine Sea marked the final destruction of Japanese naval airpower.

The US carriers were at maximum range so the American aircraft would have to find, and land on, their carriers at night.

The Great Marianas Turkey Shoot: Chronology

The Japanese attempt to smash the naval operations around the Marianas resulted in the decimation of its carrier aviation. Over four days the Japanese lost 480 aircraft. Such was the advantage enjoyed by the numerically and technologically stronger US pilots that they termed it a 'Turkey Shoot'.

1944

June 16th

The Japanese 1st Mobile Fleet and the Japanese Southern Force rendezvous in positions west of the Philippine Islands. Their destination is the Marianas Islands, with the objective of stopping a US attempt to retake the islands.

June 17th

US forces in the Pacific land on Saipan, beginning the offensive to retake the Marianas Islands. The naval component of US forces is Task Force 58 under Vice-Admiral Marc A. Mitscher. He has seven carriers at his disposal compared to the Japanese five, and 956 aircraft compared to 473 Japanese aircraft.

June 19th
8.30am

Japanese carrier aircraft and land-based aircraft from Guam and Truk attack Task Force 58. US Hellcat fighters shoot down 35 of the attackers.

9.00am

Another Japanese air strike is intercepted 80km (50 miles) from the US Fleet, having been detected by US radar at 250 km (150 miles) distance. Over 200 Japanese aircraft are shot down, and only 130 return from the first strikes out of a commitment of 373 aircraft.

9.05am

The Japanese carrier *Taiho* is torpedoed by US submarine *Albacore*.

12.20pm

The Japanese carrier *Shokaku* is badly damaged during another US submarine attack (*Cavalla*).

2.00pm

The Japanese Fleet launches its second major air strike of the day. It is misdirected and intercepted by US planes over Guam. Another 50 Japanese aircraft are lost in the engagement.

4.24pm

The *Shokaku* sinks.

4.28pm

The *Taiho* sinks.

June 20th
4.30pm

The US carriers launched their own retaliatory strike against the Japanese force, deploying 216 aircraft.

6.44pm

The Japanese carrier *Hiyo* is sunk by US dive bombers and torpedo aircraft. Two Japanese oil tankers are also sunk and the carriers *Zuikaku* and *Chiyoda* badly damaged. A further 65 Japanese aircraft are shot down.

8.45pm

US carriers lose 80 aircraft from non-combat causes following the action, most commonly from the aircraft running out of fuel and ditching, or crashing during the night landing. Total US aviation losses for the raid are 100 aircraft. The remnants of the Japanese Fleet head home.

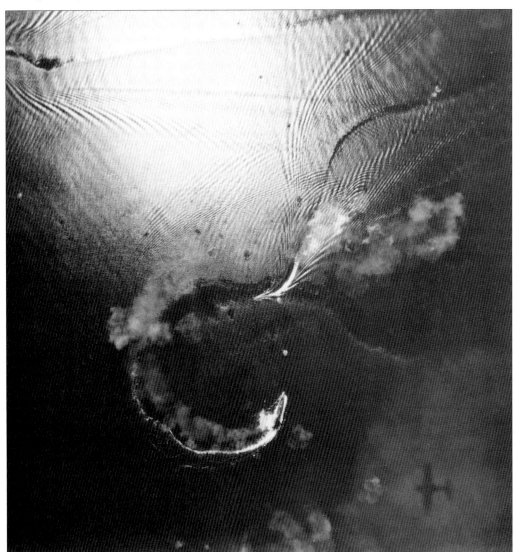

Japanese ships make frenetic evasive manoeuvres to avoid US bombs during the Battle of the Philippine Sea. With dive-bombers attacking from straight above and torpedo bombers coming in at low-level, gunnery defence aboard ships was extremely hard to coordinate.

International Events 1944

June 13th
The first German V-1 flying bomb strikes the UK.

June 17th
Two of Hitler's most prominent military leaders, von Rundstedt and Rommel, confront Hitler over what they see as disastrous tactics on the Western Front. They achieve no concessions, just promises that secret weapons will soon tip the balance in Germany's favour.

June 18th
Japanese forces of the 11th Army fighting in China capture the cities of Changsha and Chuchow.

June 20th
Soviet forces build up 166 divisions of soldiers in Belorussia in preparation for a massive offensive against German Army Group Centre.

June 22nd
The Japanese siege of Imphal, India, is finally broken after 88 days by the British 2nd Division and 5th Indian Division.

Above: Evidence of the US air victory over the Marianas is plastered to the side of this Grumman F6F Hellcat. A combination of air-combat losses, severe fuel shortages, and the devastation of land airbases meant Japanese air power could not affect the outcome of the war after mid 1944.

Below: A Grumman F6F Hellcat warms up on the deck of USS Lexington in preparation for a strike on Saipan. Some 480 F6F fighters were used in the Battle of the Philippine Sea and helped account for 400 Japanese aircraft destroyed.

Leyte Gulf

Final victory

As US forces landed in the Philippines, the Japanese navy launched a last desperate attack to stave off the inevitable.

Just four months after the Japanese reverse at the Philippine Sea the Americans staged a massive landing at Leyte, the first move in the reconquest of the Philippine islands themselves. At the head of the US battlefleet, now restyled the 3rd Fleet, Admiral William Halsey had replaced Admiral Raymond Spruance. His carrier force, still under Vice Admiral Marc Mitscher, had expanded further to nine large and eight light carriers, with nearly 1200 aircraft.

The Japanese contingency plan, 'SHO-1', included only four carriers which by then were so short of aircrews that a total of fewer than 120 aircraft could be embarked. Anticipating that any enemy counter would have to rely on land-based airpower, the American carrier groups had conducted a three-week attritional campaign so that less

than 200 Japanese land-based aircraft were left to oppose the landings, which took place between 17 and 20 October 1944 in Leyte Gulf.

Because of the wide dispersion of the oil-starved Japanese fleet, when 'SHO-1' was initiated on 17 October it involved widespread movements. Halsey's main force, covering the landing zone, was to be lured away to the north by Vice Admiral Jisaburo Ozawa's four carriers (the Northern Force, otherwise the Mobile Force, Strike Force) offered as deliberate bait. Duly uncovered, the Gulf was to be attacked at dawn on 25 October simultaneously by two powerful surface battle groups and the transports annihilated. The Central Force (Force 'A' of the 1st Strike Force, 5th Fleet) under Vice Admiral Takeo Kurita would exit via the San Bernardino Strait and

*Launched in 1914, **Fuso** was modernised from 1930–33, receiving new machinery and 2500 tons of extra armour. Together with **Yamashiro**, she formed the backbone of Nishimura's squadron at Leyte Gulf.*

attack from the north, while the Southern Force (unwisely divided in two parts under Vice Admirals Shoji Nishimura and Kiyohide Shima as Force 'C' of the 1st Strike Force and 2nd Strike Force of the 5th Fleet) would approach from the south via the Surigao Strait.

Musashi sunk

Again the far-ranging American submarines struck first. Approaching the Philippines from the west on 23 October, Kurita's powerful Central Force, which included five battleships and 10 heavy cruisers, suffered three cruisers torpedoed, two of which sank. Early on

24 October aircraft from Mitscher's carriers (T1738), operating in four groups to the east of the islands, also located the Southern Force.

With all available Japanese air power engaging TF38, sinking the light carrier USS *Princeton*, Kurita was without cover as his group crossed the Sibuyan Sea in the centre of the islands. Five separate US air strikes thus inflicted considerable damage, including the sinking of the super-battleship *Musashi*, but Kurita, though delayed by seven important hours, ploughed doggedly toward San Bernardino.

The Southern Force, with two battleships and four cruisers, was tracked across the Sulu Sea. As its approach was obviously going to be through Surigao Strait, Vice Admiral Thomas Kinkaid aimed to block it here with his 7th Fleet, the fire-support force for the US landings.

Halsey should similarly have corked Kurita in the San Bernardino Strait, but his interest was elsewhere. Ozawa, after several attempts to advertise his presence to the north, was finally 'discovered' at 1540 on 24 October: four carriers, two hybrid battleship/carriers and three cruisers. Halsey,

*Above: Kurita's squadron included the two greatest battleships ever built, **Yamato** and **Musashi**. The latter took enormous punishment from US aircraft and eventually foundered.*

The four magnificent warships of the 'Mogami' class formed the 7th Cruiser Squadron, previously commanded by Kurita when he was a rear-admiral. Two of the cruisers were lost at Leyte.

USS Pennsylvania and USS Colorado lead the way into the Lingayen Gulf. The Japanese defeat at Leyte Gulf destroyed the Imperial Navy as a fighting force.

echelon groups of escort carriers lay to the east of Samar, between him and the beaches and, though geared to a support role he could, together with shore strips, put up a goodly number of aircraft. From 0630 these little carriers were involved in a very confused action, coming even under 460mm (18.1in) shell fire from the *Yamato*. They were stoutly fought and magnificently defended by their destroyers and escort destroyers. Kurita, already rather demoralized by events, with no air cover and believing himself to be under attack from at least one of Mitscher's main carrier groups, turned back. For the loss of an escort carrier and three smaller ships, the Americans sank three Japanese heavy cruisers and almost certainly saved the whole Leyte operation.

Halsey, meanwhile, despite receiving desperate pleas for assistance, stayed to finish off Ozawa's carriers with six separate air strikes, the last of which was not launched until 1710. At 1100 he had ordered back one carrier group and Lee's battleships to plug the San Bernardino Strait. They arrived at 0100 on 26 October, some three hours after Kurita had retreated through the strait after the battle off Samar. It could easily have been a disaster.

The final gamble of 'SHO-1' had not paid off, the Japanese losing four carriers, three battleships and 10 cruisers – and their last trained aircrews. From this point on, the US Navy was never seriously threatened by the Imperial Navy.

understandably, took the bait whole. Though Kurita was in no way beaten, air strikes against him suddenly stopped as Halsey moved north, taking with him even Vice Admiral Willis Lee's fast battleship force.

Against the near-toothless Ozawa were pitted 64 warships and nearly 800 aircraft, but the San Bernardino Strait had been left wide open.

Halsey pinpointed Ozawa as early as 0200 on the fateful 25 October, at which point Kurita was just three hours short of the San Bernardino Strait and Nishimura was barging up the Surigao Strait.

Nishimura and Shima, though aware of the delay to Kurita's timetable, strove to

adhere to their own, running blindly at overwhelming opposition to reach Leyte Gulf by dawn on 25 October. With adequate time to prepare, Kinkaid placed Rear Admiral Jesse Oldendorf's six veteran battleships and eight cruisers across the northern end of the strait. To even reach them the Japanese would need to navigate the length of the waterway, first harried by 39 PT boats and then by three destroyer divisions. From 2236 on 24 October the torpedo boats attacked, mostly singly but all without success in the face of powerful defensive fire. By 0230 on 25 October, in the narrows between Leyte and Dinagat, the destroyers were taking over. Both of Nishimura's

battleships were torpedoed, *Fuso* breaking in two. Already hit by two torpedoes *Yamashiro*, now supported by only a cruiser and a destroyer, ran into Oldendorf at 0353 and was effectively obliterated. Although the other two units and Shima's small force managed to get back down the strait to temporary safety, the southern jaw of the Japanese pincer had been destroyed.

Battle off Samar

Not so the northern: even as Shima stumbled back out of the Surigao Strait at about 0530 on 25 October, Kurita came out of the San Bernardino Strait behind schedule and puzzled by lack of any opposition. By great good fortune three rear-

USS Sangamon was one of four converted fleet oilers which formed part of the escort carrier force off Samar. All the 'Sangamon' class survived Leyte and were back in action by early 1945.

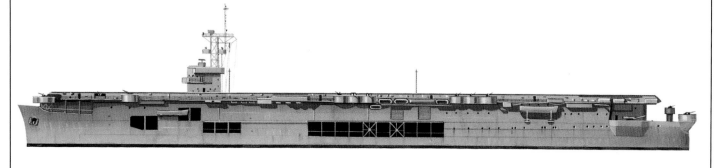

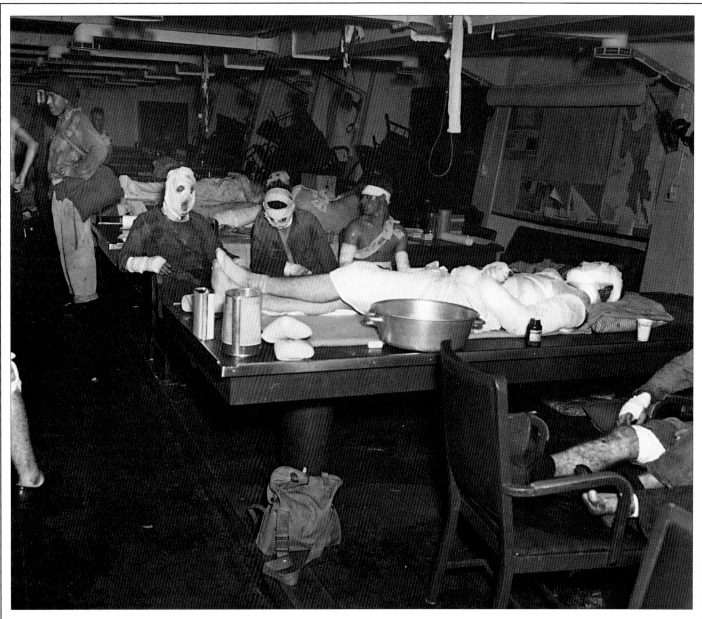

Leyte Gulf: Chronology

The sea battles around Leyte Gulf finally put paid to the Japanese Navy as a war-winning force in the Pacific theatre.

Wounded US Navy personnel from the Battle of Leyte Gulf receive treatment in a wardroom converted to a sick bay. Severe burn injuries were terribly common amongst carrier crews because of the presence of large amounts of aviation fuel and aerial munitions.

1944

October 20th
The US 6th Army lands on Leyte, beginning the operation to clear the island. A few days later, the Japanese respond with Operation Sho-Go. The Japanese Combined Fleet puts to sea en masse. It intends to draw the extremely powerful US 3rd Fleet away from Leyte to the north with Vice-Admiral Ozama's Carrier Force (containing four carriers), while two Striking Forces performed pincer attacks from the west against the US 7th Fleet.

October 23rd
The Japanese First Striking Force heading from Brunei is detected by two US submarines off Palawan Island. The submarines also sink the cruisers *Atago* and *Mayo* and damage another cruiser.

October 24th
Aircraft from the US carrier group Task Force 38 (belonging to the 3rd Fleet) begin air strikes against Japanese ships of Force A – a branch of the first striking force under Vice-Admiral Kurita heading through the Sibuyan Sea.

9.35am
US carrier *Princeton* is hit by Japanese air strikes flying from Luzon.

10.30am
The US air strikes begin. The battleships *Yamato, Musashi*, and the heavy cruiser *Myoko* are all hit, the latter forced to turn homewards.

4.30pm
The *Princeton* sinks.

7.30pm
The battleship *Musashi* sinks after taking 17 bomb and 20 torpedo hits throughout the day. Force A turns westwards back towards the San Bernardino Strait. During the evening the US 7th Fleet sends its warship group Task Force 77 southwest to deal with the threat from Vice-Admiral Nishimura's Force C (part of the first striking force) and Vice-Admiral Shima's Second Striking Force, both heading into the Surigao Strait.

October 25th
On this day the battle separates into three theatres: the battle in the Surigao Strait, the battle off Samar, and the battle off Cape Engano.

Battle off Surigao Strait
3.00am–3.40am
Forty-seven torpedoes are launched in a single salvo from US destroyers against the Japanese ships in the Surigao Strait. One battleship and four destroyers are hit.

3.51am
Eight US cruisers and six battleships launch their attack. In the following action the Japanese lose all but two of their ships – *Shima* and *Shigure* – which promptly effect an escape from the Surigao Strait. Total Japanese losses include two battleships, one cruiser and three destroyers.

Battle off Samar
Taffy 3 – an escort carrier group from the US 7th Fleet – is attacked by Kurita's still-powerful Force A. The US force is heavily outnumbered and outgunned, but over a two-hour battle they resist complete destruction. The US destroyers *Hoel, Johnston* and *Roberts* are sunk, and four other destroyers badly damaged. One US carrier, the *Gambier Bay*, is sunk at

9.07am. Yet the Japanese lose the heavy cruisers *Suzya, Chikuma* and *Chokaii*, and the *Kumano* is withdrawn from action because of damage. At 9.30am Kurita disengages and withdraws his force.

Battle off Cape Engano
US Task Force 38 consisting of 10 carriers and 22 destroyers sails northwards in the early hours of the morning to intercept Vice-Admiral Ozama's Carrier Force heading down the north off Cape Engano.

8.45am
The US carriers launch an air strike against the Japanese carriers. Further air strikes would be launched at 10.00am, 1.00pm and 5.10pm.

9.37am
The Japanese carrier *Chitose* and the destroyer *Akitsuki* are sunk by the first US air attack. The carrier *Chiyoda* is badly damaged.

2.14pm
The carrier *Zuikaku* is sunk by a US air strike.

3.26pm
The carrier *Zuiho* is sunk following a US air attack.

4.55pm
The *Chiyoda* is sunk by ships of a US Cruiser Group detached northwards from Task Force 38 to engage the Japanese.

8.59pm
The Japanese destroyer *Hatsusuki* is destroyed and sunk by the US Cruiser Group By nightfall Ozama's force is retreating fast northwards and the Japanese attempt to smash the Leyte landings has failed.

International Events 1944
October 19th
Soviet forces enter East Prussia.

October 20th
German staff in the Auschwitz concentration camp begin the destruction of documents and facilities relating to the activities within the camp.

October 20th
The Yugoslavian capital Belgrade is liberated by the Soviet 3rd Ukrainian Front and the Yugoslav partisans of Tito's Army of National Liberation.

October 20th
The former premier of Vichy France is sentenced to death for collaboration. The sentence is issued *in absentia* as Laval is living in Germany.

October 21st
The city of Aachen, Germany, is taken by US forces following a 10-day siege action and bitter house-to-house fighting.

October 22nd
Soviet forces advancing through into northern Europe come to within 45 miles (72km) of the Rastenburg, Hitler's headquarters in East Prussia.

A dramatic image of the Japanese carrier Zuikaku as it sinks off the Philippines, October 24th 1944. It took a total of seven torpedoes and nine bombs to sink the carrier. Over 800 crew died.

Return to the Philippines

Having defeated the Japanese navy at Leyte Gulf, American forces can now begin the liberation of the Philippines.

After the great carrier battle of the Marianas, American forces went on to complete the capture of Saipan, thereby providing an important base for subsequent Boeing B-29 attacks on Japan. The Americans landed on Guam on 21 July, and on Tinian four days later. The final capture of Guam on 10 August marked the end of the American campaign in the Central Pacific and the end of organized Japanese carrier warfare. The *Hiyo* had been sunk by air action, and the *Taiho* and *Shokaku* had been sunk by US submarines, while no fewer than 1223 Japanese naval aircraft had been destroyed in the two-month campaign.

Four further Japanese carriers, the *Zuikaku*, *Chitose*, *Chiyoda* and *Zuiho*

Above: The Japanese naval personnel who defended the Filipino capital had fortified Manila with thoroughness and ingenuity. It took over three weeks to overrun them, and the city was shattered.

Left: Seen from the fantail of USS Essex, the carriers USS Langley and USS Ticonderoga return to Ulithi atoll after preliminary strikes against the defences on the Philippines.

went to the bottom during the battles of Leyte Gulf. On 30 November, only 11 days after being commissioned, the huge aircraft-carrier *Shinano*, converted from a battleship, was sunk by the submarine USS *Archerfish* in Tokyo Bay. Before the end of the year the carriers *Unryu*, *Shinyo*, *Taiyo*, *Chuyo* and *Unyo* had been sunk and the *Junyo* was permanently crippled. During the same period the US Navy lost just one carrier, the light carrier USS *Princeton*.

Although the initial landings on Leyte marked the start of the Philippines campaign, the invasion of the main island, Luzon, did not take place until 9 January 1945, four divisions being put

The Nakajima Ki-84 Hayate was the most effective late war Japanese combat aircraft. Large numbers were dispatched to the Philippines on the eve of the American landings.

With twin forward-firing 20mm (0.8in) cannon and 907kg (2,000lb) bomb load, the Curtiss SB2C Helldiver was a powerful carrierborne aeroplane, but was not popular with American aircrew.

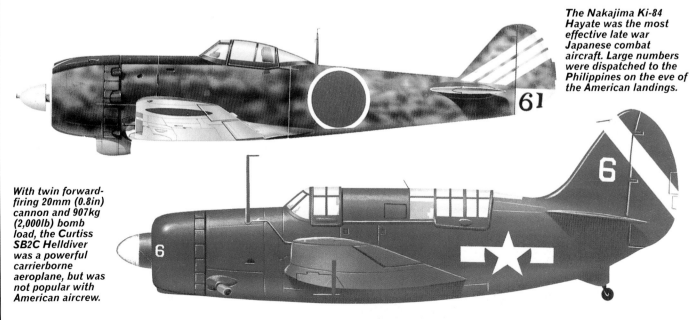

The US fleet was assailed by numerous suicide bombers. Although anti-aircraft guns could usually shoot incoming aircraft to pieces, it was not easy to destroy them entirely. With the pilot dead at the controls and the fuel tanks blazing, a kamikaze follows a ballistic trajectory towards its target.

ashore in Lingayen Gulf. Already Task Force 38 had had to contend with a powerful new enemy: atrocious weather. On 18 December a fully-fledged typhoon struck the fleet; three destroyers capsized with the loss of more than 800 men; aircraft tore loose in the carriers, starting fires as they ripped up electric cabling; the *Cowpens, Monterey* and *San Jacinto* between them lost 33 aircraft, 19 others were swept off the battleships and cruisers, and the smaller escort carriers lost a further 94. Such losses and the search for survivors in the mountainous seas delayed the ultimate assault on Luzon.

As pre-emptive strikes against Japanese air bases on Formosa were being flown by the carriers of Task Force 38 in the first week of 1945, the Lingayen Gulf assault force, carried by the US 7th Fleet under Vice Admiral Thomas C. Kinkaid, came under heavy Japanese suicide attacks as it approached the landing area. The escort carrier USS *Ommaney Bay* was hit and sunk on 4 January, and the following day the USS *Manila Bay* was damaged and suffered more than 70 casualties; on 8 January both the USS *Kitkun Bay* and the USS *Kadashan Bay* were badly damaged and had to retire from the battle.

South China Sea

On 9 January, as the American forces went ashore in Lingayen Gulf, Admiral William F. Halsey's 3rd Fleet (including TF 38), with eight fleet carriers, five light carriers, two escort carriers, six battleships, 11 cruisers and 61 destroyers, entered the South China Sea with the primary objectives of finding and destroying the Imperial Japanese navy's two hybrid battleship-carriers, *Hyuga* and *Ise*, and also of denying the Japanese an opportunity to send significant reinforcements to Luzon. Although the giant carriers were not found, the American carrier aircraft flew wide-ranging strikes over French Indo-China, China proper and Formosa, but found only a few worthwhile targets.

The rate of suicide attacks around Luzon continued to increase, the Australian cruiser HMAS *Australia* being hit five times. Fighting on the ground grew fiercer and, despite an order from General Yamashita to evacuate Manila, a Japanese admiral organized resistance by 20,000 men in the naval base. Bataan fell on 16 February, and the island of Corregidor in Manila Bay on 28 February. By then, however, the bulk of the American carrier forces had moved on to prepare for the invasion of Iwo Jima. Indeed, with the steady but bloody advance through Luzon, and the overrunning or building of airstrips on the island, it now fell to the fighter and fighter-bomber squadrons of the USAAF and US Marine Corps to provide cover over the battlefield, and to the guns of the fleet to create a curtain of fire against the suicide attacks.

Fall of Manila

On 4 March 1945, after 173 days ashore on Luzon, American forces finally captured the shattered city of Manila, having lost more than 40,000 men dead and wounded, and more than 360 aircraft. Ten days later Iwo Jima also fell to the American forces. The US Tenth Army, with the aircraft of TF58's 16 carriers in support, were poised for assault on the last stepping stone to Japan: the island of Okinawa.

A Curtiss SB2C Helldiver is readied for hurling into the sky from the deck of USS Hancock *on 25 November 1944. The softening-up attacks which preceded the landings were very effective.*

Return to the Philippines
Chronology

The retaking of the Philippines required US forces to make multiple amphibious landings around the Philippines' complex island chain. The campaign was characteristically hard-fought, with a major city battle taking place in Manila.

1944
October 20th
A massive US invasion fleet lands four divisions of troops on the island of Leyte.

December 15th
A US Task Force lands on the coast of Mindoro, a small island off south Luzon. The island falls to US troops by the end of January 1945 and provides two invaluable forward airfields for use in the Philippines campaign.

December 25th
Japanese resistance on Leyte crumbles and the island is secured by US forces. Over 80,000 Japanese troops died in the campaign. General Douglas MacArthur – commander of US forces in the Pacific – now directs his efforts towards the capture of Luzon, the main island in the Philippines.

1945
January 2nd–8th
The US 6th Army are deployed from Leyte to positions off the Lingayen Gulf, Luzon.

January 9th
I Corps and XIV Corps of the US 6th Army land at Lingayen Gulf in an uncontested amphibious operation. Once landed the two corps branch out to the south and north of the island.

January 29th
Clark Field – Luzon's key airfield –is taken by US forces. On the same day the US XI Corps is landed at San Antonio on the Luzon coastline 25 miles southwest of Clark Field and begin an eastwards advance across the top of the Bataan Peninsula.

February
Throughout the month US forces make further landings on the southwest coast of Luzon at Bataan and Nasugbu. Bataan itself is secured by the February 28th, albeit at heavy cost to both sides. Combined with the southward advance by XIV Corps, the Japanese are facing a pincer advance into the Philippine capital Manila. The fighting in Manila reaches a horrifying intensity.

March 3rd
The final pockets of Japanese resistance in Manila are stamped out. Over 16,000 Japanese soldiers and 100,000 Filipino civilians have been killed in the city battle, as well as 1000 US troops.

March 26th
San Fernando, General Yamashita's headquarters for his Japanese 14th Area Army, is taken by units from General Swift's I Corps.

April 13th
Japanese fortress defences at Corregidor, Manila Bay, are destroyed. US troops use petrol introduced into the ventilation systems to detonate internal ammunition supplies, blasting the island's concrete defences to pieces.

May–August
US troops spread out through Luzon, fighting heavily all the way. By the end of June US units have reached the northernmost coast of Luzon, though a large pocket of Japanese resistance remains in the mountainous north east. By early May US troops are moving down through the southern Bicol Peninsula, reaching the end of the peninsula by early April. During April and the end of

A Filipino nun with burn injuries stands amidst her US liberators in Manila. Over 100,000 Filipino civilians were killed in the battle for Manila alone during the Philippines campaign.

July the US 8th Army also clears the Philippine island of Mindanao, a campaign which began in late February.

August 14th
Japan announces its unconditional surrender, and over 50,000 Japanese troops on the Philippines give up their battle for the islands.

International Events
1944

December 8th
In the Pacific theatre, US forces begin a massive bombardment of Iwo Jima in preparation for an amphibious invasion. The preliminary bombardment lasts an amazing 72 days.

December 16th
Hitler launches his final major offensive of the war in the West. Over 200,000 German troops cut through the Ardennes forest in Belgium, attempting to split the Allied forces in two, and drive on to capture Antwerp. By January 28th the offensive has collapsed, costing the Germans 100,000 troops.

1945
January 24th
Hitler's esteemed general

A rare site – Japanese prisoners of war taken captive by the US 37th Division in their advance on Luzon. Most Japanese troops fought to the death during the Pacific campaign. Typically, less than 5 per cent would surrender.

Guderian tells the Führer he believes the 'war is lost'. By March Guderian is so out of favour with Hitler that he is sent away on permanent sick leave.

January 28th
Citizens of Berlin are ordered to begin digging anti-tank defences around the perimeter of the city.

March 22nd
Allied forces advancing across western Europe begin to cross the river Rhine.

March 28th
The Red Army advance through the Balkans reaches the Austrian border with units of the 2nd Ukrainian Front.

April 5th
In Moscow the Japanese ambassador is informed by Molotov that the Soviet Union will not renew its 1941 non-aggression pact with Japan.

April 21st
The western Allies are concerned over Soviet influence in Poland. The Polish government has signed a mutual assistance pact

which gives the Soviet Union a high degree of influence over Polish affairs.

April 30th
Adolf Hitler commits suicide as Soviet forces complete the capture of Berlin.

May 7th
Germany surrenders. General Alfred Jodl signs the surrender. By May 10th all fighting in Europe has ceased.

A group of Chinese colonists from the town of Mercedes, Mindanao, the Philippines, hold a welcome parade for the liberating US forces.

Strangling Japan
The submarine war in the Pacific

The Japanese Navy conquers a vast maritime empire but US submariners are soon menacing Japan's vital sea lanes.

While pre-war Japanese planning for the acquisition of a vast oceanic empire had been meticulous, the subsequent problems of sustaining it with a large merchant marine had been scarcely considered. Japan's whole strategy was, after all, posited on a short period of active hostilities, while commerce protection was a defensive concept and, therefore, not worthy of naval consideration. Even though the USA was known to have a substantial submarine force, Japan went to war with no plans for convoy organisation, few anti-submarine escorts and virtually no training.

Like the Japanese, the Americans had defined the primary functions of their submarines as reconnaissance for the surface fleet and attack on enemy warships. Unlike the Japanese, the Americans rapidly grasped the revised nature of the operational situation and went for the commerce. Designed for ocean warfare, their boats were large and capable of long, fast passages on the surface. Initially they were slow diving, while their poor submerged endurance and unhandiness was tolerable only because of poorly organised countermeasures. Nevertheless, Far Eastern waters were generally shallow and the enemy was well supplied with depth charges.

Following the progressive loss of the Philippines and the East Indies, US submarines were based on the Australian ports of Fremantle and Brisbane, under Captain John Wilkes, and on Pearl Harbor under the control of Vice Admiral Charles Lockwood. Though sharing broadly similar aims with the Germans, these two commanders did not opt for the close control exercised by Admiral Karl Doenitz, preferring instead to rely on the considerable initiative of individual skippers.

During the period of the great Japanese advances the few US submarines immediately available could do little but slow things down. On 16 December 1941 the 8660grt Japanese freighter *Atsutusan Maru* was sunk by the submarine USS *Swordfish*, acquiring the dubious privilege of being the first of several thousand losses. The first enemy warship to be sunk was the destroyer *Natsushio*, which fell victim on 8 February 1942 to the elderly 'pig-boat' *S-37* in the Macassar Strait. Three days later, USS *Shark* became the first submarine to be lost on patrol, in this case off Celebes (Sulawesi).

During the whole of the slow build-up of the submarine offensive, things were made difficult by defective torpedoes, the percentage of which reached near-crisis point and which resulted in many unsuccessful attacks, often at great risk to the crews. Torpedoes were frequently heard to hit the

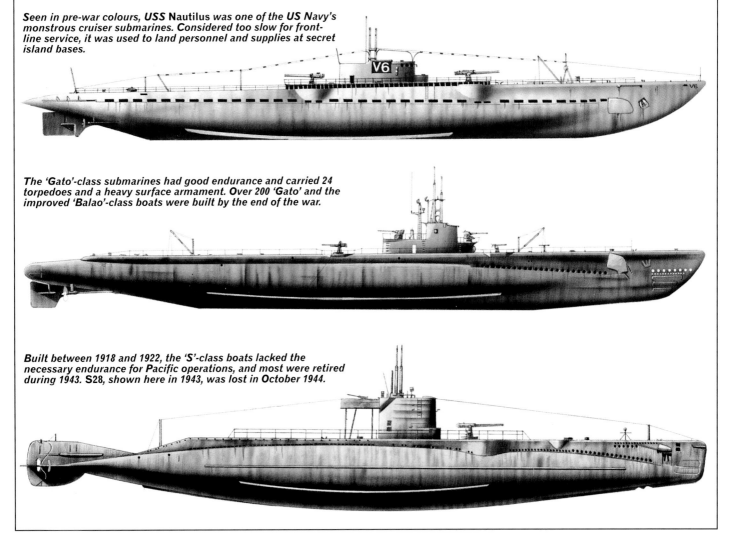

Seen in pre-war colours, USS Nautilus *was one of the US Navy's monstrous cruiser submarines. Considered too slow for front-line service, it was used to land personnel and supplies at secret island bases.*

The 'Gato'-class submarines had good endurance and carried 24 torpedoes and a heavy surface armament. Over 200 'Gato' and the improved 'Balao'-class boats were built by the end of the war.

Built between 1918 and 1922, the 'S'-class boats lacked the necessary endurance for Pacific operations, and most were retired during 1943. S28, shown here in 1943, was lost in October 1944.

Left: Death of a destroyer – her bows blown off by a torpedo, an old Japanese destroyer ploughs her way under. It was the steady attrition of merchant vessels that won the war.

War of attrition

Despite their problems, the submarines accounted for 138 Japanese merchantmen by the end of 1942, a total of 600,000grt. Three boats had been lost, but 33 more had been commissioned. In 1943 the force more than doubled these figures, gaining 56 more boats for the loss of 15. With all sources of captured tonnage now exhausted and with an inadequate new building programme, the enemy showed a net loss in available tonnage of 16 per cent on the year.

Time on station was extended for the American boats by the use of tenders or mobile forward bases, while the beginnings of a Japanese convoy system was met by the formation of 'wolf-packs', usually composed of only three boats and bearing distinctive soubriquets such as Wilkins' Wildcats and Roach's Raiders. Individual 'aces' emerged in skippers such as 'Mush' Morton who, before being sunk in USS *Wahoo* in la Perouse Strait, sank 20 ships of over 60,000grt. Overall record for tonnage destroyed went to USS *Flasher*, whose 100,000grt total still compares modestly with those of many U-boats, e.g. *U-35*'s 224 ships of 536,000grt during World War I and *U-48*'s 53 ships of 318,000grt in World War II.

By 1944 many of Japan's island garrisons were going unsupplied, and the home country lost half its imports of raw materials. Oil losses were of particular significance, shortages beginning to restrict the movement of the battle fleet itself. Targets by 1945 were becoming ever fewer for the Americans as more submarines competed with marauding carrier aircraft. Two boats after the same target actually collided under water.

Rogue torpedoes were never fully eliminated. One resulted in the loss of Dick O'Kane's USS *Tang* in the Formosa Strait as he sought to add to his score of 24 ships. During 1944/5 112 new boats joined the force, many being employed as lifeguards on the route of the now-continuous bomber streams. Over 600 aviators were thus saved to fly again.

Braving extensive minefields, the submarines spent the final months of the war penetrating even the Inland Sea. By the surrender Japan had lost over 8 million grt, of which 5 million had fallen to the submarines, which had lost 42 of their own number in return. The boats had accounted also for over 200 warships but, where this loss had only reduced the Japanese chances of winning, the destruction of the merchant fleet was a primary factor that contributed to Japan's defeat.

target without exploding.

The turning point was reached when the exasperated skipper of USS *Tinosa* hit a large stationary tanker with 11 torpedoes, of which only two exploded, the ship surviving. Belated research exposed the poor design of the firing pistols, but improved weapons (including wakeless, electric torpedoes) did not enter service until late 1943. Poor quality torpedoes encouraged several skippers to adopt a very bold surface attack using their heavy 127-mm (5-in) deck guns. An important acquisition from August 1942 was the SJ surface radar set which, with a suitable plot, enabled boats to carry out 'blind' night attacks.

Kaibokhan Type 'A' escort vessel: the Japanese had neglected to build many escorts before the war, their defensive image not endearing them to the offensively minded Imperial navy. However, these vessels carried 18 depth charges and had excellent endurance.

Strangling Japan
Chronology

During the Pacific War US submarines sank 201 Japanese warships and 1113 merchant ships. Though the contribution of the submarine arm has been frequently overlooked, US submariners sank 55 per cent of all Japanese ships lost in the war and virtually imposed a complete blockade of shipping to the Japanese mainland.

1933–1941
US Navy commissions and builds 56 new diesel-electric submarines which form the mainstay of early operations against the Japanese Navy in the Pacific.

1941
December 8th
The US Navy's submarine arm suffers its first casualty. The USS *Sealion* is destroyed by a Japanese air strike at the Navy Yard, Cavite, Philippines.

December 11th
The submarine *S 38* makes a misidentification and sinks the Norwegian merchantman *Hydra II* west of Cape Calavite, Mindoro.

1942
January 7th
The USS *Pollack* sinks a Japanese freighter off Tokyo Bay, the first sinking of a Japanese boat by a US submarine.

Above: A submarine lookout checks the skies for air activity. While a typical US submarine could sail for 21,000km (13,049 miles) on the surface, underwater endurance was limited to little more than 200km (124 miles).

Below: A US Navy submarine commanding officer looks through his periscope. The biggest problem for US submarine captains in the early years of the Pacific campaign was defective torpedoes, a high percentage not exploding upon impact because of faulty firing pistols.

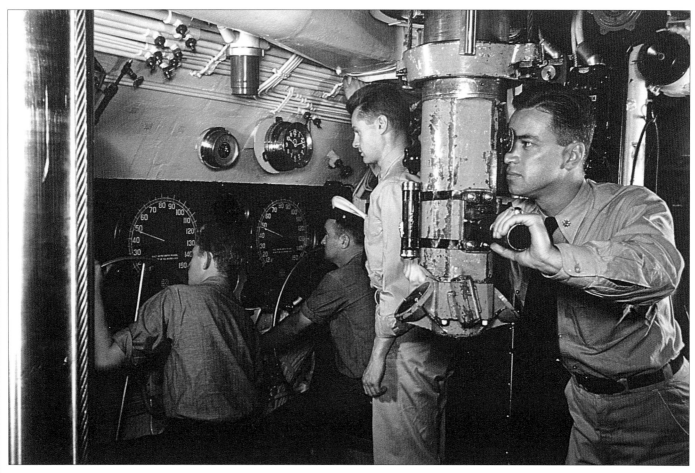

January 27th
USS *Cudgeon* becomes the first US submarine to sink an enemy submarine in action.

June 4th
At the Battle of Midway the submarine *Nautilus* (SS-168) torpedoes the Japanese carrier *Kaga*, but her torpedoes do not explode.

August 10th
Submarine *S-44* sinks Japanese heavy cruiser *Kako* near Kavieng, as it withdraws from the Battle of Savo Island.

December 17th
Submarine *Drum* lays mines in the Bungo Strait around the Japanese home islands.

1943
The year sees a major change in US Navy submarine tactics. Previously subs operated on an as-needed basis, either hunting down Japanese vessels or working in escort duties. From early 1943 they are consigned more to patrol duties on well-used Japanese shipping lanes. In addition, prior to this year US torpedoes used magnetic detonators which often malfunctioned and did not explode. Admiral Nimitz ordered the deactivation of these detonators in 1943 and the US success rate against Japanese shipping instantly climbed.

June 10th
Submarine *Trigger* (SS-237) damages the Japanese carrier *Hiyo*.

July 1943
US submarines begin to operate in the Sea of Japan.

August
US submarines fitted with a 'snorkel' mast – allowing diesel operations, air change and battery charging while submerged – are now in operation in the Pacific.

November 19th–20th
Submarine *Harder* attacks a Japanese convoy and sinks transports *Hokko Maru, Nikko Maru* and *Udo Maru* near the Marianas islands.

December 4th
Submarine *Sailfish* sinks the Japanese escort carrier *Chuyo* southeast of Honshu, though *Chuyo* is actually carrying survivors from sistership *Sculpin* sunk on November 19th.

The torpedo room of a US Navy submarine. The largest 'Narwhal' class of submarine carried 40 533mm (21in) torpedoes on board launched from 10 forward tubes.

December 25th
Submarine *Skate* torpedoes the Japanese battleship *Yamato* northeast of Truk, Carolines.

1944
February 19th
Submarine *Jack* attacks Japanese convoy of six tankers 482km (300 miles) west of Luzon, sinking four of the vessels.

June 19th
During the Battle of Philippine Sea, the submarine *Albacore* (sinks the Japanese carrier *Taiho*, while the submarine *Cavalla* sinks Japanese carrier *Shokaku*.

1945
August 6th
USS *Bullhead* is bombed and sunk by a Japanese Army aircraft near Bali, the last US submarine to be lost in the war. Eighty-four men are killed.

August 14th
Submarine *Torsk* sinks a Japanese coastal defence

vessel, the last sinking of a Japanese vessel by a US submarine in the war.

International Events
1942
May 3rd–9th
At the Battle of Coral Sea US and British naval forces turn back a Japanese invasion group destined for Port Moresby, New Guinea.

June 4th
Japan loses half of its carrier fleet during the Battle of Midway.

1943
February 7th
The US campaign to take Guadalcanal comes to a successful conclusion as 11,000 Japanese soldiers evacuate from the island.

August 17th
US troops enter the Sicilian city of Messina. The capture of Sicily is the first major Allied victory in the European

theatre since the start of the war.

1944
June 6th
The Allies open the European Second Front at Normandy, France, with amphibious landings which put ashore 326,000 men, 50,000 vehicles, and over 100,000 tons of supplies.

October 20th–25th
The Japanese Navy loses 60 ships during the Battle of Leyte Gulf, and ceases to present a significant problem to Allied advances through the Pacific theatre.

1945
May 7th
Germany signs its unconditional surrender to the Allies.

August 10th
Japan surrenders unconditionally, though Emperor Hirohito remains on the throne.

The sands of Iwo Jima

19 February 1945: on the bloodiest day in the history of the United States Marine Corps, two Marine divisions attack the fortress island of Iwo Jima.

By the end of 1944 it had become quite evident to the US commanders in the Pacific that in the near future they would have to mount a large-scale attack on the Japanese island of Iwo Jima.

Three factors made the decision inescapable. First, heavy Boeing B-29 bomber raids on the Japanese mainland, then being mounted from the Marianas, were proving prohibitively expensive as even P-51 Mustangs could not escort them on the 4500km (2800

mile) round trip; Iwo Jima lies only 1060km (660 miles) from Tokyo and possessed two airfields, one of which could take B-29s immediately. Second, even with no further advance towards Japan Iwo Jima was a highly desirable link in the defences of the newly captured Marianas. And thirdly, the island was traditionally a part of the Japanese homeland (it was administered by the Tokyo prefecture), and its fall would thus constitute a severe psychological blow to the Japanese people.

0900 hours, 20 February (D-day+1): the landings on 19 February cut the island in half, isolating Mount Suribachi (seen here in the background) from the Japanese positions in the north of Iwo Jima.

FORTRESS IWO JIMA

The tiny island of Iwo Jima was important primarily because of its airfields. In US hands they would enable fighter aircraft to escort the B-29 bomber raids on Japan. The Japanese were painfully aware of this and their garrison was well equipped and had ample time to prepare its defences.

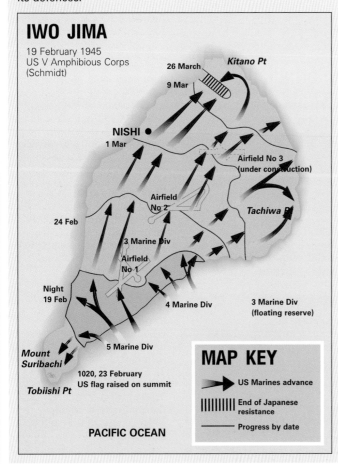

IWO JIMA
19 February 1945
US V Amphibious Corps
(Schmidt)

Kitano Pt
26 March
9 Mar
NISHI
1 Mar
Airfield No 3
(under construction)
Airfield No 2
Tachiwa Pt
24 Feb
3 Marine Div
Airfield No 1
Night 19 Feb
4 Marine Div
3 Marine Div
(floating reserve)
Mount Suribachi
5 Marine Div
1020, 23 February
US flag raised on summit
Tobiishi Pt

MAP KEY

➤ US Marines advance

||||||| End of Japanese resistance

—— Progress by date

PACIFIC OCEAN

Japanese defences

Unfortunately for the Americans the Japanese high command possessed just as keen an understanding of strategic realities, and had long appreciated the necessity of denying Iwo Jima to the Americans. As early as June 1944 the highly regarded Lieutenant General T. Kuribayashi was sent to organize the defence of the island, and given clearly to understand that in case of failure he should not expect to see his family or homeland again; the same stricture applied to the 20,000 veteran reinforcements who followed him to Iwo Jima during the months which followed. As they were provided with heavy and medium artillery, anti-aircraft batteries, heavy and light machine-guns, mortars and tanks, together with relevant ammunition all on an ample scale, their morale was in no way cast down by their predicament.

They therefore set to work with a will, dug their artillery well into the ground, and constructed successive lines of defence across the width of the island, a task in which they were considerably aided by the fact that Iwo Jima is of volcanic origin, so the soft pummice is easily quarried yet still self-supporting however deep it is cut. By the following March 4.8km

(3 miles) of tunnelling wound its way under the northern half of the island.

For the defenders this was just as well, because in order to 'soften up' the island before the landing, both the US Navy and the USAAF carried out massive bombardments. The US Navy began its assault in November 1944 with fire from the guns of six destroyers and four heavy cruisers which lasted a whole morning and was repeated at regular intervals until February, while on 8 December Consolidated B-24s and North American B-25s began an assault which was to last 72 days before climaxing on the morning of 19 February with an attack by 120 carrier-borne planes, dropping napalm along the strip of ground just inland of the proposed landing beaches. From then on the bombardment took the form of a creeping barrage from the massive guns of seven battle-ships, four heavy cruisers and three light cruisers.

Four hundred and fifty vessels of the US 5th Fleet were offshore at dawn on the morning of 19 February, and around and among them swarmed 482 landing craft of various descriptions bearing the men of eight US Marine battalions.

For the first 20 minutes

Left: 21 February – the sinister hump of Mount Suribachi looms over the US beach-head. The summit was overrun two days later, but many Japanese remained in the mountain, in a labyrinth of caves and tunnels.

Below: For the 4th Marine Division, this was their fourth amphibious assault in 13 months. The short beach rose to a low ridge and the ground beyond was swept by concealed machine-guns.

the marines, met only sporadic and scattered resistance, apparently totally unorganized. Then as the marines moved up towards a low sand ridge, concentrated fire from concealed machine-gun and mortar posts opened and a deadly rain of metal swept the beach; the most costly operation in the history of the US Marine Corps had begun.

Under fire

For a matter of seconds the shock of the sudden deluge of Japanese fire froze the marines where they lay, then training and the realities of the situation galvanized them into action. They could not stay where they were and live; they could not go back, for despite the shot and shell which furrowed the beach behind them LCVs were still swimming in through the surf and waves of supporting companies were flooding ashore and packing the beach-head.

Sheer pressure drove the leading platoons forward out of the maelstrom behind them into and over the nearest Japanese defensive positions, some of which they

destroyed, leaving others to their comrades coming up behind; and in less than an hour they had widened the beach-head to 800m (2625ft). Seven whole marine battalions were ashore with their essential equipment, forward patrols had reached the edge of the main airfield and another was in sight of the western beach.

By the end of the day 30,000 marines and their weapons and stores had been landed, and they were there to stay. Their casualties had been high (that had been expected), but the leading elements were across the neck of the island, isolating Mount Suribachi and its garrison from the main defending force, and placing the southern end of the main airfield firmly in American hands.

Battle of attrition

The ensuing four days were spent in capturing Mount Suribachi (the most famous photograph in American history, of the flag being raised by a Marine patrol on the summit, was taken on 23 February), and from then on a savage battle of attrition

was fought as the marines assaulted the defence lines to the north.

By D+10 many marine formations were down to half strength, and although the 3rd Marine Division had now been put ashore it soon found itself blocked by a positive lattice of defensive positions. In one area 915m (3000ft) wide and 200m (656ft) deep, there were 800 bunkers full of defenders – every one of whom, it was afterwards revealed, had sworn to kill at least ten marines.

It was not until D+18 that the first marine patrols reached the north-east shore of the island, and then it became possible to partition the area still in Japanese hands into small pieces and gnaw away at each piece until the defence was crushed. But at last it was done. On the night of 25/26 March the last defenders launched a final Banzai charge against their attackers, and the following

The landing beach seen from Mount Suribachi: men and supplies are unloaded on the original invasion beach after the capture of Suribachi.

morning the bodies of the 300 devoted servants of the Emperor who had carried it out littered the ground around the entrance to their last position.

By this time the first B-29 bombers had landed on the island's main airstrip, and by the end of March squadrons of P-51s were flying in to take up their role of escorting the heavy bombers against the Japanese mainland. It all formed a significant step in the defeat of Japan, but it had cost the marines 6821 killed and three times that number wounded; and of the 23,000 Japanese who had been on the island when the first landings took place, only 216 were ever taken prisoner, most of them badly wounded.

Iwo Jima was less than 25.9km^2 (10 sq miles) in area. It had taken 72 days of air bombardment, three days of concentrated naval hammering and 36 days of the most bitter infantry fighting to conquer it.

How long, and at what cost, would it take to conquer the Japanese homelands by the same methods?

The sands of Iwo Jima

Chronology

The battle to take Iwo Jima epitomised the ferocity of the Pacific campaign more than any other action. Over 20,000 Japanese and nearly 6000 US soldiers died on a barren volcanic island only 13km (8 miles) wide.

1944
June 15th
US carrier aircraft begin to make bombing raids on Iwo Jima.

1945
February 19th
The soldiers of the 4th and 5th US Marine Divisions (the 3rd Division was in reserve) land on Iwo Jima following a massive naval bombardment and an incredible 72 days of continuous preliminary air bombardment. The initial landing seems unopposed, yet after about 20 minutes a ferocious weight of firepower is being directed against the US beachhead as the defenders recover themselves.

February 20th
The first of three airfields on the island falls to the steadily advancing Marines, though every metre of progress is

Below: An aerial reconnaissance photograph of Iwo Jima. The island has almost no vegetation and the translation of its name – Sulphur Island – gives good indication of its inhospitable nature.

paid for in heavy loss of life. In the far south of the island, soldiers of the 5th Marine Division are locked in a terrible battle to clear Mount Suribachi.

February 21st
Japanese kamikaze air attacks against US ships off Iwo Jima results in the sinking of the carrier *Bismarck Sea* and the damaging of the carrier *Saratoga*.

February 23rd
Mount Suribachi is captured, and the photographer Jim Rosenthal immortalises the event with the famous image of US soldiers raising the Stars and Stripes on the summit. The battle to clear the entire island, however, will go on until March 24th.

February 24th
The 3rd Marine Division is landed on Iwo Jima. The second airstrip is taken by US troops. By this stage of the battle the Marines have occupied approximately half of the island, advancing only 6.4km (4 miles) in five days against blistering resistance.

February 25th
The 3rd Marine Division begins an offensive to clear the centre of Iwo Jima's northern plateau. It takes three days to achieve their objectives.

Above: A US soldier receives Holy Communion in the blasted landscape of Iwo Jima. Having been sparsely inhabited before the battle, the island actually became one of the most densely populated areas of earth for the 36-day duration of the battle.

March 2nd

The final airfield falls into Allied hands. About one third of the island still remains in Japanese hands. Every Japanese position is defended to the death, and the battle for Iwo Jima produced almost no Japanese survivors out of the 22,000-man garrison. On the night of the 2nd/3rd the Marines use night-attacks to surprise and overcome the defenders of Hill 362A, a key defensive strongpoint.

March 8th

Some Japanese units mount a counter-attack against the 23rd and 24th Marine battalions. The counter-attack is repelled and over 600 Japanese are killed.

March 26th

Iwo Jima is finally cleared of Japanese resistance after 36 days of fighting. The operation was originally intended to take only 14 days.

International Events 1945

February 20th

US atomic facilities in Oak Ridge, Tennessee, finally produce enough uranium (U-235) to make a single atomic weapon.

February 22nd–23rd

US troops cross the Saar and the Roer rivers, advancing deep into the heartlands of Germany. On the Eastern Front, Marshal Zhukov of the Soviet Army captures the city of Poznan in Poland.

February 25th

Tokyo is devastated by a firebomb attack from 172 long-range B-29 Superfortress bombers.

March 5th

As an act of final desperation, Hitler orders the enlistment of all male children over the age of 16 for military service.

March 10th

A colossal firebombing attack by 279 US B-29 Superfortresses over Tokyo leaves over 80,000 people dead.

March 24th

Soviet forces on the River Oder in Germany prepare to launch the final offensive to take the German capital, Berlin. In the west, US and British forces under Patton and Montgomery respectively cross the Rhine.

A soldier of the 7th War Dog Platoon, 25th Regiment 4th Marine Division, sleeps in a foxhole while his dog – Butch – stands watch. Dogs were generally used for guard duties and for tracking isolated enemy individuals and units in jungle terrain. The dogs must have had exceptional nerves to withstand the constant sounds of battle on the island.

The road to Mandalay

Triumph in Burma

Chasing the Japanese through the Burmese monsoon is a nightmare, but the British 14th Army is determined to finish the job.

By the end of August 1944 the exhausted and near-starving remnants of the Japanese 15th Army were making their painful way back from Imphal and Kohima to the relative safety of the land east of the Chindwin. They were followed, not particularly closely, by the men of Lieutenant General Sir William Slim's 14th Army, the pace dictated largely by the appalling conditions now reigning after three months

ted to Slim the latter decided that he could best aid this purpose by one simple achievement. He must destroy the Japanese Burma Area Army, now commanded by Lieutenant General Hoyotaro Kimura, reputedly one of Japan's most outstanding military leaders.

The area in which the Japanese could best be brought to battle would be, in Slim's opinion, between the Chindwin and the Irrawaddy rivers, probably in

A Japanese army signaller – the Japanese forces had to identify the main British thrust if they were to block the 14th Army.

their supplies and reinforcements must come.

By 4 December the northern prong was moving, and by 15 December the 19th Indian Division's forward units were at Indaw, ready to turn south. At about this time Slim realized that he must change his plans. Kimura would not fight him

in the Mandalay bend, after all, and was already pulling his forces back, presumably to make his stand protecting the Yenangyaung oilfields and the vital rice-fields of the Irrawaddy delta.

Slim's new plan has been claimed as one of the most daring and momentous of the war; it certainly proved spec-

Japanese troops cross the Chindwin – the Japanese knew a British offensive was coming, but were faced with the familiar problem of defending a river line.

of monsoon. Long stretches of every road or track had been washed away by weeks of continuous and torrential rain; only four-wheel drive jeeps were able to drive through with everything, from guns to food, being carried on mule-back or manhandled through by men who had not worn dry clothing since June.

In September a directive was issued to Admiral Lord Louis Mountbatten, Supreme Allied Commander, South East Asia: the opening sentence read 'Your object is the recapture of all Burma at the earliest date', and when these orders were transmit-

the huge Irrawaddy loop at Myinmu – Sagaing – Mandalay. In pursuit of this plan he sent the 19th Indian Division across the Chindwin at Sittaung to drive through Pinlebu to Indaw, then to turn south along the west bank of the Irrawaddy for Shwebo. To its south the British 2nd and 20th Indian Divisions would cross the Chindwin at Kalewa, then drive south east towards Monywa and then Myinmu beyond. The Japanese would then be caught, after a long and difficult retreat, with their backs to the Irrawaddy, here over 1.6km (1 mile) wide and across which all

BURMA LIBERATED

Using his initiative, Major-General Rees got the 19th Indian Division across the Irrawaddy at Thabeikkyin on 11 January. This diverted Japanese attention to north of Mandalay and the planned feint at Myinmu really convinced the Japanese that the main British attack was aimed straight at Mandalay. They had been completely hoodwinked.

Map legend:
- 14th Army bridgeheads
- 14th Army attacks 21 Feb-30 March
- Japanese counterattacks
- All-weather roads
- Airstrips

THABEIKKYIN — 26 February 1945, 19 Ind Div, attacks
YEU
KYAUKMYAUNG
SHWEBO
SINGU
NYAUNGWUN
BUDALIN
WETLET
XXXIII CORPS
MONYWA — 8 March 20 Ind Div attacks
8 March Br 2 Div attacks
MYINMU
KABAING
NGAZON
MANDALAY
IV CORPS
SIZON
MYOTHA
KYAUKSE
21 February 1945, 17 Ind Div, 255 Ind Tk Bde (Cowan) and 7 Ind Div (Evans)
MYINGYAN
PAKOKKU
NATOGYI
KUME
TUNGTHA
5 March village retaken
MYITCHE
KAMYE
KANDAW
PYINBIN
NYAUNGU
OYIN
WELAUNG
MAHLAING
THEDAW WUNDWIN
LETSE
SEIKTEIN
THABUKTON
CHAUK
5/29 March Jap counter attack isolates Meiktila
Jap Twenty-eighth Army (Sakurai)
MEIKTILA

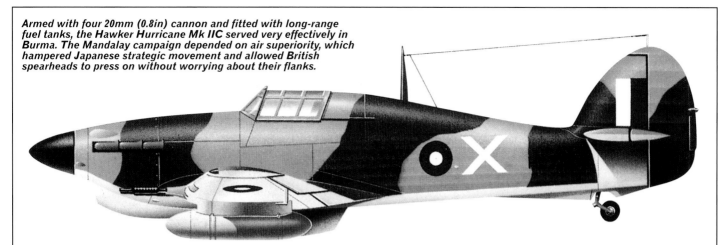

Armed with four 20mm (0.8in) cannon and fitted with long-range fuel tanks, the Hawker Hurricane Mk IIC served very effectively in Burma. The Mandalay campaign depended on air superiority, which hampered Japanese strategic movement and allowed British spearheads to press on without worrying about their flanks.

tacularly effective. Reassembling all of IV Corps except for the 19th Indian Division already poised to drive down the west bank of the Irrawaddy from Indaw, Slim transferred it to Kalemyo and directed the leading brigade (the 28th East African) down through Gangaw, Tilin and Pauk towards the Irrawaddy near Pakokku. Behind it was to come the 7th Indian Division, but some idea of the complexities involved can be gained from the fact that between the head and tail of the division as it moved lay 240km (150 miles) of quite execrable track, upon which had to travel not only the men and transport of the three brigades, but trans-porters carrying tanks and huge elements of bridging equipment: wherever the final chosen crossing-point, the river would be at least 800m (2625ft) wide.

Across the Irrawaddy

It was a magnificent feat of engineering, made the more remarkable by the fact that it was done on time, and moreover remained concealed from the Japanese until the last moment.

Slim's main objective was the Japanese centre of communication and supply between Meiktila and Thazi, without which Kimura's army group could not exist; so during January and the first half of February 1945 every effort was made to give the impression that Mandalay was the prime target. Despite the almost incredible difficulties, by 1 February the 14th Army was closed up along 320km (200 miles) of the river bank and the Japanese had no idea where the main blow would fall.

Small bridgeheads had already been formed across the Irrawaddy in the north at Thabeikkyin and Singu by the 19th Indian and British 2nd Divisions, apparently to threaten Mandalay; the 7th Indian Division arrived at Pauk on 26 January to threaten both Pakokku and Seikpyu, while at the same time the 20th Indian Division drove through Monywa and on to Myinmu.

And on 13 and 14 February, after massive artillery and air strikes which took the Japanese completely by surprise, assault brigades were flung across the river at Ngazun just west of Mandalay, and at Nyaungu south west of Pakkoku. As the first seemed larger than the second, Japanese belief that Mandalay was the main target was confirmed – and all reserves were hurried there.

By 18 February a whole new division (the 17th Indian) and a tank brigade had swept through from the borders with India into the Nyaungu bridgehead and three days later it burst out on the road to Meiktila. They were followed by the 7th Indian Division, while the 20th Indian Division to the north gradually built up the battle against the encircling Japanese at Ngazun, who were forced to bring up more strength – thus weakening the defences at Meiktila. At the same time the 19th Indian Division was moving south towards Mandalay from its bridgeheads.

On 4 March, after some of the fiercest fighting of the campaign, the 17th Indian Division took Meiktila; by the following day the whole of the east bank of the Irrawaddy was held by the 14th Army, and Mandalay itself fell on 20 March. Central Burma was now free of Japanese control – though the thousands of bodies of dead Japanese soldiers gave evidence not only of their own dedication, but of the ferocity of the battles.

Above: Victory in sight – under the exceptional leadership of Lt-Gen. Slim, 14th Army inflicted the greatest defeat the Japanese army ever suffered in a land campaign.

Right: The 11th Sikhs in pursuit – by 1945 the Indian Army was able to boast more than 2.5 million men and only a tiny number of Indians fought for the Japanese

The road to Mandalay
Chronology

The Allied campaign to retake Burma began following the successful defence of Imphal and Kohima in July 1944. Japanese forces around Mandalay were progressively outmanoeuvred by Allied forces who enjoyed better lines of supply and reinforcement and talented leaders.

1944

November 19th
Operation Extended Capital begins, the attempt by Allied forces to march on and seize the Burmese capital, Mandalay. From positions southeast of Imphal, the British XXXIII Corps takes a direct route towards Mandalay down the Chindwin river, while the British IV Corps heads south down the Gangaw valley, pushing towards the communications centre at Meiktila, 97km (60 miles) south of Mandalay, where retreating Japanese could be cut off.

December 4th
XXXIII Corps advance units cross the Chindwin and establish several bridgeheads. At the same time the 19th Indian Division advances northeast towards Baunmauk from positions at Sittaung, acting as a northerly diversion to attract Japanese forces away from Mandalay.

December 15th
19th Indian Division meets up with the US forces under General Joseph Stilwell at Banmauk, the furthest northerly point of Operation Extended Capital.

1945

January 11th
The diversionary 19th Indian Division, now heading southwards towards Mandalay along the line of the Irrawady, is met with heavy resistance by the Japanese 33rd Army as it

Air-dropped supplies fall to the West African Division in the Kaledan Valley on the Arakan front. Though ammunition and rice were the main products dropped, other containers included thousands of raincoats essential to preventing soldiers dying of exposure during the monsoons.

crosses the Irrawaddy at Thabeikkyin.

February 12th–13th
XXXIII Corps and IV Corps both make Irrawaddy crossings, IV Corps at Nyaungu and Pakkokku

roughly 160km (100 miles) southwest of Mandalay, and XXXIII Corps at Ngazun only 48km (30 miles) west of the capital.

February 17th
The 17th Indian Division,

255th Indian Tank Division, and 7th Indian Division attack out from the IV Corps bridgeheads at Nyaungu towards Meiktila.

March 3rd
Meiktila falls to the India

Elements of the infamous US infantry known as 'Merrill's Marauders' take a break from operations to clean their rifles and allow their mules to graze while awaiting an air drop from the 10th US Air Force.

units. The Japanese 15th Army vigorously counter-attacks for the rest of the month.

March 20th
Mandalay falls to XXXIII Corps. The resistance from Japanese in the city is lightened as many units are further south counter-attacking the Allied positions at Meiktila, but severe urban combat is still encountered – 1472 Allied soldiers are killed.

March 29th
Attacks by the Japanese 15th and 33rd Armies are broken off on the 29th as the Allied threat from Mandalay becomes greater. The Japanese begin to retreat southwards.

May 2nd–3rd
26th Indian Division makes an amphibious landing south of Rangoon on May 2nd and takes the city unopposed (the Japanese garrison had abandoned the city on the 2nd) on May 3rd. The war in Burma effectively comes to an end apart from localised engagements with retreating Japanese units.

International Events
1944
December 7th
British forces in liberated Greece are in combat once again in Athens, this time against an uprising of the communist National Liberation Army (ELAS).

December 31st
Hungary declares war on Germany after Russian forces in the Balkans set up a new Hungarian Provisional National Government.

1945
January 17th
Warsaw falls to the Red Army after a five-day offensive.

January 31st
The German liner *Wilhelm Gustloff* is torpedoed by a Russian submarine off the coast of East Prussia. Over 6000 German refugees aboard the ship drown.

February 16th
Budapest is taken by Soviet forces.

April 5th
Japan's Prime Minister –

General Kuniaki Koiso – resigns with his cabinet. His replacement is Admiral Baron Kantaro Suzuki, a man with a track record of anti-war diplomacy.

April 12th
US generals Eisenhower, Bradley and Patton are led around Buchenwald concentration camp. They are almost overwhelmed by the horrors of what they witness.

A wounded Japanese soldier is brought into a US Portable Surgical Hospital for treatment then questioning by intelligence officers.

Okinawa
End of an empire

The island of Okinawa is the Allies' penultimate target before the invasion of Japan itself. The Imperial Japanese navy launches a desperate attempt to save it.

An M4 Sherman flame-thrower tank burns its way forward. Although US troops used every weapon possible in the assault on Okinawa, the only way to clear a position was for a GI to get in there, rifle in hand.

In the early hours of 1 April 1945 the US 10th Army, commanded by Lieutenant General Simon Bolivar Buckner, began landing on the island of Okinawa – the main island of the Ryukyu group, 106km (66 miles) long and between 4.8 and 16.1km (3 and 10 miles) across. The operation was the largest amphibious assault yet undertaken in the Pacific and involved nearly 550,000 personnel, including 180,000 combat troops. Carrier air strikes in mid-March against the Japanese airfields on Kyushu left the facilities in ruins and destroyed some 500 aircraft, thus ensuring little interference to the landing front from that quarter. Only slight opposition faced the US forces for the first few days, the location of the Japanese garrison remaining a mystery until 5 April when it became clear that the southern half of Okinawa had been painstakingly fortified. Ensconced in a formidable network of bunkers and entrenchments were some 85,000 Japanese troops commanded by Lieutenant General Mitsuru Ushijima. Part of the force was made up of fresh conscripts, but the backbone of the defence was the veteran 62nd Division, brought back from China.

Special attack force

The infantry battle for Okinawa had barely begun when the Imperial Japanese navy launched its last major operation of the war, a kamikaze mission on the grand scale involving the magnificent battleship *Yamato*. Rejoicing in the title of the 'Special Sea Attack Force', *Yamato*, a cruiser and and a force of destroyers was dispatched on a one-way voyage to Okinawa where they were to inflict the maximum damage possible before meeting their inevitable destruction. *Yamato* was the largest and mightiest battleship of all time, displacing nearly 70,000 tons at full load; crewed by 2500 officers and ratings, she was armed with nine 460-mm (18.1-in) guns with a range of 41,150 m (45,000 yards) and over 150 anti-aircraft guns. Flying the flag of Vice Admiral Ito, she sailed from the Inland Sea on 6 April accompanied by the light cruiser *Yahagi* and eight destroyers. US submarines spotted the leviathan as she steamed past Kyushu before steering into the East China Sea. Carrierborne reconnaissance aircraft located her again on the morning of 7 April and 380 aircraft were launched from Task Force 58. Low clouds and rain squalls proved a slight inconvenience to the aircraft but *Yamato* had no fighter cover and the bombers were able to make their attacks uninterrupted.

The giant battleship greeted its deceptively puny attackers with a hail of anti-aircraft fire and manoeuvred to the best of its ability as it began to fight for its life. The US aircraft swarmed around the monstrous bulk, scoring hit after hit, but *Yamato* absorbed them without any apparent effect. But gradually she began to slow and the volume of fire coming up at the bombers noticeably diminished; meanwhile her diminutive consorts had lost all trace of formation, four of the destroyers had been sunk, and *Yahagi* went down at 1400. Half an hour later the desperate attempts at counter-flooding could postpone the end no longer and *Yamato* rolled over and sank. Her magazines exploded and a tall column of smoke some 320km (200 miles) short of Okinawa marked the grave of a proud warship and almost all of her crew.

The heroic failure of this last attempt at surface intervention was followed by a savage series of kamikaze air attacks on the US warships off shore, while Ushijima's troops stubbornly contested every yard of their island. On 19 April Buckner essayed a concentrated attack to punch a hole in the Japanese defences, but this failed with nearly 1000 casualties. For the rest of the month and into May the 10th Army battered against the 'Shuri' line in a remorseless routine of colossal bombardments followed by desperate assaults against blockhouses and bunkers cunningly sited and fanatically defended. Although the Americans knew that the casualty rate

With Okinawa as an air base, the US bombing raids on Japan would be even more effective. Acutely aware of the island's potential as an unsinkable 'aircraft carrier', the Japanese stationed the veteran 62nd Division on Okinawa and the commander was left in no doubt as to his task. Fighting on the island was a savage, close-quarter affair, with Japanese positions cunningly sited and well camouflaged.

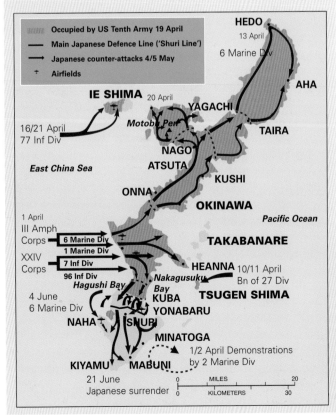

OKINAWA: THE LAST ISLAND

	Occupied by US Tenth Army 19 April
▬▬	Main Japanese Defence Line ('Shuri Line')
→	Japanese counter-attacks 4/5 May
✝	Airfields

HEDO
13 April
6 Marine Div

AHA

IE SHIMA 20 April
16/21 April 77 Inf Div
Motobu Pen
YAGACHI
TAIRA
NAGO
East China Sea
ATSUTA
KUSHI
ONNA
OKINAWA
Pacific Ocean
1 April
III Amph Corps
6 Marine Div
TAKABANARE
1 Marine Div
XXIV Corps
7 Inf Div
96 Inf Div
HEANNA 10/11 April
Nakagusuku Bn of 27 Div
Hagushi Bay Bay TSUGEN SHIMA
KUBA
4 June YONABARU
6 Marine Div
NAHA SHURI
MINATOGA
1/2 April Demonstrations
by 2 Marine Div
KIYAMU MABUNI
21 June
Japanese surrender

0	MILES	20
0	KILOMETERS	30

Rocket-armed landing craft were widely used on Okinawa, blanketing Japanese positions with high explosive, and preventing any movement by the defenders.

Yamato *continues her death ride to* Okinawa. *The destruction of the huge ship and the deaths of her 2700 crewmen availed nothing to the defenders; this great kamikaze perished in a futile holocaust.*

USS Bunker Hill – *although a pitiful gesture of despair, the kamikazes posed a major threat to the US Navy, which suffered a steady stream of casualties to them.*

guard was repulsed and the Japanese occupied new positions on Okinawa's southern tip and prepared for a last stand.

Ritual suicide

The 10th Army pushed forward for the last stage of the battle and set about the grisly task of breaking into the Japanese positions. Finally on 17 June the Japanese garrison was divided into three encircled pockets, no longer capable of a coherent defence, and some of the more recent conscripts began to surrender. Buckner broadcast a message to Ushijima urging him to stop the fighting and save the lives of his surviving soldiers, since the end was inevitable. Ironically, Buckner himself was killed on the next day when a Japanese shell blew lethal slivers of coral into him while he inspected the 8th Marines. Ushijima survived him by a week, committing ritual suicide with his chief of staff after sending a last report to Tokyo. 'Our strategy, tactics and equipment were used to the utmost and we fought valiantly... but it was nothing before the material might of the enemy.' His statement was perfectly correct: Japan was doomed.

was running wildly in their favour as the occupants of each position were killed to a man, US casualties were mounting at an alarming rate. By the end of May it seemed a breakthrough might at last be achieved, but the sudden onset of

torrential rains bogged down operations for over a week. Taking full advantage of the weather, Ushijima extracted his surviving units from the battle and began to withdraw to the south. An American attempt to break through the Japanese rear-

Most Japanese soldiers preferred death to the humiliation of surrender. However, there were some on Okinawa, mostly the younger conscripts, who surrendered unwounded.

Yamato *was the ultimate battleship in every sense: 70,000 tons of armoured elegance with the heaviest punch afloat. However, her voyage to* Okinawa *was a futile and fatalistic gesture.*

Okinawa
Chronology

Okinawa – the main island of Japan's Ryukyu group – was the focus of the last major island campaign of the Pacific War, and one of the bloodiest. Over 12,500 US servicemen lost their lives compared to 137,500 Japanese who fought to the death.

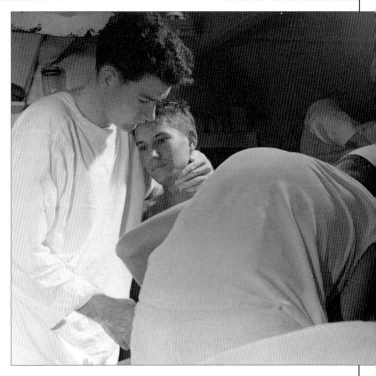

A US soldier injured on Okinawa has his wounds dressed by a US Navy medical team. The Okinawa campaign was immensely costly for the US – 12,500 servicemen were killed.

1945

March 24th–31st
The US Navy and US Air Force bombard Okinawa for over a week to soften Japanese defences for the forthcoming landings. Over 30,000 naval shells alone strike the landing areas.

March 24th
The 77th Infantry Division occupies the Kerama Islands to the south-east of Okinawa.

Injured Japanese prisoners are loaded aboard a truck with the help of local Okinawans. The number of civilian deaths on the island exceeded military casualties.

April 1st
Two US Marine divisions and two US Army divisions are landed on the southwest corner of Okinawa around Hagushi. The landings are almost entirely unopposed – the Japanese garrison commanded by General Mitsuru Ushijima is positioned inland, entrenched in the island's rocky and honeycombed structure.

April 6th
Fighting is now intense for the island. The 1st and 6th Marine Division are attempting to advance to the north of the island, while the 7th and 96th Infantry turn to clear the mountainous south.

April 6th–10th
Japanese kamikaze aircraft begin huge waves of suicide assaults against the US fleet off Okinawa. The Japanese battleship *Yamato* – the largest battleship ever built – also makes a one-way suicide trip to Okinawa, intending to

A Japanese delegation step aboard the USS Missouri to sign the official Japanese surrender on 2 September 1945, bringing to an end six years of global conflict.

wreak havoc on the US amphibious operation. She is sunk by US air attack on the afternoon of April 7th. During the Okinawan campaign 34 US Navy vessels will be sunk, mainly through kamikaze tactics.

April 10th-11th
The 27th Infantry Division lands on and takes Tsugen island off the east coast of Okinawa.

April 13th
Marines reach the northernmost tip of Okinawa, Hedo Point.

April 16th–21st
The US 77th Infantry Division conducts a five-day campaign to subdue Ie Shima, the island off the tip of the Motobu Peninsula.

April 19th
US forces assaulting into the south of the island push back the Japanese line towards Naha.

April 20th
Motobu Peninsula, a heavily defended promontory on the west of Okinawa, is cleared of Japanese resistance.

May 4th–27th
A major Japanese counter-attack in the south of the island establishes a defensive line running from Naha on the west coast to Yonabaru on the east coast. The line is subjected to constant ferocious US assaults throughout May. Finally, on May 27th, Naha is taken by US forces and they push down into the far south of the Orouku Peninsula.

June 22nd
The fighting draws to a close on Okinawa. Ushijima commits suicide

International Events 1945

March 23rd–24th
US forces under General George Patton cross the Rhine near Nierstein on March 23rd. The next day Montgomery's British, Canadian and other US units cross the river some 160km (100 miles) to the north around Wesel.

March 28th
Eisenhower orders the British and US commanders to allow the Soviets to take Berlin, and not risk lives rushing for the German capital.

April 11th
The German V-weapon development centre at Nordhausen falls into Allied hands. The Allies begin removing the technology to the west to avoid the science falling into Russian hands.

April 12th
The US President Franklin Roosevelt dies at the age of 63.

April 16th
Soviet forces surrounding Berlin begin their final assault on the German capital.

April 28th
Hitler orders the execution of Heinrich Himmler after hearing that Himmler has made peace overtures to the Allies. Himmler escaped the sentence because of Hitler's suicide two days later.

April 30th
The German capital falls to the Soviet Army after a battle which cost the Russians 300,000 dead. Adolf Hitler commits suicide.

Appendices

Military Manpower Raised, by Each of the Belligerent Nations 1939–45

Country		On entry into war	End of War	Peak Number*	Total Mobilised
[Brackets = estimated figure]					
Albania		13,000	n/a	n/a	n/a
Australia	Armed Forces	91,700	575,100	n/a	993,000
	Army	82,800	380,700	n/a	727,200
	Air Force	3500	154,500	n/a	216,900
	Navy	5400	39,900	n/a	48,900
Belgium		600,000	650,000	n/a	[900,000]
Bulgaria		160,000	450,000 (with Soviets)	n/a	1,011,000
Canada	Armed Forces	63,100	759,800	n/a	1,100,000
	Army	55,600	474,000	n/a	690,000
	Air Force	3100	193,000	n/a	222,500
	Navy	4400	92,800	n/a	99,400
China		2,500,000 (1939)	5,000,000	5,700,000	14,000,000
Denmark		6600	n/a	n/a	n/a
Finland	1939–40	127,800	200,000	n/a	n/a
	1941–44	400,000	270,000	n/a	n/a
France	Sept 1939	900,000	n/a	n/a	n/a
	1940	2,680,000	n/a	n/a	n/a
	1943–44 Italy	15,000	98,000	113,000	160,000
	1944–45 N.W. Europe	n/a	437,000	n/a	n/a
Germany	Armed Forces	3,180,000	7,800,000	9,500,000	17,900,000
	Army (Waffen SS in brackets)	2,730,000 (30,000)	6,100,000 (800,000)	6,500,000	n/a
	Air Force	400,000	1,000,000	2,100,000	n/a
	Navy	50,000	700,000	800,000	n/a
Greece	Oct 1940	430,000	n/a	n/a	n/a
	April 1941	540,000	n/a	n/a	n/a
Hungary		80,000 (1939)	210,000	n/a	n/a
India	Armed Forces	197,000	2,159,700	n/a	2,581,800
	Army	194,900	2,100,000	n/a	2,500,000
	Air Force	300	29,200	n/a	52,800
	Navy	1800	30,500	n/a	29,000
Italy	Armed Forces	1,899,600	n/a	n/a	9,100,000
	Army	1,630,000	n/a	2,563,000	n/a
	Air Force	101,000	(May 43) 200,000	n/a	n/a
	Navy	168,600	(Sept 43) 259,100	n/a	n/a
Japan	Armed Forces	1,700,000	7,200,000	n/a	9,100,000
	Army	1,500,000	5,500,000	n/a	n/a
	Navy	200,000	1,700,000	n/a	n/a
Netherlands		270,000	400,000	n/a	400,000
New Zealand	Armed Forces	13,800	192,800	n/a	n/a
	Army	11,300	157,000	n/a	n/a
	Air Force	1200	c. 27,000	n/a	n/a
	Navy	1300	5800	n/a	n/a
Norway		25,000	n/a	n/a	[90,000]

* Only when significantly different from preceeding columns.

Military Manpower Raised, by Each of the Belligerent Nations 1939–45 (continued)

Country		On entry into war	End of War	Peak Number*	Total Mobilised
Poland	1939	1,200,000	250,000	n/a	[2,400,000]
	1943–45 Italy	8600	50,000	n/a	n/a
	1944–45 N.W. Europe	28,000	n/a	n/a	n/a
	1941–45 E. Front	30,000	n/a	n/a	200,000
Rumania	1941–44	686,000	1,225,000	n/a	n/a
	1944–45 with Red Army	n/a	370,000	n/a	539,000
South Africa	Armed Forces	n/a	n/a	n/a	250,000
	Army	18,000	n/a	198,000	208,000
	Air Force	1,000	n/a	n/a	38,000
	Navy	n/a	n/a	n/a	4000
UK	Armed Forces	681,000	4,683,000	n/a	5,896,000
	Army	402,000	2,931,000	n/a	3,778,000
	Air Force	118,000	963,000	1,012,000	1,185,000
	Navy	161,000	789,000	n/a	923,000
USA	Armed Forces	5,413,000	11,877,000	n/a	16,354,000
	Army (not including USAAF)	4,602,000	5,851,000	n/a	} 11,260,000
	Air Force	354,000	2,282,000	n/a	
	Navy	382,000	3,288,000	n/a	4,183,000
	USMC	75,000	456,000	n/a	669,000
USSR	Armed Forces	9,000,000	12,400,000	13,200,000	n/a
	Army	2,900,000	6,000,000	n/a	n/a
	Air Force	n/a	n/a	n/a	n/a
	Navy	n/a	n/a	266,000	n/a
Yugoslavia	1941	150,000	n/a	n/a	[1,500,000]
	1941–45 Partisans	(Dec) 2,000	800,000	n/a	n/a

Military and Civilian Casualties of Belligerent Nations 1939–45

Country		Population	No. Served in Forces	KIA/MIA	WIA	POW	Total KIA/WIA	Total Civilian Casualties
Albania		1,100,000	n/a	n/a	n/a	n/a	n/a	n/a
Australia		6,900,000	1,340,000	29,400	39,800	26,400	69,200	n/a
Belgium	1940	8,300,000	650,000	7500	15,900	200,000	234,000	12,000
	in exile		3,500	500	n/a	n/a	n/a	n/a
Bulgaria	with Axis	6,300,000	n/a	n/a	n/a	n/a	n/a	50,000 killed, inc. 40,000 Jews
	with Russians		500,000	32,000		n/a	32,000	
Canada		11,100,000	1,100,000	39,300	532,000	9000	92,500	n/a
China		450,000,000	14,000,000	1,400,000	1,800,000	n/a	n/a	8,000,000
Czechoslovakia (in exile)		10,300,000	c. 5000	n/a	n/a	n/a	n/a	215,000 killed
Denmark		3,800,000	6,600	n/a	n/a	n/a	n/a	1000 killed
Finland	Winter War	3,800,000	n/a	24,900	43,600	n/a	78,500	3400 killed
	1941–44		n/a	65,000	158,000	n/a	223,000	
France	1940	} 42,000,000	c. 4,000,000	92,000	250,000	1,450,000	342,000	470,000
	in exile		c. 600,000	c. 30,000	c. 85,000	6500	c. 115,000	
Germany		78,000,000 (1938)	17,900,000	3,250,000	4,606,600	n/a	7,856,600	2,050,000 killed by Allies, 300,000 by Germans
Greece		7,000,000	n/a	18,300	60,000	n/a	78,300	415,000 dead, inc. 260,000 from famine
Hungary		10,000,000 (1938)	n/a	136,000	c. 250,000	n/a	c. 386,000	300,000

Military and Civilian Casualties of Belligerent Nations 1939–45 (continued)

Country		Population	No. Served in Forces	KIA/MIA	WIA	POW	Total KIA/WIA	Total Civilian Casualties
India		359,000,000	2,582,000	36,100	64,300	79,500	100,400	n/a
Italy		43,830,000	n/a	226,900	n/a	n/a	n/a	60,000 killed
Japan		72,200,000 (1937)	9,100,000	1,740,000	94,000	41,000	1,834,000	393,400 killed, 275,000 wounded/missing
Netherlands	1940	} 8,700,000	400,000	2,900	6,900	n/a	9,800 (inc. Asia)	} 150,000 killed or missing
	in exile		n/a	10,800	n/a	n/a	n/a	
New Zealand			1,600,000	n/a	12,200	19,300	8500	31,500
Norway		2,900,000	25,000	2000	n/a	n/a	n/a	3,800 killed
Poland	1939	} 34,800,000	1,200,000	66,300	133,700	787,000	200,000	4,800,000 killed in camps, plus c.500,000 other dead
	in W. Europe		c. 90,000	4500	13,000	n/a	27,500	
	with Russians		200,000	at least 40,000		n/a	at least 40,000	
Rumania	with Axis	} 19,600,000 (Dec 1937)	n/a	381,000	243,000	n/a	624,000	340,000 killed
	with Russians		540,000	170,000		n/a	170,000	
S. Africa		10,000,000	250,000	8700	14,400	14,600	23,100	n/a
UK		47,500,000	5,896,000	305,800	277,100	172,600	582,900	146,800, inc. 60,600 killed
USA		129,200,000	16,354,000	405,400	670,800	139,700	1,076,200	n/a
USSR		194,100,000	c. 30,000,000	11,000,000	n/a	c. 6,000,000	n/a	6,700,000
Yugoslavia		15,400,000	n/a	Estimates of total Yugoslav deaths 1941–45 1.5 to 1.7 million				

Battle Casualties by Service for the Major Belligerents 1939–45

Country	Service	No. Served	KIA/MIA	WIA	POW
USA	Army	c. 7,900,000	165,800	574,300	79,800
	Air Force	c. 3,400,000	54,700	17,900	40,200
	Navy	4,183,000	36,900	37,800	n/a
	Marines	669,000	19,600	67,200	n/a
USSR	Forces breakdown not available	n/a	n/a	n/a	n/a
UK	Army	3,778,000	177,800	239,600	152,076
	Air Force	1,185,000	76,300	22,800	13,100
	Navy	923,000	51,600	14,700	7400
Germany	Army	13,000,000	1,622,600	4,188,000	1,646,300
	Air Force	3,400,000	294,900	216,600	n/a
	Navy	1,500,000	149,200	25,300	n/a
Japan	Army	6,300,000	1,562,000	85,600	41,500
	Navy	2,100,000	414,900	8900	

Army Battle Casualties in Major Campaigns 1939–45

Campaign	Nationality	KIA/MIA	WIA	POW
Poland	Poles	66,300	133,700	787,000
	Germans	13,110	27,280	n/a
	Russians	900	n/a	n/a
Denmark/Norway	Danes	n/a	n/a	n/a
	Norwegians	2000	n/a	n/a
	Germans	3692	1600	n/a
France 1940	Dutch	2890	69,000	n/a
	Belgians	7500	15,850	200,000
	French	120,000	250,000	1,450,000
	British	11,010	14,070	41,340
	Germans	43,110	111,640	n/a
	Italians	1250	4780	n/a
Balkans 1941	Yugoslavs	n/a	n/a	n/a
	Greeks	19,000	70,000	n/a
	Germans	3674		n/a
	Italians	38,830	50,870	n/a
Eastern Front	Russians	c. 11,000,000	n/a	c. 6,000,000
	Germans	2,415,690	3,498,060	n/a
	Italians	84,830	30,000	n/a
	Rumanians (Germans)	381,000	243,000	n/a
	Rumanians (Russians)	17,000	n/a	n/a
	Hungarians	136,000	c. 250,000	n/a
	Poles	at least 40,000		n/a
	Bulgarians	32,000		n/a
Western Desert	British	c. 7000	n/a	n/a
	Indians	1720	3740	9750
	Australians	3150	8320	9250
	New Zealanders	6340	32,870	8520
	South Africans	2100	3930	14,250
	Germans	12,810	n/a	266,600
	Italians	20,720	n/a	
Tunisia	Americans	3620	9250	4640
	British	6230	21,260	10,600
	Indians	Included in Western Desert		n/a
	New Zealanders	Included in Western Desert		n/a
	French	Total Military Casualties = 12,920		n/a
	Germans	Included in Western Desert		n/a
	Italians	Included in Western Desert		n/a
Italy	Americans	29,560	82,180	7410
	British	89,440		n/a
	Indians	4720	17,310	46
	Canadians	5400	19,490	1000
	New Zealanders	Included in Western Desert		n/a
	Poles	2460	8640	n/a
	South Africans	710	2670	160
	French	8660	23,510	n/a
	Brazilians	510	1900	n/a
	Germans	59,940	163,600	357,090

Army Battle Casualties in Major Campaigns 1939–45 (continued)

Campaign	Nationality	KIA/MIA	WIA	POW
North West Europe	Americans	109,820	356,660	56,630
	British	30,280	96,670	14,700
	Canadians	10,740	30,910	2250
	French	12,590	49,510	4730
	Poles	1160	3840	370
	Germans	128,030	399,860	7,614,790
Pacific	Americans	55,060	162,230	30,000
	Japanese	685,230	n/a	37,280
South East Asia	British	5670	12,840	53,230
	Indians	6680	24,200	68,890
	African	860	3210	200
	Australians	1820	1370	18,130
	Americans	3650	2600	680
	Japanese	210,830	n/a	3100
China	Chinese	Total Military Casualties = 3,211,420		n/a
	Japanese	388,600	n/a	1060

Annual Allied and Axis Tank and Self-Propelled Gun production 1939–45 (units)

Nation	1939	1940	1941	1942	1943	1944	1945	Total
USA	n/a	331	4052	24,997	29,497	17,565	11,968	88,410
USSR	2950	2794	6590	24,446	24,089	28,963	15,419	105,251
UK	969	1,399	4841	8611	7476	4600	n/a	27,896
Canada	n/a	n/a	n/a	n/a	n/a	n/a	n/a	5678
Allied Total	3919	4524	15,483	58,054	61,062	51,128	27,387	227,235
Germany	247	1643	3790	6180	12,063	19,002	3932	46,857
Italy	40	250	595	1252	336			2473
Hungary	n/a	n/a	n/a	c. 500			n/a	c.500
Japan	n/a	315	595	557	558	353	137	2515
Axis Total	287	2208	4980	7989	12,957	19,355	4069	c. 52,345

German and Russian Armoured Fighting Vehicle Strengths on the Eastern Front 1941–45

Date	German	Russian
Jun 41	3671	28,800
Mar 42	1503	4690
May 42	3981	6190
Nov 42	3133	4940
Mar 43	2374	7200
Aug 43	2555	6200
Jun 44	4470	11,600
Sep 44	4186	11,200
Oct 44	4917	11,900
Nov 44	5202	14,000
Dec 44	4785	15,000
Jan 45	4881	14,200

Naval Strengths on Entry into the War

	Aircraft Carriers	Battleships	Cruisers	Destroyers	Escorts	Submarines
Australia	n/a	n/a	6	n/a	7	n/a
Brazil	n/a	2	2	13	n/a	4
Canada	n/a	n/a	n/a	6	n/a	n/a
China	n/a	n/a	6	n/a	n/a	n/a
Denmark	n/a	2	1	n/a	n/a	12
Finland	n/a	2	n/a	n/a	n/a	5
France	1	7	19	70	n/a	77
Germany	n/a	5	6	12	n/a	57
Greece	n/a	n/a	2	10	n/a	6
India	n/a	n/a	n/a	n/a	5	n/a
Italy	n/a	2	22	59	n/a	115
Japan	10	10	36	113	n/a	63
Netherlands	n/a	n/a	5	8	n/a	21
New Zealand	n/a	n/a	2	n/a	n/a	n/a
Norway	n/a	n/a	n/a	8	n/a	5
Poland	n/a	n/a	n/a	4	n/a	5
Rumania	n/a	n/a	n/a	4	n/a	n/a
UK	8	12	50	94	87	38
USA (from 12/41)	8	17	36	171	n/a	112
USSR	n/a	2	2	47	n/a	75
Yugoslavia	n/a	n/a	2	3	n/a	4

Annual Allied and Axis Naval Construction 1939–45 (units)

Nation	Ship Type	1939	1940	1941	1942	1943	1944	1945	Total
USA	Aircraft Carrier	n/a	n/a	n/a	18	65	45	13	141
	Battleship	n/a	n/a	n/a	4	2	2	n/a	8
	Cruiser	n/a	n/a	1	8	11	14	14	48
	Destroyer	n/a	n/a	2	82	128	74	63	349
	Escort	n/a	n/a	n/a	n/a	298	194	6	498
	Submarines	n/a	n/a	2	34	55	81	31	203
UK	Aircraft Carrier	n/a	2	2	n/a	2	4	4	14
	Battleship	n/a	1	2	2	n/a	n/a	n/a	5
	Cruiser	3	7	6	6	7	2	1	32
	Destroyer	22	27	39	73	37	31	13	240
	Escort	5	109	87	71	79	55	7	413
	Submarines	7	15	20	33	39	39	14	167
USSR	Aircraft Carrier	n/a	n/a	n/a	n/a	n/a	n/a	n/a	n/a
	Battleship	n/a	n/a	n/a	n/a	n/a	n/a	n/a	n/a
	Cruiser	n/a	n/a	n/a	n/a	n/a	n/a	n/a	2
	Destroyer	n/a	n/a	n/a	n/a	n/a	n/a	n/a	25
	Submarines	n/a	n/a	n/a	n/a	n/a	n/a	n/a	52
Canada	Aircraft Carrier	n/a	n/a	n/a	n/a	n/a	n/a	n/a	n/a
	Battleship	n/a	n/a	n/a	n/a	n/a	n/a	n/a	n/a
	Cruiser	n/a	n/a	n/a	n/a	n/a	n/a	n/a	n/a
	Destroyer	n/a	n/a	n/a	n/a	n/a	n/a	n/a	n/a
	Escort	n/a	n/a	n/a	n/a	n/a	n/a	n/a	191
	Submarines	n/a	n/a	n/a	n/a	n/a	n/a	n/a	n/a
Allied Total	**Aircraft Carrier**	n/a	2	2	18	67	49	17	155
	Battleship	n/a	1	2	6	2	2		13
	Cruiser	3	7	7	14	18	16	15	82
	Destroyer	22	27	41	155	165	105	76	814
	Escort	5	109	87	71	377	249	13	1102
	Submarines	7	15	22	67	94	120	45	422
Germany	Aircraft Carrier	n/a	n/a	n/a	n/a	n/a	n/a	n/a	n/a
	Battleship	n/a	n/a	n/a	n/a	n/a	n/a	n/a	n/a
	Cruiser	n/a	n/a	n/a	n/a	n/a	n/a	n/a	n/a
	Destroyer	n/a	2	5	3	7	n/a	n/a	17
	Submarines	58	68	129	282	207	258	139	1141
Italy	Aircraft Carrier	n/a	n/a	n/a	n/a	n/a	n/a	n/a	n/a
	Battleship	n/a	2	1	n/a	n/a	n/a	n/a	3
	Cruiser	n/a	2	3	1	n/a	n/a	n/a	6
	Destroyer	n/a	n/a	n/a	6	n/a	n/a	n/a	6
	Submarines	n/a	2	7	10	3	n/a	n/a	28
Japan	Aircraft Carrier	n/a	n/a	1	6	4	5	n/a	16
	Battleship	n/a	n/a	1	1	n/a	n/a	n/a	2
	Cruiser	n/a	n/a	n/a	4	3	2	n/a	9
	Destroyer	n/a	n/a	n/a	10	12	24	17	63
	Submarines	n/a	n/a	n/a	61	37	39	30	167
Axis Total	**Aircraft Carrier**	n/a	n/a	1	6	4	5	n/a	16
	Battleship	n/a	2	2	1	n/a	n/a	n/a	5
	Cruiser	n/a	2	3	5	3	2	n/a	15
	Destroyer	n/a	2	5	19	19	24	17	86
	Submarines	58	70	136	353	253	297	169	1337

Naval Losses of the Major Belligerents 1939–45

Country		Aircraft Carriers	Battleships	Cruisers	Destroyers	Escort	Submarines
(Brackets = those scuttled)							
USA	Total	11	2	10	71	10	53
	In Pacific	10	2	10	56	5	49
UK	Total	8	5	30	110	58	77
	In Mediterranean	2	1	19	45	19	41
USSR	n/a	n/a	1	3	33	n/a	c.100
Australia	n/a	n/a	n/a	3	4	2	n/a
Canada	n/a	n/a	n/a	n/a	6	11	n/a
Japan	n/a	19	8	37	134	n/a	130
Germany	n/a	n/a	9 (3)	7 (3)	44 (6)	n/a	785 (17)
Italy	n/a	n/a	1	11	84	n/a	84

Percentage of Major Belligerents' Merchant Shipping Sunk By Agent 1939–45

Agent	Nation	1939	1940	1941	1942	1943	1944	1945	Total
Submarines	Allied	55.8	54.8	50.1	80.4	80.3	74	64.2	68.1
	Axis in Med.	n/a	26.8	41	47.5	29.7	n/a	n/a	n/a
	Japanese	n/a	n/a	56.5	59.8	76.2	64.1	19.9	54.8
Aircraft	Allied	0.4	14.5	23.5	10	13.2	11.5	10.1	13.4
	Axis in Med.	n/a	21.8	26.1	39.2	36.5	n/a	n/a	33.2
	Japanese	n/a	n/a	30.1	24.6	18.5	31.7	41.7	30.8
Mines	Allied	34.8	12.8	5.3	1.3	3.4	9.2	21.3	6.5
	Axis in Med.	n/a	20.2	10.6	6	3.8	n/a	n/a	7.2
	Japanese	n/a	n/a	n/a	2.8	0.3	0.9	33.3	n/a
Surface	Allied	8.1	12.8	11.2	5.1	2.5	3.3	2.3	7.3
	Axis in Med.	n/a	11.4	13.7	3.1	3.3	n/a	n/a	6.7
	Japanese	n/a	n/a	n/a	5.3	0.2	0.4	0.4	0.9
Other	Allied	0.9	5.1	9.9	3.2	0.6	2	2.1	4.7
	Axis in Med.	n/a	19.8	8.6	4.2	26.7	n/a	n/a	16.7
	Japanese	n/a	n/a	22.3	7.5	4.8	2.9	4.7	4.5

Annual Allied and Axis Military Aircraft Production 1939–45 (units)

Nation	1939	1940	1941	1942	1943	1944	1945	Total
USA	5856	12,804	26,277	47,836	85,898	96,318	49,761	324,750
USSR	10,382	10,565	15,735	25,436	34,845	40,246	20,052	157,261
UK	7940	15,049	20,094	23,672	26,263	26,461	12,070	131,549
Canada	n/a	n/a	n/a	n/a	n/a	n/a	n/a	16,431
Other Allies	n/a	n/a	n/a	n/a	n/a	n/a	n/a	3081
Allied Total	**24,178**	**38,418**	**62,106**	**96,944**	**147,006**	**163,025**	**81,883**	**633,072**
Germany	8295	10,826	11,776	15,556	25,527	39,807	7544	189,307
Italy	1692	2142	3503	2818	967	n/a	n/a	11,122
Hungary	n/a	n/a	n/a	6	267	773	n/a	1046
Rumania	n/a	n/a	n/a	n/a	n/a	n/a	n/a	c. 1000
Japan	4467	4768	5088	8861	16,693	28,180	8263	76,320
Axis Total	**14,454**	**17,736**	**20,367**	**27,234**	**43,454**	**68,760**	**15,807**	**89,488**

Aircraft Losses Both Non-Operational and Operational 1939–45

Country	Fighters	Bombers	Other	Total
Finland	n/a	n/a	n/a	603
France (1940)	508	218	166	892
Germany	41,452	30,585	44,547	116,584
Italy	n/a	n/a	n/a	5,272
Japan	n/a	n/a	n/a	50,000
Netherlands (1940)	n/a	n/a	n/a	81
Poland (1939)	116	148	134	398
UK	10,045	11,965	n/a	22,010
USA	n/a	n/a	n/a	45,000
USSR	n/a	n/a	n/a	106,652

Annual Allied and Axis Crude Oil Production 1939–45 (m. metric tons)

Nation	1939	1940	1941	1942	1943	1944	1945	Total
USA	n/a	n/a	n/a	183.9	199.6	222.5	227.2	833.2
USSR	n/a	n/a	33	22	18	18.2	19.4	110.6
UK	n/a	11.9	13.9	11.2	15.8	21.4	16.6	90.8
Canada	1	1.1	1.3	1.3	1.3	1.3	1.1	8.4
Allied Total	**n/a**	**13**	**48.2**	**218.4**	**234.7**	**263.4**	**264.3**	**1,043**
Germany	3.1	4.8	5.7	6.6	7.6	5.6	n/a	33.4
Germany (synthetic oil only)	2.2	3.2	3.9	4.6	5.6	3.9	n/a	23.4
Italy	n/a	0.01	0.12	0.01	0.01	n/a	n/a	0.17
Hungary	n/a	0.3	0.4	0.7	0.8	1	n/a	3.2
Rumania	n/a	5	5.5	5.7	5.3	3.5	n/a	25
Japan	n/a	n/a	n/a	1.8	2.3	1	0.1	5.2
Axis Total	**3.1**	**10.1**	**11.7**	**14.8**	**16**	**11.1**	**n/a**	**67**

Index

Page numbers in *italics*
refer to picture captions.